Emotions and the Family

Emotions and the Family has been co-published simultaneously as *Marriage & Family Review*, Volume 34, Numbers 1/2/3/4 2002.

Emotions and the Family

Richard A. Fabes
Editor

Emotions and the Family has been co-published simultaneously as *Marriage & Family Review*, Volume 34, Numbers 1/2/3/4 2002.

NEW YORK AND LONDON

First published 2002 by Haworth Press, Inc.
10 Alice Street, Binghamton, NY 13904-1580 USA

This edition published 2016 by Routledge
711 Third Avenue, New York, NY 10017, USA
2 Park Square, Milton Park, Abingdon, Oxon, OX14 4RN

Routledge is an imprint of the Taylor & Francis Group, an informa business

Emotions and the Family has been co-published simultaneously as *Marriage & Family Review*™, Volume 34, Numbers 1/2/3/4 2002.

© 2002 by The Haworth Press, Inc. All rights reserved. No part of this work may be reproduced or utilized in any form or by any means, electronic or mechanical, including photocopying, microfilm and recording, or by any information storage and retrieval system, without permission in writing from the publisher.

The development, preparation, and publication of this work has been undertaken with great care. However, the publisher, employees, editors, and agents of The Haworth Press and all imprints of The Haworth Press, Inc., including The Haworth Medical Press® and Pharmaceutical Products Press®, are not responsible for any errors contained herein or for consequences that may ensue from use of materials or information contained in this work. Opinions expressed by the author(s) are not necessarily those of The Haworth Press, Inc. With regard to case studies, identities and circumstances of individuals discussed herein have been changed to protect confidentiality. Any resemblance to actual persons, living or dead, is entirely coincidental.

Cover design by Jennifer Gaska

Library of Congress Cataloging-in-Publication Data

Emotions and the family / Richard A. Fabes, editor.
    p. cm.
"Emotions and the Family has been co-published simultaneously as Marriage & family review, vol. 34, no. 1/2/3/4 2002."
Includes bibliographical references and index.
    ISBN 0-7890-2050-5 (hardcover : alk. paper) – ISBN 0-7890-2051-3 (softcover : alk. paper)
    1. Family–Psychological aspects. 2. Emotions. I. Fabes, Richard A. II. Marriage & family review.

HQ734.E583 2003
306.85–dc21

2002155852

ISBN 13: 978-0-7890-2051-2 (pbk)

ABOUT THE EDITOR

Richard A. Fabes is Professor and Chair of the Department of Family and Human Development at Arizona State University. He completed his MS and PhD in Child Development from Oklahoma State University. Since graduating in 1982, he has published over 100 research articles, books, and chapters. His work has appeared in the best journals, including *Developmental Psychology, Child Development, Journal of Marriage and Family, Family Relations, Journal of Family Psychology, Psychological Bulletin,* and *Journal of Personality and Social Psychology*. His primary research interest is social/emotional development and the role that parents and peers play in influencing emotional and social behavior. Currently, he is Associate Editor of *Merrill-Palmer Quarterly* and a member of the Society for Research in Child Development, the American Psychological Association, and the National Council on Family Relations.

Emotions and the Family

CONTENTS

PART I: GENERAL FAMILY/MARRIAGE PROCESSES

Introduction   3
    Richard A. Fabes
    Carlos Valiente
    Stacie A. Leonard

A Family-Wide Model for the Role of Emotion
    in Family Functioning   13
    E. Mark Cummings
    Marcie C. Goeke-Morey
    Lauren M. Papp

A Meta-Analysis of Family Expressiveness and Children's
    Emotion Expressiveness and Understanding   35
    Amy G. Halberstadt
    Kimberly L. Eaton

"When My Mommy Was Angry, I Was Speechless":
    Children's Perceptions of Maternal Emotional Expressiveness
    Within the Context of Economic Hardship   63
    C. Cybele Raver
    Mary Spagnola

Psychosocial Moderators of Emotional Reactivity to Marital
    Arguments: Results from a Daily Diary Study   89
    David M. Almeida
    Katherine A. McGonagle
    Rodney C. Cate
    Ronald C. Kessler
    Elaine Wethington

Emotional and Relational Consequences of Coping
in Stepfamilies   115
   Anita DeLongis
   Melady Preece

Affect Pattern Recognition: Using Discrete Hidden
Markov Models to Discriminate Distressed
from Nondistressed Couples   139
   William A. Griffin

The Role of Emotions in Marriage and Family Therapy:
Past, Present, and Future   165
   Debra A. Madden-Derdich

PART II: DEVELOPMENTAL AND PARENT-CHILD PROCESSES

The Contribution of Older Siblings' Reactions to Emotions
to Preschoolers' Emotional and Social Competence   183
   Katharine Strandberg Sawyer
   Susanne Denham
   Elizabeth DeMulder
   Kimberly Blair
   Sharon Auerbach-Major
   Jennifer Levitas

Children's Understanding of Emotion Communication
in Families   213
   Carolyn Saarni
   Maureen Buckley

Maternal Sensitivity and Infant Emotional Reactivity:
Concurrent and Longitudinal Relations   243
   Tracy L. Spinrad
   Cynthia A. Stifter

Children's Emotional Reactions to Stressful Parent-Child
Interactions: The Link Between Emotion Regulation
and Vagal Tone   265
   John Mordechai Gottman
   Lynn Fainsilber Katz

The Coping with Children's Negative Emotions Scale (CCNES): Psychometric Properties and Relations with Children's Emotional Competence   285
   Richard A. Fabes
   Richard E. Poulin
   Nancy Eisenberg
   Debra A. Madden-Derdich

Parental Contributions to Preschoolers' Understanding of Emotion   311
   Susanne Denham
   Anita T. Kochanoff

Children's Emotional Regulation and Social Competence in Middle Childhood: The Role of Maternal and Paternal Interactive Style   345
   David J. McDowell
   Mina Kim
   Robin O'Neil
   Ross D. Parke

Index   367

PART I:
GENERAL FAMILY/ MARRIAGE PROCESSES

Introduction

Richard A. Fabes
Carlos Valiente
Stacie A. Leonard

PART I:
GENERAL FAMILY/MARRIAGE PROCESSES

A family is a place where minds come in contact with one another. If these minds love one another the home will be as beautiful as a flower garden. But if these minds get out of harmony with one another it is like a storm that plays havoc with the garden.

–Buddha

In this quote from Buddha, the dynamic role that emotions play in family life is insinuated. "The family is the place where minds come in contact with one another" reflects the fact that the emotional lives of family members interact, influence, and confront one another. Sometimes these emotional interactions and confrontations are relatively calm and benign, sometimes they are filled with rapture and affection, and sometimes they are like a storm of anger, rage, fear, and anxiety that plays havoc with family harmony and relationships. Moreover, emotions are involved in almost every aspect of family development: from the beginnings of family formation (e.g., dating, courting, attraction, and marriage), to the transition to parenthood (e.g., pregnancy, birth, bonding, and attachment), parenting (e.g., socialization and discipline), as well as the dissolution of family relationships (e.g., divorce and death). Thus, in many ways, the fabric of family life is woven together by the complex interplay of the emotions of its members. As a result, behavior often is at its emotional peak at home. Families, therefore, provide a natural laboratory for the investigation of emotional experience and expression.

Given its centrality to everyday family life and family interaction, it is surprising that, with few exceptions (e.g., Blechman, 1990; Brody, 1999; Gottman, Katz, & Hooven, 1997; Halberstadt, 1991; Saarni, 1993), theoretical and empirical work focusing specifically on emotions and the family are relatively rare. The purpose of this volume is to highlight theory and research on the role that emotions play in family life and in the relationships among family members. Although contributors differ in regard to their specific focus on emotions, they are in agreement about the adaptive function of emotions. All contributors portray family members' interactions and competence as dependent on the way emotions are experienced and expressed within the family.

The papers in this volume reflect the dramatic change that has taken place in how we view emotions. Emotions no longer are viewed primarily as a function of *intrapsychic* processes, but now are viewed to have important *interpsychic* functions. Thus, emotions are considered to have social functions that help regulate, guide, and influence the actions, behaviors, and emotions of others (Saami, Mumme, & Campos, 1998).

Frijda (1986) discussed the social functions of emotions and argued that one principle can be derived that covers the social functions of emotions: the principle of *relational activity*. Relational activity refers to actions that establish or modify a relationship between an individual and his or her environment. Emotional behaviors are considered to meet this definition and thus possess the functional significance associated with relational activity.

The conceptualization of emotions from a relational perspective has significant implications for our understanding of families and emotions–emotions have important functions that affect family interactions. To illustrate these qualities, we adapted Frijda's (1986) description of the qualities of different emotional states to include how these different emotions affect family interaction patterns (e.g., their relational activity in regard to family interactions–see Table 1). For example, the emotion of anger has a behavioral tendency that reflects attack and threat (e.g., agonistic). The effect of this tendency on the relationship between an individual and his or her family reflects an effort to establish control or dominance. Insult and derision also can be derived as consequences of

TABLE 1. Emotions and Their Relation to Family Interactions

Emotion	Behavioral Tendency	Relational Activity Associated with Family Interaction Patterns
Desire	Approach	Enhanced access and availability
Fear	Avoidance	Withdrawal or seeking protection
Happiness	Contact	Maintenance of interaction
Interest	Attending to	Recognizable orientation and awareness
Disgust	Avoidance	Rejection
Anger	Agonistic	Establishment of control or dominance
Anxiety	Inhibition	Increased caution and tension
Sadness	Deactivation	Acknowledgment of submissiveness and elicitation of concern

Adapted from Frijda, 1986.

the relational activity of anger. Thus, by this conceptualization, emotions are thought to organize and reorganize family interactions and patterns of family relationships.

It also is important to point out that family relationships and family developments affect the organization and reorganization of family members' emotional lives. Changes associated with childbirth, marriage, divorce, and death produce major emotional reorganizations in family members. In turn, these emotional reorganizations have the potential to affect the quality of subsequent family relationships and developments.

The articles in this collection reflect this new and dynamic view of emotions. Although they focus on different topics, they all acknowledge the interpersonal nature of emotions and their role in family life and family interactions. There are two parts to this volume. The papers in the first half focus on general family and marriage processes related to emotions and the family. The focus of the second half is concentrated more on developmental and parent-child processes. The distinction between these two is arbitrary and there is considerable overlap in the topics reflected in both parts.

Readers will be exposed to a wide variety of approaches to the study of emotions and family functioning. These differences reflect an important question in the study of emotion: namely, how do we best study processes that are as internal and private as are emotions? Because emotions are inherently intrinsic qualities, measuring these qualities presents serious methodological challenges and problems. Added to this problem is the fact that emotional expressions can be controlled and manipulated. Thus, the overt qualities associated with the expression of emotion may or may not precisely reflect the true internal state. A family member may smile while being angry or exaggerate an expression of sadness without truly feeling as sad as they appear. In contrast, a family member may appear calm and unemotional but be seething with rage inside. These manipulations and deceptions of the expression of emotion are not limited to adults. Children quickly learn that they can get what they want by faking or exaggerating certain emotions (e.g., pretend crying or throwing a fake temper tantrum) and by the end of preschool, children learn to control certain emotional expressions that are inappropriate for their gender (Birnbaum & Chemelski, 1984; Brody, 1985).

If you want to know how someone is feeling, researchers generally have relied on asking people how they feel or felt. The advantages of using self-reports of emotion are obvious–they are easy to administer and can provide a relatively differentiated measure of emotion (Batson, 1987). The value of self-reports of emotion, however, rests on two assumptions: (1) that individuals know what they are feeling, and (2) that they will accurately tell us what they are feeling. Some individuals have difficulty identifying and reporting the emotions they are feeling. This is especially true for young children, but also can be true for adults. Emotions can be blends that are difficult to label (e.g., feeling both attraction and repulsion) and sometimes the context of the emotion makes it difficult to identify precisely what one is feeling. Even when individuals know what they are feeling, they may not want to communicate their true feelings. Thus, self-reports of emotions are susceptible to distortions due to social desirability, self-presentation, and demand characteristics of the situation.

In search for measures of emotion that are more accurate, sensitive, and more objective, researchers have turned to non-verbal measures of emotion. You will see this in several of the papers in this collection. Facial (Griffin, Part I), behavioral (Spinrad & Stifter, Part II), and physiological (Gottman & Katz, Part II) measures of emotion reflect the different ways that emotions may be measured. Even when self-reports are used, many different approaches are reflected, including daily diary reports (Almeida et al.; DeLongis & Preece; Cummings et al., Part I), questionnaires (Halberstadt & Eaton, Part I; Fabes et al., Part II), and story measures (Raver & Spagnola, Part I; Denham et al., Part II).

Moreover, the authors in this volume take different approaches to the specific aspect of family-emotion dynamics on which they concentrate. Some focus on the marital relationship (Almeida et al., Griffin, Part I), others focus on the parent-child relationship (e.g., McDowell et al., Part II), whereas others focus on sibling (Denham et al., Part II) or stepfamily relationships (DeLongis & Preece, Part I). Others focus on families as a whole (e.g., Saarni & Buckley, Part II). Even more impressive is the wide array of family contexts emphasized in the different papers–ranging from a focus on specific relationships within a family, to families in therapy (Madden-Derdich, Part I), to a more molar view of the impact of contextual influences on family emotionality (Raver & Spagnola, Part I). This last aspect is critical because we know little about how larger social forces (e.g., cultural and ethnic values) moderate and mediate the relation between emotions and family dynamics.

The articles presented in this volume go a long way toward addressing the complexities associated with understanding the role that emotions play in family functioning. Several directions are identified for new avenues of research, theory, measurement, and analysis. We hope that these articles spur more attention to study of emotions–both positive and negative–and family dynamics.

PART II:
DEVELOPMENTAL
AND PARENT/CHILD PROCESSES

When you're drawing up your list of life's miracles, you might place near the top the first moment your baby smiles at you ... Today, she looked right at me. And she smiled. . . . Her toothless mouth opened, and she scrunched her face up and it really was a grin. . . . The sleepless nights, the worries, the crying–all of a sudden it was all worth it. . . . She is no longer just something we are nursing and carrying along–somewhere inside, part of her knows what's going on, and that part of her is telling us that she's with us.

–Bob Greene (1985, pp. 34-35)

In his journal of the early years of his daughter's life, reporter Bob Greene (Greene, 1985) dramatically depicts the important role that emotions and emotional behaviors play in children's development and in influencing parent-child relationships. He notes the impact that his daughter's first smile had on him, washing away a lot of the concern, worry, and fatigue of early parenting and enhancing his commitment and enthusiasm for parenting and being a parent. More importantly, he reveals the implicit belief that emotions make us human and contribute significantly to the meaning of parent-child relationships. His daughter's smile was interpreted to mean that she was gaining awareness of her relationship to her family environment and that she was becoming more of an interactive partner in the parent-child relationship. Moreover, her smile meant that parenting no longer merely involved the daily caregiving activities of feeding, cleaning, and carrying, but that she was telling him that "she's with us"–becoming a member of the family and a more active contributor to family relationships.

As noted in the Introduction of Part I of this volume, emotions are involved in almost every aspect of family development. Certainly, emotions are intimately involved in almost as many aspects of the parent-child relationship. Parents' emotions influence children's development and emotions (Halberstadt, 1991) and children's development and emotions influence parents' emotions and behavior (Dix, 1991).

These dynamics reflect the fact that emotions are transactional in nature–they reflect the interplay between the qualities individuals bring to their environments and the diversity of environments individuals experience (Sameroff, 1987). An example of the transactional nature of emotions and parent-child interactions is presented in Figure 1. As depicted in this figure, a complicated childbirth may make a mother anxious and nervous about her fragile newborn child. The mother's anxiety during the first months of the infant's life may cause her to be uncertain and inappropriate in her interactions with the infant. In response to such inconsistency, the infant may become fussy and difficult. This fussiness decreases the pleasure the mother obtains from the child and, as a result, she spends less time with her infant. One outcome of her withdrawal is that the child may develop feelings of anger, resentment, and insecurity. In this example, the outcome (the child's insecurity and anger) was not caused by the complicated birth nor by the mother's subsequent anxiety. The most direct cause is the mother's displeasure and avoidance in interacting with her child–but this conclusion would be a serious oversimplification of a complex sequence of emotion-related transactions that occurred over time. Clearly, there is a need for more research that is transactional and focuses on the bi-directional effects of parent-child emotionality.

Introduction

For much of this century, a focal issue in the study of children's development has been the process of socialization (Bugental & Goodnow, 1998). Although attention has been paid to the effects and correlates of parental warmth and hostility on children's development (Maccoby & Martin, 1983), until recently, there has been considerably less attention paid with how family members' socialize each others' emotions and emotion-related behavior (Eisenberg, Cumberland, & Spinrad, 1998). The papers contained in this volume make a significant contribution to this relatively neglected area of family research and reflect the diversity of topics related to this area of inquiry. For example, the papers focus on a variety of emotion-related processes ranging from parental interactive styles (McDowell et al.) to parental responsiveness (Spinrad & Stifter) to how parents react to children's emotions (Fabes et al.). Moreover, these papers focus on various parent subsystems–ranging from the study of the impact of individual mothers and fathers to the study of the marital system (Cummings et al., Part I). Although most of the papers in this portion of the work focus on parent-child relationships, the Sawyer et al. paper focuses on another important family influence on emotional development–namely, the impact of siblings. This is important because interactions with siblings provide a context for a wider range of emotional experiences than do parent-child interactions and interactions with siblings have been found to be typified by greater emotional intensity than the exchanges that characterize other family interactions (Katz, Kramer, & Gottman, 1992). Thus, emotions and family interactions vary depending on the specific nature of the individual family members involved in the interactions.

The papers in Part II also vary in regard to the nature of emotion-related outcomes. Some papers focus more on emotional reactivity (Spinrad & Stifter), whereas others are more concerned with how this reactivity is regulated (McDowell et al.; Gottman & Katz). Some authors focus more on general emotional competence (McDowell et al.; Fabes et al.), whereas others focus more on specific elements of general emotional competence, such as understanding and communication of emotion (Denham & Kochanoff; Sawyer et al.; Saarni & Buckley). A bias in all of the research is that almost all of the papers focus on the influence of parents' behavior on child outcomes. One notable exception is the work of Fabes et al. who specifically developed a scale that measures parents' reactions to children's negative emotions–focusing on how children's negative emotions influence parental behaviors and emotional reactions. But even in our paper, the outcome for the study is how these parental responses influence children's emotion-related responding.

FIGURE 1. Transactional Depiction of the Relation of Emotions and Parent-Child Interactions.

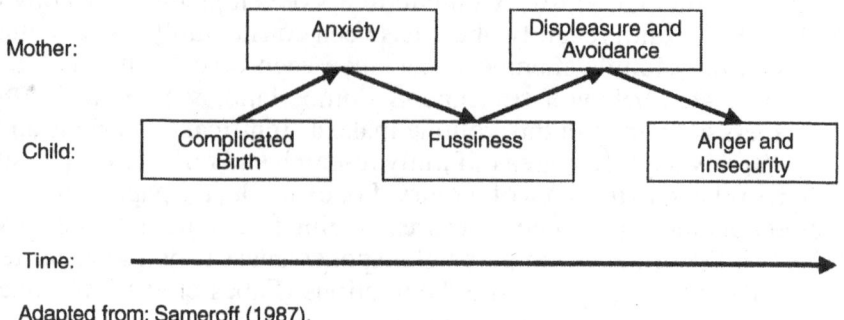

Adapted from: Sameroff (1987).

Clearly, there is a need for greater study as to how children affect the organization and reorganization of parental (and sibling) emotions and behaviors (cf. Dix, 1991).

These papers also cover a wide, but not complete, age range of children's development. The study of children's emotions from infancy through middle-school is well represented. Absent from this is the study of the relations of family and emotions in adolescents–an area that needs more work devoted to it.

In the introduction to Part I, we noted some of the problems associated with measuring emotions, particularly in regard to self-reports of emotion. Most researchers who study emotions wish for better measures than we now have. The need for measures of emotion that are more accurate, sensitive, reliable, and objective is clear and breakthroughs in the study of emotion and families will require the use of new sources of evidence to supplement the popular measures currently used. In our view, the most likely area for a measurement breakthrough is the physiological domain. Although we can still learn a lot about emotions by asking people how they feel, the use of physiological measures appears to be the key to new developments in the measurement of emotion. The Gottman and Katz paper reflects this new potential. In addition to heart rate and its various indexes (e.g., mean heart rate, heart rate variability, vagal tone), emotion researchers also have turned to the use of other physiological measures such as: electrodermal activities (e.g., skin conductance; Fabes, Eisenberg, & Eisenbud, 1993), temperature (Ekman, Levenson, & Friesen, 1983), facial electromyograms (e.g., facial muscle contractions; Wilson & Cantor, 1985), brain waves (Calkins, Fox, & Marshall, 1996), blood pressure (Prkachin, Williams-Avery, Zwaal, & Mills, 1999), and hormones such as cortisol (a stress-related hormone; Stansbury & Gunnar, 1994). Although rarely done, we believe that these measures can be used to examine physiological linkages and affective exchanges among family members (cf. Levenson & Gottman, 1983). Thus, the use of physiological measures to assess emotions among family members may provide new insights in the ways that emotions affect, and are affected by, the ways that family members relate to, interact with, and influence one another.

We wish to thank the authors for their willingness to contribute to this important book. Appreciation also goes to Gary Peterson and Sue Steinmetz, co-editors of *Marriage & Family Review*, for their advice and assistance in getting the papers to press. Finally, thanks goes to all those individuals who helped with the reading and reviewing of the papers. Their advice helped shape the quality of the work. Together, we hope this volume generates more interest in understanding better the relation between emotions and family life.

AUTHOR NOTE

Support for Richard Fabes was provided in part by a grant from the National Institute of Mental Health (RO1 MH60838). Support for Carlos Valiente and Stacie Leonard was provided by a Cowden Fellowship Award from the Department of Family and Human Development, Arizona State University.

Address correspondence to: Richard A. Fabes, Department of Family and Human Development, Box 872502, Arizona State University, Tempe, AZ 85287-2502 (E-mail: rfabes@asu.edu).

REFERENCES

Batson, C. D. (1987). Self-report ratings of empathic concern. In N. Eisenberg & J. Strayer (Eds.), *Empathy and its development* (pp. 356-360). New York: Cambridge University Press.

Birnbaum, D. W., & Chemelski, B. E. (1984). Preschoolers' inferences about gender and emotion: The mediation of emotionality stereotypes. *Sex Roles, 10*, 505-511.

Blechman, E. A. (Ed.). (1990). *Emotions and the family: For better or for worse.* Hillsdale, NJ: Erlbaum.

Brody, L. (1999). *Gender, emotion, and the family.* Cambridge, MA: Harvard University Press.

Brody, L. R. (1985). Gender differences in emotional development: A review of theories and research. Special Issue: Conceptualizing gender in personality theory and research. *Journal of Personality*, *53*, 102-149.

Bugental, B. B., & Goodnow, J. J. (1998). Socialization processes. In W. Damon & N. Eisenberg (Eds.), *Handbook of child psychology* (Vol. 3, pp. 389-462). New York: Wiley.

Calkins, S. D., Fox, N. A., & Marshall, T. R. (1996). Behavioral and physiological antecedents of inhibited and uninhibited behavior. *Child Development*, *67*, 523-40.

Dix, T. (1991). The affective organization of parenting: Adaptive and maladaptative processes. *Psychological Bulletin*, *110*, 3-25.

Eisenberg, N., Cumberland, A., & Spinrad, T. L. (1998). Parental socialization of emotion. *Psychological Inquiry*, *9*, 241-273.

Ekman, P., Levenson, R. W., & Friesen, W. V. (1983). Autonomic nervous system activity distinguishes among emotions. *Science*, *221*, 1208-1210.

Fabes, R. A., Eisenberg, N., & Eisenbud, L. (1993). Behavioral and physiological correlates of children's reactions to others in distress. *Developmental Psychology*, *29*, 655-663.

Frijda, N. H. (1986). *The emotions*. New York: Cambridge University Press.

Gottman, J. M., Katz, L. F., & Hooven, C. (1997). *Meta-emotion: How families communicate emotionally*. Mahwah, NJ: Erlbaum.

Greene, B. (1985). *Good morning, merry sunshine*. New York: Penguin Books.

Halberstadt, A. G. (1991). Toward an ecology of expressiveness: Family socialization in particular and a model in general. In R. S. Feldman & B. Rime (Eds.), *Fundamentals of nonverbal behavior. Studies in emotion & social interaction.* (pp. 106-160). New York: Cambridge University Press.

Katz, L. F., Kramer, L., & Gottman, J. M. (1992). Conflict and emotions in marital, sibling, and peer relationships. In C. U. Shantz & W. W. Hartup (Eds.), *Conflict in child and adolescent development* (pp. 122-149). Cambridge, England: Cambridge University Press.

Maccoby, E. E., & Martin, J. A. (1983). Socialization in the context of the family: Parent-child interaction. In P. H. Mussen & E. M. Hetherington (Eds.), *Handbook of child psychology: Vol 4. Socialization, personality, and social development* (pp. 1-101). New York: Wiley.

Prkachin, K. M., Williams-Avery, R. M., Zwaal, C., & Mills, D. E. (1999). Cardiovascular changes during induced emotion: An application of Lang's theory of emotional imagery. *Journal of Psychosomatic Research*, *47*, 255-67.

Saarni, C. (1993). Socialization of emotion. In M. Lewis & J. M. Haviland (Eds.), *Handbook of emotions*. (pp. 435-446). New York, NY: Guilford Press.

Saarni, C., Mumme, D. L., & Campos, J. J. (1998). Emotional development: Action, communication, and understanding. In W. Damon & N. Eisenberg (Eds.), *Handbook of child psychology* (Vol. 3, pp. 237-310). New York: Wiley.

Sameroff, A. J. (1987). The social context of development. In N. Eisenberg (Ed.), *Contemporary topics in developmental psychology* (pp. 273-291). New York: Wiley.

Stansbury, K., & Gunnar, M. R. (1994). Adrenocortical activity and emotion regulation. *Monographs of the Society for Research in Child Development*, *59*, 108-134.

Wilson, B. J., & Cantor, J. (1985). Developmental differences in empathy with a television protagonist's fear. *Journal of Experimental Child Psychology*, *39*, 284-299.

A Family-Wide Model for the Role of Emotion in Family Functioning

E. Mark Cummings
Marcie C. Goeke-Morey
Lauren M. Papp

SUMMARY. A family-wide perspective is essential for comprehensive understanding of the influence of emotions on child and marital functioning. After reviewing a family systems perspective on emotions, a specific family-wide model (i.e., an emotional security hypothesis) is outlined. Exploratory analyses based on a new diary methodology are presented examining interconnections between emotions and behaviors among family members during marital conflict situations in the home. Results based on both mothers' and fathers' reports indicated that emotions and behaviors in the marital subsystem were linked to children's emotional and behavioral reactions in a manner consistent with an emotional security hypothesis. Implications for a family-wide model of emotion and directions for future research are discussed. *[Article copies available for a fee from The Haworth Document Delivery Service: 1-800-HAWORTH. E-mail address: <docdelivery@haworthpress.com> Website: <http://www.HaworthPress.com> © 2002 by The Haworth Press, Inc. All rights reserved.]*

KEYWORDS. Emotion, marital relationships, family systems

E. Mark Cummings, Marcie C. Goeke-Morey, and Lauren M. Papp are affiliated with the University of Notre Dame.

Preparation for this paper was supported in part by a grant from the National Institute of Child Health and Human Development (HD 36261) to the first author.

[Haworth co-indexing entry note]: "A Family-Wide Model for the Role of Emotion in Family Functioning." Cummings, E. Mark, Marcie C. Goeke-Morey, and Lauren M. Papp. Co-published simultaneously in *Marriage & Family Review* (The Haworth Press, Inc.) Vol. 34, No. 1/2, 2002, pp. 13-34; and: *Emotions and the Family* (ed: Richard A. Fabes) The Haworth Press, Inc., 2002, pp. 13-34. Single or multiple copies of this article are available for a fee from The Haworth Document Delivery Service [1-800-HAWORTH, 9:00 a.m. - 5:00 p.m. (EST). E-mail address: docdelivery@haworthpress.com].

© 2002 by The Haworth Press, Inc. All rights reserved.

A distinguished body of research has evolved indicating the significance of emotions to children's functioning and development (Denham, 1998; Fabes & Eisenberg, 1992; Harris, 1989; Saarni, 1999). However, with a few notable exceptions (Cummings & Davies, 1996; Denham & Grout, 1992; Gottman, Katz, & Hooven, 1997), research and theory have only begun to advance the study of the role of emotions in child and family functioning from a family-wide perspective. A family-wide perspective is undoubtedly essential for a comprehensive understanding of the effects of emotions on child and family functioning. This paper is concerned with conceptual themes toward advancing a family-wide model of the role of emotions in child and family functioning. Given the centrality of methodology to the potential for new advances in understanding (Cummings, Davies, & Campbell, 2000), attention is also given to a new methodology being employed to study these questions and the ways in which the current investigation contributes to the understanding and study of these issues. Moreover, to illustrate directions for future research, exploratory analyses are presented that examine interconnections between emotions and behaviors among family members.

A FAMILY SYSTEMS PERSPECTIVE ON EMOTIONS

Families are appropriately viewed as relational environments with systems qualities (Cox & Paley, 1997). Thus, a systems theory perspective may be usefully applied to outlining the complex patterns of mutual influence that characterize family functioning. Accordingly, such a perspective emphasizes viewing families as organized wholes, with the wholes having influences above and beyond those of its parts. For example, overall family emotional expressiveness may constitute a context for children's reaction to family emotion, beyond effects due to the emotional qualities of specific family subsystems (Cassidy, Parke, Butkovsky, & Braungart, 1992). Thus, a child whose family experiences indicate that highly emotional exchanges have benign outcomes in families may not be disturbed by emotionally-charged interactions (e.g., between parents and children or between husbands and wives), whereas a child from a family environment in which such exchanges often have negative outcomes may respond with distress. Thus, larger units within the family are pertinent to an understanding of emotion as influences within the family (triadic subsystems, for example, mother, father and child as a relation unit, or the whole family system as a unit of contextual influence) (Cox & Paley, 1997).

At the same time, it also follows from systems theory that the family is appropriately seen as composed of multiple distinct subsystems, with each exercising influence on the others and on the whole. Accordingly, the actions and emotions of family members are necessarily interdependent, having a reciprocal and continuous influence on other family members, with each individual or dyadic unit inextricably embedded within the larger family system. Thus, a family systems model advocates against simple linear models of causality or the assumption that one can adequately understand family influences by focusing exclusively on certain individual subsystems (Emery, Fincham, & Cummings, 1992). For example, in order to fully understand child functioning, it is important to consider the emotions and actions of multiple family subsystems (e.g., parent-child, marital, siblings, and child) rather than simply the emotions and actions of a single family system (e.g., child or parent-child).

Applied to a family-wide model of emotions, systems theory predicts that the emotions and behaviors of each subsystem are related to the emotions and behaviors of other subsystems. Thus, it would be expected that the emotions of one marital partner would influence the emotions of the other in interaction. As another example, family systems may include mothers, fathers, and children, that is, triadic or even more complex systems, with interrelations thus expected between the emotions and behaviors of marital partners and children.

The research literature indicates that among the subsystems that merit particular consideration with regard to family influences are the individual as a subsystem, the marital subsystem, the parent-child subsystem, and the sibling subsystem (Cummings et al., 2000). However, these subsystems are not necessarily equal in the pattern of emotional influence on children and other family systems. Traditional research has emphasized the importance of the influence of emotions in the parent-child subsystem for children's own emotional functioning, frequently to the exclusion of the study of possible effects of other family subsystems. More recent research suggests that the emotional qualities of the marital (or other interadult) subsystem may actually have more pervasive implications for the quality of child, marital, parent-child, and sibling subsystems, as well as overall family functioning (Cowan & Cowan, 2001; Cummings, 1998; Cummings, Goeke-Morey, & Graham, 2001). Accordingly, a central theme of this paper is the need for a family-wide perspective on emotions that goes beyond considering emotions in the parent-child subsystem to considering relations between emotions and behaviors in the marital and child subsystems as well.

However, a limitation of traditional systems theory is that these notions are for the most part theoretically rather than empirically based. Moreover, many questions are left unanswered, based solely on the theoretical principles of systems theory, including the degree to which emotions in one subsystem affect emotions and behavior in the others, or the relative size of effects attributable to different subsystems. There are endless possibilities for patterns, levels, and directions of influence, with no basis for deciding amongst the alternatives based solely on systems theory. Thus, the contribution toward a family-wide model of emotions of systems theory is a general heuristic for outlining a family-wide model but it remains for family research to articulate the specific process models for the role of emotions in families.

FAMILY RESEARCH DIRECTIONS

Marital conflict has proven to be a particularly significant category of emotional event in the family with regard to child, marital, and family functioning (Cummings & Davies, 1994). Emotionality in the marital subsystem, especially during interparental conflict, has been shown repeatedly to have direct effects on children's emotions and behaviors (e.g., Cummings, 1987), and indirect effects by influencing the quality of emotional communications in the parent-child subsystem (e.g., Jouriles & Farris, 1992). Furthermore, researchers using a number of different analogue paradigms have isolated the emotional qualities of interparental communications as influential in terms of children's emotions and behaviors (e.g., Shifflett-Simpson & Cummings, 1996). Moreover, family systems researchers (e.g., Easterbrooks & Emde, 1988) have suggested that the marital dyad is the most important and influential family relationship, and that when this relationship is distressed, family responsibilities and coping skills suffer (Gilbert, Christensen, & Margolin, 1984). Minimally, consideration of the marital relationship when studying child development is necessary for any complete account of socialization influences (Fincham, 1998).

Traditional correlational research has long indicated links between marital conflict and child adjustment (Cummings & Davies, 1994; Grych & Fincham, 1990). More recent observational studies of the functioning of triadic family contexts involving marital conflict and children's functioning are informative regarding dynamic processes underlying or mediating the effects between marital exchanges and children's responses in triadic contexts, particularly including the role of emotions. In one such study, Easterbrooks, Cummings, and Emde (1994) reported that toddlers showed more positive behaviors than distressed or mediating behaviors when their parents demonstrated harmonious or positive expressions during a marital problem-solving task. On the other hand, expressions of distress between the parents, although relatively uncommon in this context, were significantly related to children's distress.

In another recent study, Kitzmann (2000) reported that family processes involving mothers, fathers, and their 6- to 8-year-old sons, became disrupted after conflictual marital interactions compared to pleasant marital interactions. Lower levels of family cohesion as well as higher levels of unbalanced alliances were found following marital disagreements. In addition, fathers demonstrated significantly less support and engagement toward their sons following the conflictual discussion compared to the pleasant discussion.

Along similar lines, Davis, Hops, Alpert, and Sheeber (1998) suggested that a triadic family approach is more informative than the traditional dyadic perspective when investigating marital conflict's impact on adolescents' development. Using a sequential analysis procedure, this laboratory study found that conflictual mother-father interactions led to subsequent aggressive functioning during triadic family interactions for both boys and girls, suggesting that children model their parents' hostile or aggressive conflict strategies in their own interpersonal relationships. Moreover, adolescents' aggressive and dysphoric responses to interparental aggression sequences contributed to the prediction of their overall aggressive and depressive functioning when general marital satisfaction was included as a control variable.

An assumption of this study is that the meaning rather than the specific content of marital communications is particularly important when considering effects on both parents and children (Fincham, 1998). Given this assumption, the use of parental reports of their own, their partners' and their children's emotions may tell us more in important ways about current and past family functioning in the home than could be obtained from an outside observer in the laboratory. Consistent with this conceptual and methodological perspective, self-reports of emotional reactions and perceptions of others' emotional responses through procedures such as home diaries may provide a particularly valuable window into emotional processes.

An initial diary study used mothers' home reports to examine young children's reactions to naturally occurring marital anger and affection expressions and simulated emotion expressions (Cummings, Zahn-Waxler, & Radke-Yarrow, 1981). Findings suggested that marital conflict induced distress and anger in 10- to 20-month-old infants which was markedly different from their reaction to marital harmony. In a follow-up study, Cummings, Zahn-Waxler, and Radke-Yarrow (1984) found that children's reactions to expressions of anger and affection in the home changed over time. Six- to 7-year-old children overtly expressed their emotions (e.g., cry, yell, laugh) significantly less often during interparental anger situations than they did as toddlers, and they were much more likely to intervene in marital conflict situations, as evidenced by the significantly higher rate of mediation attempts (Cummings et al., 1984).

In a more recent diary study (O'Hearn, Margolin, & John, 1997), mothers and fathers completed daily reports of marital conflict that occurred in front of their child. Children from homes with physical marital conflict were more likely to evidence negative emotions (e.g., appear sad or frightened), become hostile (e.g., misbehave or appear angry), or attempt to control exposure to marital conflict (e.g., leave the room) than children from nonphysical conflict or low conflict families. In addition, children from either physical or nonphysical high conflict families were more likely to take sides during marital conflict episodes than children from low conflict homes.

These studies suggest that both in the laboratory and in the home, emotions and behaviors in one family subsystem influence emotions and behaviors in others. Theoretical as well as empirical directions are needed for further advances in the study of the role of emotions in families. In particular, given the vast number of possible interrelations and processes that are possible, theory is needed to delimit and define the function of emotions in interpersonal functioning in families, including marital relations and children, thereby providing a model and framework to guide systematic tests of the role of emotions in families. In the next section, we build upon past work (Cummings & Davies, 1996), and outline testable propositions toward a model regarding a proactive and active role of emotions in child and family functioning.

EMOTIONAL SECURITY HYPOTHESIS: A SPECIFIC FAMILY-WIDE MODEL OF EMOTIONS

The traditional view considers emotions to be feeling states as relatively passive correlates of more powerful or cognitive functions, but as

Barrett and Campos (1987) discuss, a paradigm shift is occurring. Theories are moving away from views that emotions are of secondary importance to a functional perspective emphasizing the personal meaningfulness and the functional importance of emotions. Moreover, traditional views hold that emotions primarily result from "intrapsychic" events and processes. Newer views of emotion, including the functionalist perspective, hold that emotions also result from "interpsychic" or "interpersonal" events and processes.

The functionalist perspective on emotions suggests that emotions serve an adaptive, organizational function for an individual. Campos, Campos, and Barrett (1989) define *emotions* as "processes of establishing, maintaining, or disrupting the relations between the person and the internal or external environment, when such relations are significant to the individual" (p. 395). Emotions are posited, in effect, to be integral to the internal monitoring system for the individual, appraising events, organizing experiences, and motivating and guiding behavior (Bretherton, Fritz, Zahn-Waxler, & Ridgeway, 1986).

Consistent with a functionalist perspective on emotions, Davies and Cummings (1994) suggest that children's emotional responses reflect their evaluation of the meaning that marital conflict has for their own well-being and the well-being of their families. This emotional security hypothesis is a process model that posits that emotions are integral to children's appraisals about situations (such as marital conflict), and organize and guide their behavior so as to maximize their sense of emotional security.

Cummings and Davies (1996) define emotional security as ". . . a set goal by which children regulate their own functioning in social contexts, thereby directing social, emotional, cognitive, and physiological reactions" (p. 126). Thus, for children, the primary goal of maintaining a sense of emotional security is what motivates them to act and react in the face of a family stressor such as marital conflict (Davies & Cummings, 1998). That is, children have a set goal of emotional security, a state at which they feel safe and secure about themselves and their families. When something upsetting occurs, such as witnessing destructive marital conflict, children are moved from that place of security. Children then react so as to reestablish their sense of emotional security.

Davies and Cummings (1994; Cummings & Davies, 1996) describe three interrelated processes by which emotional security impacts children's functioning. First, they suggest that children's sense of emotional security affects their ability to regulate their own emotional arousal, including their affective state, behavioral expressions, and physiological reactions. Second, children's emotional security guides them to regulate their exposure to family stressors such as marital conflict by attempting to control their parents' behavior or emotion, or by removing themselves from the exposure. Third, emotional security affects children's cognitive appraisals of the internal representations they have about the nature of the relationships within their family. Together, these components of emotional security serve to mediate the effect of marital dysfunction on children's adjustment (Davies & Cummings, 1998).

Framed within a contextualistic perspective and consistent with a general systems model, children's sense of emotional security is seen as a function of the interaction between environment and individual factors (Davies & Cummings, 1994; Cummings & Davies, 1996). Thus, factors such as history of marital functioning, parent-child relationships, parental characteristics (such as depression), and individual differences in children (e.g., temperament), all influence emotional security.

Consistent with a functionalist perspective on emotion, Goeke-Morey (1999) has also suggested that children's emotional responses provide a basis for classifying parental marital conflict behaviors as constructive, destructive, or productive by serving as an index of their emotional security. Marital conflict behaviors that elicited more negativity than positivity in children, reflecting a reduction in emotional security, were classified as destructive. These included such behaviors as using physical aggression, making threats, yelling, withdrawing, or giving the cold shoulder. Behaviors that elicited more positivity than negativity in children, reflecting an increase in emotional security, were classified as constructive. These included such acts as holding hands, making a sincere joke, being supportive, apologizing, and compromising. Finally, behaviors that elicited equally low levels of negativity and positivity, reflecting a lack of difficulty from a security perspective, were classified as productive. These included such behaviors as calmly discussing the problem, suggesting solutions, or reaching a partial resolution, such as agreeing to disagree or giving in. Thus, children's emotional responding reflects their felt security in the face of various types of marital conflict; using the emotional criteria, three categories of conflict emerge: destructive, productive, and constructive.

A child's emotional security derives from interactions (present and past) between the individual and the functioning of the family as a whole (Cummings & Davies, 1996). Thus, pertinent to a family-wide model of the role of emotions in families, Cummings and Davies (1996) explicitly extended the emotional security hypothesis to include the possible influence of multiple family systems on children's emotional security. Thus, according to this model, sibling-sibling relations, child-grandparent relations, and broader contextual elements of family functioning (e.g., emotional relationships with other individuals within and outside of the family) should each be considered potential influences on children's emotional security (see also Waters & Cummings, 2000).

Serving to emphasize the role of emotionality, recent empirical tests of the roles of the three components of emotional security in mediating relations between marital conflict and children's adjustment have produced the most consistent support for emotional regulation as a mediator of children's functioning due to marital conflict histories. For example, using a latent variable path analysis, Davies and Cummings (1998) examined whether the links between marital relations and 6- to 9-year-old children's adjustment were mediated by response processes indicative of emotional security. Analyses supported theoretical pathways whereby the interrelated components of emotional security mediated the relationship between marital dysfunction and children's adjustment. Emotional reactivity (e.g., vigilance, distress) and internal representations in the context of interparental relations were each identified as mediators of relations between marital conflict and child adjustment. However, emotional reactivity was related to both externalizing and internalizing symptoms, whereas internal representations of marital relations were only related to internalizing.

In summary, we have provided a general conceptual framework for a family-wide perspective on emotions from a systems perspective. Moreover, we have described a specific process model that emphasizes the function of emotions in organizing and directing children's reactions to family interactions (i.e., the emotional security hypothesis). We next consider an example of a future direction in research toward advancing the family-wide study of the role of emotions in family functioning. Consistent with these conceptions, we present ongoing research from our laboratory that addresses gaps in the current methodology and further explores interrelations between marital and child emotions and behaviors.

TOWARD A NEW DIARY METHODOLOGY

The current study is based on parental diary reports and expands upon previous investigations concerned with the question of examining marital conflict behaviors and children's responses in everyday contexts. A number of directions in parental diary development have been designed to improve this methodology, particularly with regard to the role of emotions in family functioning. A key new direction is to more extensively train mothers and fathers to accurately describe what happens at home. A frequent limitation of investigations using diary methods in the past was that adults were not informed with regard to definitions of terms or tested with regard to their understanding of the categories for home reporting. Moreover, in response to the limitations of requiring parents to make dictated narrative records, the present diary report only requires parents to complete a brief checklist concerning marital and child responses during interparental interactions. Consequently, accessibility of this methodology is increased to a broader sampling of adults, including adults with relatively limited verbal skills. Finally, consistent with an emphasis on the role of emotions in guiding children's and parents' behavior that is posited here, reporting on the perceptions of father, mother, and child emotions across a range of emotions (positive, sad, mad, scared) is a focus of the diary report protocol. Thus, the current methodology is designed to increase the breadth, precision, and user-friendliness of the assessment of marital and child functioning by means of parental diary reports (Cummings, Goeke-Morey, & Dukewich, 2001).

The present methodology also provides an advance over previous diary methodologies by improving the conceptualization as well as measurement of interparental discord. Notably, children are affected by everyday differences of opinion between parents that are handled in a constructive or destructive manner (Cummings & Davies, 1994). While most research has narrowly focused on highly negative forms of marital conflict, inclusion of a broader range of everyday marital interactions around differences between the parents is likely to advance understanding of the role of marital relations in children's functioning. Accordingly, *couple conflict* in the present research is broadly defined as any major or minor interparental interaction that involves a difference of opinion, whether it is mostly negative or mostly positive. This encompassing definition of couple conflict is expected to provide a more complete picture of marital relations and children's experiences with marital interactions within families.

METHOD

Participants

Participants in this study were 55 families with at least one child between the ages of 4-11 (28 boys and 27 girls). Ninety-five percent of the couples were married; 5% cohabitated. Forty-nine percent of couples (43% of mothers and 31% of fathers) reported that their marriages were disharmonious (indicated by a score of less than 100 on at least one of the spouse's Marital Adjustment Test; Locke & Wallace, 1959). Mothers' mean age was 33 years (range = 21-43) and fathers' mean age was 36 years (range = 24-44). In addition, 100% of mothers reported graduating high school and 42% graduating college or beyond; 100% of fathers reported graduating high school and 54% graduating college or beyond. Ninety percent of families were Caucasian, 4% African American, 4% biracial, and 2% Hispanic. Family annual income ranged from less than $10,000 to more than $80,000 per year with an average annual income of between $25,000 and $40,000. Families were recruited through newspaper advertisements and flyers distributed at daycare centers and community events and were paid $60 to participate.

Materials

Marital Daily Record. The Marital Daily Record (MDR) is an instrument that parents completed independently at home to describe specific instances of marital conflict. Among other elements, couples reported their own emotions and behaviors experienced throughout a marital conflict interaction, as well as their perception of their partners' emotions and behaviors. The emotions assessed include positivity, anger, sadness, and fear. For the analyses discussed in this paper, anger, sadness, and fear were also summed to create a negativity composite. The behaviors include a variety of destructive (e.g., making threats), productive (e.g., discussing the problem calmly), and constructive (e.g., compromising) behaviors used both during and to end the conflict interaction. For these analyses, each endorsed behavior in a particular category was summed to created composites of destructive, productive, and constructive behaviors.

Child Response Record. Parents completed the Child Response Record (CRR) when their child was able to see or hear the interaction reported on the MDR. On the CRR, parents marked the degree to which they believed their child felt happy, angry, sad, and afraid throughout the marital conflict episode. Again, anger, sadness, and fear were summed to create a negativity composite. Parents also endorsed the behaviors used by their child, including a variety of mediational (e.g., helped out), extremely insecure (e.g., was aggressive), avoidant (e.g., avoided us), and secure behaviors (e.g., continued activity), which were summed to create composite scores.

Procedure

During the initial laboratory visit, parents were led through a standard training procedure for completing the MDR and CRR. They were taught to complete an MDR following any interparental discussions in which (a) some difference of opinion needed to be worked through, (b) the parents were upset with each other, *or* (c) both of the above. Parents were instructed to describe every conflict interaction that fit that description, whether or not the disagreement was resolved, and were asked to complete the MDR as soon as possible after the interaction ended.

Parents' received extensive training regarding each element of the MDR and the CRR. Terms and behavioral categories were described in detail, with definitions and examples provided for each. Parents received folders containing blank MDRs and detailed written instructions that reviewed the information parents learned during the training session. In addition, parents watched short video clips of adult actors simulating each behavior on the MDR. These video clips served both to give parents a visually presented example of the behaviors and to measure parents' ability to identify the behaviors on the MDR after receiving the training and before completing the measures at home. Mothers and fathers discussed misidentified behaviors with the research assistant until all behaviors were fully understood.

In addition, parents received practice completing the entire MDR during the training session. Mothers and fathers watched a videotape of actors simulating a series of relatively complex marital conflict situations, similar to those experienced by couples at home. The situations included a range of positive and negative behaviors and emotions, providing parents with examples of a broad range of constructive and destructive marital interactions. Parents completed the practice MDRs on their own, and then reviewed them with the research assistant, who answered questions and verified that all of the relevant sections were completed. Throughout the laboratory visit, parents were given ample opportunity to ask questions about any aspect of the forms. Mothers and fathers then left the lab and completed MDRs and CRRs independently at home regarding their everyday marital interactions over the span of 6 days.

Mothers and fathers returned for a second laboratory session several weeks later, bringing the MDRs and CRRs they had completed at home. During this visit, parents again watched the video clips of the behaviors included on the MDR and completed the behavior-matching task. In addition, mothers and fathers again completed MDRs for the more complex, simulated conflict interactions between two adults represented as marital partners.

The procedure ensured that parents received considerable training on the definitions of the behaviors used and how and when to complete MDRs and CRRs at home. By obtaining records from both mothers and fathers, we gained the opportunity to consider the perspective of each member of the marital subsystem, rather than relying exclusively on the report of one spouse, traditionally the wife, as the definitive view. This allowed for consideration and comparison of both partners' perceptions of marital and family functioning in the home.

RESULTS

Exploratory analyses are presented pertaining to the role of mothers', fathers', and children's emotions and behaviors in dyadic and triadic marital conflict situations. Analyses are concerned with the relations between husbands' and wives' emotions in the context of everyday marital interactions and the emotions and behaviors of children who are present for these marital events. Consistent with the family-model for the role of emotions in families advanced here, it was expected that the emotions experienced or expressed by one member or dyad within the family would be related to emotions experienced or expressed by other members of the family (i.e., marital emotions would be related to children's emotions and behaviors). Moreover, given that emotions are posited here to play a central role in organizing and directing responses in family interactions, it was expected that interparental emotions would be even more closely related to children's emotional and behavioral responses than other categories of interparental behaviors (e.g., forms of conflict behaviors).

In the present study, over the span of 6 days, wives reported a total of 264 marital conflict episodes; children were present for 45.1%. Husbands reported a total of 204 marital conflict episodes; children were present for 38.7%. One hundred fifty-four of those conflicts were common between husbands and wives. It is interesting to speculate as to the cause of the discrepancy between husbands' and wives' reports. It could be that husbands and wives perceive marital interactions differently to the point that they do not always view the same instances as conflict. It is also possible that wives were simply more willing to report conflicts or are more diligent in the completion of the checklists than were husbands. Means and standard deviations for study indices are presented in Tables 1 and 2.

TABLE 1. Means and Standard Deviations for Parents' Reports of Conflict Emotions and Behaviors

	Fathers' reports				Mothers' reports			
	Father		Mother		Father		Mother	
	MI[a]	CP[b]	MI[a]	CP[b]	MI[c]	CP[d]	MI[c]	CP[d]
Emotions								
Positivity	105.74 (78.01)	108.43 (85.12)	108.21 (74.36)	111.76 (82.02)	106.84 (82.61)	113.43 (81.05)	111.84 (80.89)	118.97 (84.39)
Negativity	140.14 (119.87)	153.71 (121.06)	160.19 (139.64)	155.37 (115.37)	129.06 (102.51)	132.13 (100.62)	184.77 (139.58)	186.77 (138.24)
Anger	71.39 (63.08)	86.23 (72.99)	86.99 (76.55)	94.57 (80.13)	81.50 (70.46)	84.93 (72.50)	96.21 (76.44)	98.98 (80.31)
Sadness	51.30 (71.56)	49.29 (67.80)	49.08 (64.37)	36.96 (45.95)	32.03 (46.78)	33.04 (46.06)	61.89 (72.46)	63.33 (73.77)
Fear	17.45 (22.25)	18.19 (20.91)	24.12 (29.60)	23.84 (26.16)	15.53 (24.60)	14.16 (18.25)	26.67 (34.38)	24.46 (29.26)
Behaviors								
Destructive	1.40 (1.26)	1.78 (1.37)	1.32 (1.30)	1.45 (1.49)	1.18 (1.25)	1.22 (1.24)	1.41 (1.31)	1.45 (1.27)
Productive	1.32 (.95)	1.30 (1.08)	1.13 (.88)	1.14 (.90)	1.24 (.92)	1.29 (.99)	1.23 (.89)	1.28 (.96)
Constructive	.90 (.95)	.85 (1.01)	.66 (.82)	.67 (.80)	.89 (1.01)	.88 (.98)	.70 (.87)	.66 (.72)

Note. MI = All marital interactions; CP = Marital interactions for which the child was present Means: (standard deviations). [a]n = 204; [b]n = 79; [c]n = 264; [d]n = 119.
Possible ranges: Individual Emotions: 0-290; Destructive: 0-7; Productive and Constructive: 0-5.

How Do Fathers' and Mothers' Emotions Relate to Children's Emotions and Concern During Marital Conflict?

Table 3 shows the intercorrelations between mothers' and fathers' reports of their emotions within the marital subsystem and their children's emotions and concerns. Both mothers and fathers reported that when parents expressed more anger, sadness, fear, and negative emotionality in marital conflict, children were more concerned. Moreover, children generally experienced more negative emotions and less positive emotions when their parents expressed negative emotions during marital conflict. Although mothers and fathers reported that neither their own

TABLE 2. Means and Standard Deviations for Parents' Reports of Children's Reactions to Marital Conflicts

	Fathers' reports[a]	Mothers' reports[b]
Concern	82.85 (70.64)	67.79 (61.47)
Emotions		
Positivity	145.04 (77.92)	161.68 (73.90)
Negativity	126.65 (215.72)	94.77 (99.88)
Anger	34.16 (64.75)	24.55 (32.08)
Sadness	50.05 (70.37)	42.53 (48.91)
Fear	42.43 (97.48)	27.70 (42.71)
Behaviors		
Extreme Insecurity	.28 (.68)	.36 (.79)
Mediation	1.08 (1.32)	1.03 (1.27)
Avoidance	.11 (.36)	.06 (.27)
Security	2.68 (.99)	2.65 (1.27)

Note. [a]n = 79, [b]n = 119. Means: (standard deviations).
Possible ranges: Concern and Individual Emotions: 0-290;
Extreme Insecurity and Mediation: 0-5; Avoidance: 0-1; Security: 0-3.

nor their partners' positivity throughout marital conflict was related to children's level of concern or children's negative emotional responses, they each reported that their partners' positive emotionality was related to their children's positive emotionality.

How Do Fathers' and Mothers' Emotions Relate to Children's Behaviors?

Next we consider the relation between fathers' and mothers' emotions in marital conflict and children's mediating, avoiding, secure, and

TABLE 3. Correlations Between Parents' Emotions and Children's Emotions Throughout Marital Conflict Episodes

	C Concern	C Positivity	C Negativity	C Anger	C Sadness	C Fear
F Positivity	−.005	.229*	−.073	−.092	−.090	.002
	.184	*.113*	*.135*	*.063*	*.099*	*.185*
F Negativity	.363***	−.200*	.334***	.154 ^	.343***	.272**
	*.279**	*−.352****	*.402****	*.307***	*.513****	*.314***
F Anger	.327***	−.221*	.261**	.153 ^	.253**	.206*
F Sadness	.231*	−.086	.238**	.065	.281**	.186*
	.117	*−.242**	*.391****	*.322***	*.434****	*.337***
F Fear	.117	−.005	.199*	.073	.178^	.208*
	*.254**	*−.311***	*.554****	*.411****	*.588****	*.527****
M Positivity	.094	.150	−.013	−.058	−.046	.066
	.085	*.200 ^*	*−.078*	*−.091*	*−.113*	*−.030*
M Negativity	.315***	−.084	.366***	.167 ^	.456***	.208*
	.192 ^	*−.286**	*.344***	*.262**	*.408****	*.293***
M Anger	.131	.045	.163^	.157 ^	.243**	−.016
	.139	*−.251**	*.240**	*.190 ^*	*.277**	*.206 ^*
M Sadness	.301***	−.119	.327***	.115	.447***	.166 ^
	.074	*−.158*	*.218 ^*	*.178*	*.277**	*.164*
M Fear	.371***	−.219*	.457***	.070	.358***	.607***
	*.293***	*−.215 ^*	*.399****	*.262**	*.464****	*.375****

Note. Standard text reflects mother report (n = 119); text in italics reflects father report (n = 79). F = Fathers' emotions; M = Mothers' emotions; C = Children's emotions.
^ $p \leq .10$. * $p \leq .05$. ** $p \leq .01$. *** $p \leq .001$.

extremely insecure behaviors during marital conflict. Correlations based on the report of mothers and fathers are presented in Table 4.

Mothers reported that children engaged in extremely insecure behaviors (such as crying, freezing, misbehaving, yelling at parents, being aggressive) when fathers were angry or evidenced negative emotionality, but that mothers' emotion was not related to extremely insecure behaviors by the children. Mothers further reported that children's mediation (involvement in the parents' conflict through such acts as comforting,

TABLE 4. Correlations Between Parents' Emotions and Children's Behaviors Throughout Marital Conflict Episodes

	C Extreme Insecurity	C Mediation	C Avoidance	C Security
F Positivity	−.139 *.094*	−.094 *−.071*	.012 *−.082*	−.065 *−.052*
F Negativity	.186* *.030*	.276** *.302***	.015 *.187^*	.048 *−.130*
F Anger	.254** *−.186^*	.270** *.227**	.052 *.180*	.079 *−.180*
F Sadness	.039 *.203^*	.156^ *.197^*	−.037 *.106*	−.011 *−.034*
F Fear	−.086 *.166*	.055 *.318***	−.029 *.114*	−.018 *−.016*
M Positivity	−.048 *.028*	−.036 *−.059*	.034 *−.189^*	−.091 *−.056*
M Negativity	.073 *−.007*	.220* *.174*	.201* *.020*	−.043 *−.010*
M Anger	−.061 *−.154*	.130 *.033*	.159^ *.012*	−.101 *.038*
M Sadness	.145 *.281**	.225* *.143*	.169^ *−.030*	.038 *−.006*
M Fear	.147 *−.052*	.118 *.416****	.087 *.105*	−.021 *−.151*

Note. Standard text reflects mother report (n = 119); text in italics reflects father report (n = 79). F = Fathers' emotions; M = Mothers' emotions; C = Children's behaviors.
^ $p \leq .10$. * $p \leq .05$. ** $p \leq .01$. *** $p \leq .001$.

helping out, taking sides) was related to mothers' and fathers' negative emotionality and sadness, and to fathers' anger. Mothers reported that their negative emotionality, anger, and sadness was related to children's avoidance, but that fathers' emotions were not. Finally, children's secure behaviors (such as continuing activity or watching) were not related to parents' emotions during conflict.

The fathers' perspective provided a similar story, although different in a few notable ways. Similar to mothers, fathers reported a significant relation between their anger and their children's extreme insecurity, but fathers also described that both mothers' and fathers' sadness was related to children's extreme insecurity. Fathers reported that their negative emotionality, anger, and sadness were related to children's mediation, but also reported that mothers' and fathers' fear was related to that type of behavior in children. Fathers described that their negative emotionality was related to children's avoidance, and that their wives' positivity was inversely related to children's avoidance. Fathers' reports did not indicate a significant relation between children's secure behaviors and parents' emotions during marital conflict.

DISCUSSION

The exploratory analyses presented in this paper support the complex interdependence and reciprocity of emotion within the family system, specifically with regard to marital conflict. When children were considered in relation to the marital subsystem, results indicate the interconnectedness of emotions between different individuals in everyday family environments. Even in a context defined only by the behavior in one subsystem (the marital), members of another subsystem (the child) affect and are affected emotionally by the interaction. The appraisal and regulatory functions of emotion were indicated by these data.

Interestingly, parents' emotions were more closely related to children's emotions than to children's behaviors. These data thus advance the notion that emotions play an important, even central, role in family functioning. Moreover, the powerful findings for emotions are consistent with the notion of the directing, organizing, and motivating function of emotion posited by the emotional security hypothesis and a functionalist perspective on emotion. Furthermore, the similarity in patterns of responding to the two different reporters of family emotions and behaviors (e.g., the mother and the father) adds to confidence in the pattern of findings.

The present review thus outlines conceptual, empirical and methodological directions for a family-wide model for the role of emotions in family functioning. Not surprisingly, given the complexity and elusiveness of the subject of emotional processes in interpersonal relations in the family, many questions remain. For example, despite the acknowledgment of the role of both emotion and cognition in children's appraisals of marital conflict and other family processes (Davies & Cummings, 1994; Grych & Fincham, 1990), little is known about the relations between cognition and emotion at the level of the dynamic processes underlying the appraisal of everyday family events. Moreover, the strong assertions of a functionalist perspective for the role of emotions in appraising, organizing and directing children's responses to family events require much further investigation. Nonetheless, recent work indicates an active and proactive role of emotional environments and emotional processes in family functioning (Cummings & Davies, 1994; Gottman et al., 1997). Notably, the theory and operationalization of variables advanced by the emotional security hypothesis (Cummings & Davies, 1996; Cummings, Goeke-Morey, & Papp, 2001; Davies & Cummings, 1998) provides a specific and testable proving ground for examining the role that emotions play in family functioning, pertinent to the evaluation of the tenets of a functionalist perspective on emotions.

This study explored correlational relationships between emotions and behaviors. An important next step is to utilize more sophisticated statistical techniques in order to more fully understand the complex nature of diary data from a systems perspective. Multilevel modeling, such as HLM could be employed to more thoroughly examine the relationship between elements of parental conflict and children's emotional and behavioral responding. Multilevel modeling would allow us to obtain separate estimates of these relationships for each conflict episode and to efficiently aggregate these estimates so that averages for individual families could be obtained. This technique would also allow investigation of the relation between elements of conflict measures with the MDR and other family variables.

Innovations in methodology will continue to be integral for breaking new ground in the study of emotions from a family-wide perspective in naturalistic family contexts (Cummings, 1995). As every direction in methodology has strengths and weaknesses, a thorough understanding of process is most likely to emerge from a coordinated use of multiple methodological directions (Cummings et al., 2000). In terms of substantive topics, future directions should include more study of the moderators of established relations, that is, for whom and under what circumstances the relations hold (e.g., variations by culture, ethnicity, SES). Finally, there is an urgent need for the investigation of developmental process and causal relations in prospective longitudinal designs. It is hoped that this review will serve as an impetus for investigators to tackle these and related questions about the role of emotions in family life from a family-wide perspective.

REFERENCES

Barrett, K. C., & Campos, J. J. (1987). Perspectives on emotional development II: A functionalist approach to emotions. In J. Osofsky (Ed.), *Handbook of infant development* (2nd Ed.) (pp. 555-578). New York: Wiley.

Bretherton, I., Fritz, J., Zahn-Waxler, C., & Ridgeway, C. (1986). Learning to talk about emotions: A functionalist perspective. *Child Development, 57,* 529-548.

Campos, J. J., Campos, R. G., & Barrett, K. C. (1989). Emergent themes in the study of emotional development and emotion regulation. *Developmental Psychology, 25,* 394-402.

Cassidy, J., Parke, R. D., Butkovsky, L., & Braungart, J. M. (1992). Family-peer connections: The roles of emotional expressiveness within the family and children's understanding of emotions. *Child Development, 63,* 603-618.

Cowan, P. A., & Cowan, C. P. (2001). What an intervention design can tell you about how parents affect children's academic achievement and social competence. In M. M. Bristol-Power, J. G. Borkowski, & S. L. Landesman (Eds.), *Parenting and the child's world: Multiple influences on intellectual and socio-emotional development* (pp. 75-97). Hillsdale, NJ: Lawrence Erlbaum Associates, Inc.

Cox, M. J., & Paley, B. (1997). Families as systems. *Annual Reviews of Psychology, 48,* 243-267.

Cummings, E. M. (1987). Coping with background anger in early childhood. *Child Development, 58,* 976-984.

Cummings, E. M. (1995). Usefulness of experiments for the study of the family. *Journal of Family Psychology, 9,* 175-185.

Cummings, E. M. (1998). Children exposed to marital conflict and violence: Conceptual and theoretical directions. In G. W. Holden, R. Geffner, & E. N. Jouriles (Eds.), *Children exposed to marital violence: Theory, research, and applied issues* (pp. 55-93). Washington, DC: American Psychological Association.

Cummings, E. M., & Davies, P. T. (1994). *Children and marital conflict: The impact of family dispute and resolution.* New York, NY: The Guilford Press.

Cummings, E. M., & Davies, P. T. (1996). Emotional security as a regulatory process in normal development and the development of psychopathology. *Development and Psychopathology, 8,* 123-139.

Cummings, E. M., Davies, P. T., & Campbell, S. (2000). *Developmental psychopathology and family process.* New York, NY: The Guilford Press.

Cummings, E. M., Goeke-Morey, M. C., & Dukewich, T. L. (2001). The study of relations between marital conflict and child adjustment: Challenges and new directions for methodology. In J. H. Grych & F. D. Fincham (Eds.), *Child development and interparental conflict* (pp. 39-63). Cambridge, MA: Cambridge University Press.

Cummings, E. M., Goeke-Morey, M. C., & Graham, M. A. (2001). Interpersonal relations as a dimension of parenting. In M. M. Bristol-Power, J. G. Borkowski, & S. L. Landesman (Eds.)., *Parenting and the child's world: Multiple influences on intellectual and socio-economic development* (pp. 251-263). Hillsdale, NJ: Lawrence Erlbaum Associates, Inc.

Cummings, E. M., Goeke-Morey, M. C., & Papp, L. M. (2001). Couple conflict, children, and families: It's not just you and me, Babe. In A. Booth, A. Crouter, & M.

Clements (Eds.), *Couples in conflict* (pp. 117-147). Mahwah, NJ: Lawrence Erlbaum Associates, Inc.

Cummings, E. M., Zahn-Waxler, C., & Radke-Yarrow, M. (1981). Young children's responses to expressions of anger and affection by others in the family. *Child Development, 52*, 1274-1282.

Cummings, E. M., Zahn-Waxler, C., & Radke-Yarrow, M. (1984). Developmental changes in children's reactions to anger in the home. *Journal of Child Psychology and Psychiatry, 25*, 63-74.

Davies, P. T., & Cummings, E. M. (1994). Marital conflict and child adjustment: An emotional security hypothesis. *Psychological Bulletin, 116*, 387-411.

Davies, P. T., & Cummings, E. M. (1998). Exploring children's emotional security as a mediator of the link between marital relations and child adjustment. *Child Development, 69*, 124-139.

Davis, B. T., Hops, H., Alpert, A., & Sheeber, L. (1998). Child responses to parental conflict and their effect on adjustment: A study of triadic relations. *Journal of Family Psychology, 12*, 163-177.

Denham, S. A. (1998). *Emotional development in young children*. New York, NY: The Guilford Press.

Denham, S. A., & Grout, L. (1992). Mothers' emotional expressiveness and coping: Relations with preschoolers' social-emotional competence. *Genetic, Social, and General Psychology Monographs, 118*, 73-101.

Easterbrooks, M. A, Cummings, E. M., & Emde, R. N. (1994). Young children's responses to constructive marital disputes. *Journal of Family Psychology, 8*, 160-169.

Easterbrooks, M. A., & Emde, R. N. (1988). Marital and parent-child relationships: The role of affect in the family system. In R. A. Hinde & J. Stevenson-Hinde (Eds.), *Relationships within families: Mutual influences* (pp. 83-103). London, England: Oxford University Press.

Emery, R. E., Fincham, F. D., & Cummings, E. M. (1992). Parenting in context: Systemic thinking about parental conflict and its influence on children. *Journal of Consulting and Clinical Psychology, 60*, 909-912.

Fabes, R. A., & Eisenberg, N. (1992). Young children's coping with interpersonal anger. *Child Development, 63*, 116-128.

Fincham, F. D. (1998). Child development and marital relations. *Child Development, 69*, 543-574.

Gilbert, R., Christensen, A., & Margolin, G. (1984). Patterns of alliances in non-distressed and multiproblem families. *Family Processes, 23*, 75-87.

Goeke-Morey, M. C. (1999). *Children and marital conflict: Exploring the distinction between constructive and destructive marital conflict behaviors*. Unpublished doctoral dissertation, University of Notre Dame, Notre Dame, IN.

Gottman, J. M., Katz, L. F., & Hooven, C. (1997). *Meta-emotion: How families communicate emotionally*. Mahwah, NJ: Lawrence Erlbaum Associates, Inc.

Grych, J. H., & Fincham, F. D. (1990). Marital conflict and children's adjustment: A cognitive-contextual framework. *Psychological Bulletin, 108*, 267-290.

Harris, P. L. (1989). *Children and emotion: The development of psychological understanding*. Oxford, England: Basil Blackwell, Inc.

Jouriles, E. N., & Farris, A. M. (1992). Effects of marital conflict on subsequent parent-son interactions. *Behavior Therapy, 23*, 355-374.

Kitzmann, K. M. (2000). Effects of marital conflict on subsequent triadic family interactions and parenting. *Developmental Psychology, 36*, 3-13.

Locke, H. J., & Wallace, K. M. (1959). Short marital-adjustment and prediction tests: Their reliability and validity. *Marriage and Family Living, 21*, 251-255.

O'Hearn, H. G., Margolin, G., & John, R. S. (1997). Mothers' and fathers' reports of children's reactions to naturalistic marital conflict. *Journal of the American Academy of Child and Adolescent Psychiatry, 36*, 1366-1373.

Saarni, C. (1999). *The development of emotional competence.* New York, NY: The Guilford Press.

Shifflett-Simpson, K., & Cummings, E. M. (1996). Mixed message resolution and children's responses to interadult conflict. *Child Development, 67*, 437-448.

Waters, E. & Cummings, E. M. (2000). A secure base from which to explore close relationships. *Child Development, 71*, 164-172.

A Meta-Analysis of Family Expressiveness and Children's Emotion Expressiveness and Understanding

Amy G. Halberstadt
Kimberly L. Eaton

SUMMARY. We assessed associations between family styles of expressing emotion and children's expressive styles and skill in understanding emotion. We used a meta-analytic strategy for synthesizing the studies in these two areas, and we examined moderating variables of emotion valence, age group, and measurement diversity in the relationship between family expressiveness and outcomes in children. For emotional expressiveness, positive family expressiveness and positive children's expressiveness were consistently associated across age, but negative family expressiveness and negative children's expressiveness were linearly and curvilinearly related across age, with a U-shaped relationship. For emotion understanding, positive family expressiveness and children's understanding were not related at any age. Negative and negative-submissive family expressiveness and children's emotion under-

---

Amy G. Halberstadt and Kimberly L. Eaton are affiliated with North Carolina State University.

Address correspondence to either author at: Department of Psychology, North Carolina State University, Raleigh, NC 27695-7801 (E-mail: Halbers@unity.ncsu.edu or Keaton@unity.ncsu.edu).

The authors thank Judith A. Hall for generously sharing her expertise in meta-analyses, and Julie C. Dunsmore, Nancy McElwain, Rick Fabes, and the anonymous reviewers for their helpful comments on the manuscript.

[Haworth co-indexing entry note]: "A Meta-Analysis of Family Expressiveness and Children's Emotion Expressiveness and Understanding." Halberstadt, Amy G., and Kimberly L. Eaton. Co-published simultaneously in *Marriage & Family Review* (The Haworth Press, Inc.) Vol. 34, No. 1/2, 2002, pp. 35-62; and: *Emotions and the Family* (ed: Richard A. Fabes) The Haworth Press, Inc., 2002, pp. 35-62. Single or multiple copies of this article are available for a fee from The Haworth Document Delivery Service [1-800-HAWORTH, 9:00 a.m. - 5:00 p.m. (EST). E-mail address: docdelivery@haworthpress.com].

© 2002 by The Haworth Press, Inc. All rights reserved.

standing tended to be related across age, both linearly and curvilinearly (an inverted U-shaped relationship). Explanations for these relations and future goals for research are discussed. *[Article copies available for a fee from The Haworth Document Delivery Service: 1-800-HAWORTH. E-mail address: <docdelivery@haworthpress.com> Website: <http://www.HaworthPress.com> © 2002 by The Haworth Press, Inc. All rights reserved.]*

KEYWORDS. Family expressiveness, meta-analysis, children's emotionality

The family is a hotbed of emotion. Parents and children report experiencing both positive and negative emotions throughout the course of development, and these emotional experiences can be intense and frequent. Siblings also evoke powerful feelings that are both positive (e.g., love, loyalty, adoration), and negative (e.g., anger, jealousy, and envy).

Not only are emotions intense and frequent in family settings, but individuals are more likely to express their emotion experiences to family members, compared to strangers, acquaintances, or colleagues at work (Matsumoto, Takeuchi, Andayani, Kouznetsova & Krupp, 1998). A common folk theory of emotion is that emotions can be more freely expressed at home, and should be relatively more regulated outside the home: "If you can't express your emotions at home, then where can you?"[1] Even children in elementary school report that they are more willing to show emotions with family members than with friends (Zeman & Garber, 1996).

There is also tremendous variation in overall expressiveness within families. First, individuals vary in both the frequency and intensity of experiencing discrete emotions (e.g., Halberstadt & Carpenter, 1993; Larsen, Diener, & Emmons, 1986). Second, individuals living in families experience their emotions within a social context, and other family members may act to suppress, modify, or intensify each others' emotions. For example, some families may encourage family members to suppress an emotion, either because they do not value emotion or because they perceive emotion to be dangerous (Dunsmore & Halberstadt, 1997; Halberstadt, Dunsmore, McElwain, Eaton, & McCool, 2001). In other families, however, individuals may actively seek to intensify emotions of other family members. Third, emotion can be contagious whether or not family members intend to affect others' emotional states (e.g., Hatfield, Cacioppo, & Rapson, 1994; Levenson, 1996).

It is theoretically logical that parental variations in felt and expressed emotion intersect with the lives of their developing children. For example, parents' reactions to children's emotions, parents' discussions of emotion with their children, parents' own styles of expressing emotion, and parental selection and modification of situations (also known as "niche picking") all have implications for children's emotional experiences. These parent-child emotional experiences influence both how children express their emotional experiences, and how they interpret others' emotional experience and expressions (Dunsmore & Halberstadt, 1997; Frederickson, 1998; Halberstadt, 1991; Parke & McDowell, 1998).

Because research evaluating parents' emotion-related socialization behaviors is well reviewed (Eisenberg, Cumberland, & Spinrad, 1998, and subsequent commentaries; Halberstadt, Crisp, & Eaton, 1999), we proceed to a more in-depth analysis of emotion expression in families, its associations with two kinds of outcomes for children, and life-span effects. We are particularly interested in lifespan effects for two reasons. First, it makes sense that parental influence, if it exists, develops over time, so we would expect that children would not necessarily be influenced by parental goals immediately. Indeed, some evidence for this exists in the family expressiveness literature; for example, fathers' and mothers' socialization behaviors that are not related to their children's skill at the same time of measurement have implications for their children's emotion understanding two years later (Denham & Kochanoff, 2001). Second, folklore suggests that children distance themselves from their parents in early adolescence, but become more like their parents as they get older. Research supports this lay perception of the changes over time and suggests that (a) it is not just movement away from parental models and support, but a switch of allegiance from parents to peers, and (b) the process begins in preadolescence (Buhrmester & Furman, 1987; Furman & Buhrmester, 1992).

Halberstadt et al. (1999) reviewed the literature on parental expression of emotion, and found nine groupings of outcome data. As predicted, children in expressive families were themselves emotionally expressive. Family expressiveness was also related to individuals' emotionality, understanding of emotion, social competence, intra-familial relationships and adult interpersonal relationships, self-esteem and personal adjustment, and academic achievement. Perhaps most interesting was how the relationships between family expressiveness and various outcome variables changed when valence of family expressiveness and age of the children were examined.

To examine these relationships more closely, we studied the two groupings for which there were 20 or more studies found in the narrative review (Halberstadt et al., 1999), and we used meta-analyses. For expression of emotion, the narrative review suggested that positive family expressiveness is consistently associated with individuals' positive expressiveness throughout the lifespan, but negative family expressiveness is only associated with negative expressiveness in older children (e.g., as they move into the middle childhood years and beyond). Using meta-analysis, a statistical technique that is sensitive to the magnitude of effects, we hoped to identify age differences that would not be detected in a narrative review. Particularly for negative expressiveness, we wanted to further explore the possibility that age was moderating the relationship between family and self-expressiveness. Again, we were interested in assessing the magnitude of the relationship, and at various times in the lifespan.

We were also able to distinguish between negative emotions that tend to be more submissive (e.g., sadness, apology, not handling tension well, embarrassment) and those that tend to be more dominant (e.g., anger, contempt, blaming, expressing dislike, criticizing). We wondered if families would be more similar in their expression of negative-submissive emotions than negative-dominant emotions. Because children's expression of negative-submissive emotion may be more socially acceptable than expression of negative-dominant emotions, children might model their parents' negative-submissive style more than their negative-dominant style. In families that are highly negative-dominant, there may be greater costs when children express negative-dominance back to parents. The power dynamics of negative-dominant expression might also change as children get older. For example, negative-dominance in infants and toddlers might be treated as part of the developmental process or initially as "cute," but by preschool and elementary school, negative dominance would not be tolerated by parents, especially parents who display high levels of negative-dominant emotions. In adolescence and college, when parents have less control over their children's behavior, children may become more like their parents than their parents would like. Thus, the relationship for negative dominance might change with age.

For understanding of emotion, the narrative review suggested different relationships for family expressiveness as a function of emotional valence. That is, positive expressiveness in the family was related to children's emotion understanding, but negative expressiveness in the family was not consistently related to children's emotion understanding. Again, age seemed to matter, with children from more expressive families demonstrating relatively greater skill early on, compared to children from less expressive families. This relationship seemed to reverse over time, however, with less expressive families demonstrating relatively greater skill than children from more expressive families during college and adulthood. It would make sense that young children, when presented with clear and frequent displays of prototypical expressions of emotion, would develop recognition skill more quickly, compared to children in less expressive homes, where emotion expression is less frequent and less fully displayed. By the college years, however, children from less expressive homes would have developed skill in recognizing prototypical expressions, and also the less intense or even fragmentary emotion expressions that children from more expressive homes may not be looking for or recognizing when they are present. Thus, for both positive and negative family expressiveness, we were interested in assessing the magnitude of the relationship, and at various times in the lifespan.

We also hypothesized that type of negative affect in the family was a relevant consideration. For example, when families are more expressive of negative-submissive emotions, which are by their nature more introspective, children may pay more attention to their emotions and understand them better. When families are more expressive of negative-dominant emotions, however, their negative expressiveness may impede development of understanding because the child is focusing on self-protective mechanisms such as escape. If so, then the relation between family negative-submissiveness and children's emotion understanding would be more positively related than the relation between family of negative-dominance and children's emotion understanding.

METHOD

The data set was generated by searching APA's PsychInfo database using terms related to expressiveness in the family context or between family members, and by soliciting reprints and preprints from researchers known to be active in family socialization of emotion. We further restricted the sample by excluding studies that did not report any effect sizes (see Table 1 for a list of the studies). As in Halberstadt et al. (1999), we distinguished between global, positive, and negative expressiveness. All findings reported for discrete emotions such as happiness, joy, surprise and interest, as well as dimensional emotions such as "positive," were included under the rubric of positive expressiveness. All findings for discrete emotions such as sadness, fear, anger, and disgust, as well as dimensional emotions such as "negative," "negative-submissive," and "negative-dominant," were included under the rubric of negative expressiveness. The negative expressiveness category was further analyzed by examining separately the findings that were reported as negative-submissive (sadness, fear and reported "negative submissive" findings) and negative-dominant (anger and reported "negative dominant" findings).

We examined correlation coefficients as the effect size estimates. When results were reported as t or F tests with 1 numerator degree of freedom, we derived r from t and F. We combined the effect sizes by transforming them to a Fisher's Zr, conducted the analyses, and then transformed the results back to r for ease of interpretability. Failures to support hypotheses as well as significant effects were included in the data set. Thus, if a study reported significant findings for mothers' negative expressiveness and fathers' positive expressiveness, and the researchers had collected the data to test mothers' positive and fathers' negative expressiveness as well, we assumed that the failure to report those relationships implied nonsignificant findings. For all such missing data, we imputed a correlation of $r = 0$. Because this was a conservative test of the hypotheses, parallel analyses were conducted including and excluding these null findings. Analyses excluding null findings provided slightly larger effects, but they did not differ significantly from those including the null findings in size or patterning by valence or age. Thus, we report the most conservative results (including the imputed zero correlations) below.

Many studies had multiple methods and multiple findings per study, with a mean of 13 findings per study for expressiveness and 8 findings per study for understanding. The unit of analysis in a meta-analytic review is the study, however, so each study can contribute only one effect size to any calculation. Thus, if a study reported three tests of the relationship between negative family expressiveness and children's expressiveness of negative emotion, and one test of the relationship between positive family expressiveness and children's expressiveness of positive emotion, the mean of the first three findings represented that study's finding in the negative expressiveness analyses, and the single effect for positive expressiveness represented that study's finding in the positive expressiveness analysis.

Mean effect sizes were weighted by the inverse of their variance, to recognize the increased power of studies with larger sample sizes. Following Cohen (1988), we interpret correlations of .10 as small, .30 as medium, and .50 as large. The significance level of the combined studies was estimated using Stouffer's method of adding Zs. To determine whether each group of studies shared a common population, we calculated a homogeneity statistic, Q, which has an approximate chi-square distribution with $k-1$ degrees of freedom. A significant Q statistic indicates that the variance in study effect sizes is significantly greater than we would expect by chance if the studies shared a common population effect size (Shadish & Haddock, 1994). We conducted planned linear and quadratic contrasts of age groups and linear contrasts of measurement diversity.

We also calculated a fail-safe N for each significant combined Z by squaring the sum of the individual Z scores, dividing by 2.706, and subtracting the number of studies present in that analysis (Rosenthal, 1991). The fail-safe N estimates the number of additional studies with null effects that would be needed to render the obtained results non-significant. Rosenthal suggests that an adequate fail-safe N is at least $5(k) + 10$, where k is the number of studies in the meta-analysis.

Participant ages were coded into one of these categories: infants/toddlers (ages 0-3), preschool (ages 3-4), kindergarten-elementary (ages 5-12), or adolescent/college (ages 13-21).[2] We also developed a measure of the extent to which researchers used multiple methods and times of measurement to assess the independent and dependent variable. We anticipated that correlations in studies that measured family expressiveness (FE) and children's expressiveness simultaneously, and used the same measurement procedures, were likely to be larger than correlations in studies that measured family and child expressiveness at different times or in different contexts. The four levels of measurement diversity were: (1) when FE and the outcome variable were both measured using the same method at the same time/setting, (2) when FE and the outcome variable were measured using the same method, but at a different time/setting or the same method at the same time but with very different measures, (3) when FE and the outcome variable were measured using the same method, but with different measures and different times or different methods at the same time, or (4) when FE and the outcome variable were measured using different methods at different times or settings. Although this is only a rough measure, we hoped it would be of some help in assessing how robust findings were when time, context, and types of measurements varied.

TABLE 1. Studies Used in Family Expressiveness–Self-Expressiveness and Family Expressiveness–Emotion Understanding Analyses

Study	Participant Population	Family Expressiveness–Self-Expressiveness Emotion Type	Family Expressiveness–Emotion Understanding Emotion Type
Barth & Steingard (1994)	College	P, N, NS, ND	
Berenbaum & James (1994)	College	N	P, N, NS, ND
Bronstein, Briones, Brooks, & Cowan (1996)	Adolescent	G, P	
Burrowes & Halberstadt (1987)	College & adult	G, P, N	
Camras, Ribordy, Hill, Martino, Sachs, Spaccarelli, & Stefani (1990)	Preschool - 1st Grade	G, P, N, NS, ND	P, N, ND
Cantor (1995)	Elementary		G, P, N
Cassidy, Parke, Butkovsky, & Braungart (1992)	Kindergarten/1st grade	P, N	G, P, N
Cummings, Zahn-Waxler, & Radke-Yarrow (1981)	Toddler	P, N, ND	
Daly, Abramovitch, & Pliner (1980)	Kindergarten		G
Denham (1989)	Toddler	P, N, NS, ND	
Denham, Cook, & Zoller (1992)	Preschool		G
Denham & Grout (1992)	Preschool		P, N, NS
Denham & Grout (1993)	Preschool	P, N	
Denham, Renwick-DeBardi, & Hewes (1994)	Preschool	N, NS, ND	
Denham, Zoller, & Couchoud (1994)	Preschool	G	G, P, N, NS, ND
Dunn, Bretherton, & Munn (1987)	Toddler	G	
Dunn, & Brown (1994)	Preschool		N
Dunn, Brown, Slomkowski et al. (1991)	Preschool		G
Dunn, Brown, & Beardsall (1991)	Elementary		G, P, N
Eisenberg, Fabes, Schaller et al. (1991)	College		P, N, NS, ND
Garner & Power (1996)	Preschool	P, N	P, N, NS, ND
Garner, Jones, Gaddy, & Rennie (1997)	Preschool	G	G
Garner, Robertson, & Smith (1998)	Preschool	P	
Halberstadt, Study 1 (1983)	College		G
Halberstadt, Study 2 (1983)	College		G

Study	Age Group	Codes
Halberstadt (1981/1986)	College	G, P, N, NS, ND
Halberstadt (1984,1986)	College	
Halberstadt, Fox, & Jones (1993)	Kindergarten	G
Hall (1978), in Halberstadt (1983)	Kindergarten	G
Isley, O'Neil, Clatfelter, & Parke (1999)	Kindergarten	P, N
Jones, Abbey, & Cumberland (1997)	Kindergarten–3rd grade	P, N, NS, ND
Jones, Eisenberg, & Fabes (1996)	Elementary	P, N, NS, ND
King & Emmons (1990)	College	G
Kring & Gordon (1998)	College	G
Lacks & Uzgiris (1995)	Toddler	G
Ludemann (1993)	Preschool	P, N, NS, ND
Malatesta & Haviland (1982)	Infant	P, N, NS, ND
Malatesta, Culver, Tesman, & Shepard (1989)	Infant/Toddler	P, N, NS, ND
Malatesta, Grigoryev, Lamb, Albin, & Culver (1986)	Infant	P, N, NS, ND
Nixon (1997)	Preschool	P, N
Stifter & Grant (1993)	Infant	P, N
Stifter & Moyer (1991)	Infant	P
Taylor (1979), in Halberstadt, 1983	College	G
Weissbrod & Kendziora (1997)	Preschool	P
Zuckerman (1979), in Halberstadt (1983)	College	G

Note. G = global; P = positive; N = negative; NS = negative-submissive; ND = negative dominance.

RESULTS

Family and Child Expressiveness

We found 29 studies that reported effect sizes for the relationship of family expressiveness (FE) with children's self-expressiveness (SE) of the same emotion type. Reliability for identifying findings relevant for these analyses was assessed by the two authors for five studies. Overall percent agreement was 87%, and the second author's decisions were used when disagreements occurred. We first examined studies that measured FE in a global way, without regard to the valence of the emotion being expressed. Next, we examined studies that distinguished positive and negative expressiveness. Within negative expressiveness, we further examined negative-submissiveness and negative-dominant expressiveness separately.

Global family expressiveness and global child expressiveness. These studies measured overall levels of expressiveness in the family without regard to possible differences in positive and negative expressiveness. Thus, these effects are separate measures, and not means of the findings presented below on positive and negative expressiveness. As shown in Table 2, results suggested a moderate relationship between FE and SE, $r = .25$. This was a highly robust finding, with a fail-safe N of 115 studies. Table 3 reports the weighted mean correlations by age group. These, and the trends found in the linear and quadratic contrasts for age, suggested a decline from toddlerhood to preschool, stability through elementary school, and then a slight rebound in adolescence/college, $Zs = -1.45$ and 1.37, ps $< .10$, for the linear and quadratic contrasts.

The linear contrast of measurement diversity indicated that studies with multiple measures and methods reported significantly lower correlations than those that used a single measure or method to assess expressiveness, $Z = -1.84$, $p < .05$. Surprisingly, the weighted mean correlations for measurement diversity were somewhat stable across the first three levels, despite variations in time and context, but dropped sharply when multiple methods, measures, and times of measure were used (weighted mean correlations for diversity levels 1 to 4 = .22, .34, .53, .12, respectively). The drop in magnitude for the highest level of measurement diversity did not appear confounded with sample age, as studies in that group included preschool, kindergarten/elementary, and adolescent/college participants.

Positive family expressiveness and positive child expressiveness. Nineteen studies assessed the relationship between positive FE and

TABLE 2. Meta-analysis of Relationships Between Family Expressiveness and Children's Expressiveness by Emotion Type

Emotion type	Unweighted mean r	Weighted mean r	95% Confidence Interval	k	n	Z	p =	Q
Global	.25	.25	.17, .33	11	531	5.80	.00001	14.86
Positive	.26	.27	.21, .33	19	966	8.50	.00001	50.95***
Negative	.13	.09	.03, .15	17	989	2.80	.00254	20.83
NS	.11	.13	.02, .24	8	338	2.40	.00814	8.89
ND	.15	.10	−.002, .21	9	356	1.91	.02775	16.71*

Note. Weighted mean r = mean effect size weighted by $N - 3$; k = number of studies contributing independent effect sizes; n = total number of participants; Z = measure of significance of weighted mean effect size; p = level of probability of weighted mean effect size; Q = test of homogeneity; NS = negative-submissive; ND = negative-dominant.
*$p < .05$. **$p < .01$. ***$p < .001$.

children's self-expressiveness of positive emotion. As shown in Table 2, results suggested a moderate relationship between FE and SE, $r = .27$, which was highly robust, with a fail-safe $N = 428$ studies. An unexpected finding was the highly heterogeneous nature of this group of studies; $Q = 50.95, p < .001$.

The weighted mean correlations in Table 3 suggested a decline from the infant/toddler years to the preschool years, and little change from there through adolescence/college. However, the planned age contrasts were not significant. Further, 10 of the 13 studies of infants, toddlers and preschoolers used a single measure or time of measurement to assess parental and child expressiveness. Thus, age groups were confounded with measurement diversity, which was significant in a planned linear contrast, $Z = -3.31, p < .01$. The weighted mean correlations for diversity levels 1 to 4 = .42, .16, .06, .11, respectively.

The heterogeneity of this data set was surprising, as positive expressiveness has traditionally been perceived as a theoretically cohesive construct. Because neither age trends nor measurement diversity differences account for this variability, we remain somewhat mystified by this variability for positive expressiveness, and also the robustness of the relationship between family and child expressiveness, which was maintained despite the heterogeneity.

Negative family expressiveness and negative child expressiveness. Seventeen studies assessed the relationship between negative FE and children's self-expressiveness of negative emotion. As shown in Table 2, FE and SE are only slightly related, $r = .09$.[3] Although the combined z-score suggests that it is extremely unlikely that the true population correlation is zero, the fail-safe N of 54 studies is lower than the $5k+10$ studies suggested by Rosenthal (1991) as a standard, so it is reasonable to assume there may be enough unpublished studies with null results to render this effect size nonsignificant.

The weighted mean correlations in Table 3 indicate a decline from infancy/toddlerhood to preschool, an increase in elementary school and a decrease in college participants. This pattern was significant in the planned quadratic contrast for age, $Z = 1.70, p < .05$.

The planned linear contrast for measurement diversity was also significant, $Z = -2.03, p < .05$. Larger effect sizes occurred in studies using a single method or time of measurement, and smaller effect sizes in studies with more varied methodology. Weighted mean correlations for diversity levels 1 to 4 = .19, .01, .03, .07, respectively. However, age groups and measurement diversity levels were not confounded with each other.

TABLE 3. Relationship of Family Expressiveness and Self-Expressiveness by Emotion Type Within Age Groups

Emotion Type	Infant/Toddler		Preschool		Kindergarten/Elementary		Adolescence/College		Age contrasts	
	k	Weighted mean r	k	Weighted mean r	k	Weighted mean r	k	Weighted mean r	(linear)	(quadratic)
Global	2	.46	3	.17	1	.16	5	.25	-1.45+	1.37+
Positive	7	.34	6	.21	3	.25	3	.20	-.74	.58
Negative	6	.14	5	.04	3	.12	3	.06	-.01	1.70*
NS	4	.12	2	.00	1	.08	1	.46	1.76*	1.24
ND	5	.21	2	-.17	1	.07	1	.27	-.80	3.17***

Note. Weighted mean r = mean effect size weighted by $N - 3$; k = number of studies contributing independent effect sizes.
+$p < .10$. *$p < .05$. **$p < .01$. ***$p < .001$

Negative-submissive family expressiveness and negative-submissive child expressiveness. Eight studies assessed the relationship between negative-submissive FE and children's negative-submissive expressiveness. As shown in Table 2, results suggest a small relationship between FE and SE, $r = .13$. Although the combined Z-score suggests that it is extremely unlikely that the true population correlation is zero, the fail-safe N of 6 studies suggests that there may well be enough unpublished studies with null results to render this effect size nonsignificant.

The weighted mean correlations in Table 3 indicated a decrease from infancy/toddlerhood to preschool, followed by an increase in elementary school and then again in college, and this was significant in the planned linear contrast for age, $Z = 1.76, p < .05$. The linear contrast of measurement diversity was not significant.

Negative-dominant family expressiveness and negative-dominant child expressiveness. Nine studies assessed the relationship between negative-dominant FE and children's negative-dominant expressiveness. As shown in Table 2, results suggested a small relationship between FE and SE, $r = .10$. The studies were also heterogeneous, $Q = 16.71, p < .05$, suggesting that the effect may be moderated by another variable. Although the combined Z-score suggests that it is extremely unlikely that the true population correlation is zero, the fail-safe N of 10 studies again suggests that there may be enough unpublished studies with null results to render this effect size zero.

The weighted mean correlations in Table 3 indicated a decrease from infancy/toddlerhood to preschool, followed by an increase in elementary school, and then again in college. This pattern was significant in the planned quadratic contrasts, $Z = 3.17, p < .001$.

The planned linear contrast for measurement diversity was also significant, $Z = -3.40, p < .001$. The finding of larger effect sizes in the studies using a single method or time of measurement, and smaller effect sizes in the two studies with more varied methodology must be interpreted cautiously, however, as diversity levels 3 and 4 contained only one study each. Weighted means for diversity levels 1, 3, and 4 = .18, .07, −.31, respectively. However, age group and measurement diversity levels were unrelated.

Overall, these studies suggest a small but significant effect of family expressiveness of emotion on children's developing expressiveness of emotion. Although all of the studies were correlational in nature, and thus directionality cannot be determined, it was consistently clear that a pattern of relationships exists. Children in expressive families were themselves more expressive, and, for negative expressiveness, the relationships between family and child were strongest when children were quite young and again when they reach young adulthood. It may be that similarity in negative expressiveness declines gradually with age as children experiment with styles that differ from those of their parents, and increases in college as independence is achieved and differentiation from the parental model is less important. Further, although type of measurement had some impact on the size of the effects, as predicted, the effects for age appeared to be independent and unconfounded by measurement effects.

Family Expressiveness and Children's Emotion Understanding

Analysis of the effect of family expressiveness on children's understanding of emotion was examined in 23 studies using the same constructs of global, positive and negative expressiveness that characterized the research on children's self-expressiveness (see Table 1 for the full list of studies). Reliability for identifying findings relevant for these analyses was assessed by the two authors for five studies. Overall percent agreement was 93%, and the second author's decisions were used when disagreements occurred. Results for analyses with emotion understanding are summarized in Tables 4 and 5.

Global family expressiveness. The correlation between overall levels of FE and children's emotion understanding approached zero in 15 studies, $r = .03$. However, the heterogeneity of these results, $Q = 33.72$, $p < .01$, suggested that analyses within levels of a moderator variable, such as age or measurement diversity, may reveal important relationships.

The weighted mean correlations by age group, in Table 5, indicate that the relationship between global FE and emotion understanding increased from preschool to kindergarten/elementary school, but was negative in college. As predicted, age was a significant moderator, whether tested with linear or quadratic contrasts; $Zs = -2.98$ and $-2.64, ps < .01$. There was no significant effect for measurement diversity.

Positive family expressiveness. The correlation between positive FE and children's emotion understanding also approached zero in 13 studies, $r = .03$.[3] Neither age nor measurement diversity was a significant moderator.

Negative family expressiveness. As with the expressiveness studies, we analyzed all studies on negative family expressiveness, whether negativity was assessed specifically (e.g., sadness or anger) or in an undifferentiated way (combining various aspects of negative expressive-

TABLE 4. Meta-analysis of Relationships Between Family Expressiveness and Children's Emotion Understanding by Emotion Type

Emotion type	Unweighted mean r	Weighted mean r	95% Confidence Interval	k	n	Z	p =	Q
Global	.03	.03	−.05, .11	15	627	.61	.27107	33.72**
Positive	.003	.03	−.03, .10	13	901	1.01	.15635	17.98
Negative	−.02	−.03	−.09, .04	14	939	−.90	.81657	21.63
NS	−.02	−.08	−.15, −.001	8	675	−1.98	.02358	17.46*
ND	.02	.03	−.05, .11	8	667	.75	.22548	6.74

Note. Weighted mean r = mean effect size weighted by $N − 3$; k = number of studies contributing independent effect sizes; n = total number of participants; Z = measure of significance of weighted mean effect size; p = level of probability of weighted mean effect size; Q = test of homogeneity; NS = negative-submissive; ND = negative-dominant.
*$p < .05$. **$p < .01$. ***$p < .001$.

TABLE 5. Relationship of Family Expressiveness and Emotion Understanding by Emotion Type Within Age Groups

Emotion Type	Preschool		Kindergarten/Elementary		Adolescence/College		Age contrasts	
	k	Weighted mean r	k	Weighted mean r	k	Weighted mean r	(linear)	(quadratic)
Global	5	.09	4	.17	6	−.15	−2.98**	−2.64**
Positive	6	−.03	4	.01	3	.09	.79	−.41
Negative	7	−.04	4	.05	3	−.07	.30	−1.61+
NS	4	.06	1	−.09	3	−.17	−2.19*	.71
ND	4	.01	1	.08	3	.03	−.21	−.38

Note. Weighted mean r = mean effect size weighted by $N − 3$; k = number of studies contributing independent effect sizes.
+ $p < .10$. * $p < .05$. ** $p < .01$. *** $p < .001$.

ness). This procedure allowed us to create the largest data set possible for analyzing the relationship between negative family expression and children's emotion understanding. We also examined negative-submissiveness and negative-dominant expressiveness separately.

The correlation between negative FE and children's emotion understanding approached zero in 13 studies, $r = -.03$. The weighted mean correlations and the quadratic trend reported in Table 5 suggested that the relationship between negative FE and emotion understanding increased from preschool to elementary school, but became negative again in college. The planned linear contrast of measurement diversity was not a significant moderator.

Negative-submissive family expressiveness. For expressiveness of negative-submissive emotions such as sadness and crying, the correlation between FE and children's emotion understanding was small but significant in 8 studies, $r = -.08$. This finding suggested, over all age groups, that children from more expressive homes (for negative-submissiveness) were less skilled at emotion understanding than children from less expressive homes. Again, the heterogeneity of these results, $Q = 17.46, p < .05$, suggested that analyses within levels of a moderator variable, such as age or measurement diversity, may be especially useful. As expected, the weighted mean correlations in Table 5 indicated a decline from the preschool studies to the elementary school studies, and then a decline again in college, and this pattern was significant in the linear contrast, $Z = -2.19, p < .05$. The planned linear contrast of measurement diversity was not significant.

Negative-dominant family expressiveness. For expressiveness of negative-dominant emotions such as anger or hostility, the correlation between FE and children's emotion understanding approached zero in 8 studies, $r = .03$. The weighted mean correlations and planned contrasts for age in Table 5 indicated little difference over age. The linear contrast of measurement diversity was not a significant moderator.

DISCUSSION

Altogether, the meta-analyses on emotional expressiveness confirmed relationships between emotional expressiveness in the family and in children. The effects for global and positive expressiveness were moderate in size and quite robust, as demonstrated by the large failsafe Ns. The meta-analyses demonstrated that the relationship of negative expressiveness between families and children was significant, but small and possibly eliminated by unpublished studies. Perhaps of greater significance, the meta-analyses provided us with sensitive analyses of age effects, and the linear and quadratic effects for all analyses with negative expressiveness demonstrated that age moderated the relationship between negative expressiveness and self-expressiveness. Together, these effects suggested a decline in the relationship between familial and child expressiveness from the infant/toddler years to preschool and kindergarten. With the introduction into peer life and school, the relations began to attenuate, and stayed fairly low throughout elementary school. By the college years, the relationships were positive again and of moderate magnitude. Thus, children seem to come full circle in similarity to their families.

The meta-analyses also highlighted the difference in magnitude of the associations between family and child expressiveness by valence. The overall effect size for the relationship between family and child expressiveness for positive expressiveness was more than twice the size of any of the overall effect sizes for negative expressiveness. It may be that these effect sizes reflect underlying biological dispositional similarities within families, but the negative expressiveness effects appear weaker due to variations in parental control of children's negative expressiveness. That is, familial dispositions for expressiveness styles may be more apparent for positive expressiveness because there are fewer social constraints regarding positive expressiveness in our culture, and so the dispositional styles are less modified by socialization strategies of parents.

Alternatively, it may be that parental socialization strategies create positive relationships for positive expressiveness, but children's negative temperamental qualities override parental styles of and values for expressiveness (Goldsmith, Buss, & Lemery, 1997). Yet another possibility is that parents do not try to control levels of positive expressiveness as much as negative expressiveness, so when children naturally imitate family styles there are few attempts to modify their behavior. However, when children imitate family styles of negative expressiveness, parents that are high in negative expressiveness may send additional (and forceful) messages of "Do as I say, not as I do!" Additionally, there may be especially strong consequences in highly negatively dominant families for children being negatively dominant themselves. This would nicely explain the decline in the relationship between familial and child negative expressiveness, beginning in preschool, and a reversion to family styles when children are in adolescence and college, and have become both more independent and powerful in the family. At that point in the lifespan, the myriad examples of family styles of negative expressiveness may have more of an effect on the developing child's behavior than strictures and consequences imposed by parents.

The significant relations for measurement diversity suggest that the more similar the methods, the higher the associations between variables. Studies that assess expressiveness at different times and in different contexts do not, however, necessarily provide more accurate assessments of the magnitude of the relationship. Rather, children learn early in life that different rules for behavior apply in different contexts, and those lower correlations may reflect children's more complex understanding of expressiveness rules in different contexts.

The meta-analyses on emotion understanding provide limited support for an overall relationship between family expressiveness and children's emotion understanding, with only one significant effect (negative-submissiveness in the family was negatively related to emotion understanding). Even when we examined only studies for which we had exact statistics (omitting studies with nonsignificance for which we had to assign a zero), the relationship between family expressiveness and emotion understanding changed minimally. This is in contrast to the "eyeball analyses" reported in Halberstadt et al. (1999), when narrative and simple counting procedures were used to assess the relationship.

There were, however, age-moderated relationships between family emotional expressiveness and children's emotion understanding. In three of the five emotion valence categories that we examined, the meta-analyses revealed a trend or significant linear or quadratic effect of age moderating the relationship between family expressiveness and children's emotion understanding. For global and negative-submissive emotions, familial expressiveness was increasingly related to poorer emotion understanding in children over time. Also, for global and negative emotions, a curvilinear relationship between family expressiveness and emotion understanding emerged, such that familial expressiveness tended to be increasingly related to emotion understanding from the preschool years to the elementary school years, but was negatively related by the college years. These meta-analyses provide the first empirical evidence of the curvilinear relations that have been hypothesized for some time (Camras et al., 1990; Halberstadt, 1991).

We also predicted different patterns in emotion understanding based on family levels of negative-submissiveness and negative-dominance. We predicted that children in families with higher levels of negative-submissiveness would become fairly skilled in emotion understanding, due to the more introspective nature of these emotions, compared to children in families with higher levels of negative-dominance, which might invoke self-protective mechanisms. The meta-analyses, however, indicated little difference between the two. Perhaps negative-submissiveness does not work to encourage an introspective approach to emotion so much as a ruminating approach, or perhaps the effects of negative-submissiveness in the family depend upon the target, with introspection occurring when children are not the targets but the observers of negative-submissive affect. Additionally, the self-protective behaviors that may emerge when negative-dominance behaviors occur in day-to-day interactions of family life may not be activated by artificial laboratory tasks, with stories and photographs about non-related others.

Sample heterogeneity. One of the difficulties of meta-analysis is the variability across samples due to multiple ways of measuring the constructs of interest. In this group of studies, family and child expressiveness were studied using questionnaires, observations, analysis of the emotion content of narratives, and with parent diaries. Children's emotion understanding was measured with vignette/interview designs and lab observations, and at least four different kinds of emotion understanding were measured: receptive expressive, stereotypical and non-stereotypical knowledge. The variability in methods adds noise to the data, thereby decreasing the likelihood of effects emerging. However, variability also increases confidence in the findings that do emerge as significant; they are clearly robust across different measures and contexts.

Family features. Although child and parent gender were analyzed too infrequently to include in a meta-analysis, individual studies suggest that parental gender matters. For example, stronger relationships between parental expressiveness and self-expressiveness emerge in same-gender dyads compared to cross-gender dyads (Cassidy, Parke, Butkovsky, & Braungart, 1992; Isely, O'Neil, Clatfelter, & Parke, 1999). It is also important to remember that caregiving time in the US still tends to be unequally distributed, with mothers much more likely to be the primary caregiver, or providing more caregiving than fathers. If boys and girls are brought up primarily by women, and boys perceive a need to differentiate from women as part of the gendering messages of the culture, then children's gender, caregiver gender, and family sex-role stereotype may also affect relations between family and children's expressiveness (Brody, 1999).

Although most of the studies we examined did not assess marital satisfaction, research on children's facial communicative skill (which is sometimes related to the more spontaneous expressiveness that we did analyze) suggests that boys with unhappily married parents were less skilled at producing emotion displays than boys with happily married parents (Shortt, Bush, McCabe, Gottman, & Katz, 1994). Family size may also matter, in that families with more members may well provide a more emotionally expressive environment, simply by virtue of having more people in the same amount of space. It is likely that sheer volume of interactions will increase (although rate of interactions may be stable) and, thus, more emotional events will be occurring within sight and hearing of children.

Within families, parental homogeneity versus heterogeneity may affect both emotion expressiveness and understanding in children (Dunsmore & Halberstadt, 1997). When parents are alike, children may more readily come to develop their parents' style of expressiveness, and when parents differ, children may develop an amalgamation of parental styles, or may develop a style most similar to the same-sex or the more nurturing parent. We imagine that children growing up in homes where parents have similar expressiveness styles will develop understanding about emotions at earlier ages than when parents use different styles of expressing emotions. When parents have different styles, children's understanding of emotion may be delayed (much like language learning when children are learning multiple language systems simultaneously), but their understanding of emotion may ultimately become more complicated and sophisticated than children whose parents are more homogenous in their expressiveness.

Assessing features of emotion understanding. Our meta-analyses are restricted to the studies that have been conducted, but other dimensions might moderate the relationship between family expressiveness and emotion understanding. For example, whose emotions are to be understood? That is, is the child being asked to assess the emotions of others or to assess his/her own emotions. Second, are the emotions depicted prototypical emotions, or do the expressions include blends or fragments? Solving a problem for which all the pieces are present may involve a very different set of skills than solving a problem for which several parts of the solution must be inferred. Third, what is being measured? There are actually many different kinds of skills, some of which have been measured in the collection of studies we have examined (e.g., emotion recognition, emotion situation knowledge, recognizing conflicting emotions, etc.) and some of which have not (e.g., knowing within the flow of an interaction that a message has been sent, Halberstadt, Denham & Dunsmore, 2001; recognizing idiosyncratic styles of communicating, Halberstadt et al., 2001; recognizing emotional transitions in others, Mayer & Salovey, 1997).

Skill versus children's interpretive structures. Although children's accuracy in recognizing emotion cues is associated with family expressiveness in different ways through the lifespan, the real effects of family styles of expressing emotions may be to convey many messages about how to interpret the world around the child. For example, the social referencing literature clearly demonstrates that children use parental expressions as guides in approaching or withdrawing from both physical and social stimuli (Sorce, Emde, Campos, & Klinnert, 1985). Children look to their trusted family members for guidance as to whether the physical or social environment is safe or not safe. Parental expressions of fear, worry, and anxiety, which are accumulated over time, may provide children with an overall message that the world is not a safe place, and may provide them with a filter with which they interpret others' behaviors. Thus, our focus on accuracy in recognizing emotions in comparison to interpreting socioemotional situations may cause us to underestimate the effects of family influence.

Developmental issues. For children's expressiveness (but not for emotion understanding), we were able to distinguish between very young children (infant/toddlers), children who are more aware of peer relations and importance (preschoolers), and children who are in formal settings in which peers clearly create and maintain cultures (kindergarten and elementary school). We were unable to distinguish, for either domain, between the early and later elementary school years, or adolescence, although there may well be substantial developmental progress that may occur over those years (Harter & Buddin, 1987). Thus, several valuable time periods are ripe for study.

In conclusion, we now know that familial positive expressiveness has robust associations with children's positive expressiveness, and that familial negative expressiveness has age-related associations with children's negative expressiveness, including both a linear pattern and curvilinear patterns that are U-shaped. Additionally, familial positive expressiveness does not appear to be related to children's emotion understanding, but familial negative expressiveness has age-related associations with children's emotion understanding, including both a linear pattern and a curvilinear pattern that is inverted U-shaped. In our discussion, we have attempted to open new questions and strategies for future research. It is rewarding to be able, with meta-analysis, to specify some answers to specific questions, and to open the stage for new ways to consider family socialization of emotion.

NOTES

1. Willingness to express emotion with family members also appears to vary by culture; for example, although American, Japanese, and Koreans report being more expressive with their families than with colleagues or strangers, Russians report being more controlled in emotional expressiveness with family members than with colleagues (Matsumoto et al., 1998).

2. One study with children from preschool to first grade (Camras et al., 1990) was included in the preschool category because the mean age of the children was at the preschool level. Additionally, one study combining adults with college students (and reporting no differences by sample age) was included in the college category (Burrowes & Halberstadt, 1987).

3. It may be noted that overlap between the positive and negative expressiveness analyses, and between the NS and ND analyses, was substantial. This overlap is an asset, however, because the valence differences that emerged cannot be due to the vagaries of different populations or different methods.

REFERENCES

Barth, J. M., & Steingard, B. (1994, April). *Family expressivity and college students' intimate relationships.* Poster presented at the Conference for Human Development, Pittsburgh, PA.

Berenbaum, H., & James, T. (1994). Correlates and retrospectively reported antecedents of alexithymia. *Psychosomatic Medicine, 56,* 353-359.

Brody, L. R. (1999). *Gender, emotion, and the family.* Cambridge: Harvard University Press.

Bronstein, P., Briones, M., Brooks, T., & Cowan, B. (1996). Gender and family factors as predictors of late adolescent emotional expressiveness and adjustment: A longitudinal study. *Sex Roles, 34,* 739-765.

Buhrmester, D., & Furman, W. (1987). The development of companionship and intimacy. *Child Development, 58,* 1101-1113.

Burrowes, B. D., & Halberstadt, A. G. (1987). Self- and family-expressiveness styles in the experience and expression of anger. *Journal of Nonverbal Behavior, 11,* 254-268.

Camras, L. A., Ribordy, S., Hill, J., Martino, S., Sachs, V., Spaccarelli, S., & Stefani, R. (1990). Maternal facial behavior and the recognition and production of emotional expression by maltreated and nonmaltreated children. *Developmental Psychology, 26,* 304-312.

Cantor, E. (1995). *The socialization of emotion understanding in deaf children: The role of the family.* Unpublished doctoral dissertation, University of Denver, Denver.

Cassidy, J., Parke, R. D., Butkovsky, L., & Braungart, J. M. (1992). Family-peer connections: The roles of emotional expressiveness within the family and children's understanding of emotions. *Child Development, 63,* 603-618.

Cohen, J. (1988). *Statistical power analysis for the behavioral sciences.* Hillsdale, NJ: Lawrence Erlbaum Associates.

Cummings, E. M., Zahn-Waxler, C., & Radke-Yarrow, M. (1981). Young children's responses to expressions of anger and affection by others in the family. *Child Development, 52,* 1274-1282.

Daly, E. M., Abramovitch, R., & Pliner, P. (1980). The relationship between mothers' encoding and their children's decoding of facial expressions of emotion. *Merrill-Palmer Quarterly, 26,* 25-33.

Denham, S. A. (1989). Maternal affect and toddlers' social-emotional competence. *American Journal of Orthopsychiatry, 59,* 368-376.

Denham, S. A., Cook C., & Zoller, D. (1992). Baby looks very sad: Implications of conversations about feelings between mothers and preschoolers. *British Journal of Developmental Psychology, 10,* 301-315.

Denham, S. A., & Grout, L. (1992). Mothers' emotional expressiveness and coping: Relations with preschoolers' social-emotional competence. *Genetic, Social, and General Psychology Monographs, 118,* 75-101.

Denham, S. A., & Grout, L. (1993). Socialization of emotion: Pathway to preschoolers' emotional and social competence. *Journal of Nonverbal Behavior, 17,* 205-227.

Denham, S. A., & Kochanoff, A. T. (2002). Parental contributions to preschoolers' understanding of emotion. *Marriage & Family Review, 34*(3/4), 311-343.

Denham, S. A., Renwick-DeBardi, S., & Hewes, S. (1994). Emotional communication between mothers and preschoolers: Relations with emotional competence. *Merrill-Palmer Quarterly, 40,* 488-508.

Denham, S. A., Zoller, D., & Couchoud, E. A. (1994). Socialization of preschoolers' emotion understanding. *Developmental Psychology, 30,* 928-936.

Dunn, J., & Bretherton, I., & Munn, P. (1987). Conversations about feeling states between mothers and their young children. *Developmental Psychology, 23,* 132-139.

Dunn, J., & Brown, J. (1994). Affect expression in the family, children's understanding of emotions, and their interactions with others. *Merrill-Palmer Quarterly, 40,* 120-137.

Dunn, J., Brown, J., & Beardsall, L. (1991). Family talk about feeling states and children's later understanding of other's emotions. *Developmental Psychology, 27,* 448-455.

Dunn, J., Brown, J., Slomkowski, C., Tesla, C., & Youngblade, L. (1991). Young children's understanding of other people's feelings and beliefs: Individual differences and their antecedents. *Child Development, 62,* 1352-1366.

Dunsmore, J. C., & Halberstadt, A. G. (1997). How does family emotional expressiveness affect children's schemas? In K. C. Barrett (Ed.) *New Directions in Child Development, The communication of emotion: Current research from diverse perspectives* (Vol. 77, pp. 45-68). San Francisco: Jossey-Bass Publishers.

Eisenberg, N., Fabes, R. A., Schaller, M., Miller, P., Carlo, G., Poulin, R., Shea, C., & Shell, R. (1991). Personality and socialization correlates of vicarious emotional responding. *Journal of Personality and Social Psychology, 61,* 459-470.

Eisenberg, N., Cumberland, A., & Spinrad, T. L. (1998). The socialization of emotion: Reply to commentaries. *Psychological Inquiry, 9,* 317-333.

Frederickson, B. L. (1998). Cultivated emotions: Parental socialization of positive emotions and self-conscious emotions. *Psychological Inquiry, 9,* 279-281.

Furman, W., & Buhrmester, D. (1992). Age and sex differences in perceptions of networks of personal relationships. *Child Development, 63*, 103-115.

Garner, P. W., Jones, D. C., Gaddy, G., & Rennie, K. M. (1997). Low-income mothers' conversations about emotions and their children's emotional competence. *Social Development, 6*, 37-52.

Garner, P. W., & Power, T. G. (1996). Preschoolers' emotional control in the disappointment paradigm and its relation to temperament, emotional knowledge, and family expressiveness. *Child Development, 67*, 1394-1407.

Garner, P. W., Robertson, S., & Smith, G. (1998). Preschool children's emotional expressions with peers: The roles of gender and emotion socialization. *Sex Roles, 36*, 675-691.

Goldsmith, H. H., Buss, K. A., & Lemery, K. S. (1997). Toddler and childhood temperament: Expanded content, stronger genetic evidence, new evidence for the importance of environment. *Developmental Psychology, 33*, 891-905.

Halberstadt, A. G. (1981). *The relationship between family expressiveness and nonverbal communicative behavior*. Unpublished doctoral dissertation. The Johns Hopkins University.

Halberstadt, A. G. (1983). Family expressiveness styles and nonverbal communication skills. *Journal of Nonverbal Behavior, 8*, 14-26.

Halberstadt, A. G. (1984). Family expression of emotion. In C. Z. Malatesta & C. E. Izard (Eds.), *Emotion in adult development* (pp. 235-252). Beverly Hills, CA: Sage.

Halberstadt, A. G. (1986). Family socialization of emotional expression and nonverbal communication styles and skills. *Journal of Personality and Social Psychology, 51*, 827-836.

Halberstadt, A. G. (1991). Towards an ecology of expressiveness: Family expressiveness in particular and a model in general. In R. S. Feldman & B. Rimé (Eds.), *Fundamentals in nonverbal behavior* (pp. 106-160). Cambridge: Cambridge University Press.

Halberstadt, A. G., & Carpenter, S. L. (1993, March). Anger within family relationships. In Diane C. Jones (Chair), *Emotions and the family*. Symposium conducted at the meeting of the Society for Research in Child Development, New Orleans, LA.

Halberstadt, A. G., Crisp, V. W., & Eaton, K. L. (1999). Family expressiveness: A retrospective and new directions for research. In P. Philippot, R. S. Feldman, & E. J. Coats (Eds.). *The social context of nonverbal behavior* (pp. 109-155). NY: Cambridge University Press.

Halberstadt, A. G., Denham, S., & Dunsmore, J. C. (2001). Affective social competence. *Social Development, 10*, 79-119.

Halberstadt, A. G., Dunsmore, J. C., McElwain, N., Eaton, K. L., & McCool, A. (2001). Parents' beliefs about feelings. Unpublished data.

Halberstadt, A. G., Fox, N. A., & Jones, N. A. (1993). Do expressive mothers have expressive children? The role of socialization in children's affect expression. *Social Development, 2*, 48-65.

Harter, S., & Buddin, B. J. (1987). Children's understanding of the simultaneity of two emotions: A five-stage developmental acquisition sequence. *Developmental Psychology, 23*, 388-399.

Hatfield, E., Cacioppo, J. T., & Rapson, R. L. (1994). *Emotional contagion.* New York, NY: Cambridge University Press.

Isley, S., O'Neil, R., Clatfelter, D., & Parke, R. D. (1999). Parent and child expressed affect and children's social competence: Modeling direct and indirect pathways. *Developmental Psychology, 35,* 547-560.

Jones, D. C., Abbey, B. B., & Cumberland, A. (1998). The development of display rule knowledge: Linkages with family expressiveness and social competence. *Child Development, 69,* 1209-1222.

Jones, S. M., Eisenberg, N., & Fabes, R. A. (1996). *Parents' emotion behaviors and children's social competence: The mediating role of children's affective displays.* Unpublished manuscript, Arizona State University, Tempe.

King, L. A., & Emmons, R. A. (1990). Conflict over emotional expression: Psychological and physical correlates. *Journal of Personality and Social Psychology, 58,* 864-877.

Kring, A. M., & Gordon, A. H. (1998). Sex differences in emotion: Expression, experience, and physiology. *Journal of Personality and Social Psychology, 74,* 686-703.

Lacks, J. M., & Uzgiris, I. C. (1995, March). *Affective imitation in relation to the genesis of empathy.* Paper presented at the meeting of the Society for Research in Child Development, Indianapolis, IN.

Larsen, R. J., Diener, E., & Emmons, R. A. (1986). Affect intensity and reactions to daily life events. *Journal of Personality and Social Psychology, 51,* 803-814.

Levenson, R.W. (1996). Biological substrates of empathy and facial modulations of emotion: Two facets of the scientific legacy of John Lanzetta. *Motivation and Emotion, 20,* 185-204.

Ludemann, P. M. (1993, March). *Family factors and preschoolers' facial expression production and recognition.* Paper presented at the meeting of the Society for Research in Child Development, New Orleans, LA.

Malatesta, C. Z., Culver, C., Tesman, J. R., & Shepard, B. (1989). The development of emotion expression during the first two years of life. *Monographs of the Society for Research in Child Development 54* (1-2, Serial No. 219).

Malatesta, C. Z., & Haviland, J. M. (1982). Learning display rules: The socialization of emotion expression in infancy. *Child Development, 53,* 991-1003.

Malatesta, C. Z., Grigoryev, P., Lamb, C., Albin, M., & Culver, C. (1986). Emotion socialization and expressive development in preterm & full-term infants. *Child Development, 57,* 316-330.

Matsumoto, D., Takeuchi, S., Andayani, S., Kouznetsova, N., & Krupp, D. (1998). The contribution of individualism vs. collectivism to cross-national differences in display rules. *Asian Journal of Social Psychology, 1,* 147-165.

Mayer, J. D., & Salovey, P. (1997). What is emotional intelligence? In P. Salovey & D. J. Sluyter (Eds.), *Emotional development and emotional intelligence: Educational implications* (pp. 3-34). New York: Basic Books, Inc.

Nixon, C. L. (1997). *Family experiences and early social-cognition: Links to social behavior.* Unpublished doctoral dissertation, Pennsylvania State University, Erie.

Parke, R. D., & McDowell, D. J. (1998). Toward an expanded model of emotion socialization: New people, new pathways. *Psychological Inquiry, 9,* 303-309.

Rosenthal, R. (1991). *Meta-analytic procedures for social research.* Beverly Hills, CA: Sage.

Shadish, W. R. & Haddock, C. K. (1994). Combining estimates of effect size. In H. Cooper & L.V. Hedges, *The handbook of research synthesis* (pp. 261-281). NY: Russell Sage Foundation.

Shortt, J. W., Bush, L. K., McCabe, J. L., Gottman, J. M, & Katz, L. F. (1994). Children's physiological responses while producing facial expressions of emotions. *Merrill-Palmer Quarterly, 40,* 40-59.

Sorce, J. F., Emde, R. N., Campos, J. J., & Klinnert, M. D. (1985). Maternal emotional signaling: Its effect on the visual cliff behavior of 1-year-olds. *Developmental Psychology, 21,* 195-200.

Stifter, C. A., & Grant, W. (1993). Infant responses to frustration: Individual differences in the expression of negative affect. *Journal of Nonverbal Behavior, 17,* 187-204.

Stifter, C. A., & Moyer, D. (1991). The regulation of positive affect: Gaze aversion activity during mother-infant interaction. *Infant Behavior & Development, 14,* 111-123.

Weissbrod, C. S., & Kendziora, K. T. (1997, April). *Parental positive socialization and emotion in the prediction of children's emotional expression.* Poster presented at the meeting of the Society for Research in Child Development, Wash., DC.

Zeman, J. & Garber, J. (1996). Display rules for anger, sadness, and pain: It depends on who is watching. *Child Development, 67,* 957-973.

"When My Mommy Was Angry, I Was Speechless": Children's Perceptions of Maternal Emotional Expressiveness Within the Context of Economic Hardship

C. Cybele Raver
Mary Spagnola

SUMMARY. This study examined relations among poverty-related risk, mothers' self-report of negative emotional expressiveness, and children's representations of maternal anger and sadness (N = 46). Children's accuracy was lower when identifying negative emotions than when identify-

---

C. Cybele Raver is affiliated with Irving B. Harris Graduate School of Public Policy Studies, University of Chicago. Mary Spagnola is affiliated with the Department of Psychology, Syracuse University.

Address correspondence to: C. Cybele Raver, Associate Professor, Irving B. Harris Graduate School of Public Policy Studies, University of Chicago, 1155 E. 60th Street, Chicago, IL 60637 (E-mail: raver@src.uchicago.edu).

Support for this research was provided by the National Science Foundation grant (#SBR-9616454), the McCormick-Tribune Foundation, and a Faculty Scholars Award from the William T. Grant Foundation, to the first author. Many thanks to the families and administrators of participating Head Start centers in Tompkins County, NY and the city of Rochester, NY. The authors are grateful for the exemplary research assistance of Joylyn Somersel, Barbara Esqudero, Todd Jusko and Melissa Leibman. They also thank Elizabeth Gershoff and the volume editor and reviewers for their helpful comments.

[Haworth co-indexing entry note]: "'When My Mommy Was Angry, I Was Speechless': Children's Perceptions of Maternal Emotional Expressiveness Within the Context of Economic Hardship." Raver, C. Cybele, and Mary Spagnola. Co-published simultaneously in *Marriage & Family Review* (The Haworth Press, Inc.) Vol. 34, No. 1/2, 2002, pp. 63-88; and: *Emotions and the Family* (ed: Richard A. Fabes) The Haworth Press, Inc., 2002, pp. 63-88. Single or multiple copies of this article are available for a fee from The Haworth Document Delivery Service [1-800-HAWORTH, 9:00 a.m. - 5:00 p.m. (EST). E-mail address: docdelivery@haworthpress.com].

© 2002 by The Haworth Press, Inc. All rights reserved.

ing positive emotions. Significant differences between children exposed to high versus low levels of maternal negative expressiveness were found. Children of highly negative mothers were less accurate in identifying maternal anger, used fewer anger-related terms, and described maternal anger as significantly less intense. These children also were significantly more likely to generate punitive solutions to child anger and irrelevant/incomplete solutions to maternal sadness than were children with less emotionally negative mothers. Support was also found for the negative impact of poverty-related risk on emotional processes within the family. These findings are discussed in light of models of emotion socialization, risk, and resilience among low-income families. *[Article copies available for a fee from The Haworth Document Delivery Service: 1-800-HAWORTH. E-mail address: <docdelivery@haworthpress.com> Website: <http://www.HaworthPress.com> © 2002 by The Haworth Press, Inc. All rights reserved.]*

KEYWORDS. Maternal emotional expressiveness, economic hardship, emotion socialization

Recently, researchers have focused considerable attention on ways that parents directly and indirectly influence their children's development of emotional competence (Denham, Mitchell-Copeland, Strandberg, Auerbach & Blair, 1997; Eisenberg, Fabes, Minore, Mathy, Hanish & Brown, 1994; Eisenberg & Fabes, 1992; Fabes, Leonard, Kupanoff & Martin, 2001; Garner, Jones, Gaddy & Rennie, 1997; Gottman, Katz & Hooven, 1996). Previous research suggests that high levels of expressed parental anger and distress may have a profound negative impact on children's ability to handle and interpret their own negative emotions (Cummings & Davies, 1994; Eisenberg, Cumberland & Spinrad, 1998; Fabes et al., 2001; Garner, Robertson & Smith, 1997). Yet, although children are hypothesized to learn about their own and others' emotions, at least in part, from adults' expressiveness (Denham & Grout, 1993; Denham, Zoller & Couchoud, 1994), we know less about the ways that children encode and represent episodes of parental emotional dysregulation (see Cummings, Vogel, Cummings & El-Sheikh, 1989; Dunn & Hughes, 1998 for exceptions). That is, how do young children perceive and interpret parental expressions of anger and sadness? This may be a particularly important question to ask among families facing serious economic hardship, where the psychological stress associated with poverty has been hypothesized to have a negative impact on parents' emotional equilibrium and children's emotional competence (Conger, Ge, Elder, Lorenz & Simons, 1994; Halpern, 1990; McLoyd, 1990). Given that approximately one quarter of all young children live in poverty, our need to learn more about the impact of poverty-related stressors on families' emotional processes is particularly pressing (Garner & Spears, 2000; U.S. Bureau of the Census, 1992).

To address this need, we are currently conducting an ongoing set of studies on the ways in which family expressiveness and emotion socialization practices may mediate the negative impact of economic hardship on children's development of effective emotional knowledge, self-regulation and subsequent competence with peers. The following study represents a preliminary examination of children's perceptions of their mothers' emotional expressiveness, collected during a recent follow-up visit with some of the low-income families participating in our research. With these data, our objectives were (1) to explore the nature of low-income children's reports of mothers' emotional expressiveness, using a story-stem technique adapted from Denham (1997) and Roberts and Strayer (1987); (2) to determine whether children's reports of maternal anger and sadness were related to mothers' self-reports of negative emotional expressiveness, using a standardized self-report measure (Halberstadt, Cassidy, Stifter, Parke & Fox, 1995); and finally, (3) to examine relations between a number of poverty-related, ecological stressors and both maternal and child report of mothers' emotional expressiveness.

WHAT DO CHILDREN KNOW ABOUT EMOTIONS?

By the age of 4, children are generally able to distinguish sadness, anger, fear and happiness, correctly identifying them from pictures or drawings (Cassidy, Parke, Butovsky & Braungart, 1992; Denham, Zoller & Couchoud, 1994; Garner et al., 1997). In addition, preschool-aged children can generally identify the appropriate or correct emotion for a given hypothetical scenario, naming sadness, for example, for a child who has dropped her ice cream cone, and happiness for a child who has just received a gift (Garner, Jones & Miner, 1994). By age 6, children are able to distinguish finely-grained negative emotional displays and can accurately gauge the emotional intensity expressed by adults (Cummings et al., 1989). Children who know more about the causes and consequences of emotions are believed to be better able to respond appropriately to displays of anger, sadness, and distress among friends and family members: Emotion understanding is thus viewed as a key form of social cognition supporting children's emotion regulation and social competence with peers and adults (Campos, Campos & Barrett, 1989; Cassidy et al., 1992; Denham, 1997).

Although there has been increasing interest in children's knowledge of appropriate emotions to be expressed in hypothetical situations involving other children, less is known regarding children's conceptions of *their own* families' emotions and their perceptions of the emotional climate experienced in their own households. Recent studies have turned our attention toward children's understanding of their mothers' responsiveness or sensitivity to child emotions (e.g., Denham, 1997; Levine, Stein & Liwag, 1999), but there has been very little work, to date, on children's perceptions of mothers' emotional expressiveness (see McHale, Nuegebauer, Asch & Schwartz, 1999, as an exception). One reason for this may be that research on children's perceptions of family emotional climate may be hampered by methodological obstacles: Systematic interviews regarding parents' angry and sad outbursts may be too psychologically taxing or threatening to young children (Buchsbaum, Toth, Clyman, Cicchetti & Emde, 1992; McHale et al., 1999). A standardized but flexible story-stem narrative-elicitation procedure provides a less threatening alternative (Bretherton, Ridgeway & Cassidy, 1990). The story-stem narrative procedure allows children to produce psychologically complex narratives that may be less prone to the pressures of social desirability, while also allowing for some experimenter follow-up questions, clarification, control and standardization (Light, 1986; Murray, Woolgar, Biers & Hipwell, 1999).

There has been much support for narrative story-stem techniques as a rich source of information on children's representations of parent and child behavior (see Kochanska, Padavich & Koenig, 1996; Macfie, Toth, Rogosch, Robinson, Emde & Cicchetti, 1999; Oppenheim, Nir, Warren & Emde, 1997). Such techniques have been employed to assess children's schemas of family relationships (Bretherton et al., 1990; Cicchetti & Toth, 1997) and consequences of emotion within the family (Denham, 1997; Roberts & Strayer, 1987). One critique of narrative story-stem techniques has been that children's responses may involve wish fulfillment, fantasy, and representations of actual experiences, leading to less congruence with external measures (Oppenheim et al., 1997). Previous research suggests that children's narrative reports do, however, correspond with external measures (e.g., Kochanska et al., 1996) are relatively stable over time, and are not merely reflective of language skills or level of emotional understanding (McHale et al.,

1999). Reassured by prior empirical support for the utility of story-stem narrative techniques, we chose to use this methodology to elucidate young children's schemas regarding the quality and intensity of their own and their mothers' emotional expressions during routine family interactions.

Specifically, we adapted previous emotionally oriented narrative techniques (Denham, 1997; Roberts & Strayer, 1987) to tap children's (a) *accuracy* in identifying emotions when the protagonist of the story was the child's mother, (b) children's depictions of negative emotional *intensity* when describing mothers' emotions, assessed through both the frequency of emotion label use and from Likert-type ratings (see Cummings et al., 1989), and (c) children's enactments of their own and their mothers' *resolutions* or coping strategies in response to each other's negative emotions (see also Covel & Miles, 1992; Denham et al., 1995; Fabes et al., 1999). Our goal is to complement recent empirical emphasis on adults' representations of the family's emotional experience (Gottman et al., 1996), by examining mothers' emotional expressiveness from the child's point of view. In conducting this research, we also aimed to expand the methodologies available for the study of families' styles of emotional expressiveness. If accurate, children's reports of adults' affect could be particularly valuable as the field moves toward the use of more sophisticated statistical techniques such as structural equation modeling, where latent constructs such as family emotional expressiveness can be best predicted by the collection of multiple observed variables from more than one informant.

SOURCES OF INDIVIDUAL DIFFERENCES IN CHILDREN'S REPRESENTATIONS OF EMOTION: FAMILIAL AND EXTRAFAMILIAL INFLUENCES

At first glance, it would seem relatively obvious to expect that mothers' reports of their own expressiveness of anger and sadness should be positively related to children's reports of the frequency and intensity of mothers' negative emotions during the narratives procedure. Previous research by McHale et al. (1999) supports this view, with preschool-aged children spontaneously producing more aggression-laden stories to open story-stems among families where mothers reported higher levels of family conflict. Based on these findings, children of mothers who report expressing high levels of anger and sadness might be expected to rate their mothers as highly expressive in depictions of family interactions during semi-structured play.

This picture is complicated, however, by previous research suggesting that children from highly emotionally negative families show deficits in emotion knowledge. That is, children with parents who express high levels of negative emotions show lower understanding of angry and sad emotions than do their counterparts from low-expressive and moderately expressive families (Denham et al., 1994; Garner & Power, 1996; Garner et al., 1994). Similarly, children whose parents experience greater personal distress and respond more punitively to child expressions of negative emotions have been found to avoid emotional situations and to show difficulties handling negative emotions in the school context (Eisenberg & Fabes, 1994; Fabes et al., 1999). Also, children from maltreating families have been found to have particular difficulty identifying and discussing feelings of anger when presented with emotion understanding assessments (Rogosch, Cicchetti & Aber, 1995; Shipman & Zeman, 1999).

In assessing children's reports of mothers' emotions, therefore, an alternative hypothesis might be that children from highly emotionally negative households have less knowledge of angry and sad emotions, and would therefore be less accurate in identifying others' negative expressions, using these labels less often. Similarly, children from emotionally negative families may actively defend against their own overarousal and stress by minimizing, ameliorating, or cognitively reinterpreting instances of parental anger (Cummings & Cummings, 1988; Thompson, 1994). This study tests these competing hypotheses by examining whether children with highly negative mothers are more accurate, describe their mothers as more emotionally intense, and propose more competent resolutions to situations evoking anger and sadness than do children with less negative mothers. Alternately, the family's emotionally negative climate may interfere with children's acquisition of negative emotion terms and with their interpretation of emotionally negative events. This interference often leads children of highly negative mothers to be less accurate and less forthcoming when ascribing negative feelings to their mothers, than would children from less negative households.

Investigators have increasingly examined parents' emotional socialization as a key source of individual differences in children's emotional development. This emerging body of research, however, has yet to take into account fully the ways that extrafamilial environmental contexts may influence parents' emotional expressiveness and parental socialization of children's emotional skills. Specifically, a decade of research examining the negative impact of poverty on child outcomes suggests that economic hardship takes a particularly harsh toll on parents' ability to provide sensitive, warm caregiving for their children (Dodge, Pettit & Bates, 1994; Halpern, 1990). Similarly, poverty has been found to take a toll on children's emotional dysregulation, as demonstrated by numerous findings that children exposed to longer periods of poverty manifest higher rates of internalizing and externalizing behaviors (Bolger, Patterson, Thompson & Kupersmidt, 1995; Dodge et al., 1994). It is likely that families experiencing multiple poverty-related stressors also experience greater psychological distress and correspondingly, express more negative emotion in the home (see Conger et al., 1994; Sampson & Laub, 1994). Low-income children who face increasing parental emotional dysregulation may, themselves, have greater difficulty processing emotional information and managing emotional displays. Conversely, children in more emotionally positive households may be buffered from the negative impact of stressors associated with economic hardship.

THE PRESENT STUDY

Although longitudinal data are needed to test this mediating model, a good first step would be to examine the ways in which high ecological risk may affect mothers' self-report of negative emotional expressiveness as well as children's perceptions of maternal anger and sadness. Previous research has demonstrated the utility of a cumulative risk approach to the study of the impact of economic hardship on social and emotional processes (Deater-Deckard, Dodge, Pettit & Bates, 1998; Seifer, Sameroff, Baldwin & Baldwin, 1992). Accordingly, we expected that mothers who experienced the cumulative risks of parenting singly, combined with higher numbers of stressful life events and living on lower income would report higher levels of negative emotional expressiveness than would low-income women who experienced comparatively fewer risks. We also expected that the cumulative ecological risks experienced by the family would affect children's understanding and interpretation of family emotions. Consequently, we examined whether cumulative risk and mothers' self-reports of negative emotional expressiveness were separately and jointly associated with children's responses to emotionally-laden story stems.

Thus, the following study asks three questions. First, how accurate are low-income children, generally, in identifying appropriate emotions, when given story-stems centering on their mothers' anger, sadness, and happiness? Second, are individual differences in mothers' emotional expressiveness related to a set of poverty-related ecological risks? Third, are individual differences in children's depictions of maternal anger and sadness related to both (a) mothers' self-reports of negative emotional expressiveness and (b) the cumulative ecological risks that the family faces? And if so, how do maternal expressiveness and cumulative risk work independently and jointly in predicting children's responses to story stems about emotions? In keeping with recent research (e.g., Denham et al., 1994; Ramey, Ramey & Lanzi, 1998), the following study compared narratives produced by 6-year-old children of more negatively expressive (labeled "high negative") mothers versus less negatively expressive (labeled "low-negative") mothers, facing higher versus lower levels of cumulative risk, to answer these questions.

METHOD

Sample

As part of a follow-up of a larger, longitudinal study of the relations between parents' positive emotion socialization practices and their children's development of emotional and social competence, 46 families participated in this study. Participating children represented 68% of the cohort previously assessed one and a half years earlier in the spring of the Head Start school year. (Attrition was due to our inability to locate the family (13%), relocation of families (7%), parental refusal (8%), and assessment problems or equipment failure (3%)).

Families participating in the most recent assessment were not found to differ significantly from nonparticipating families on any demographic or risk-related measure (see below). Families were of low-income status upon recruitment into the study two years earlier, as defined by Head Start eligibility requirements. At the time of the follow-up assessment, children's ages ranged from 59 to 83 months ($M = 75$ months, $SD = 4.70$) and were currently enrolled in either kindergarten or first grade in either a rural or urban site, located in upstate New York, approximately 100 miles from each other. The resulting sample consisted of 22 families from the rural site (with equal numbers of boys and girls) and 24 families (with 9 boys and 15 girls) from the urban site.

As expected, samples in rural versus urban sites were racially segregated, with white families comprising 86% of the rural sample and African American families comprising 71% of the urban sample. The majority of mothers in the sample were single (65.5%), with no differences in families' marital status between sites. Rural and urban families did differ, however, in levels of maternal education ($F(1, 44) = 10.24, p < .01$) and family income, $F(1, 44) = 4.03, p = .05$, with rural mothers reporting more years of education ($M_{rural} = 12.77, SD = 1.41$) than urban mothers ($M_{urban} = 11.50, SD = 1.28$) and higher levels of income ($M_{rural} = \$22,181, SD = \$7,531$), on average, than urban mothers ($M_{urban} = \$18,083, SD = \$6,310$). Despite these differences, it is important to note that the majority of both groups lived on low incomes (\$24,000 or less), facing multiple poverty-related stressors (see below). Rural and urban samples did not significantly differ on measures of maternal emotional expressiveness (see below), nor did they differ on measures of emotion frequency, intensity, and resolutions to story stems. Boys and girls also did not differ on measures of maternal emotional expressiveness, emotion frequency, intensity, or on resolutions to the story stems. Boys and girls across the rural and urban subsamples were therefore combined for all analyses that follow.

Procedures

Data for the analyses outlined below were collected during a visit to families' homes. All mother-reported data in this paper was collected during an interview that included a demographic questionnaire, questionnaires to assess mothers' emotion expressiveness (SEFQ, Halberstadt, Cassidy, Stifter, Parke & Fox, 1995) and mothers' experiences with stressful life events in the past 12 months (FILE-M, MCubbin & Patterson, 1981). While mothers were being interviewed, a second interviewer met with the child to complete a narrative elicitation/story stem task (adapted from Denham, 1997, and Roberts & Strayer, 1987) to obtain children's reports of their own and their mothers' emotions, emotional intensity, and resolutions to emotionally laden scenarios. Following the interviews, parents were reimbursed \$20 for their participation.

Maternal-Report Measures. Mothers' expressiveness of negative emotions was assessed with the negative dominant and negative submissive subscales of the Self-Expressiveness in the Family Questionnaire (SEFQ, Halberstadt et al., 1995). The SEFQ is a self-report measure of the predominant style of emotion expressiveness used by the respondent within the context of everyday family life. It correlates moderately with observed measures of parents' expressed affect during laboratory tasks (Cassidy et al., 1992; Halberstadt et al., 1995) and has been found to be reliable and valid with low-income and middle-income samples (Garner et al., 1994; Greenberg et al., 1999). High scores on this scale indicate high levels of negative emotion expressiveness, and mothers were divided into "high negative" and "low negative" groups based on a median split.

Level of cumulative poverty-related risk was calculated by a family (a) falling above the median on the Family Inventory of Life Events (FILE–McCubbin & Patterson, 1981), a 71-item measure of negative life events experienced by the respondent or her immediate family, (2) falling below the combined sample mean on income, and (3) single-parenthood status. Thus, mothers could face 0 ($N = 8$), 1 ($N = 12$), 2($N = 18$), or 3($N = 8$) risks, with rural families no more likely than urban families to face differing levels of risk (chi square = 2.97, ns). Families were then categorized as facing low (0 or 1) risks or high (2 or more) risks. Using this dichotomy, 20 families faced "low risk" and 26 families faced "high risk."

Child-Report Measures. Children's narratives regarding their own and their mothers' emotions were assessed using a narrative story-stem technique adapted from Denham (1997). Children were introduced to mother, child, and playmate dolls (matched on the child's gender and race) and household furniture that would be used in the stories. Children were told "Let's pretend that this is you, and this is your mother, and this is a friend who comes over to play sometimes," and "Let's pretend that these are your kitchen and living room. We'll use the story people and the furniture to tell some stories about how things happen in your home." Children were also shown a card with three yellow circles of varying sizes and were told that the circles represented "a little," "pretty much" and "really, or a lot." Children were told "I will begin the story, but then I want you to finish it. Sometimes, I will ask you some questions about what is happening." An example of a typical sequence of experimenter questions and child responses is given in Table 1.

Six story stems were employed in assessing children's perceptions of their own and their mothers' emotions as well as each story character's reactions and resolutions to the emotional scenario. Specific story stems are shown in Table 2. Story stems by Denham (1997) and Roberts and Strayer (1987) were originally designed to elicit children's representations of the consequences of children's emotional displays, including mothers' responsiveness to child distress. These story stems were al-

TABLE 1. Example of Story-Stem Response with Mother as Target (First Six Conversational Turns Presented).

Experimenter	Child
1. "You and your Mom are at the kitchen table. Mom made cabbage for dinner. You don't like cabbage. You say 'I don't like it, and I won't eat it.' What happens next?"	"She spanks me."
2. "How does Mom feel when you say you won't eat the cabbage?"	"Mad."
3. (Pointing to circles) "Does Mom feel a little mad, pretty mad, or really mad?"	"A little mad."
4. "What do you do when Mom is mad?"	"I just go sit and watch T.V."
5. "How do you feel?"	"Mad, too."
6. "Do you feel a little mad, pretty mad, or really mad?"	"Pretty mad."

TABLE 2. Story-Stems Administered to Children

	Happy story	Sad story	Angry/Mad story
Child report on mother	You and your Mom are in the living-room, sitting on the couch. You come in and say "Mom, I have a surprise for you." And you give her a present. (1)	You and your Mom are in the kitchen, sitting and talking. You both have ice-cream cones. Mom drops hers by mistake. (2)	You and your mom are at the kitchen table. Mom made cabbage for dinner, and you don't like cabbage. You say "I don't like it, and I won't eat it." *
Child report on self	You and your Mom are in the kitchen. Your Mom says "Wait here, I'll be right back." And she goes to the cupboard/ refrigerator and gets your favorite dessert. ** (3)	You and your Mom are in the living room, sitting on the couch. You are getting ready to read your favorite book. You reach over to the table to get the book, and you fall off the couch and hurt your knee. (4)	You and your friend are in the living room, while your Mom is in the next room. You have your favorite toy. Your friend tries to take your toy away from you.

* Children were probed for foods that they did not like. For children who were unfamiliar with, or liked cabbage, another disliked food was substituted.
** "dessert" was substituted for "ice cream" to avoid confusion with story stem #2.

tered to (1) probe maternal as well as child emotions, and (2) to elicit children's attributions of maternal feeling states, as we were interested in children's own encoding and evaluation of *mothers'* emotions and emotional intensity of "what happens in their house." For example, we removed Denham's (1997) recommendation that the experimenter enact angry emotional displays (e.g., an experimenter-modeled fight between two dolls) and sad displays (e.g., "Now she's crying"). After adapting these stories, the content of each of Denham's (1997) story stems remained unambiguous, with the exception of one. Correspondingly, we replaced one "sad" story by Denham (1997) with a story designed to tap child sadness involving the child falling and hurting a knee.

After introducing the scenario, children were first asked to name the emotion that the target of the story would feel (with either self or mother as target). Following verbalization of the emotion, children were asked to indicate how (happy, sad, angry) they/their mother felt, by pointing at one of three circles on the Likert-style rating card, described above. Following the identification and rating of the emotion felt by the target, children were asked to identify the emotion and emotional intensity felt by the other character in the story. Inter-rater percentage agreement on both emotion and intensity were 100%. For this paper, analyses were restricted to (1) children's accuracy when identifying mothers' emotions for happy, sad and angry stories, with mothers as the protagonist, (2) children's ratings of mothers' negative emotional intensity, indexed by (a) the frequency of children's use of the "angry/mad" or "sad" emotion labels whenever discussing maternal emotions across all stories (including those where the mother was the protagonist and those where the child was the story protagonist) and (b) the child's rating of maternal sadness or anger, using the Likert-type scale, whenever the child discussed maternal negative emotions. Lastly, we analyzed (3) children's depictions of their own and their mothers' resolutions, or coping strategies, when presented with story-stems depicting scenarios of maternal and child sadness and anger, described below.

Children's depictions of the resolutions or coping strategies that they or their mothers would enact were also adapted from Denham (1997) and Roberts and Strayer (1987). Following previous research, we coded the following categories: "comforts, " "provides directives/discipline," (e.g., "mom sends me to my room."), "discussion of emotion-eliciting events and feelings," "matches emotion," "takes pragmatic action to solve the distressing problem" (e.g., "I help mom clean it up" in response to fallen ice cream story stem), "withdraws/ignores" and "don't know/irrelevant" responses. We also added a category for "aggresses" (e.g., "I kick over the table"). We then combined these codes into the following categories, which were guided conceptually by those used in Denham's (1997) work: (1) competent/solves problem (including comforts, takes pragmatic action, emotion matches, and discussion of emotional events/feelings), (2) directs/disciplines, (3) aggresses, withdraws, or ignores, and (4) incomplete/irrelevant (e.g., child answers "I don't know" or provides odd, non-related response). We used these codes for both mothers' responses to children's emotions and children's responses to their mothers' emotions. Cohen's kappa for this coding system was .75.

RESULTS

In analyzing our data, we first examined whether the low-income 6-year-olds in this study varied in their understanding and descriptions of maternal emotions. We then examined whether our independent variables of interest (i.e., maternal expressiveness and cumulative ecological risk) were themselves inter-related. We then examined ways that children from "high negative" versus "low negative" households, facing relatively high versus relatively low risk, differed in the accuracy, intensity, and responsiveness with which they described maternal negative emotions. Each of these sets of analyses is provided, in turn, below.

How Do Low-Income 6-Year-Olds Describe Maternal Emotions?

Descriptive statistics are first provided, regarding children's knowledge and depictions of maternal negative emotions. First, to assess children's accuracy in identifying the correct emotion for each story stem, we conducted a repeated measures Analysis of Variance (ANOVA) with Emotion (happy versus sad versus angry story stem) as the within-subjects factor. Repeated measures ANOVA revealed a main effect for Emotion ($F(2, 86) = 41.19$, $p < .001$). Post-hoc paired-sample t-tests suggest that although children were highly accurate when identifying maternal happiness ($M_{happy} = .98$, $SD = .15$), they were significantly less accurate when identifying maternal sadness ($M_{sad} = .69$, $SD = .47$), $t(1, 44) = 3.85$, $p < .001$. Children were significantly even less accurate when identifying maternal anger ($M_{anger} = .44$, $SD = .50$), $t(1, 44) = -2.69$, $p = .01$.

Regarding emotional intensity, children reported their mothers as sad an average of 2.17 times ($SD = 1.37$, Range = 0-5) across all story stems. On average, children rated their mothers' sadness as close to "pretty sad" (Mean intensity for sadness = 1.82, SD = 1.11). Regarding anger, children described their mothers as angry or "mad" 1.35 times, on average (SD = 1.18, Range = 0-4). Mean intensity of children's appraisals of maternal anger = 1.63, SD = 1.37. Mothers' assessments of their own negative emotional expressiveness, using the combined Negative Dominant and Negative Submissive subscales of the SEFQ (Halberstadt et al., 1995), yielded a mean score of 89.97, SD = 25.24.

Is There Any Preliminary Evidence that Ecological Risks Are Related to Mothers' Emotional Expressiveness?

As expected, mothers in families facing higher incidence of stressful life events and lower income reported greater negative emotional expressiveness (r (1, 44) = .36, $p < .05$, and r (1, 44) = $-.45$, $p < .01$, respectively). Expressiveness of negative emotions was unrelated to mothers' marital status. Subsequently, a cumulative risk index was formed, and 2-way Multivariate Analyses of Variance (MANOVAS) were then conducted with high vs. low expressiveness and high vs. low risk as between-group factors in examining differences in children's reports of maternal emotional expressiveness. The purpose of these analyses, in turn, was to examine the combined contributions of maternal emotional expressiveness and the risks experienced by the family on children's understanding and report of negative emotions. Differences in children's report of their mothers' negative emotional expressiveness are examined first in terms of accuracy, then in terms of intensity, and finally in terms of the quality of maternal responsiveness, below.

Are Individual Differences in Children's Accuracy Related to Their Mothers' Self-Report of Negative Emotional Expressiveness and to Ecological Risk?

Considerable variance was found for children's accuracy in identifying maternal negative emotions for the story stems depicting maternal anger and sadness. Consequently, we first examined whether individual differences in children's accuracy were related to levels of maternal expressiveness and levels of poverty-related ecological risk. With children's accuracy in identifying appropriate emotions for story-stems describing maternal anger and sadness as dependent variables, MANOVAS were conducted with high versus low negative emotional expressiveness and high versus low cumulative environmental risk as between-group factors. The results of the MANOVA revealed a main effect only for negative emotional expressiveness, Hotelling's Trace $(2, 40) = 8.53, p < .01$. Follow-up univariate ANOVAs revealed that children with more negative mothers were significantly less accurate $(M_{High} = 0.17, SD = .39)$ in identifying maternal anger than were children with less emotionally negative mothers $(M_{low} = .70, SD = .47), F(1, 41) = 17.35, p < .001$ (see Figure 1). No significant differences were found for children's levels of accuracy when responding to the story stem depicting maternal sadness.

Are Children's Ratings of Mothers' Emotional Intensity Related to Mothers' Self-Reports and to Ecological Risk?

We next examined the frequency of children's use of negative emotion terms across the six stories, calculating children's frequency of use of "angry/mad" and "sad" emotion labels when describing mothers' responses to various hypothetical scenarios. Two-way MANOVAS with frequency of references to maternal anger and maternal sadness as dependent variables and maternal negative expressiveness (high versus low) and cumulative environmental risk (high versus low) as between-groups factors were carried out. Results for these analyses revealed marginal main effects for maternal negative expressiveness, Hotelling's Trace $(2, 41) = 2.67, p < .10$ and for cumulative risk, Hotelling's Trace $(2, 41) = 2.52, p < .10$, and a significant 2-way inter-

FIGURE 1. Children with highly expressive mothers are significantly less accurate for the story stem depicting maternal anger than are children of less expressive mothers.

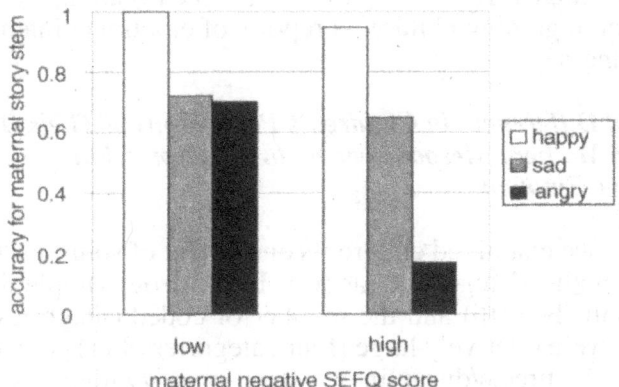

action of expressiveness × risk, Hotelling's Trace (2, 41) = 5.22, p = .01. Follow-up univariate analyses revealed that children of highly expressive mothers made significantly fewer references to anger (M_{high} = 1.08, SD = .22) than did children of less expressive mothers (M_{low} = 1.80, SD = .21), $F(1,42)$ = 5.42, $p < .05$. Conversely, children facing high levels of ecological risk made marginally more references to maternal anger (M_{high} = 1.74, SD = .20) than did children facing low levels of risk (M_{low} = 1.14, SD = .23), $F(1, 42)$ = 3.73, $p < .10$. A significant Negative Expressiveness × Cumulative Risk interaction for the frequency of children's references to maternal anger ($F(1, 42)$ = 10.68, $p < .01$) was also found. A post-hoc Tukey Test suggests that it was children from high risk/low expressive families (M = 2.60, SD = 1.08) that reported significantly higher frequency of maternal anger than each of the other three groups, Ms ranged from .87 (SD = 1.09) to 1.29 (SD = .95), $p < .05$.

Finally, we calculated the mean intensity scores for maternal sadness and anger across all episodes whenever children ascribed angry and sad emotions to their mothers, across all six stories. With mean intensity ratings for maternal anger and sadness as dependent variables, MANOVAs (with negative expressiveness and cumulative risk as between-group factors) revealed a marginal main effect for maternal emotional expressiveness only, Hotelling's Trace (2, 41) = 2.88, $p < .08$. Follow-up univariate ANOVAS revealed that children with high negative mothers reported significantly lower *mean* levels of emotional intensity for maternal anger than did children with low negative mothers, $F(1, 44)$ = 9.39, $p < .05$. Children with high negative mothers rated their mothers as a little angry (M_{high} = 1.18, SD = .30) on average, as compared to children with low negative mothers, who rated their mothers as "pretty angry," on average (M_{low} = 2.13, SD = .28) (see Figure 2). No differences were found regarding children's reports of emotional intensity for maternal sadness.

Individual Differences in Children's Perceptions of Their Own and Their Mothers' Responsiveness to the Expression of Negative Emotion

Finally, we examined children's enactment of solutions to their own and their mothers' anger and sadness. Because our sample size was relatively small (N = 46) and the number of coded categories for coping strategies were relatively large [four categories of (1) competent/solves problem, (2) directs/disciplines, (3) aggresses/withdraws/ignores and

FIGURE 2. Children with highly expressive mothers rate maternal anger as significantly less intense than do children of less expressive mothers.

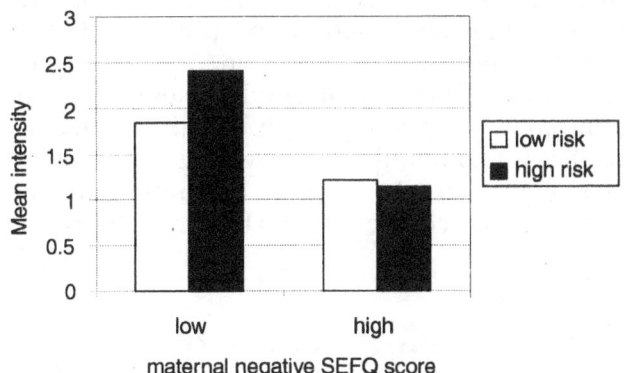

(4) incomplete/irrelevant], our last set of analyses of children's enactments of solutions to their own and their mothers' negative emotion are restricted to testing the independent effects of high versus low expressiveness and high versus low risk, separately.

For the story depicting maternal sadness, children narrated either a competent solution (61%), a solution involving withdrawing from or ignoring their mother (13%), or an irrelevant/incomplete solution to the problem (26%). Children with high negative mothers were significantly more likely to provide irrelevant or incomplete solutions to the problem than were children of low negative mothers, $\chi^2 (1, 44) = 7.62, p < .05$. No differences were found in the responses of children facing high and low risk. In the story describing maternal anger, children generated a wider range of responses, with 37% withdrawing or ignoring, 11% suggesting aggressive solutions, 24% suggesting competent solutions, and 26% suggesting incomplete/irrelevant solutions. Children of high negative and low negative mothers were equally likely to provide each type of solution. However, chi square analyses revealed that children of high risk families were significantly more likely to provide aggressive or withdrawn solutions to maternal anger than were children of low-risk families, $\chi^2 (1, 44) = 8.42, p < .05$.

Regarding maternal responsiveness to child sadness, the bulk of children reported mothers using competent solutions, with only 7% of children suggesting aggressive or disciplinary solutions, and 17% of the children suggesting irrelevant/incomplete solutions. No differences were found between the responses given by children of high versus low negative mothers, nor were any found between children facing low or high risk. Finally, the majority of children suggested that mothers would provide competent solutions to child anger, but 15% of children suggested that mothers would provide directive or disciplinary solutions, and an equal number of children suggested irrelevant/incomplete solutions. Children with high negative mothers were marginally more likely than children of low negative mothers to enact solutions involving maternal discipline or punishment, $\chi^2 (1, 44) = 4.98, p < .08$. No differences were found between children facing high and low risk.

DISCUSSION

With this study, we set out to learn more about young children's schemas regarding the quality and intensity of their mothers' emotional expressions during routine family interactions. In keeping with previous research (Fabes et al., 1991), we found that young children were more accurate in identifying positive emotions than in identifying negative emotions in others. Interestingly, the low-income 6-year-olds in this study had marked difficulty in identifying maternal anger, as compared to 6-year-olds in previous research (Cummings et al., 1989; Fabes et al., 1991). Descriptive analyses reveal that the children in this study were on average, accurate in identifying mothers as angry only 44% of the time, whereas kindergartners in the Fabes et al. (1991) study were able to accurately identify anger in real episodes of emotion expression among peers 83% of the time. A simple explanation for this might be that the story stem designed to elicit depictions of maternal anger (e.g., a mother who prepares a child's least favorite food for dinner and then faces child's refusal to eat it) was more ambiguous or less salient than the stimuli presented in prior research. Our finding of a coherent pattern of individual differences in children's depictions of maternal anger, based on family emotional climate and level of ecological risk, suggests a more complex interpretation is warranted.

The Role of Mothers' Expressiveness of Negative Emotions

First, children of highly negative mothers were significantly less likely to be accurate than were children of less negative mothers when shown the story-stem designed to elicit depictions of maternal anger. Children of highly negative mothers accurately identified mothers as angry only 17% of the time (whereas children of low negative mothers were accurate roughly 70% of the time), suggesting that children facing emotionally negative climates may be actively minimizing or avoiding attributions of anger (Thompson, 1994).

Second, we also found an intriguing pattern of individual differences in children's depictions of mothers' negative emotions, their intensity, and their solutions. Children with highly negative mothers were significantly less likely to use "angry" or "mad" as labels for mothers' emotional states throughout the story-stem procedure, and reported their mothers as *less* emotionally intense than did children of less emotionally negative mothers. Although at first it may seem surprising that children's ratings of maternal emotional intensity were inversely related to mothers' own self-reports, our findings lend support to the view that high levels of maternal negative emotional expressiveness may inhibit rather than promote children's development of emotion understanding (see previous research by Denham and colleagues, 1994, 1997). Given these results, we suggest that investigators may need to rely on the perspectives of other adults in the household, rather than on children, when seeking multiple measures of mothers' emotional expressiveness.

Third, children of highly negative mothers were also significantly more likely to suggest that their mothers would use discipline or punishment in response to a scenario depicting child anger than were children from less emotionally negative households. Thus, children appear aware of parental punitiveness following child anger, as has been described by previous researchers (Fabes et al., 1999; Fabes et al., 2001). Similarly, children with highly negative mothers were significantly more likely to give incomplete or irrelevant responses to the story stem designed to depict maternal sadness, than were children with less emotionally negative mothers. Children from highly negative households may have a more limited repertoire of competent responses when dealing with parental distress, and may view themselves as less competent agents. These differences in children's renderings of optimal coping strategies, or solutions to emotions suggest that children from highly negative households may have fewer tools to solve social problems when they arise, as hypothesized by previous investigators (e.g., Cassidy et al., 1992; Denham, 1997; Eisenberg & Fabes, 1992; Garner & Spears, 2000; Jones & Garner, 1997).

Taken together, these findings lend support to a model of emotion socialization whereby parents who vent strong feelings of anger and sadness may inadvertently increase their children's chances of developing later difficulty in managing their own and others' emotions (Gottman et al., 1996; Zahn-Waxler et al., 1990). Perhaps these children become "flooded" or dysregulated by frequent exposure to maternal distress (see Snyder et al., 1989), shifting cognitive resources toward managing and monitoring their own emotional state and away from interpreting the situational and social cues surrounding their parent's displays of anger or sadness. Future studies are needed to determine whether children from emotionally volatile households have greater trouble at later times with regulating their arousal, encoding, processing, or recalling emotionally salient stimuli. The possibility should be considered that these consequences result from some combination of regulating, processing and monitoring their own and others' negative emotions during ongoing family interactions and in later encounters with peers (see Eisenberg et al., 1998; Fabes et al., 1999; Jones & Garner, 1997).

Other results provide support for models of resilience for low-income children and their families (e.g., Garcia Coll et al., 1995). Specifically, we found that low-income mothers who were able to inhibit intense expressions of sadness and anger had children who were more accurate in identifying anger, more able to discuss anger, and more able to generate competent solutions to sadness, than were children of parents who were emotionally negative. We suspect that these children, in turn, may be more able to accurately interpret, self-regulate, and respond prosocially to peers' anger and distress, leading to a greater likelihood of acceptance and preference by peers (see Garner & Spears, 2000; Raver et al., 1999). We are conducting additional studies to examine links between low-income parents' positive parenting practices, emotional expressiveness, and children's self-regulatory, self-monitoring and emotion knowledge skills in efforts to more fully map the pathways leading to social competence.

The Role of Ecological Risk

This study also highlights ways in which the emotional climate within household is negatively affected by ecological risks commonly faced by low-income families (Conger et al., 1994; McLoyd, 1990). Specifically, we found that mothers who faced a higher number of risks (including very low income, high exposure to stressful life events, and the strain of parenting alone) also reported higher levels of anger and sadness. These findings also underscore the need to better understand how some mothers are able to maintain a positive emotional climate, despite mounting pressures inside and outside the home (Conger et al., 1994; Jones & Garner, 1998). For example, low-income mothers increasingly must meet the challenge of maintaining emotional equilibrium while balancing both parenting and work, facing stringent welfare reform policy mandates and few needed resources such as childcare or transportation (Menaghan & Parcel, 1995; Raver & Leadbeater, 1999).

Important questions remain unanswered. For example, what psychological and structural factors help or hinder low-income women in providing emotionally positive, nurturing environments for children during this rapidly changing economic and policy shift? Numerous investigations are currently underway to answer these questions (Duncan & Chase-Lansdale, 2000; Kalil & Eccles, 1998; Raver, 2000).

Importantly, this study also yielded preliminary evidence that ecological risk has a negative impact on children's understanding of emotion and on their perceptions of maternal emotional expressiveness. Specifically, children from high risk households (and low, but not high levels of maternal negative expressiveness) used marginally more anger terms to describe their mothers, than did children of low risk mothers. Regarding children's depictions of their own and their mothers' responsiveness in the face of expressions of anger and sadness, children facing higher levels of cumulative risk were more likely to enact solutions where they either took aggressive action against their mothers or where they ignored or withdrew from their mothers. These data provide important empirical support for researchers' concerns regarding the developmental "cost" of poverty-related stressors for young children's optimal social and emotional development.

It is important to note that the findings of this study should be qualified in light of the study's small sample size and its cross-sectional design. We are concerned, for example, with the paucity of findings regarding children's attributions of maternal sadness. Parents may feel freer to express frustration rather than sadness with their children, with young children often clearly able to recognize instances where they have made their parents angry (Dunn & Hughes, 1998); young children may consequently have clearer and more defined scripts or schema for the causes and consequences of maternal anger than they do for maternal sadness (Saarni, 1997). In addition, we cannot determine from our data whether children's depictions of maternal anger were affected by differences in children's level of emotional arousal, differences in their emotional self-regulatory skill, differences in emotion knowledge, or simply, differences in their vocabulary or general cognitive competence. Lastly, this study was not able to examine the ways in which child temperament may have affected maternal emotional expressiveness and child emotional competence. Future research would benefit from assessing individual differences in child temperament, language and cognitive skill, using parent and teacher reports as well as multiple measures of emotion knowledge and emotion regulation (e.g., Jones & Garner, 1998; Raver & Leadbeater, 1999; Shipman & Zeman, 1999).

Despite these limitations, this study provides a springboard for future research on low-income children's schemas regarding their families' emotional climates. First, through the lens of a transactional model (Cicchetti & Toth, 1997), we speculate that it is not just children, but also adults, who are affected by family emotional climate. Stressed parents may become increasingly emotionally dysregulated when interacting with a child who is less emotionally skilled. Conversely, a transactional model also points to the cyclic manner in which relative emotional equilibrium in the household may be maintained: Mothers who are able to competently regulate their own emotions may have children who develop greater accuracy, sensitivity, and responsiveness to their own as well as parental emotions (see Eisenberg et al., 1998; Fabes et al., 1999; Garner & Spears, 2000). By examining parents' emotional expressiveness from children's perspectives, we hope to sharpen empirical attention on multiple members of the family, emphasizing that the psychosocial and emotional development of both parents and children are important.

Second, this study points to the value of using an ecologically oriented approach to elucidate the ways that factors inside and outside the family may influence the resolution of developmental, stage-salient issues such as the achievement of emotional competence. Poverty has been found repeatedly to take a harsh toll on parents' psychological well-being and their subsequent ability to provide sensitive care (Halpern, 1990). We need to go further, however, in understanding the emotional sequelae of upswings and downturns in families' economic fortunes. What are the social and emotional ramifications of families' loss of welfare benefits, mandated work participation, or recent promotions at a new job? How do the timing and severity of these changes affect families' emotional experiences and children's subsequent attainment of key emotional competencies? By examining basic developmental processes among families facing economic hardship, we hope to underscore the ways in which families' emotional worlds are not only affected by interpersonal processes unfolding within households, but are also seriously affected by the socioeconomic forces surrounding them.

REFERENCES

Bolger, K. E., Patterson, C. J., Thompson, W. W., & Kupersmidt, J. B. (1995). Psychosocial adjustment among children experiencing persistent and intermittent family economic hardship. *Child Development, 66,* 1107-1129.

Bretherton, I., Ridgeway, D. & Cassidy, J. (1990). Assessing internal working models of the attachment relationship: An attachment story completion task for three year olds. In Greenberg, M. T., Cicchetti, D., and Cummings, E. M. (Eds.), *Attachment in the preschool years; Theory, research, and intervention* (pp. 273-308). Chicago: University of Chicago Press.

Buchsbaum, H. K., Toth, S. L., Clyman, R. B., Cicchetti, D., & Emde, R. N. (1992). The use of a narrative story stem technique with maltreated children: Implications for theory and practice. *Development and Psychopathology, 4,* 603-625.

Campos, J. J., Campos, R. G. & Barrett, K. C. (1989). Emergent themes in the study of emotional development and emotion regulation. *Developmental Psychology, 25,* 394-402.

Cassidy, J., Parke, R. D., Butkovsky, L., & Braungart, J. M. (1992). Family-peer connections: The roles of emotional expressiveness within the family and children's understanding of emotions. *Child Development, 63,* 603-618.

Cicchetti, D. & Toth, S. L. (1997). Transactional ecological systems in developmental psychopathology. In Luthar, S. S., Burack, J. A., Cicchetti, D., & Weisz, J. R. (Eds.), *Developmental psychopathology: Perspectives on adjustment, risk, and disorder* (pp. 317-349). New York, NY, USA: Cambridge University Press.

Conger, R. D., Ge, X., Elder, G. H., Lorenz, F.O., & Simons, R. L. (1994). Economic stress, coercive family process and developmental problems of adolescents. *Child Development, 65,* 541-561.

Covel, K. & Miles, B. (1992). Children's beliefs about strategies to reduce parental anger. *Child Development, 63,* 381-390.

Cummings, E. M. & Cummings, J. L. (1988). A process-oriented approach to children's coping with adults' angry behavior. *Developmental Review, 8,* 296-321.

Cummings, E. M. & Davies, P. (1994). *Children and marital conflict: The impact of family dispute and resolution. Guilford series on social and emotional development.* New York, NY, USA: The Guilford Press.

Cummings, E. M.,Vogel, D., Cummings, J. S. & El-Sheikh, M. (1989). Children's responses to different forms of expression of anger between adults. *Child Development, 60,* 1392-1404.

Deater-Deckard, K., Dodge, K. A., Bates, J., & Pettit, G. (1998). Multiple risk factors in the development of externalizing behavior problems: Group and individual differences. *Development and Psychopathology, 10,* 469-493.

Denham, S.A. (1997). "When I have a bad dream, Mommy holds me": Preschoolers' conceptions of emotions, parental socialization, and emotional competence. *International Journal of Behavioral Development, 20,* 301-319.

Denham, S. A. & Grout, L. (1993). Socialization of emotion: Pathways to preschoolers' emotional and social competence. *Journal of Nonverbal Behavior, 17,* 205-227.

Denham, S. A., Mason, T. & Couchoud, E. A. (1995). Scaffolding young children's prosocial responsiveness: Preschoolers' responses to adult sadness, anger and pain. *International Journal of Behavioral Development, 18,* 489-504.

Denham, S. A., Mitchell-Copeland, J., Strandberg, K., Auerbach, S., & Blair, K. (1997). Parental contributions to preschoolers' emotional competence: Direct and indirect effects. *Motivation and Emotion, 21,* 65-86.

Denham, S. A., Renwick-DeBardi, S. & Hewes, S. (1994). Emotional communication between mothers and preschoolers: Relations with emotional competence. *Merrill-Palmer Quarterly, 40,* 488-508.

Denham, S. A., Zoller, D., & Couchoud, E. A. (1994). Socialization of preschoolers' emotion understanding. *Developmental Psychology, 30,* 928-936.

Dodge, K. A., Pettit, G. S., & Bates, J. E. (1994). Socialization mediators of the relation between socioeconomic status and child conduct problems. *Child Development, 65,* 649-665.

Duncan, G. J. & Chase-Lansdale, P. L. (2000). Welfare reform and child well-being. Paper presented to the Blank/Haskins conference on "The New World of Welfare Reform," Washington, DC.

Dunn, J., & Hughes, C. (1998). Young children's understanding of emotions within close relationships. *Cognition and Emotion, 12,* 171-190.

Eisenberg, N., Cumberland, A., & Spinrad, T. L. (1998). Parental socialization of emotion. *Psychological Inquiry, 9,* 241-273.

Eisenberg, N. & Fabes, R.A. (1992). Emotion, regulation, and the development of social competence. In Clark, Margaret S. (Ed) et al., *Emotion and social behavior. Review of personality and social psychology, Vol. 14* (pp. 119-150). Newbury Park, CA, USA: Sage Publications.

Eisenberg, N., & Fabes, R. A. (1994). Mothers' reactions to children's negative emotions: Relations to children's temperament and anger behavior. *Merrill-Palmer Quarterly, 40,* 138-156.

Eisenberg, N., Fabes, R. A., Minore, D., Mathy, R., Hanish, L. & Brown, T. (1994). Children's enacted personal strategies: Their relations to social behavior and negative emotionality. *Merrill-Palmer Quarterly, 40,* 212-232.

Fabes, R. A., Eisenberg, N., Nyman, M., & Michealieu, Q. (1991). Young children's appraisals of others' spontaneous emotional reactions. *Developmental Psychology, 27,* 858-866.

Fabes, R.A., Eisenberg, N., Jones, S., Smith, M., Guthrie, I., Poulin, R., Shepard, S. & Friedman, J. (1999). Regulation, emotionality, and preschoolers' socially competent peer interactions. *Child Development, 70,* 432-442.

Fabes, R. A., Leonard, S. A., Kupanoff, K., & Martin, C. L. (2001). Parental coping with children's negative emotions: Relations with children's emotional and social responding. *Child Development, 72,* 907-920.

Garcia Coll, C. T, Meyer, E. C., & Brillon, L. (1995). Ethnic and minority parenting. M. H. Bornstein et al. (Eds). *Handbook of parenting, Vol. 2: Biology and ecology of parenting* (pp. 189-209). Mahwah, NJ, USA: Lawrence Erlbaum Associates, Inc.

Garner, P. W., Jones, D. C., Gaddy, G. & Rennie, K. M. (1997). Low-income mothers' conversations about emotions and their children's emotional competence. *Social Development, 6,* 37-52.

Garner, P. W., Jones, D. C., & Miner, J. L. (1994). Social competence among low-income preschoolers: Emotion socialization practices and social cognitive correlates. *Child Development, 65,* 622-637.

Garner, P. W. & Power, T. G. (1996). Preschoolers' emotional control in the disappointment paradigm and its relation to temperament, emotional knowledge, and family expressiveness. *Child Development, 67,* 1406-1419.

Garner, P.W., Robertson, S., & Smith, G. (1997). Preschool children's emotional expressions with peers: The roles of gender and emotion socialization. *Sex Roles, 36,* 675-691.

Garner, P. W. & Spears, F. M. (2000). Emotion regulation in low-income preschoolers. *Social Development, 9,* 246-264.

Gottman, J. M., Katz, L. F., & Hooven, C. (1996). Parental meta-emotion philosophy and the emotional life of families: Theoretical models and preliminary data. *Journal of Family Psychology, 10,* 243-268.

Greenberg, M.T., Lengua, L. J., Coie, J. D., Pinderhughes, E. E., Bierman, K., Dodge, K. A. Lochman, J. E., & McMahon, R. J. (1999). Predicting developmental outcomes at school entry using a multiple-risk model: Four American communities. *Developmental Psychology, 35,* 403-417.

Halberstadt, A. G., Cassidy, J., Stifter, C. A., Parke, R. D. & Fox, N. A. (1995). Self-expressiveness within the family context: Psychometric support for a new measure. *Psychological Assessment, 7,* 93-103.

Halpern, R. (1990). Poverty and early childhood parenting: Toward a framework for intervention. *American Journal of Orthopsychiatry, 60,* 6-18.

Jones, D. C. & Garner, P. W. (1997). Socialization of emotion and children's emotional competence: Variations on a theme. *Psychological Inquiry, 9,* 297-299.

Kalil, A. & Eccles, J. S. (1998). Does welfare affect family processes and adolescent adjustment? *Child Development, 69,* 1597-1613.

Kochanska, G., Padavich, D. L., & Koenig, A. L. (1996). Children's narratives about hypothetical moral dilemmas and objective measures of their conscience: Mutual relations and socialization antecedents. *Child Development, 67,* 1420-1436.

Levine, L. J., Stein, N. L., & Liwag, M. D. (1999). Remembering children's emotions: Sources of concordant and discordant accounts between parents and children. *Developmental Psychology, 35,* 790-801.

Light, P. (1986). Context, conservation, and conversation. In M. Richards & P. Light (Eds.), *Children of Social Worlds* (pp. 170-190). Cambridge: Polity Press.

Macfie, J., Toth, S. L., Rogosch, F. A., Robinson, J., Emde, R. N. & Cicchetti, D. (1999). Effect of maltreatment on preschoolers' narrative representations of responses to relieve distress and of role reversal. *Developmental Psychology, 35,* 460-465.

McCubbin, H. I., & Patterson, J. M. (1981). *Systematic assessment of family stress, resources and coping: Tools for research, education, and clinical intervention.* St. Paul, MN: Family Social Science.

McHale, J. P., Neugebauer, A., Asch, A. R., & Schwartz, A. (1999). Preschoolers' characterizations of multiple family relationships during family doll play. *Journal of Child Clinical Psychology, 28,* 256-268.

McLoyd, V. C. (1990). The impact of economic hardship on Black families and children: Psychological distress, parenting, and socioemotional development. *Child Development, 61,* 311-346.

Menaghan, E. & Parcel, T. L. (1994). Social sources of change in children's home environments: The effects of parental occupational experiences and family conditions. *Journal of Marriage & the Family, 57,* 69-84.

Murray, L., Woolgar, M., Biers, S., & Hipwell, A. (1999). Children's social representations in dolls' house play and theory of mind tasks, and their relation to family adversity and child disturbance. *Social Development, 8,* 179-200.

Oppenheim, D., Emde, R. N., & Warren, S. (1997). Children's narrative representations of mothers: Their developmental associations with child and mother adaptation. *Child Development, 68,* 127-138.

Oppenheim, D., Nir, A., Warren, S., & Emde, R. N. (1997). Emotion regulation in mother-child narrative co-construction: Associations with children's narratives and adaptation. *Developmental Psychology, 33,* 284-294.

Ramey, C. T., Ramey, S. L. & Lanzi, R. G. (1998). Differentiating developmental risk levels for families in poverty: Creating a family typology (pp. 187-205). In M. Lewis et al. (Eds). *Families, risk and competence.* Mahwah, NJ: Lawrence Earlbaum Associates, 350 pp.

Raver, C. C. (2000). Maintaining emotional equilibrium in the context of economic hardship: Relations between psychological well-being, negative emotional expressiveness, and optimal parenting among low-income families in urban and rural contexts. Unpublished manuscript.

Raver, C. C. & Leadbeater, B. J. (1999). Mothering under pressure: Environmental, child, and dyadic correlates of maternal self-efficacy among low-income women. *Journal of Family Psychology, 4,* 1-12.

Roberts, W. & Strayer, J. (1987). Parents' responses to the emotional distress of their children: Relations with children's competence. *Developmental Psychology, 23,* 415-422.

Rogosch, F. A., Cicchetti, D. & Aber, L. J. (1995). The role of child maltreatment in early deviations in cognitive and affective processing abilities and later peer relationship problems. *Development and Psychopathology, 7,* 591-609.

Saarni, C. (1997). Coping with aversive feelings. *Motivation and Emotion, 21,* 45-63.

Sampson, R. J. & Laub, J. H. (1994). Urban poverty and the family context of delinquency: A new look at structure and process in a classic study. *Child Development, 65,* 523-540.

Seifer, R., Sameroff, A. J., Baldwin, C. P., & Baldwin, A. L. (1992). Child and family factors that ameliorate risk between 4 and 13 years of age. *Journal of the American Academy of Child and Adolescent Psychiatry, 31,* 893-903.

Shipman, K. L. & Zeman, J. (1999). Emotional understanding: A comparison of physically maltreating and nonmaltreating mother-child dyads. *Journal of Clinical Child Psychology, 28,* 407-417.

Snyder, J., Edwards, P., McGraw, K., Kilgors, K., & Holton, A. (1994). Escalation and reinforcement in mother-child conflict: Social processes associated with the development of physical aggression. *Development and Psychopathology, 6,* 305-321.

Thompson, R. (1994). Emotion regulation: A theme in search of definition. *Monographs of the Society for Research in Child Development, 59* (2-3, Serial No. 240).

U.S. Bureau of the Census (1992). *Poverty in the United States: 1992.* Series P60-185.

Zahn-Waxler, C., Kochanska, G., Krupnick, J. & McKnew, D. (1990). Patterns of guilt in children of depressed and well mothers. *Developmental Psychology, 26,* 51-59.

Psychosocial Moderators of Emotional Reactivity to Marital Arguments: Results from a Daily Diary Study

David M. Almeida
Katherine A. McGonagle
Rodney C. Cate
Ronald C. Kessler
Elaine Wethington

SUMMARY. Several studies document that marital arguments negatively affect mental health. Yet it is also evident that considerable variability exists in emotional reactivity to marital arguments. One such piece of evidence is that wives are more emotionally reactive than are husbands. Using a close relationships perspective, this study explores reasons for this variability by identifying psychosocial characteristics of individuals and their marriages. The analysis is based on a daily diary study of 166 married couples who completed questionnaires each day for six weeks. These couples represent a subsample of a prior general population community panel study. Results show that wives' emotional reactivity is best explained by a model that includes extraversion, marital

---

David M. Almeida is affiliated with the University of Arizona, Katherine A. McGonagle is affiliated with the University of Michigan, Rodney C. Cate is affiliated with the University of Arizona, Ronald C. Kessler is affiliated with Harvard University, and Elaine Wethington is affiliated with Cornell University.

[Haworth co-indexing entry note]: "Psychosocial Moderators of Emotional Reactivity to Marital Arguments: Results from a Daily Diary Study." Almeida, David M. et al. Co-published simultaneously in *Marriage & Family Review* (The Haworth Press, Inc.) Vol. 34, No. 1/2, 2002, pp. 89-113; and: *Emotions and the Family* (ed: Richard A. Fabes) The Haworth Press, Inc., 2002, pp. 89-113. Single or multiple copies of this article are available for a fee from The Haworth Document Delivery Service [1-800-HAWORTH, 9:00 a.m. - 5:00 p.m. (EST). E-mail address: docdelivery@haworthpress.com].

© 2002 by The Haworth Press, Inc. All rights reserved.

trust, being in a first marriage, and the percentage of total family income earned by the wife. Husbands' emotional reactivity is best explained by how frequently the couple argues on average, support from relatives, acute life events, and total family income. The paper concludes with a discussion of the implications for research on the mental health effects of marital distress. *[Article copies available for a fee from The Haworth Document Delivery Service: 1-800-HAWORTH. E-mail address: <docdelivery@haworthpress.com> Website: <http://www.HaworthPress.com> © 2002 by The Haworth Press, Inc. All rights reserved.]*

KEYWORDS. Marital conflict, psychological distress, daily diary

Marriage provides a peaceful and satisfying haven for many people and is known to provide significant protection from many psychological problems (Coyne & Downey, 1991). However, studies have established an association between marital conflict and such psychopathological conditions as depression (Beach et al., 1998), eating disorders (Van den Brouke, Vandereycken, & Norre, 1997), and alcohol abuse (O'Farrell, Choquette, & Birchler, 1991). Also, Paykel and colleagues (1969) found that the most common life event preceding the onset of clinical depression was an increase in marital arguments. Further, it has been suggested that chronic emotional upset or reactivity stemming from marital arguments is the key link between interpersonal conflict and psychological distress (Lazarus, 1999; Lazarus & Folkman, 1984). On the other hand, it is obvious that many people are able to avoid psychological distress in the face of considerable marital conflict. However, it is less clear what factors may protect or make marital partners more vulnerable to the negative effects of marital arguments. The present study is a preliminary attempt to identify psychosocial factors that may buffer (or exacerbate) emotional reactivity to marital conflict. The study utilizes a 6-week daily diary study of 166 marital couples all of whom participated in a previous study of life events, social support, coping, and mental health. During the diary portion of the study, participants completed daily questionnaires on marital arguments and psychological distress.

Our conceptual perspective in this study draws heavily on the Close Relationships Framework (Kelley et al., 1983). According to this framework, the basic data of a dyadic relationship are chains of behavioral, cognitive and affective events that are causally connected between two individuals over time. This framework contends that the various stable characteristics of marital partners, their marriages, and the environment serve as causal conditions for these chains of events. These characteristics exist on four levels: individual, relationship, social environment, and physical environment. The four levels are viewed as reciprocally tied to each other. Figure 1 illustrates the application of the Close Relationships Framework to the present study. The bottom portion of the figure shows the daily linkages between marital arguments (i.e., behavioral events) and psychological distress (i.e., affective events). The solid arrows represent reactivity to marital conflict. Emotional reactivity is operationalized as the likelihood an individual will report psychological distress on days they have a marital argument compared to days they do not have an argument. The top of the figure illustrates how stable individual, relationship, and social environmental variables serve as possible moderators of the relationship between marital arguments and the accompanying daily psychological distress. The dotted arrows in the figure illustrate this moderating process. Evidence about how these types of psychosocial characteristics may moderate reactivity to marital arguments is provided below.

INDIVIDUAL FACTORS

Gender. The gender of marital partners is one factor that is related to the emotional distress that accompanies marital arguments. Research has demonstrated that emotional distress which stems from a marital argument is more pronounced for wives than husbands (Almeida & Kessler, 1998; Bolger, DeLongis, Kessler, & Schilling, 1989a). This suggests that wives may be more reactive than husbands to marital arguments. Consequently, in the present study, we examine various moderators of the argument-distress relationship separately by gender.

Personality. It is expected that various personality factors of marital partners will play a role in the association of emotional reactivity to marital arguments. For example, people's positive views of themselves should provide some protection against stress. In fact, a considerable amount of research has demonstrated the role of *mastery* and *self-esteem* in helping people cope with stress in their lives (Pearlin, 1999), including marital arguments (Pearlin & Schooler, 1978).

Other personality factors may affect how people process and interpret the stress in their lives. Personality theorists have identified *neuroticism* as one potentially important characteristic that affects how people interpret and react to their daily experiences (Costa & McCrae,

FIGURE 1. Close Relationships Framework Applied to the Examination of Emotional Reactivity to Marital Arguments.

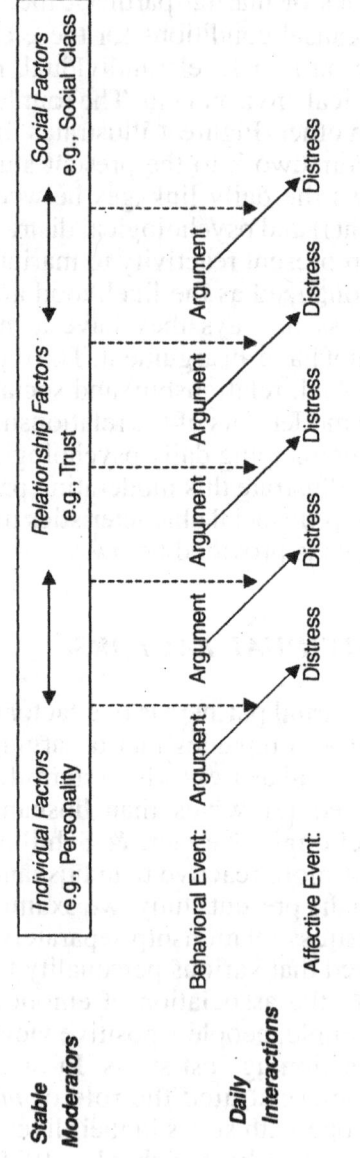

1992). People with low levels of neuroticism tend to experience life more rationally and seem relatively impervious to the strains of everyday life. Research has shown that people high in neuroticism engage in more frequent conflict (Bolger & Zuckerman, 1995), have higher levels of unpleasant affect during social interaction (Barrett & Pietromonaco, 1997), and engage in less agreeable behavior (Cote & Moskowitz, 1998).

Others have suggested that people's orientations toward others in the form of *interpersonal dependency* and *introversion* may exacerbate emotional reactivity to stressful events such as marital conflicts (Barnett & Gotlib, 1988). Consistent with that suggestion, one study demonstrated that feelings of interpersonal dependency are related to the onset of intense depression (Stader & Hokanson, 1998), while another found that dependent individuals had significant increases in dysphoria following negative interpersonal events (Lakey & Ross, 1994). Similarly, introverts also have been found to be more susceptible to post-traumatic stress disorder (Schnurr, Friedman, & Rosenberg, 1993) and to react with more physiological arousal to social stress (Hinton & Craske, 1977) than extraverts.

Finally, it is plausible that one's *sex role orientation* may predispose marital partners to certain ways of reacting to arguments. For example, past research has shown that couples who hold traditional sex role orientations tend to have less satisfying relationships than those with non-traditional orientations (Shaver, Papalia, Clark, & Koski, 1996). More important to this study, wives in traditional marriages reported more negativity (feeling sad, worthless, shy, etc.) in their lives than in non-traditional types of marriages. Unfortunately, similar data for husbands are not available.

RELATIONSHIP FACTORS

Marital history. We know of no studies that have addressed the impact of marital duration on reactivity to marital conflict. However, it has been shown that the impact of frequent marital arguing on divorce increases with time in the marriage (McGonagle, Kessler, & Gotlib, 1993), suggesting that arguments get more severe over time. Such evidence raises the possibility that emotional reactivity may increase with longer duration of marriage. In addition, although remarried individuals disagree less frequently than first marrieds, the higher divorce rates of remarried couples suggest that emotional reactivity may be greater among that group.

Economic contribution of spouses. It has been suggested that marital dynamics are affected when wives earn a significant portion of the total family income. Specifically, husbands may feel threatened in their roles as primary wage earners when wives contribute significantly to the family income. It has been demonstrated that as wives' income increases relative to total household income, marital satisfaction decreases (Moore & Waite, 1981). This may produce an interpersonal climate where emotional reactivity and arguments are likely to increase.

Trust and intimacy. We know of no studies that have addressed the ability of marital trust and intimacy to ameliorate emotional reactivity to arguments. However, marital trust and intimacy do moderate the effects of stresses in other role domains such as work (e.g., House, 1981). In addition, several studies have demonstrated that individuals positively disposed toward a partner tend to make relatively benevolent attributions about their partners' negative behaviors (Holmes & Rempel, 1986). Thus, a trusting marital environment may engender a positive climate that leads to less emotional reactivity.

Frequency of arguments. There is evidence that couples who have frequent negative interactions are more reactive to recent negative marital interactions than couples whose negative interactions are rare (Jacobson, Follete, & McDonald, 1982). This suggests that the *frequency of couples' arguments* (i.e., chronicity) will affect reactivity to any single argument.

Social support. We know of no study that has directly examined the influence of social support on reactivity to marital arguments, although the stress-moderating effect of social support has been documented in studies of more global measures of stress (Cohen & Syme, 1985). Research findings demonstrating strong effects of friend and relative support on well-being (e.g., Holahan & Moos, 1981) raises the possibility that non-spousal support may moderate the effects of marital stress.

SOCIAL ENVIRONMENT FACTORS

Stress. The evidence is mixed as to whether emotional reactivity to marital arguments is magnified by the existence of other *acute or chronic stressors* in a person's life. Consistent with the existence of such an effect, Brown and Harris (1978) found that experiencing an acute stressor in the context of a poor marriage increased the risk of major depression. However, McGonagle and Kessler (1990) found no evidence that the distressing effects of chronic marital problems were exacerbated by acute stresses.

Children. Our review of the literature failed to find any research that directly examined how the presence of children affects vulnerability to marital arguments. One line of research has shown that the addition of children predicts decreases in marital quality (Belsky & Pensky, 1988) and increases in psychological distress (McLanahan & Adams, 1987), inferentially suggesting that children may exacerbate the emotional impact of marital arguments. Relatedly, the close spacing of children (child density), as well as the number of children, have been suggested as factors that influence marital satisfaction (Figley, 1973). The alternative possibility, that children may decrease emotional reactivity, is suggested by evidence that multiple roles promote well-being because negative effects of stresses in one role are offset by positive experiences in other roles (Barnett & Baruch, 1985).

Socioeconomic status. Research on socioeconomic differences in marital interaction has shown that blue-collar couples are more reactive to marital conflict than white-collar couples and that this difference can be traced to the higher levels of job distress of blue-collar workers (Krokoff, Gottman, & Roy, 1988). This finding is supported by further research showing that level of education reduces the effects of marital strain through effective coping (Pearlin & Schooler, 1978).

In summary, the present study provides some preliminary evidence concerning the within-person covariation of marital arguments and distressed mood, as well as how the psychosocial characteristics described above moderate this covariation. The findings contribute to the literature for two reasons. First, data from the larger project allowed us to examine possible moderators of the links between marital arguments and emotional distress that exist at various levels of analysis. Such studies have not yet been conducted. This may lead to the development of more refined research questions and hypotheses in subsequent research. Second, the method of data collection used a daily diary procedure over six weeks to gather information on day-to-day events and reactions in marriage as they naturally occur. This method is an improvement on retrospective designs that are subject to substantial recall biases as well as laboratory studies that are prone to problems of external validity (Larson & Almeida, 1999).

METHOD

Sample and Design

Respondents were husbands and wives consisting of 166 married couples, all of whom had previously participated in a community survey of stress and coping. The original sample consisted of 778 intact couples from the Detroit metropolitan area. The response rate in the original survey was 73%. Of these, we attempted to recontact and recruit 489 couples by telephone to participate in a diary study which took place 3 years later (the remaining 289 couples were excluded due to participation in an earlier study). We were able to trace and recruit only 166 couples in which both spouses agreed to participate, yielding a couple-level response rate of 34%. A nonresponse adjustment weight was constructed to compensate for two types of nonresponse. First, prior analysis found very few differences between couples in the diary subsample and those in the larger community survey (see Bolger, DeLongis, Kessler, & Wethington 1989a). Diary couples, however, tended to report less marital conflict and slightly lower levels of distress. Second, the data were weighted to adjust for these differences. The data were also weighted to correct for misrepresentation of the target population.

Respondents completed a short daily diary questionnaire on each of 42 consecutive days (6 weeks). Diaries were distributed and returned by mail each week. Seventy-four percent of the respondents completed the full set of 42 diary days and 89% completed 28 days or more. Data were obtained on 12,054 diary days in all and on 11,578 days on which both husband and wife in a couple reported. We base our analysis on the latter subsample (see Bolger et al., 1989a for more details on the design and sample).

Measures

Outcome variable. The outcome variable was extent of psychological distress as assessed daily using an inventory of 18 mood items from the Affects Balance Scale (Derogatis, 1975) designed to measure anxiety (e.g., nervous, tense, afraid), hostility (e.g., irritable, angry, resentful) and depression (e.g., helpless, worthless, depressed). Based on their emotional state over the past 24 hours, respondents rated each of the 18 items on a 4-point scale ranging from "not at all" to "a lot." Responses to all items were combined and rescaled to create a summary measure of distressed mood which ranged from 0 (all items endorsed "not at all") to 4 (all items endorsed "a lot"). The summary measure was then standardized. The scale had high internal consistency (Cronbach's alpha = .91 for husbands and .92 for wives).

Predictor variables. Described below are two categories of predictor variables used in the analysis. The first was the occurrence of a marital argument on a given day, based on information obtained from the daily diary survey. The second category consisted of psychosocial characteristics obtained from the original baseline survey that may moderate the relation between marital arguments and psychological distress.

Marital arguments. The diary included a checklist of 21 stressors that occurred over the past 24 hours, including arguments with spouse, children and others. Respondents checked which arguments, if any, they experienced over the prior 24 hours. If multiple arguments occurred, respondents indicated the argument that was the most serious one of their day. We focus here on arguments with the spouse that were either the only argument of the day or, in the case of multiple arguments, the most serious argument. A prior report showed that nearly all respondents in the diary subsample reported having a marital argument at least some of the time, with the vast majority reporting average frequencies between one to two marital arguments per month (McGonagle, Kessler, & Schilling, 1992).[1] Marital arguments were dummy-coded (0 = no, 1 = yes).

Moderator variables. Consistent with the Close Relationships Framework (Kelley et al., 1983), we included possible moderator variables drawn from the individual, relationship, and social environment levels. The individual variables measured were mastery, self-esteem, neuroticism, extraversion, interpersonal dependency, and sex role orientation. *Mastery* was measured with four items (alpha = .61) from Pearlin and Schooler (1978). Respondents' answered on a 4-point scale of "strongly agree" to "strongly disagree." For example, one item was "I often feel helpless in dealing with the problems of life." *Self-esteem* was tapped with six items (alpha = .72) from Rosenberg (1965) using the same agree-disagree format as above. An example item was "At times I think I'm no good at all." *Neuroticism* was measured with 11 items (alpha = .78) from Eysenck and Eysenck (1976). Items asked respondent's to indicate a "yes," "no," or "sometimes" response to a series of questions such as, "Would you call yourself a nervous person?" *Extraversion* was assessed by 9 items (alpha = .80) from Eysenck and Eysenck (1976). The response format was the same as for neuroticism. One item was "In general, do you enjoy meeting new people?" *Interpersonal dependency* was tapped by six items (alpha = .61) using a four-point agree-disagree response format as described above (Hirschfeld et al., 1977). A sample item was "The idea of losing a close friend is terrifying to me." *Sex-role orientation* was measured with three items (alpha = .69) from Huber and Spitze (1983) and Mason, Czajka, and Arber (1976), again on an agree-disagree continuum. One item read "It is more important for a wife to help her husband's career than to have one herself." All of the individual variables were standardized prior to analysis.

The relationship variables included several single-item indicators: *length of marriage*; *first vs. remarriage*; *percent of wives income to total income*; *average frequency of arguments*; *marital intimacy* ("how much can you open up to your spouse about things that are really important to you?"); and *marital trust* ("how much can you trust your spouse to keep his/her promises to you?"). In addition, two short 4-point scales (two items each) had respondents indicate the level of *perceived support from friends* (e.g., "express interest in how you are doing") and *perceived support from family* (e.g., "make you feel that they care about you"). Participants indicated the level of support on a scale of "often to never." Coefficient alphas for these support measures were .60 and .74.

The social environment variables were: *number of children ages 0-12*; *number of children ages 13+*; *number of children outside home*; *spacing of children*; *child density*; *total income*, and *years of education*. Lastly, *chronic difficulties*; and *acute life events* were assessed using 87 items from McGonagle and Kessler (1990) that assessed ongoing difficulties (e.g., persistent financial problems) and acute life events (e.g., death of a close friend) not related to the marriage. All of the moderator variables were standardized to a mean of 0 and variance of 1.

Analysis Strategy and Statistical Model

The moderating effects of psychosocial characteristics on the relationship between marital arguments and daily mood were analyzed using Hierarchical Linear Modeling (HLM; Bryk & Raudenbush, 1992; Mason, Wong, & Entwistle, 1984), a method that allows simultaneous estimation of both (a) a separate within-person model of regression slopes and intercepts for each respondent and (b) a single between-person model in which the within-person slopes and intercepts are treated as dependent variables regressed on person-level predictor variables. For the present analyses the within-person model assesses the daily covariation of distressed mood and occurrence of a marital argument. This model can be expressed as:

$$DM_{it} = a_{0i} + a_{1i}ARG_{it} + e_{it} \quad (1)$$

where DM_{it} is the Distressed Mood of Person$_i$ on Day$_t$, ARG_{it} is a dummy variable indicating whether Person$_i$ experienced a marital argument as the most serious argument of Day$_t$ (coded 1 for those who reported yes and 0 for those who reported no), a_{0i} is the intercept for Person$_i$'s level of distressed mood, a_{1i} is the slope indicating the effects of marital arguments, and e_{it} is the random component or error associated with Distressed Mood of Person$_i$ on Day$_t$.

A distinctive feature of HLM is that the intercepts and slopes can vary across persons. Therefore, between-person models of within-person variability can be formulated. In our analysis, the intercepts and slopes in Equation (1) were modeled to vary as a function of the moderator variables as follows:

$$a_{0i} = b_0 + b_1 MOD_i + d_i \quad (2)$$

$$a_{1i} = b_2 + b_3 MOD_i + g_i \quad (3)$$

Equations 2 and 3 show that level of distressed mood (a_{0i}) and the slope of distressed mood on arguments (a_{1i}) are functions of a moderator and a random component. Substituting Equations 2 and 3 into Equation 1, a single multi-level equation can be obtained showing daily distressed mood as a function of a moderator, marital arguments, and their joint effects:

$$DM_{it} = (b_0 + b_1 MOD_i + d_i) + (b_2 + b_3 MOD_i + g_i)ARG_{it} + e_{it} \quad (4)$$

which reduces to:

$$DM_{it} = b_0 + b_1 MOD_i + b_2 ARG_{it} + b_3(MOD_i \times ARG_{it}) + d_i + g_i ARG_{it} + e_{it} \quad (5)$$

Equations 4 and 5 represent conventional linear models except that the structure of the random component is more complex. As a result of this complexity, neither the b coefficients nor the covariances among the random components can be appropriately estimated using standard linear regression methods such as OLS. Recent developments in statistical theory and computation, however, allow for maximum-likelihood estimation of these coefficients using the EM algorithm (Dempester, Laird, & Rubin, 1977). This estimation procedure takes into consideration the amount of data available from each person, so that missing data on some days are taken into account by giving more weight to persons with complete data than those with some missing data.

Control variables were included in the model to adjust for time-varying correlates of arguments and mood. These include day of the week (six dummy variables) and the linear and quadratic forms of a variable defining the number of days that had elapsed since the respondent first began filling out the diary.

Day of the week was controlled because prior research has documented systematic day-of-the-week variation in mood (e.g., Stone, Hedges, Neale, & Satin, 1985). We controlled for length of time in the study in order to capture any tendency of respondents to change how they completed the diaries in response to boredom, novelty, or fatigue. Previous research has shown that the number of stressors reported by diary respondents declines over time (DeLongis, Folkman, & Lazarus, 1988).

The first step of our analysis was to assess the bivariate relationships among gender, marital arguments and the moderator variables. In the second step, we estimate the moderating effects of the psychosocial characteristics on the relationship between marital arguments and daily mood in 23 separate models (i.e., one model per moderator) using the statistical model described above. In the third step, all significant moderators in the previous analyses were assessed simultaneously to choose best-fitting models.

RESULTS

Gender and Psychosocial Characteristics: Bivariate Associations

We initially examined whether the psychosocial variables were associated with gender. Variations in these characteristics are generally what we would expect based on prior research (see Table 1). Wives reported significantly higher levels of neuroticism [$t(165) = 3.2, p < .01$], extraversion [$t(165) = 4.0, p < .01$], interpersonal dependency [$t(165) = 3.3, p < .01$], and nontraditional sex-role orientation [$t(165) = 2.8, p < .01$] than did husbands. There were no sex differences in levels of mastery or self-esteem. Husbands and wives reported equal levels of marital intimacy and wives reported significantly higher levels of marital trust than husbands [$t(165) = 4.8, p < .01$]. Wives also reported higher levels of perceived support from friends and relatives [$t(165) = 6.6, p < .01$;

TABLE 1. Description of the Psychosocial Moderator Variables

Moderator Variables	Husband		Wife	
	M	SD	M	SD
A. Individual Factors				
Neuroticism	−.18	.98	.06	.96
Extraversion	−.20	1.0	.10	.94
Mastery	.08	.98	−.04	.93
Self-Esteem	.10	.96	−.05	.91
Interpersonal Dependency	−.12	.95	.13	1.01
Sex-Role Orientation	.01	.92	.22	.94
B. Relationship Factors				
Marital Intimacy	.80	.21	.84	.22
Marital Trust	.01	.68	.31	.88
Perceived Friend Support	−.25	1.11	.25	.84
Perceived Relative Support	−.11	1.12	.14	.89
Average Number of Marital Arguments	.10		.10	
Years Married	17.11	12.31		
First- vs. Remarriage	.84	.37		
Percent Wives' Income	.17	.18		
C. Social Environmental Factors				
Chronic Difficulties	.44	.59	.45	.60
Acute Life Events	.07	.28	.09	.31
Number Children Aged 0-12	.74	1.10		
Number Children Aged 13>	1.68	1.00		
Mean Number Children Away from Home	1.11	1.62		
Child Spacing	3.41	1.92		
Child Density	.26	.22		
Total Income	47724	23745		
Years Education	13.61	2.51	13.42	2.01

$N = 166$ couples

$t\ (165) = 3.3,\ p < .01$]. There were no sex differences in reports of chronic and acute stress or in years of education.

Moderating Effects on the Relationship Between Marital Arguments and Daily Mood

Table 2 presents results from 23 separate HLM equations testing buffering effects of psychosocial characteristics on husbands' and wives' daily mood. The coefficients in the table are the slope moderating effects (b_3) described in Equation 3. In such a large series of tests, it is likely that a few coefficients will be significant merely by chance. To adjust for this, we used a more conservative criterion for statistical sig-

TABLE 2. Gross Moderating Effects of Daily Reactivity to Marital Arguments

Variable	Husbands (n = 5205 days) b	t	Wives (n = 5331 days) b	t
A. Individual Factors				
Self-esteem	.024	2.6*	-.061	-4.2**
Mastery	.023	2.4	-.055	-4.2**
Dependence	-.027	-2.6*	.047	3.7*
Neuroticism	.007	0.9	.057	4.8**
Extraversion	-.011	-0.9	-.068	-5.2**
Sex-Role Orientation	.032	3.0*	.024	1.7
B. Relationship Factors				
Marital Trust	-.008	-1.4	-.034	-3.1*
Marital Intimacy	.019	2.1	-.058	-4.2**
Friend Support	-.005	-0.6	.011	0.8
Relative Support	.026	2.8*	-.023	-1.8
Average Number of Marital Arguments	.045	5.2**	.006	0.5
Years Married	-.012	-1.1	.023	1.7
First- or Remarriage	-.002	-0.2	-.071	-5.0**
Percent Wives' Income	.012	1.3	.057	4.2**
C. Social Environmental Factors				
Chronic Difficulties	-.013	-1.4	.013	1.1
Acute Life Events	.025	2.6*	.011	0.8
Number Children Aged 0-12	.031	3.5*	-.026	-2.2
Number Children Aged 13>	.015	1.6	-.013	-1.0
Mean # Children Away from Home	-.026	-2.8*	.012	1.1
Child Spacing	.003	0.3	-.021	-1.6
Child Density	-.002	-0.2	.041	3.5*
Total Income	.022	2.6*	-.016	-0.9
Years of Education	.013	1.2	.028	2.0

*$p < .01$, **$p < .001$

nificance ($p < .01$). It is also important to evaluate the significance of the overall series of 23 coefficients rather than focus on separate coefficients. We did this by considering the significance of the moderators across the entire set of 23 equations. Among wives, 10 of 23 buffering effects were significant at the .01 level, which is considerably more than we would expect by chance. Nine of these effects are significant among husbands.

As shown in Table 2, the pattern of significant results for wives within each of the three categories were generally in the directions that we would expect based on prior research. The coefficients reflecting wives reactivity to a marital argument decreased with increases in self-esteem, mastery, extraversion, marital trust and intimacy, and being first-married. Reactivity was exacerbated by high levels of dependency, neuroticism, many children relative to years married, education, and percentage of total family income earned by the wife. Extraversion and being first-married have the most powerful effects on wives reactivity. For husbands, reactivity to spousal arguments is buffered by increases in dependency and number of children outside the home and exacerbated by high self-esteem, a non-traditional sex-role orientation, support from relatives, average number of marital arguments, frequent life events, young children in the home, and high household income. High levels of average number of marital arguments most powerfully predict husbands' reactivity.

In the next analysis, the subset of significant moderators that best explained distressed mood was chosen by simultaneously entering all significant moderators from the previous analysis into a single HLM equation. This analysis allowed us to examine the unique moderating effects of each variable while controlling their relations to each other. The results presented in Table 3 showed that reactivity to marital arguments was best explained by a 4-variable model for both husbands and for wives. No other buffering effects uniquely contributed to these models at the .01 level. The coefficients presented in the table are interactions between the presence of a marital argument on a given day and the significant moderator controlling for other moderators. Among husbands, daily reactivity to a marital argument increased as the relative

TABLE 3. Net Moderating Effects of Daily Reactivity to Marital Arguments

Variable	Husbands (n = 5205 days)	
	b	t
Relative Support	.021	2.1*
Acute Life Events	.025	2.2*
Average Number Marital Argument	.047	4.9***
Total Income	.035	3.1**
Variable	Wives (n = 5331 days)	
	b	t
Extraversion	−.051	−3.6***
Marital Trust	−.032	−2.0*
First- vs. Remarriage	−.067	−3.7***
Percentage of Income Earned by the Wife	.035	2.1*

*p < .01, **p < .001, ***p < .0001

support, acute life events, average frequency of marital arguments and household income increased. Wives' reactivity was exacerbated by higher contributions to household income and attenuated by increases in extraversion, marital trust, and being in their first marriage.

DISCUSSION

The results of the present study provide information about characteristics associated with vulnerability to a particularly debilitating form of daily stress. Such information may increase our understanding about how risk factors and resources that affect day-to-day distress are implicated in the development and course of psychiatric disorder. In general, these results reveal that emotional reactivity to marital arguments is highly dependent on a range of psychosocial factors. Indeed, we found evidence of gross stress-buffering effects in each of the three sets of psychosocial factors. These results stand in contrast to a prior report showing that how *frequently* couples engage in marital disagreements does not generally depend upon a wide variety of psychosocial factors (McGonagle et al., 1992). That is, over a time period of approximately one month, the occurrence of a marital disagreement is nearly universal regardless of SES, children, etc. Our results in combination with these prior findings suggest that psychosocial factors may be more important in how individuals react to marital arguments than how often they have such arguments.

Among the most noteworthy of results were the striking gender differences in individual moderators of reactivity. Although two individual variables (dependence and self-esteem) were significant for both husbands and wives, the direction of the correlation was reversed by gender (see discussion below). In addition, there were gender differences in all three categories of variables (individual, relationship, and social environment) used in this study.

Individual Moderators

For wives, each stable individual characteristic had significant buffering effects on reactivity to marital arguments (with the exception of sex-role orientation). Specifically, high levels of mastery, self-esteem, and extraversion, as well as low levels of dependency and neuroticism, attenuated reactivity. These findings are broadly consistent with prior research documenting the buffering effects of personality (an individual characteristic) on marital stress. An intriguing finding in this study is that husbands' reactivity was affected by personality but in a different direction than we expected. Husbands with higher self-esteem and lower dependency were more upset by arguments, although these effects disappeared in the net models.

This gender difference may be understood in light of evidence that personality plays a greater role in coping with stressful life events that are highly threatening (Lazarus & Folkman, 1984) or uncontrollable (Pearlin & Schooler, 1978). Such research suggests that the gender differences that we observed may be due to wives perceiving marital arguments as more threatening and uncontrollable than did husbands. This hypothesis is consistent with the fact that wives are significantly more upset by marital arguments than are husbands (Bolger et al., 1989a) and with evidence that marital happiness is more highly associated with wives' overall happiness than with husbands' (Glenn, 1975). This same hypothesis may help explain the findings that other individual moderators, self-esteem, low dependency, and non-traditional sex-roles, were positively related to husbands' reactivity on a marital argument day. That is, perhaps the marital relationship is similarly central to the emotional well-being of these non-traditional husbands as it is for wives. In the future we plan to conduct a comparative analysis of the link between various family relationships and emotional well-being among husbands and wives as a function of various components of their self-image, including personality characteristics and sex-role orientation.

Relationship Moderators

Three relationship factors (marital trust, marital intimacy, and the percent of total income earned by the wife) were significant moderators for wives, but not for husbands. As levels of marital trust and intimacy increased, reactivity to marital arguments decreased. Research with couples (Holmes & Rempel, 1986) has shown that a climate of positivity in relationships can lead to relatively benevolent attributions for negative behavior on the part of the partner. Such a positive interpersonal climate may moderate reactivity to marital arguments. Wives in this study expressed higher levels of marital trust than husbands. If a threshold exists for trust to moderate reactivity, it may be that the levels of trust by husbands in this study were too low to trigger such a buffering effect.

One relationship factor did exacerbate emotional reactivity for wives, but not husbands. The percentage of wives' income relative to total income exacerbated emotional reactivity to marital arguments for wives.

This may be due to increased workplace demands that accompany wives' increased participation in the labor market. Previous research has shown that wives who work for pay outside the home and have children experience more psychological distress than do their husbands (Thoits, 1986).

In addition to the above gender differences, the average number of marital arguments moderated the link between marital arguments and emotional reactivity for husbands, but not for wives. This result extends prior research by showing that not only are daily perceptions of marital quality undermined by recent negative interactions among couples who generally have frequent negative interactions (Jacobson et al., 1982), but that *emotional* reactivity is elevated as well. Why this would occur for husbands and not wives is not completely clear given that prior research has shown that wives are more reactive to marital arguments than their husbands (Almeida & Kessler, 1998). Some clues may be gained by evidence that husbands are more physiologically reactive to stress and find negative affect more aversive (Gottman & Levenson, 1988). Perhaps husbands are less likely to admit or acknowledge that they are upset because it is aversive to them and will only report negative feelings when they experience persistent arguments. Thus, it may be that it is more difficult for husbands' arousal rates to return to baseline than wives' in the context of chronic marital distress. This possibility could be tested in future research by conducting a comparative analysis of habituation processes among husbands and wives.

Social Environmental Moderators

Several gender differences appeared for the social environmental moderators. The social environment was relatively more influential in moderating reactivity to marital arguments for husbands than for wives. Support from relatives, acute life events, number of children under 12 years old, number of children outside the home, and total income moderated reactivity for husbands but not wives. Having children who were close in age exacerbated wives' reactivity.

An explanation of the finding that support from relatives exacerbated emotional reactivity for husbands but not for wives may lie in gender differences in the seeking of social support. That is, prior research shows that distress levels initiate support seeking (Kessler, Kendler, Heath, Neal, & Eaves, 1992) and it is plausible that the threshold of distress at which support seeking is initiated is higher for husbands than it is for wives. Further examination of this issue would make an important contribution to the literature on gender differences in social support.

Our analyses revealed a weak, but significant, exacerbating effect of acute life events on husbands' reactivity, but not on wives' reactivity. This gender difference is somewhat puzzling and has no obvious explanation. However, in the context of the other findings for husbands, a very tentative explanation can be offered. Most of the significant moderators for husbands vs. wives can be seen as sources of general stress (e.g., children in the home, total income). It may be that acute life events are simply a part of the general stress that exacerbates reactivity for husbands, but not wives.

We found significant associations between the presence of children in the home and reactivity to marital arguments for husbands, but not for wives. However, these effects were weak and disappeared in the net models. It is noteworthy that these findings are relevant to prior research, which has generally found that the transition to parenthood is associated with decrements in marital quality (Belsky, Spanier, & Rovine, 1983), by demonstrating that this decline may occur through the exacerbation of reactivity to marital conflicts. For husbands only, it is the number of children under 12 years of age in the home that increases reactivity to arguments, while the number of children outside the home decreases reactivity to arguments. For wives, it is the presence of children that are close in age that exacerbates reactivity to marital arguments.

Our results showed that husbands, but not wives, become more distressed by a marital argument as household earnings increased. One plausible explanation is that high income is presumably positively correlated with job demands, suggesting that increased emotional reactivity to marital arguments occurs, in part, through perceptions of the argument as an additional demand on time and energy. It is important to note that the percentage of wives' earnings to household income failed to affect husbands' reactivity. In subsequent analyses not presented here, we examined the possibility that the impact of wives' income on husbands' reactivity to marital arguments varies as a function of husbands' sex-role orientation. We found no evidence that traditional husbands were more reactive than non-traditional husbands as a function of their wives' earning power. A challenge for future research is to sort out the complicated associations between mental health and wives' employment and earnings.

Limitations and Implications

Limitations of the present study should be noted. First, information was obtained in only 34% of the couples approached to participate in the study. Although attempts were made to correct this problem through weighting procedures, external validity is somewhat compromised by our response rate. It is, nevertheless, comparable to rates obtained in other studies of married couples (e.g., Hiller & Philliber, 1985).

Another limitation is that our measurement of marital arguments and distressed mood was somewhat crude and incomplete. First, it is important to point out that information on arguments and distressed mood come from the same reporter. Thus findings reported here could be partly due to this shared method variance. In addition, we were only able to capture a limited portion of the variability that no doubt exists in perceptions of argument severity by excluding from our analysis those person-days on which a serious argument with an individual other than the spouse occurred. Regarding incompleteness, prior research shows that particular components of marital disagreements, including frequency, style and outcome, are differentially distressing (McGonagle et al., 1992). Furthermore, these findings raise the possibility that the results reported here differ as a function of these various components. Thus, a challenge for future research on daily marital stress is the development of more sophisticated measures of marital distress, including marital arguments.

Despite these limitations, the results of the present study take an important step in elucidating the link between marital arguments and psychological distress by drawing attention to how various psychosocial features in the lives of married couples influence vulnerability to marital arguments. The findings also lend considerable support to the utility of the Close Relationships Framework for understanding emotion in marriage. According to this framework, dyadic relationships fundamentally consist of chains of behavioral, cognitive and affective events that are causally connected between two individuals over time. In addition, this framework contends that various stable characteristics of relationship partners, their relationships, and the environment serve as causal conditions for these chains of events. In keeping with the theme of this volume on emotions in families, we applied this framework to the examination of the daily linkages between marital arguments (i.e., behavioral events) and psychological distress (affective events). Our diary design and analytic strategy permitted us to provide direct evidence that individuals report higher levels of psychological distress on days they have a marital argument compared to days they do not have an argument. Furthermore, we were able to test how stable characteristics of individuals, relationships, and the social environment moderate these daily linkages. Indeed, there was evidence of gross moderating effects of each of the three sets of psychosocial factors that were examined.

We believe that the findings presented here set the stage for further application of the Close Relationships Framework. First, our results were based on concurrent within-day associations. Subsequent research should investigate the temporal sequencing between marital arguments and psychological distress by testing whether arguments on Day 1 are related to distress on Day 2, or whether arguments predict *change* in distress from Day 1 to Day 2 (cf. Larson & Almeida, 1999). Second, more work needs to be conducted on the mechanisms underlying the stable moderators. In the present analysis, the number of significant moderators was substantially reduced in the net model. This suggests that many of the significant moderators work indirectly through others. The Close Relationships Framework posits various pathways of potential causality. For example, neuroticism (a gross effect only) may moderate argument-emotional reactivity through its impact on marital trust (a net effect). Third, dynamic moderators of the daily linkages between marital arguments could also be explored. Our findings certainly provide evidence that some people are more likely to react to marital arguments than other people based on stable characteristics about themselves and their relationships. However, we do not test how fluctuating circumstances of day-to-day life buffer or exacerbate the emotional effects of marital arguments. For example, emotional reactivity to marital arguments may be heightened on days when other stressors occur. Also, future work might address how the occurrence of positive affect on specific days buffers reactivity to arguments. Finally, the Close Relationships Framework contends that causal processes are largely reciprocal in nature. However, there is almost no research on how the daily emotional lives of couples feeds back to influence more stable properties of individuals or relationships. The use of daily diary designs, in conjunction with longitudinal methods, could be fruitful in suggesting answers to these questions of reciprocity. Using dairy designs embedded in a Close Relationships Framework might provide some clues for this potentially exciting avenue of research.

NOTE

It has been suggested that the frequency of marital arguments in this sample is relatively low. We do not believe that this poses a problem for the study. First, twenty percent of the couples reported arguments between two per month and more than one per week. Consequently, the sample represents a fairly broad spectrum of argument frequency. Second, there is little evidence to guide researchers in determining which couples are "high" in marital arguments versus "low" in marital arguments.

REFERENCES

Almeida, D. M., & Kessler, R. C. (1998). Everyday stressors and gender differences in daily distress. *Journal of Personality and Social Psychology, 75,* 670-680.

Barnett, R. C., & Baruch, G. K. (1985). Women's involvement in multiple roles and psychological distress, *Journal of Personality and Social Psychology, 49,* 135-145.

Barnett, P. A., & Gotlib, I. H. (1988). Psychosocial functioning and depression: Distinguishing among antecedents, concomitants, and consequences. *Psychological Bulletin, 104,* 97-126.

Barrett, L., & Pietromonaco, P. (1997). Accuracy of the five-factor model in predicting perceptions of daily social interactions. *Personality and Social Psychology Bulletin, 23,* 1173-1187.

Beach, S., Tesser, A., Fincham, F., Jones, D., Johnson, D., & Whitaker, D. (1998). Pleasure and pain in doing well, together: An investigation of performance-related affect in close relationships, *Journal of Personality and Social Psychology, 74,* 923-938.

Belsky, J., & Pensky, E. (1988). Marital change across the transition to parenthood. *Marriage & Family Review, 12,* 133-56.

Belsky, J., Spanier, G. B., & Rovine, M. (1983). Stability and change in marriage across the transition to parenthood, *Journal of Marriage and the Family, 45,* 567-577.

Bolger, N., DeLongis, A., Kessler, R. C., & Schilling, E. A. (1989a). Effects of daily stress on negative mood. *Journal of Personality and Social Psychology, 57,* 808-818.

Bolger, N., DeLongis, A., Kessler, R. C., & Wethington, E. (1989b). The contagion of stress across multiple roles. *Journal of Marriage and the Family, 51,* 175-183.

Bolger, N., & Zuckerman, A. (1995). A framework for studying personality in the stress process. *Journal of Personality and Social Psychology, 69,* 890-902.

Brown, G. W., & Harris, T. O. (1978). *Social origins of depression.* New York: Free Press.

Bryk, A. S., & Raudenbusch, S. W. (1992). *Hierarchical linear models: Application and data analysis.* Newbury Park: Sage.

Cohen, S., & Syme, S. L. (eds.), (1985). *Social support and health.* San Diego, CA: Academic Press.

Costa, P., & McCrae, R. (1992). *Revised NEO Personality Inventory (NEO-PI-R) and NEO Five-Factor Inventory (FFI) professional manual.* Odessa, FL: Psychological Assessment Resources.

Cote, S., & Moskowitz, D. (1998). On the dynamic covariation between interpersonal behavior and affect: Prediction from neuroticism, extraversion, and agreeableness. *Journal of Personality and Social Psychology, 75,* 1032-1046.

Coyne, J., & Downey, G. (1991). Social factors and psychopathology: Stress, social support, and coping processes. *Annual Review of Psychology, 42,* 401-425.

Delongis, A., Folkman, S., & Lazarus, R. S. (1988). The impact of daily stress on health and mood: Psychological and social resources as mediators. *Journal of Personality and Social Psychology, 54,* 486-495.

Dempster, A. P., Laird, N. M., & Rubin, D. B. (1977). Maximum likelihood from incomplete data via the EM algorithm. *Journal of the Royal Statistical Society, Series B, 39,* 1-8.

Derogatis, L. R. (1975). *Affects balance scale.* Baltimore, MD: Clinical Psychometrics Research Unit.

Eysenck, H. J. & Eysenck, S. B. G. (1976). *Psychoticism as a dimension of personality.* London: Hodder & Stoughton.

Figley, C. (1973). Child density and the marital relationship. *Journal of Marriage and the Family, 35,* 272-282.

Glenn, N. (1975). The contribution of marriage to the psychological wellbeing of males and females. *Journal of Marriage and the Family, 37,* 594-600.

Gottman, J. M., & Levenson, R. W. (1988). The social psychophysiology of marriage. In P. Noller & M. A. Fitzpatrick (Eds.), *Perspectives on Marital Interaction.* (pp. 182-200). Philadelphia, PA: Multilingual Matters.

Hiller, D. V., & Philliber, W. W. (1985). Maximizing confidence in married couple samples. *Journal of Marriage and the Family, 35,* 729-732.

Hinton, J., & Craske, B. (1977). Differential effects of test stress on the heart rates of extraverts and introverts, *Biological Psychology, 5,* 23-28.

Hirschfeld, R. M. A., Klerman, G. L., Cough, H. G., Barrett, J., Korchin, S. J., & Chodoff, P. (1977). A measure of interpersonal dependency. *Journal of Personality Assessment, 41,* 610-618.

Holahan, C. J., & Moos, R. H. (1981). Social support and psychological distress: A longitudinal analysis. *Journal of Abnormal Psychology, 90,* 365-370.

Holmes, J., & Rempel, J. (1986, August). *Trust and conflict in close relationships.* Invited Address at the Meeting of the American Psychological Association, Washington, DC.

House, J. S. (1981). *Work stress and social support.* Reading, MA: Addison-Wesley.

Huber, J., & Spitze, C. (1983). *Sex stratification: Children, housework and jobs.* New York: Academic Press.

Jacobson, N., Follette, W. C., & MacDonald, D. W. (1982). Reactivity to positive and negative behavior in distressed and nondistressed married couples. *Journal of Consulting and Clinical Psychology, 50:* 706-714.

Kelley, H. H., Berschied, E., Christensen, A., Harvey, J. H., Huston, T. L., Levinger, G., McClintock, E., Peplau, L. A., & Peterson, D. R. (1983). *Close Relationships.* San Francisco: W. H. Freeman.

Kessler, R. C., Kendler, K. S., Heath, A., Neale, M. G., & Eaves, L. (1992). Social Support, depressed mood, and adjustment to stress: A genetic epidemiological investigation. *Journal of Personality and Social Psychology, 62:* 257-272.

Krokoff, L. J., Gottman, J. M., & Roy, A. (1988). Blue-collar and white-collar marital interaction and communication orientation. *Journal of Social and Personal Relationships, 5,* 201-221.

Lakey, B., & Ross, L. (1994). Dependency and self-criticism as moderators of interpersonal and achievement stress: The role of initial dysphoria. *Cognitive Therapy and Research, 18,* 581-599.

Larson, R., & Almeida, D. M. (1999). Emotional transmission in the daily lives of families: A new paradigm for studying family processes. *Journal of Marriage and the Family, 61,* 5-20.

Lazarus, R. S. (1999). *Stress and emotion.* New York: Springer Publishing.
Lazarus, R. S., & Folkman, S. (1984). *Stress, appraisal, and coping.* New York: Springer.
Mason, K. O., Czajka, J. L., & Arber, S. (1976). Change in U.S. women's sex-role attitudes. *American Sociological Review, 41*: 573-593.
Mason, W. M., Wong, G. Y., & Entwistle, B. (1984). Contextual analysis through the multilevel linear model. In S. Leinhardt (Ed.), *Sociological methodology 1983-1984* (pp. 72-103). San Francisco: Jossey-Bass.
McGonagle, K. A. & Kessler, R. C. (1990). Chronic stress, acute stress and depressive symptoms. *American Journal of Community Psychology, 18*, 681-706.
McGonagle, K. A., Kessler, R. C., & Schilling, E. A. (1992). The frequency and determinants of marital arguments in a community sample. *Journal of Social and Personal Relationships, 9*, 507-524.
McGonagle, K. A., Kessler, R. C., & Gotlib, I. H. (1993). The effects of marital disagreement style, frequency and outcome on marital stability. *Journal of Social and Personal Relationships, 10*, 385-404.
McLanahan, S. S. & Adams, J. (1987). Parenthood and psychological well-being. In W. R. Scott & J. F. Short (Eds.), *Annual Review of Sociology* (pp. 237-257). Palo Alto, CA: Annual Reviews.
Moore, K. A., & Waite, L. J. (1981). Marital dissolution, early motherhood and early marriage. *Social Forces, 60*, 20-40.
O'Farrell, T., Choquette, K., & Birchler, G. (1991). Sexual satisfaction and dissatisfaction in the marital relationships of male alcoholics seeking marital therapy. *Journal of Studies on Alcohol, 52*, 441-447.
Paykel, E. S., Myers, J. K., Dienelt, M., Klerman, G. L., Lindenthal, J. J., & Pepper, M. P. (1969). Life-events and depression. *Archives of General Psychiatry, 31*, 753-760.
Pearlin, L. I. (1999). Stress and mental health: A conceptual overview. In A. Horwitz, V. Allan, & T. Scheid (Eds.), *A handbook for the study of mental health: Social contexts, theories, and systems* (pp. 161-175). New York: Cambridge.
Pearlin, L. I., & Schooler, C. (1978). The structure of coping. *Journal of Health and Social Behavior, 19*, 2-21.
Rosenberg, M. (1965). *Society and the adolescent self-image.* Princeton: Princeton University Press.
Schnurr, P., Friedman, M., & Rosenberg, S. (1993). Preliminary MMPI scores as predictors of combat-related PTSD symptoms. *American Journal of Psychiatry, 150*, 479-483
Shaver, P. R., Papalia, D., Clark, C. L., & Koski, L. R. (1996). Androgyny and attachment security: Two related models of optimal psychology. *Personality and Social Psychology Bulletin, 22*, 582-597.
Stader, S., & Hokanson, J. (1998). Psychosocial antecedents of depressive symptoms: An evaluation using daily experiences methodology. *Journal of Abnormal Psychology, 7*, 17-26.
Stone, A. A., Hedges, S. M., Neale, J. M., & Satin, M. S. (1985). Prospective and cross-sectional mood reports offer no evidence of a "blue monday" phenomenon. *Journal of Personality and Social Psychology, 49*, 56-58.

Thoits, P. (1986). Multiple identities: Examining gender and marital status differences in distress. *American Sociological Review, 51*, 259-272.

Ulbrich, P. M. (1988). The determinants of depression in two-income marriages. *Journal of Marriage and the Family, 50*, 121-131.

Van den Brouke, S., Vandereycken, W., & Norre, J. (1997). *Eating disorders and marital relationships.* London: Routledge.

Emotional and Relational Consequences of Coping in Stepfamilies

Anita DeLongis
Melady Preece

SUMMARY. One hundred and fifty-four remarried couples were interviewed at two time-points 20 months apart and provided ratings of closeness and tension in their relationships with both their own children and their stepchildren. The difference in emotional relationship quality for stepchildren and own children was described as the "stepgap." Eighty-one of these couples also completed structured diaries daily for 1 week reporting on daily family stressors and ways of coping. Compromise, confrontation, and interpersonal withdrawal were examined as ways of coping with interpersonal stress. Multilevel modeling was used to analyze family data. Results suggest that in stepfamilies where wives use

---

Anita DeLongis and Melady Preece are affiliated with the University of British Columbia.

Address correspondence to either Melady Preece, Department of Psychology, University of British Columbia (E-mail: melady@home.com) or Anita DeLongis, Department of Psychology, University of British Columbia, 2136 West Mall, Vancouver, British Columbia, Canada, V6T 1Z4 (E-mail: adelongis@psych.ubc.ca).

This research was supported by research grants from the Social Sciences and Humanities Research Council of Canada to Anita DeLongis, and a doctoral fellowship awarded to Melady Preece by the British Columbia Health Research Foundation. Parts of the paper are based on Melady Preece's dissertation. The authors wish to thank Jennifer Campbell, Richard Fabes, David Kenny, Tess O'Brien, Tom Snijders, and the anonymous reviewers for their comments and suggestions.

[Haworth co-indexing entry note]: "Emotional and Relational Consequences of Coping in Stepfamilies." DeLongis, Anita, and Melady Preece. Co-published simultaneously in *Marriage & Family Review* (The Haworth Press, Inc.) Vol. 34, No. 1/2, 2002, pp. 115-138; and: *Emotions and the Family* (ed: Richard A. Fabes) The Haworth Press, Inc., 2002, pp. 115-138. Single or multiple copies of this article are available for a fee from The Haworth Document Delivery Service [1-800-HAWORTH, 9:00 a.m. - 5:00 p.m. (EST). E-mail address: docdelivery@haworthpress.com].

© 2002 by The Haworth Press, Inc. All rights reserved.

confrontation to cope with family stressors, husbands withdraw emotionally from stepchildren. When husbands withdraw consistently, emotional closeness between wives and stepchildren deteriorates, and tension between wives and their own children increases. *[Article copies available for a fee from The Haworth Document Delivery Service: 1-800-HAWORTH. E-mail address: <docdelivery@haworthpress.com> Website: <http://www.HaworthPress.com> © 2002 by The Haworth Press, Inc. All rights reserved.]*

KEYWORDS. Stepfamilies, emotionality, coping

The rate of divorce currently approaches 50% of all marriages. The vast majority of divorced adults will either remarry or establish common-law relationships. Many of these adults will bring children from a previous union into their new situation, creating a stepfamily. It has been estimated that between 25% and 40% of North American children will live in a stepfamily for a time (Glick, 1989). Most of them will be children of divorce, already at increased risk for adjustment problems (Amato & Keith, 1991; Hetherington, 1991).

Remarriage has the potential to positively influence the overall functioning of a family previously headed by a single parent. In the best possible scenario, the addition of a new stepparent can provide economic advantages, as well as emotional and child-rearing support. However, the promise of improved family well-being often goes unrealized. It has been noted that stepfamilies are often less cohesive and more stressful than nuclear families and parent-child relationships are generally more detached, negative, and conflicted (Bray & Berger, 1993). Research has also shown that the presence of stepchildren is a major contributor to the somewhat greater rate of divorce among couples with stepchildren relative to those without stepchildren (Booth & Edwards, 1992; White & Booth, 1985).

PROBLEMS AND CHALLENGES OF STEPFAMILY LIFE

One factor often implicated in the high failure rate among stepfamilies is that members of a new stepfamily must cope with a number of stressors unique to the remarried family structure. These can be so problematic as to outweigh any advantages. For example, establishing and maintaining a strong marital bond is more challenging when the stepparent must simultaneously work to construct a functional stepparent-stepchild relationship. Similarly, while working to develop a close marital relationship, remarried parents also need to sustain a close relationship with their children from a previous union, and to resolve the loyalty conflicts that are likely to emerge (Hetherington & Jodl, 1994).

Although the quality of the stepparent-stepchild relationship is perhaps the most important relationship in predicting overall stepfamily happiness, it is also the most stressful stepfamily relationship. It is well documented that stepfamilies experience stress (Crosbie-Burnett, 1989), but little is known about how stepfamilies cope with stress on a daily basis, or how coping affects the quality of stepfamily relationships. Because many stepparent-stepchild relationships do not have the solid foundation created by early childhood bonding experiences, the way parents cope with family stress may have an even greater impact on the stepparent-stepchild relationship than on parent-child relationships that began at birth.

INTERPERSONAL RELATIONSHIPS AND INTERPERSONAL EMOTIONS

Interpersonal interactions are one of the primary elicitors of human emotions. Both the disruption and the development of relationships in stepfamilies are likely to elicit strong emotions. Love, warmth, closeness, and affection are considered interpersonal emotions because they are evoked as the result of one person's relationship with another. Such feelings are most often associated with positive affect, except in the unfortunate case when they go unreciprocated. Close relationships tend to be characterized by greater emotional intensity, positive affect, and caring and commitment (Perlman & Fehr, 1987). Further, although both positive and negative emotions are elicited in most relationships, in close relationships, positive emotions tend to predominate (Parks & Floyd, 1996).

Interpersonal tension, on the other hand, is often accompanied by both anger and anxiety. In a relational sense, a feeling of tension describes the anxious, angry emotions experienced when unresolved and often unexpressed negative affect is elicited by contact with another. However, as such tension cannot be entirely hidden, it tends to "leak" out in one way or another. In this study, closeness and tension are used as descriptors of the subjective emotional tone of the parent-child relationships in stepfamilies.

CONSIDERING THE "STEPGAP"

One of the most important determinants of the quality of the relationship between the children and parents in a stepfamily is whether the parent is a parent-from-birth or a stepparent. Stepparents and stepchildren experience each other in a way that is fundamentally different from the way parents-from-birth and their children experience each other (Papernow, 1988). Generally speaking, emotional and relational ties between stepparents and stepchildren are weaker than ties between parents-from-birth and their children. Further, research has shown that in homes where prior-marriage children of both parents are present, parents report differential treatment of children (Hetherington & Camara, 1985). Differential treatment of children in stepfamilies may lead to resentment and have long-term implications for the quality of relational ties (Anderson, Hetherington, Reiss, & Howe, 1994).

Certainly the importance of the stepparent-stepchild bond is not limited to the time during which the child is living in the stepfamily. Families remain important sources of identity and social support long after children have grown and left home. However, stepchildren's perception of available support has been found to be substantially lower than that of biological children (White, 1994). This may be due in large part to the quality of the relationship children experience with both their own parents and their stepparents. Over the long term, it is to be expected that the behavior of both parents and stepparents will affect parent-child relationships in the stepfamily, and affect the way children perceive the family and their place in it.

The term "stepgap" has been coined as a way of referring to differences between stepchildren and children-from-birth in terms of parent-child relationship quality (Preece, 2000). It was expected that the stepgap would be an important predictor of parent-child relationship quality. It was also expected that the degree of this gap would be moderated by how parents coped with stressful events within the stepfamily. Because of the mutual interdependence of emotional reactions to stress within a family unit (Berscheid, 1993), we expected that parents' coping would have continuing effects on relationship quality that would reverberate through the system and be detectable even over the long-term.

STRESS AND COPING IN THE STEPFAMILY

Coping is defined as an individual's efforts to manage those demands appraised as either taxing or exceeding available resources (Folkman, Lazarus, Dunkel-Schetter, DeLongis, Gruen, 1986). Two broad functions of coping have generally been emphasized: problem-focused and emotion-focused. Problem-focused coping involves attempts to change the person-environment relation directly, whereas emotion-focused coping is geared toward managing negative emotions generated by the stressful situation. When coping with stressors that are primarily interpersonal, however, an additional function emerges. This function, termed relationship-focused coping, describes those modes of coping that are intended to manage, regulate, or preserve relationships during stressful periods (DeLongis & O'Brien, 1990).

Research in the area of stress and coping has indicated that those daily stressors with the greatest impact on mood and health are often interpersonal in nature (Bolger, DeLongis, Kessler, & Schilling, 1989). Further, a number of researchers have concluded that interpersonal factors have a strong influence on every aspect of the stress and coping process (Taylor, Repetti, & Seeman, 1997). However, the effectiveness of coping strategies has most often been considered in relation to the individual's own outcomes. Within the family, where the maintenance of good relationships is critical to well-being, the way parents cope with family stress may have direct implications for the quality of family relationships. From this perspective, the most relevant outcome to consider when examining the effectiveness of coping strategies used with family stressors is subsequent relationship quality.

Some studies have indicated that remarried couples may possess poorer conflict resolution and problem-solving skills than couples in first marriages (e.g., Larson & Allgood, 1987). However, whether this means that remarried couples are typically deficient in their use of coping strategies, or whether stepfamily parents are merely overwhelmed by the degree of stress in their lives, is unclear. The emotional quality of social relationships may be an important determinant of both the coping strategies individuals select and their ability to implement those strategies effectively (O'Brien & DeLongis, 1997; Schreurs & de Ridder, 1997). In a stepfamily, strained relationships may both constrain the choice of coping strategies and limit the efficacy of strategies employed.

WAYS OF COPING WITH FAMILY STRESS

Researchers in the communication literature have identified three interpersonally-based options available to individuals faced with a relationship conflict (Sillars, Colletti, Parry, & Rogers, 1982), which they describe as: (1) avoidance and withdrawal, (2) verbal competition, aggression, and confrontation, or (3) cooperation and compromise. Research has also pointed to the importance of withdrawal, confrontation, and compromise as strategies used to cope with interpersonal stress (Buss, 1992; Repetti, 1992). The *Brief Ways of Coping* (BWOC) is a coping measure developed for use in diary studies. One of the notable features of this scale is the inclusion of ways of coping that are primarily interpersonal in nature. Three subscales of this measure correspond to the constructs discussed above, and were examined in this study to determine their influence on relational outcomes.

Compromise. Compromise can be described as belonging to the class of "positive and direct" behaviors (Sillars et al., 1982). Although little research has focused on the construct of compromise, *per se*, there are a number of similar, more often studied, constructs that are relevant. For example, a theory of accommodation processes has been advanced that bears some resemblance to the construct of compromise. Accommodation is defined as an individual's willingness to engage in a constructive reaction given a partner's potentially destructive behavior (Rusbult, Verette, Whitney, Slovik, & Lipkus, 1991). Accommodation tends to be associated with features of the relationship. In particular, individuals are more likely to accommodate in relationships where they have a high level of commitment. It was also proposed that there might be a social cost to the decision to accommodate. In a healthy relationship, a fair degree of mutuality in the process of accommodation is expected. However, if one partner carries most of the accommodative burden in the relationship, that partner will probably experience some personal distress as a consequence.

Compromise can also be thought of as a method of cooperating in a social dilemma. A social dilemma can be defined as a situation in which two or more persons in an interdependent relationship are faced with a conflict between maximizing personal (selfish) interests and maximizing collective (family) interests (Komorita, Parks, & Hulbert, 1992). From this perspective, one of the most important determinants of an individual's decision to cooperate is their expectation of reciprocity. The norm of reciprocity predicts that individuals tend to help those who have helped them in the past, and to retaliate against those who have injured them. In other words, individuals are more cooperative when they expect that others will also cooperate. It has been suggested that the idea of reciprocity is at the heart of all stable relationships, and is a basic norm in all social interactions (Thibault & Kelley, 1959).

Confrontation. Confrontation can be thought of as a "negative and direct" method of coping with conflict. It has been suggested that such competitive, dominating behaviors are more likely to be employed to deal with interpersonal conflict when people are most concerned with themselves rather than with involved others (Rahim, 1983). Although confronted individuals may concede defeat in the short term, the probability of future cooperation will likely be reduced due to the experience of such negative emotions as resentment, anger, and sadness. Equally problematic, immediate success provides reinforcement to the confronter, thus encouraging individuals to continue employing similar strategies. Over time, such interaction patterns may lead to the escalation of hostile and aggressive behaviors (Patterson, 1982).

The use of confrontive coping has been linked with negative psychological outcomes (Folkman et al., 1986). When coping with marital tension, confrontation has been associated with higher levels of distress for both participants in a dyadic interaction (Daylen, 1993). In this study, confrontation is conceptualized as a hostile and somewhat aggressive manner of achieving the outcomes one desires. It describes a method of coping that includes expressions of anger and a refusal to back down, accompanied by demands that the other concede.

Withdrawal. Withdrawal can be thought of as an "indirect" conflict management behavior. Some researchers have pointed out that withdrawal can have either a positive or a negative intent. For example, Repetti (1992) conceptualized withdrawal as a method of decreasing arousal after a stressful encounter. In her conceptualization, withdrawal was proposed to be an unconscious behavior, and included such activities as reading the paper or listening to music. In another conceptualization, withdrawal was identified as the conflict management behavior most likely to be taken when concern for the self and concern for the other are both low (Rahim, 1983). In the stress and coping literature, behaviors such as those described above also correspond to a coping strategy called "distancing," which involves removing oneself from the problem, and not allowing it to "get to you."

In this research, the construct named "interpersonal withdrawal" (to distinguish it from other forms of withdrawal) also includes items describing a more punitive and negative tone. It is conceptualized as an angry but non-communicative response and includes such behaviors as:

withdrawing from the other person, giving them "the silent treatment," sulking, as well as efforts to "keep my feelings to myself" and to "keep others from knowing about the problem."

METHOD

Sample

Couples were recruited from the lower mainland of British Columbia, Canada, by means of newspaper and radio advertisements, notices in school newsletters, posters on community bulletin boards, and solicitation at several local stepfamily groups. The requirements for participation were that couples be either married or living together, and have a child from a previous union living in the home at least 25% of the time. Interested couples were asked to telephone the project office for more information.

Procedure

Upon contacting the project office, couples were sent a letter describing the study's goals and procedures. If couples determined that they met the qualifications and wished to participate, preliminary demographic information was obtained. In the telephone interviews parents were asked to rate the level of closeness and tension in their relationship with each of their own children and each of their stepchildren. Following the telephone interviews, participants were mailed a set of structured diaries to be completed each evening over a period of one week. Participants were asked to complete the diary independently and to return them in the stamped envelopes provided. Approximately 20 months after the initial interview, couples were re-contacted for a second telephone interview. In this interview, participants again answered questions regarding the emotional quality of their family relationships.

Data Available for Analysis

There were 154 couples that participated in the initial interview. Of these, 142 also participated in the second interview approximately 2 years later. In addition, 81 couples returned completed diaries (a couple diary response rate of 53%). Only the descriptions of relationship quality with minor children (those between the ages of 2 and 21) were used in this research because adult children spent little or no time in the stepfamily home and were thus unlikely to be affected by parents' ways of coping with daily stressors. Children under the age of 2 were excluded because reports of relationship quality with babies were described as lacking in tension. Further, relationship quality for children from the current union was not included, as these children were not anyone's stepchildren, and differed qualitatively from those children who were from previous unions. For children from the current union, age was also completely confounded with their status, as these children were always the youngest in the stepfamily.

Sample Characteristics

The median annual family income for the families in the study was $68,000 (CDN) per year, indicating a comfortable middle-class standard of living. This is only slightly higher than the average family income reported by Statistics Canada (1995) for the area where they lived ($64,778). However, the large range (from $14,000 to $340,000) for this sample suggests a heterogeneous sample in terms of income. Husbands had significantly greater personal income than did wives ($M = \$52,940$, $SD = \$3,720$ and $M = \$25,930$, $SD = \$1,923$, respectively, $t(153) = 8.26, p < .001$). The mean education level of individuals participating in the study was 13.86 (ranging from 8 to 17) years, and there was no significant difference in educational level between husbands and wives. This educational level is close to the average for the area in which they lived (Statistics Canada, 1995). Husbands were significantly older than their wives ($M = 40.24$, and $M = 37.17$, $t(154) = 5.564$, $p < .001$). This is consistent with previous research showing that remarried adults are more likely to be in age-heterogamous marriages than are those adults in their first marriages (Booth & Edwards, 1992).

The modal number of previous marriages for both husbands and wives was one. In fact, 93% of the participants reported at least one previous union. Of the total number of men and women participating in the study, 88% of husbands and 91% of wives were either divorced or separated from their previous partner. Only 5% of the husbands and 2% of the wives had been widowed. Although the requirement for participation in the study was that one stepchild live in the household for three months per year, data from all children between the ages of 2 and 21, whether living in the stepfamily household or not, were included in the analyses. The mean number of children in each stepfamily was 3.14, ranging from 1 to 8. The average age of the children in each family was

11.19, ranging from 2.4 to 19.8 years. The average length of time the stepfamily had been in existence was 4.57 years (ranging from 1 to 16). Of all the stepfamilies, 31% had children from the current union.

In this sample, at least 42% of the husbands' children lived with their fathers either "most of the time" or "all of the time." Further, 41% of fathers reported no consistent arrangement as to the amount of time their children spent in the stepfamily home. For wives, 79% of their children from a previous union lived in the stepfamily home either "most of the time" or "all of the time," and 74% of wives' children had their mother as the custodial parent.

Characteristics of diary sample. Couples who completed diary data were compared to those who did not on a variety of demographic variables, including education, income, years in the stepfamily, the number of children from the current union, the average age of children in the stepfamily, and the average amount of time children spent in the stepfamily household. The only significant difference between couples who completed diaries and those who did not was that among stepfamily couples that completed diary data, the children were older on average ($M = 12.02$, and $M = 9.79$, respectively, $t(153) = 2.94, p < .01$).

Measures

Parent-child relationship quality was assessed with parents' ratings of items regarding closeness and tension with each child at both Time 1 and Time 2. Husbands and wives were asked to rate on a 5-point scale how close they felt to each child, and to what extent the relationship with each child was characterized by tension. In each case, a rating of 1 indicated "not at all" and 5 meant "very."

Diary Measures. Reports of coping in the diary were aggregated for use as contextual variables. Each evening participants were instructed to select a family stressor that had occurred that day. Compromise, confrontation, and interpersonal withdrawal as ways of coping with daily family stressors was measured with the *Brief Ways of Coping* (BWOC). This scale is the result of previous psychometric work (Preece, DeLongis, & O'Brien, 1997) and a final factor analysis using the current data set (Preece, DeLongis, O'Brien, & Campbell, 2001). Participants were asked to describe their use of each strategy on a 3-point scale, indicating either a 1 (not at all), a 2 (a little) or a 3 (a lot). Compromise ($\alpha = .73$) was assessed with items such as, "Tried to find a solution that was fair to all involved," and "Tried to meet the other person half-way." Confrontation ($\alpha = .70$) was measured with items such as, "Stood my ground and fought for what I wanted," and "Tried to get the person responsible to change his or her mind." The Interpersonal Withdrawal scale ($\alpha = .75$) contained items such as, "Withdrew from the other person(s) involved," and "Gave the other person(s) involved the silent treatment."

Statistical Analyses

In this research, the characterization of families as complex groups led to the application of multilevel modeling as a statistical technique for the analysis of data with a hierarchical nesting structure. In the case of families, children can be thought of as being nested within the parental structure (Snijders, 1995). All children in the family have the same parents (or stepparents), so their relationship outcomes are not independent. An indicator variable was used in the analyses to consider the "stepgap" as a factor predicting relationship quality at the children's level of analyses. This variable was coded "+ 1" for wives' children from a previous marriage and "− 1" for husbands' children from a previous marriage.

RESULTS

Means and standard deviations for the study variables are reported separately for husbands and wives for both own children and stepchildren (see Table 1). Husbands and wives reported feeling significantly closer to their own children than to their stepchildren both at Time 1 and at Time 2. A slightly different pattern of results emerged for tension, however, with husbands reporting no differences in tension at Time 1, and only a trend towards less tension with their own children than with their stepchildren at Time 2. Wives reported significantly less tension with their own children than with their stepchildren at both time points. Correlations between relationship quality ratings indicate that at Time 2, there was a significant correlation between husbands' ratings of tension with their own children and with their stepchildren. For wives, on the other hand, correlations between ratings of closeness and tension with own children and with their stepchildren were significant at Time 1, but were reduced at Time 2.

TABLE 1. Means and Standard Deviations of Reports of Relationship Quality (Aggregated by Parent)

Relationship Quality	Own Children		Stepchildren		Paired Statistics		
	M	SD	M	SD	r	df	t
Husbands							
Time 1 Closeness	4.19	0.86	3.59	0.96	0.12	89	4.68***
Time 2 Closeness	3.99	1.15	3.52	1.11	0.17	81	2.92**
Time 1 Tension	2.22	0.99	2.40	0.93	0.11	89	−1.33
Time 2 Tension	2.16	1.13	2.42	1.19	0.41***	81	−1.87'
Wives							
Time 1 Closeness	4.62	0.78	2.96	1.19	0.33**	96	13.72***
Time 2 Closeness	4.44	0.77	2.63	1.10	−0.02	89	12.69***
Time 1 Tension	1.93	1.15	2.82	1.28	0.44***	96	−6.85***
Time 2 Tension	2.15	1.03	2.53	1.19	0.12	89	−2.40*

' $p < .10$, * $p < .05$, ** $p < .01$, *** $p < .05$

In Table 2, the means, standard deviations, and intercorrelations among the aggregated coping scores are presented separately for husbands and wives. These mean scores represent the average coping across all reports by each individual for the 7 days of the diary study. Correlations between husbands' and wives' coping variables were significantly related. Paired t-tests revealed that the only significant mean difference between husbands and wives average reports of coping was for confrontation, with wives reporting significantly greater use of confrontation than their husbands. An interesting dynamic is suggested by the significant correlation between wives' use of confrontation and husbands' use of compromise.

Effects of Parents' Coping on Time 2 Relationship Quality

The results of the analyses considering the long-term effects of coping on relationship quality are presented in Table 3. The analyses used coping to predict closeness and tension in the parent-child relationships at Time 2, controlling for relationship quality at Time 1.

Deviance reduction statistics. Deviance is a measure of model fit that can also be used as a measure of improvement of model fit for subse-

TABLE 2. Intercorrelations, Means, and Standard Deviations of Aggregated Coping Variables

		1	2	3	4	5	6
Wives							
1	Compromise	---					
2	Confrontation	0.43***	---				
3	Int. Withdrawal	0.24*	0.17	---			
Husbands							
4	Compromise	0.40***	0.27*	0.13	---		
5	Confrontation	0.20	0.41***	0.06	0.28*	---	
6	Int. Withdrawal	0.21	0.13	0.44***	0.11	0.23*	---
	Mean[a]	1.44	1.55$_a$	1.31	1.40	1.43$_b$	1.26
	SD	0.30	0.40	0.22	0.30	0.33	0.28

Note. $N = 81$
[a] Means with different subscripts differed significantly between husbands and wives according to a paired t-test.
* $p < .05$, ** $p < .01$, *** $p < .001$

quent models. In each case, the statistic compares the more elaborated model to the simpler previous models.

Husbands' Time 2 closeness. Time 1 closeness was a significant predictor of Time 2 closeness, and the stepgap did not have an independent effect on changes in closeness over time, after controlling for husbands' and wives' coping. As would be expected, the child level predictors resulted in a significant reduction in deviance. There was also a trend towards a significant reduction in deviance for husbands' coping as a set. No individual way of coping had a significant main effect, however. After controlling for husbands' and wives' average coping, wives' confrontation had a significant effect on the stepgap, which was allowed to vary as a random effect. The interactions between wives coping and the stepgap (as a set) also resulted in a significant reduction in deviance. This result supported our expectation that wives' coping would moderate the stepgap in husbands' reports of relationship quality.

The significant interaction between wives' confrontation and stepgap in closeness was broken down and portrayed graphically in Figure 1. To plot this interaction, the sample was divided into husbands' stepchildren and husbands' own children and the multilevel model was run separately for each group. The results indicated that those wives

TABLE 3. Husbands' and Wives' Average Coping as Predictors of Time 2 Relationship Quality Between Husbands and Children in Stepfamilies

| | Husbands' T2 Relationship Quality | | | | | |
| | Closeness | | | Tension | | |
Predictor variables	B	SE	t	B	SE	t
Intercept	3.68	0.06	60.28***	2.16	0.07	29.35***
Child level predictors						
Time 1 Relationship quality	0.54	0.06	9.04***	0.21	0.07	2.97**
Stepgap[a]	0.04	0.07	0.65	−0.04	0.08	−0.46
Parents' Coping						
Husbands' Compromise	−0.06	0.26	−0.24	0.04	0.31	0.14
Husbands' Confrontation	0.29	0.21	1.35	0.31	0.25	1.21
Husbands' Interpersonal Withdrawal	−0.12	0.26	−0.48	0.66	0.31	2.17*
Wives' Compromise	−0.36	0.26	−1.41	−0.36	0.31	−1.17
Wives' Confrontation	0.11	0.19	0.57	−0.15	0.23	−0.65
Wives' Interpersonal Withdrawal	0.27	0.31	0.89	0.08	0.37	0.21
Cross-level interactions (Coping x Stepgap)						
Husbands' Compromise × Stepgap	0.52	0.29	1.83[ꞌ]	−0.02	0.32	−0.07
Husbands' Confrontation × Stepgap	0.16	0.24	0.68	0.17	0.27	0.64
Husbands' Int. Withdrawal × Stepgap	−0.28	0.28	−0.99	−0.07	0.33	−0.20
Wives' Compromise × Stepgap	0.13	0.28	0.44	−0.09	0.32	−0.28
Wives' Confrontation × Stepgap	−0.47	0.21	−2.23*	−0.12	0.24	−0.52
Wives' Int. Withdrawal × Stepgap	−0.35	0.35	−0.99	0.28	0.39	0.72
Deviance Reduction Statistics:	Dev.	df	χ^2	Dev.	df	χ^2
Null model	577.60			566.54		
Child level predictors	520.43	4	57.17***	553.64	4	12.90*
Husbands' Coping	513.85	3	6.58[ꞌ]	546.39	3	7.25[ꞌ]
Wives' Coping	512.93	3	0.92	543.68	3	2.71
Husbands' Coping × Stepgap	511.12	3	1.81	543.46	3	0.22
Wives' Coping × Stepgap	502.62	3	8.50*	542.61	3	0.85

Note: $N = 70$, $n = 200$.
[a] Stepgap compares wives' children (+1) to husbands' children (−1)
[ꞌ] $p < .10$, * $p < .05$, ** $p < .01$, *** $p < .001$

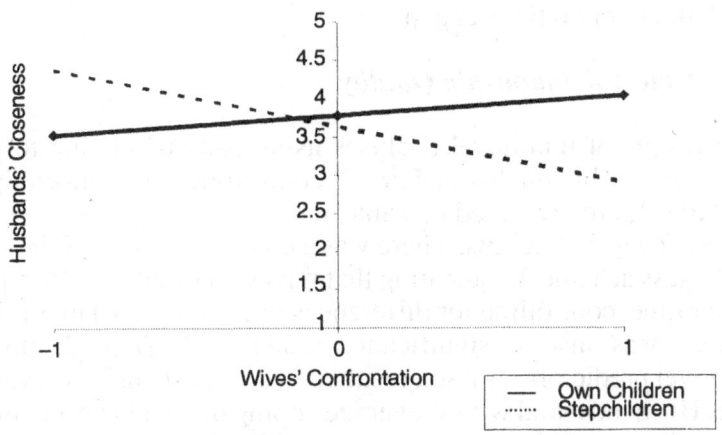

FIGURE 1. Wives' Confrontation × Stepgap Interaction Predicting Husbands' Closeness to Children in Stepfamily at Time 2.

who reported higher levels of confrontation had husbands who reported less closeness to their stepchildren. The slope describing the relationship between husbands' closeness to stepchildren and wives use of confrontation was significant ($B = -.74$, $t(49) = -2.07$, $p < .05$). However, the slope describing the relationship between husbands' closeness to his own children and wives use of confrontation was not significant ($B = .25$, $t(48) = .73$, $p > .10$). These results suggest that in families with mothers who interact with their children in an aggressive, confrontational manner, stepfathers report a decrease in emotional closeness with their stepchildren over time.

Husbands' Time 2 Tension. Husbands' reports of tension at Time 1 were significant predictors of the level of tension they reported at Time 2, and although the stepgap did not contribute to any changes in tension, after controlling for Time 1 tension and parents' coping, child level predictors resulted in a significant reduction in deviance. In addition, there was a significant main effect of husbands' typical use of interpersonal withdrawal predicting higher levels of tension at Time 2, controlling for Time 1 levels. There was also a trend towards a significant reduction in deviance as a result of the inclusion of husbands' coping in the model as a set. This result can be interpreted as indicating that husbands who reported higher levels of interpersonal withdrawal experienced an increase in levels of tension at Time 2 whereas husbands who reported lower levels of interpersonal withdrawal experienced a decrease in tension. Wives' coping did not have a significant effect on husbands' reports of tension at Time 2, and neither husbands' nor wives' coping as a set had an effect on the stepgap.

Wives' Time 2 Relationship Quality

The results of multilevel analyses using parents' coping to predict wives' relationship quality at Time 2, controlling for relationship quality at Time 1, are presented in Table 4.

Wives' Time 2 closeness. There was a continued effect of the stepgap on closeness at Time 2, indicating that wives reported a widening of the gap over time, controlling for differences in closeness at Time 1. Time 1 closeness was also a significant predictor of Time 2 closeness. Child-level predictors, as a set, resulted in a significant reduction in deviance. Husbands' and wives' average coping did not have any main effects on closeness. However, after controlling for average coping, both husbands' and wives' use of interpersonal withdrawal had significant effects on the stepgap slope. These interactions were broken down separately for both stepchildren and own children in the same manner as the interaction shown in Figure 1.

When probed, the interactions indicated that husbands' greater typical use of interpersonal withdrawal to cope with family stressors was related to wives' reports of lower levels of closeness with stepchildren at Time 2. This slope was significant in the smaller sample of stepchildren ($B = -.97$, $t(50) = -2.04$, $p < .05$). The effect of husbands' interpersonal withdrawal was not evident, however, for wives' reports of closeness with own children ($B = .07$, $t(52) = .163$, $p > .10$).

The interaction between wives' interpersonal withdrawal and the stepgap slope was also further examined. Results indicated that wives' use of interpersonal withdrawal had a greater effect on closeness with their own children than with their stepchildren. Although neither slope was significant on its own, the significant interaction suggests that the slopes are different from each other. Note that the variance in the stepgap slopes between wives was not significant. Therefore, neither set of coping interactions resulted in a significant reduction in deviance as there was no significant variance to explain. These findings suggest that for most wives, differences in closeness between stepchildren and own children are fairly stable, and therefore are subsumed in the Time 1 closeness predictor.

TABLE 4. Husbands' and Wives' Average Coping as Predictors of Time 2 Relationship Quality Between Wives and Children in Stepfamilies

	Wives' T2 Relationship Quality					
	Closeness			Tension		
Variable	B	SE	t	B	SE	t
Intercept	3.57	0.08	42.87***	2.30	0.09	24.59***
Child level predictors						
Time 1 relationship quality	0.58	0.07	7.96***	0.46	0.08	5.71***
Stepgap[a]	0.54	0.08	6.60***	−0.05	0.08	−0.63
Parents' Coping						
Husbands' Compromise	0.01	0.38	0.01	−0.51	0.41	−1.25
Husbands' Confrontation	0.43	0.28	1.52	0.34	0.32	1.06
Husbands' Interpersonal Withdrawal	−0.38	0.33	−1.13	0.53	0.38	1.42
Wives' Compromise	0.19	0.33	0.56	0.09	0.38	0.23
Wives' Confrontation	−0.17	0.26	−0.67	−0.11	0.29	−0.38
Wives' Interpersonal Withdrawal	−0.27	0.43	−0.63	0.39	0.48	0.83
Cross-level interactions (Coping × Stepgap)						
Husbands' Compromise × Stepgap	0.42	0.32	1.30	−0.13	0.36	−0.35
Husbands' Confrontation × Stepgap	−0.29	0.23	−1.26	0.23	0.28	0.83
Husbands' Int. Withdrawal × Stepgap	0.53	0.26	2.01*	0.63	0.31	2.00*
Wives Compromise × Stepgap	0.05	0.27	0.19	0.02	0.32	0.06
Wives' Confrontation × Stepgap	0.06	0.21	0.26	0.20	0.25	0.77
Wives' Int. Withdrawal × Stepgap	−0.68	0.34	−2.00*	−0.35	0.40	−0.88
Deviance Reduction Statistics:	Dev.	df	χ^2	Dev.	df	χ^2
Null model	733.45			691.24		
Child level predictors	574.14	4	159.31***	656.67	4	34.57***
Husbands' Coping	570.38	3	3.77	647.90	3	8.77*
Wives' Coping	568.48	3	1.89	647.39	3	0.51
Husbands' Coping × Stepgap	564.03	3	4.45	642.48	3	4.91
Wives' Coping × Stepgap	560.01	3	4.02	641.37	3	1.12

Note. $N = 74$, $n = 209$
[a]Stepgap compares wives' children (+1) to husbands' children (−1)
†$p < .10$, * $p < .05$, ** $p < .01$, *** $p < .001$

Wives' Time 2 tension. Wives' reports of tension at Time 1 were significant predictors of tension at Time 2. Although the inclusion of husbands' coping in the model also resulted in a significant reduction in model deviance, no form of coping had a significant effect on its own. However, husbands' greater typical use of interpersonal withdrawal did have a moderating effect on the stepgap for wives' reports of tension with children in the stepfamily. This interaction was broken down and portrayed graphically in Figure 2.

Figure 2 indicates that as husbands' use of interpersonal withdrawal increased, wives reported greater tension with their own children ($B = 1.20$, $t(52) = 2.758, p < .01$). However, for stepchildren, the slope was non-significant ($B = .34, t(50) = .694, p > .10$). The significant cross-level interaction indicates that these slopes are significantly different from each other, and suggests that husbands' use of interpersonal withdrawal has an influence on wives' relationship quality with their own children. This result provides support for the hypothesis that husbands' coping would moderate wives' Time 2 stepgap.

DISCUSSION

The results of this research illustrate the influence that parents' ways of coping with family stress have on the emotional tone of stepfamily relationships. They also suggest that these ways of coping are consistent enough that a one-week sample of self-reported interpersonal coping behaviors can predict changes in relationship quality almost 2 years later.

FIGURE 2. Husbands' Interpersonal Withdrawal × Stepgap Interaction Predicting Wives' Closeness to Children in Stepfamily at Time 2.

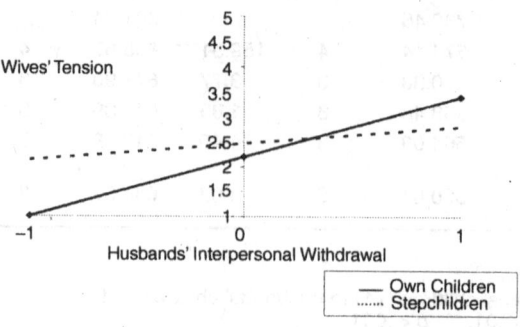

Parents' Typical Ways of Coping with Family Stressors

Wives who reported greater typical use of confrontation to cope with family stressors tended to have husbands who subsequently reported a decrease in closeness to their stepchildren, as compared to husbands whose wives reported lower typical use of confrontation. This result suggests a dynamic that may be involved in promoting the disengaged parenting style typical of stepfathers (Hetherington, 1993). Due to stepfathers' lack of a socially defined role, they may feel uncomfortable about intervening in mother-child conflicts. Additionally, wives may make it clear to their husbands that their participation in mother-child disagreements is not appreciated, particularly if the husband takes the child's side. In contrast, stepchildren are not likely to develop a close relationship with stepfathers who will not intervene in a negative conflictual interaction, and a decrease in closeness would be the inevitable result.

Our results also highlight the negative impact of husbands' interpersonal withdrawal on their wives' relationships with both their own children and their stepchildren. Wives whose husbands reported higher levels of withdrawal reported an increase in tension with their own children, and a decrease in closeness with their stepchildren. Comments made in open-ended sections of the diary further emphasized how husbands' coping behaviors can affect mothers' relationships with their children from a previous union. As one frustrated stepmother remarked, "The biggest problem I have is my husband's total lack of involvement with his children, and his unwillingness to be a father to them. And nobody accepts me as his children's step-mother, not his kids, not his parents, not his ex-wife, no one." Another mother noted, "My teen-aged daughter is pregnant, and I want to be there for her, but my husband gets really jealous. He is suffocating me, and I need to be available to my daughter. She needs me right now."

A husband who withdraws consistently may be an individual who does not cope well with stress. Such a coping response may indicate a lack of proactive coping strategies, and may preclude the development of a cohesive stepfamily unit, due either to husbands' unwillingness or inability to extend themselves in an effortful way. Alternatively, husbands who withdraw consistently may be reacting to the unexpected complexities of stepfamily life. If their initial coping efforts are not successful, they may begin to increasingly withdraw as the most effective way to avoid family tension. Unfortunately, the results presented here also suggest that wives' efforts to grow closer to their stepchildren and maintain good relations with their own children may be thwarted by their husbands' lack of active participation in stepfamily life.

Taken together, these results suggest that in stepfamilies where wives report using higher amounts of confrontation to cope with family stressors, husbands may withdraw emotionally from their stepchildren. Further, when husbands withdraw consistently, emotional closeness between wives and stepchildren deteriorates, and tension with wives' own children tends to increase. In addition, the "stepgap" effect indicates that parents' ways of coping impact relationships with their own children and with their stepchildren in very different ways. Such an effect suggests that stepparents' efforts to treat their stepchildren "just like their own" may not always be the best strategy for the maintenance of warm relations.

Implications of This Research

Our results suggest that wives' use of confrontation and husbands' use of interpersonal withdrawal are related to the deterioration of emotional relationships with children in stepfamilies. However, no long-term effects of compromise were revealed. In a daily process examination of stepfamilies (Preece, 2000), findings indicated that compromise had its effects on a day-to-day basis. In particular, parents' use of compromise predicted parents' reports of increased affection from their own children, but not their stepchildren, on the following day. It may be that the use of compromise is not particularly stable over long periods of time, and thus could not be expected to predict across the two-year period involved in this study. Alternatively, the one week window of coping behaviors examined here may not have been sufficient to provide an accurate picture of parents' use of compromise.

It has been suggested that the act of cooperation involves a state of hopeful vulnerability in which one makes an offer while simultaneously incurring a risk (Sheldon, 1999). The risk is that the other individual may not reciprocate. In a stepfamily, the coping strategies employed were expected to have different effects on parents' relationships with their own children and with their stepchildren because of different levels of vulnerability and expectations of reciprocity.

It is not difficult to imagine a scenario in which a mother's behavior could affect relationship quality in different ways throughout the stepfamily system. Perhaps the wife in a stepfamily may react negatively to a family conflict. She may become angry and confrontational, or she may withdraw. Due to a sense of loyalty, the mother's children may take her side. They may choose to blame their stepfather, and perhaps his children as well, for their mother's upset. The father's children, on the other hand, are likely dealing with loyalty conflicts of their own. They may find in their stepmother's behavior an opportunity to blame their father for his new wife's behavior, and perhaps even for remarrying in the first place.

The results reported here also highlight the paradoxical nature of interpersonal withdrawal as a coping strategy. An examination of the short-term effects of parental coping (Preece, 2000) indicated that when parents withdrew in response to a family stressor, they were rewarded by a decrease in tension the next day. However, the longitudinal data presented here suggest that if withdrawal becomes a common coping response, it may increase levels of tension with children in the stepfamily. Thus, a coping strategy that is effective in the short-term may become an instigator of the very conditions it was employed to avoid.

CONCLUSIONS

The interdependence of emotional experience and expression within a family system are highlighted by the results of this research. People bring their emotional states into interactions with others, and these emotions may affect how they behave. Certainly, both close relational partners and enemies may induce strong emotional reactions. In stepfamilies, the distinctions between the two may be somewhat blurred, but strong emotions will continue to be evoked. This study suggests that an ability to avoid aggressive and hostile ways of handling conflict, a willingness to remain engaged and open, and a commitment to the promotion of a cooperative environment, are essential parental qualities for the creation of a well-functioning stepfamily unit.

REFERENCES

Amato, R., & Keith, B. (1991). Consequence of parental divorce for children's well-being: A meta-analysis. *Psychological Bulletin, 10,* 26-46.

Anderson, E. R., Hetherington, E. J., Reiss, D., & Howe, G. (1994). Parents' nonshared treatment of siblings and the development of social competence during adolescence. *Journal of Family Psychology, 8,* 303-320.

Berscheid, E. (1993). Emotion. In H. H. Kelly, E. Berscheid, A. Christensen, J. H. Harvey, T. L. Huston, G. Levinger, E. McClintock, L. A. Peplau, & D. R. Peterson (Eds.), *Close relationships* (pp. 110-168). San Francisco, CA: Freeman.

Bolger, N., DeLongis, A., Kessler, R. C., & Schilling, E. A. (1989). The emotional effects of daily stress. *Journal of Personality and Social Psychology, 57*, 808-818.

Booth, A., & Edwards, J. N. (1992). Starting over: Why remarriages are more unstable. *Journal of Family Issues, 13*, 179-194.

Bray, J., & Berger, S. H. (1993). Development issues in stepfamilies research project: Family relationships and parent-child interactions. *Journal of Family Psychology, 7*, 76-90.

Buss, D. M. (1992). Manipulation in close relationships: Five personality factors in interactional context. *Journal of Personality, 60*, 477-499.

Coleman, M., & Ganong, L. (1990). Remarriage and stepfamily research in the 80s: New interest in an old family form. *Journal of Marriage and the Family, 52*, 925-940.

Crosbie-Burnett, M. (1989). Application of family stress theory to remarriage: A model for assessing and helping stepfamilies. *Family Relations, 38*, 323-331.

Daylen, J. (1993). *Gender differences in spouses coping with marital tension.* Unpublished doctoral dissertation, University of British Columbia.

DeLongis, A. & O'Brien, T. (1990). An interpersonal framework for stress and coping: An application to the families of Alzheimer's patients. In M. A. P. Stephens, J. H. Crowther, S. E. Hobfoll, & D. L. Tennenbaum (Eds.). *Stress and coping in later-life families* (pp. 221-238). Washington, D.C.: Hemisphere Publishers.

Folkman, S., Lazarus, R. S., Dunkel-Schetter, C., DeLongis, A., & Gruen, R. J. (1986). Dynamics of a stressful encounter: Cognitive appraisal, coping, and encounter outcomes. *Journal of Personality and Social Psychology, 50*, 992-1003.

Glick, P. C. (1989). The family life cycle and social change. *Family Relations, 38*, 123-129.

Hetherington, E. M. (1991). The role of individual differences in family relations in coping with divorce and remarriage. In P. Cowan & E. M. Hetherington (Eds.), *Advances in family research: Vol. 2. Family transitions* (pp. 165-194). Hillsdale, NJ: Erlbaum.

Hetherington, E. M. (1993). An overview of the Virginia Longitudinal Study of Divorce and Remarriage with a focus on early adolescence. *Journal of Family Psychology, 7*, 39-56.

Hetherington, E. M., & Camara, K. A. (1985). Families in transition: The processes of dissolution and reconstitution. *Review of Child Development Research, 7*, 398-439.

Hetherington, E. M., & Jodl, K. M. (1994). Stepfamilies as settings for child development. In A. Booth & J. Dunn (Eds.), *Stepfamilies: Who benefits? who does not?* (pp. 55-79). Hillsdale, NJ: Lawrence Erlbaum.

Komorita, S. S., Parks, C. D., & Hulbert, L. G. (1992). Reciprocity and induction of cooperation in social dilemmas. *Journal of Social Psychology, 61*, 607-617.

Larson, J. H., & Allgood, S. M. (1987). A comparison of intimacy in first-married and remarried couples. *Journal of Family Issues, 8*, 319-331.

O'Brien, T. B., & DeLongis, A. (1997). Coping with chronic stress: An interpersonal perspective. In B. H. Gottlieb (Ed.), *Coping with chronic stress* (pp. 161-190). New York: Plenum.

Papernow, P. L. (1988). Stepparent role development: From outsider to intimate. In W. R. Beer (Ed.), *Relative strangers: Studies of stepfamily processes* (pp. 54-82). Totowa, NJ: Rowman & Littlefield.

Parks, M. R., & Floyd, K. (1996). Meanings for closeness and intimacy in friendship. *Journal of Social and Personal Relationships, 13,* 85-107.

Patterson, G. R. (1982). *Coercive family process.* Eugene, OR: Castalia.

Perlman, D., & Fehr, B. (1987). The development of intimate relationships. In D. Perlman & S. Duck (Eds), *Intimate relationships: Development, dynamics, and deterioration* (pp. 13-42). Newbury Park, CA: Sage.

Preece, M. (2000). Exploring the stepgap: How parents' ways of coping with daily family stressors impact stepparent-stepchild relationship quality in stepfamilies. Unpublished doctoral dissertation, University of British Columbia, Vancouver, Canada.

Preece, M., DeLongis, A., & O'Brien, T. (June, 1997). *The social dimension of emotional expression.* Poster session presented at the annual meeting of the International Network on Personal Relationships, Oxford, Ohio.

Preece, M., DeLongis, A., O'Brien, T., & Campbell, J. (2001). *Agentic and communal appraisals: Application to coping in stepfamilies.* Manuscript submitted for publication.

Rahim, J. A. (1983). A measure of styles of handling interpersonal conflict. *Academy of Management Journal, 26,* 368-376.

Repetti, R. L. (1992). Social withdrawal as a short-term coping response to a daily stressor. In H. S. Friedman (Ed.), *Hostility, coping, and health* (pp. 151-165). Washington, D.C.: American Psychological Association.

Rusbult, C. E., Verette, J., Whitney, G. A., Slovik, L. F., & Lipkus, I. (1991). Accommodation processes in close relationships: Theory and preliminary empirical evidence. *Journal of Personality and Social Psychology, 60,* 53-78.

Schreurs, K. M. G., & de Ridder, D. T. D. (1997). Integration of coping and social support perspectives: Implications for the study of adaptation to chronic diseases. *Clinical Psychology Review, 17,* 89-112.

Sheldon, K. M. (1999). Learning the lessons of tit-for-tat: Even competitors can get the message. *Journal of Personality and Social Psychology, 77,* 1245-1253.

Sillars, A. L., Colletti, S. F., Parry, D., & Rogers, M. A. (1982). Coding verbal conflict tactics: Nonverbal and perceptual correlates of the "Avoidance-Distributive-Integrative" distinction. *Human Communication Research, 10,* 317-350.

Snijders, T.A.B. (1995). Multilevel models for family data. In J. J. Hox, B. F. van der Meulen, J. M. A. M. Janssens, J. J. F. ter Laak, & L.W.C. Tavecchio (Eds.), *Advances in family research.* Amsterdam: Thesis Publishers.

Statistics Canada (1995). *Canadian families: Diversity and change.* www.statcan.ca. Ottawa: Statistics Canada.

Taylor, S. E., Repetti, R. L., Seeman, T. (1997). Health psychology: What is an unhealthy environment and how does it get under the skin? *Annual Review of Psychology, 48,* 411-447.

Affect Pattern Recognition: Using Discrete Hidden Markov Models to Discriminate Distressed from Nondistressed Couples

William A. Griffin

SUMMARY. Self-report affect sequences generated during a conversation between spouses were used to illustrate how Hidden Markov Model (HMM) methodology can classify couples according to marital quality. This pattern recognition technique allows an investigator to characterize processes that generate observable phenomena–in these data, expressed affect. I introduce the conceptual foundations and, briefly, the methodology of HMM and discuss its potential use in social and behavioral research. To illustrate the potential value of this method, I show how sequences of self-reported affect, derived in real-time during a laboratory interaction be-

---

William A. Griffin is affiliated with the Marital Interaction Laboratory, Department of Family and Human Development.

Address correspondence to: William A. Griffin, Marital Interaction Lab, Department of Family and Human Development, YHE 2502, Arizona State University, Tempe, AZ 85287 (E-mail: William.Griffin@asu.edu).

This work was supported by a grant from the National Institute of Mental Health (1 RO1 MH51184-01A1).

The author would like to thank Gordon Gunnell for help with data preparation and his review of the manuscript, and Vicenç Quera and Jialong He for comments on earlier drafts of this manuscript. Information about available software is posted on the author's Website: www.public.asu.edu/~atwag.

[Haworth co-indexing entry note]: "Affect Pattern Recognition: Using Discrete Hidden Markov Models to Discriminate Distressed from Nondistressed Couples." Griffin, William A. Co-published simultaneously in *Marriage & Family Review* (The Haworth Press, Inc.) Vol. 34, No. 1/2, 2002, pp. 139-163; and: *Emotions and the Family* (ed: Richard A. Fabes) The Haworth Press, Inc., 2002, pp. 139-163. Single or multiple copies of this article are available for a fee from The Haworth Document Delivery Service [1-800-HAWORTH, 9:00 a.m. - 5:00 p.m. (EST). E-mail address: docdelivery@haworthpress.com].

© 2002 by The Haworth Press, Inc. All rights reserved.

Thibault, J. W., & Kelly, H. H. (1959). *The social psychology of groups.* New York: Wiley.

White, L. (1994). Stepfamilies over the life course: Social support. In A. Booth & J. Dunn (Eds.), *Stepfamilies: Who benefits? who does not?* (pp. 109-137). Hillsdale, NJ: Lawrence Erlbaum.

White, L. K., & Booth, A. (1985). The quality and stability of remarriages: The role of stepchildren. *American Sociological Review, 50,* 689-698.

tween 30 married partners, can successfully discriminate between distressed and nondistressed marital relationships. *[Article copies available for a fee from The Haworth Document Delivery Service: 1-800-HAWORTH. E-mail address: <docdelivery@haworthpress.com> Website: <http://www.HaworthPress.com> © 2002 by The Haworth Press, Inc. All rights reserved.]*

KEYWORDS. Affect recognition, hidden Markov models, marital relationships

Imagine that a married couple is sitting in a university laboratory engaged in a conversation about their relationship and that the way each spouse feels about the other spouse is generated by an attribution set–a cognitive structure that evolved during the couple's history, that is maintained by current events and is reflected in the ongoing discussion. Further, assume that each verbal statement and nonverbal behavior is a manifestation of internal feelings generated by the attribution set. It could be argued that such overt behaviors accurately and fully reflect the internal states or that, at minimum, they reflect some leakage of those emotions, or finally, it is possible that the overt behaviors are masking the internal states.

Irrespective of the position held by the reader about the correspondence between what is felt and what is displayed, it is assumed that fundamental differences exist between happy and unhappy couples. A natural scientific question arises from this assumption: What are the important differences between couples who report being distressed and those that report being nondistressed? Next, the question turns to the composition of the differences–is it the behaviors or is it the underlying emotion that discriminates between these types of relationships? Is it both? These questions become easier to answer by introducing a few additional assumptions: first, behaviors and emotions in a couple are inexorably interrelated, that is, each reflects the same phenomena–the quality of the relationship; and second, equally accurate measurement of either one has similar discriminatory power. If we hold these assumptions to be true, then the emphasis on identification shifts from the modality of the data (i.e., internal vs. external) to the development of mechanisms for pattern recognition.

Maximizing the ability to discriminate between distressed and nondistressed couples requires access to unbiased or minimally biased data and a quantitative method of recognizing patterns. To date, investigators in the area of marital dyad research have shown impressive gains in dissecting couple interaction, using either data from observation coding (e.g., MICS, see Weiss & Heyman, 1990; SPAFF, Gottman, 1994) or referencing internal affect ratings (Griffin, 1993)–but there has been a conspicuous absence of pattern recognition research. This paper addresses this dearth by introducing and illustrating a method of classifying patterns of human behavior, or in this case, patterns of reported affect, using the Hidden Markov Model (HMM) approach, an applied mathematical modeling technique currently employed in engineering and biology to classify sub-types of a system using the sequential features exhibited by the system.

WHY CLASSIFY?

"Thinking without the positing of categories and of concepts in general would be as impossible as is breathing in a vacuum" (Einstein, as cited in Auyang, 1998). It is difficult not to use categories to help understand or simplify the intricacies of a network of interactions that occur in complex systems (Watts, 1999). We categorize phenomena, especially those that arise from complex systems, hoping to understand, at least scientifically, the processes that generate the observed features. Although the pursuit of discerning discrete categories within any complex system necessarily requires ignoring some information, the value of positing two or more categories characterized by unique distributions of features may help clarify the composition and processes of the system. This long held supposition indigenous to the physical sciences is equally applicable to individuals, couples, and families and their behaviors and emotions (Bar-Yam, 1997).

Our general tendency is to describe an individual or a couple according to some vague attribute thought to be universally understood. We might say, for example, *he seems depressed*, or *they appear to be a happy couple*. In these comments, *depressed* and *happy* are the words of consequence. They denote an emotional or affective state; in the former, *depression* refers to a generally accepted idea that the person is sad or despondent, and in the latter example, *happy* refers to the state of the couple–that is, as a dyad, they seem to like each other. Moreover, in the former, the emotional condition is described using other affect terms (i.e., sad, despondent) whereas with the couple, the descriptor is also an affect term, but it refers to the condition of the relationship, not the individuals. This difference, though subtle, is important because although it is assumed that the individual possesses the affect state, the individuals comprising the couple do not–instead, the affect state is possessed by their relationship. At the colloquial level this might suffice as information about his or their affective disposition; however, it is inadequate for scientific research. It is at the scientific level that the subtle difference noted above becomes important: for the individual, depression has a clear nosological foundation, and with it, associated characteristics having physical features (e.g., weight loss, inability to concentrate, insomnia, crying)–but the attributed affective condition of the couple does not. There is no empirically based system that categorizes couples as happy vs. unhappy.[1] Marital dyads, however, can be distressed or nondistressed, and data indicate that nondistressed couples report being individually happier than individuals in distressed marriages (Weiss & Heyman, 1990). Intuitively, this should be no surprise.

We have shifted, at least conceptually, from couples possessing an affect (i.e., being happy) to their relationship having a qualitative affective characteristic: distress. Moreover, if we assume that expressed affect, ranging from positive to negative, by an individual within a marriage can be associated with marital distress, it follows that the characteristics of the jointly expressed affect (i.e., sequence, distribution) by a couple during a marital interaction should discriminate between distressed and nondistressed couples. Restating this as a research question: *Do joint affect configuration patterns displayed by a couple discriminate between distress levels?* The immediate response is a qualified yes, with the qualification coming from two points. First, most assessed affect in the marital interaction literature comes from observer-coded data and not from real-time self-report data, leaving open the possibility for observer and investigator bias (Gottman, 1994). The most obvious exception to this general statement is the work of Gottman and Levenson (1985) and Griffin (1993); both used the subjects' immediate recall of the feelings experienced during the interaction with the spouse.

The second qualification comes from the analytic methods used to differentiate the couples by distress levels. Researchers in this area have been vocal about the need to retain the sequential and temporal integrity of the data stream, and yet, the majority of supporting evidence that couple affect discriminates is derived from traditional parametric statistics (e.g., ANOVA) utilizing summary indices (e.g., means, z scores). Obviously, to answer the research question above and address the noted qualified response, we need an analytic method that retains the integrity of the affect sequence, characterizes its pattern, and then determines if the pattern differs by distress level.

This idea that sequences are patterned and that the pattern contains information, either in a utilitarian (e.g., mental health diagnoses) and mathematical sense (i.e., information theory; see Applebaum, 1996), is consistent with the search for sequence patterning in couple and family behavior that has occurred for at least 30 years (see Gottman & Notarius, 2000). To date, most attempts to classify sequential behavior generated from marital interaction have come from non-traditional, though often quite eloquent, statistical methods initially employed to be descriptive (e.g., sequential analysis, Bakeman & Gottman, 1997; Bakeman & Quera, 1995; Griffin & Gottman, 1990). They usually operate by generating the odds of two groups being different (e.g., z-scores or odds ratios), but such analytic techniques are not useful as pattern recognition devices. For example, with an adequate sample of distressed and nondistressed couples, sequential techniques would show that the distressed couples are more likely to be negative and have longer cycles of negative reciprocity (Weiss & Heyman, 1990), or that with event-history analysis, females' negative affect states are longer (Griffin, 1993; 1995), but neither analytic approach can pick a couple at random and, with any technique inherent in the method, quantify the likelihood that the particular couple chosen is either distressed or nondistressed. And that is probably the question most often asked of a social scientist who studies couples–specifically, *based on the observed behavior, is the couple distressed or nondistressed?* The question addresses a pattern recognition problem, and fortunately, advances in applied mathematics combined with increases in the computational power of computers have made recognizing patterns mainstream work in several areas of biology (Durbin, Eddy, Krogh, Mitchison, 1998), computer science, and engineering (e.g., speech recognition; Deller, Proakis, Hansen, 1993). These techniques are also applicable to the behavior of humans and their expressions of affect.

MARKOV MODELS

At the core of the HMM is the general Markov assumption that in a sequence of events the future is knowable from the present and that having additional knowledge of the past does not enhance prediction. More formally, a finite Markov chain representing a sequence of events is a stochastic process with a finite number of states in which the probability of being in a particular state at the $(n + 1)$ st step depends only on the state occupied at the nth step; this process is assumed to be stationary

(Olinick, 1978). We make this concept more tangible by showing how it describes a process characterizing a simple system. Consider a system that is, at any time, in one of a set of N distinct states, indexed by $\{1,2,\ldots,N\}$. At discrete times the system undergoes a change of state according to a set of probabilities associated with the state. We denote the time instants associated with state changes as $t = 1,2,K$ and we denote the actual state at time t as q_t. A full probabilistic description of the above system would require, in general, specification of the current state (at time t), as well as all the predecessor states. For the special case of a discrete-time, first-order, Markov chain, the probabilistic dependence is truncated to just the preceding state; that is,

$$P[q_t = j | q_{t-1} = i, q_{t-2} = k, \ldots] = P[q_t = j | q_{t-1} = i]. \qquad (0.1)$$

This observable Markov model outputs from the modeled process a set of states at each instant of time, where each state corresponds to an observable event.[2] Implicit in the model is the assumption that each state corresponds to a deterministically observable event. That is, the observed output is assumed to derive from its source via a non-random process. Colloquially speaking, *What you see reflects what is* (e.g., happiness begets a smile). But what happens when we relax this latter assumption? Asked differently, what is observed if the state stochastically, rather than deterministically, generates an output? The answer: You observe the outcome of the process but not the process–it is hidden. In other words, the overt manifestation of a system may be expressed in one of several forms. For example, a smile–a behavior typically associated with happiness–may occur as a perfunctory response (e.g., at a job interview) and have minimal correspondence to the internal state of the individual; or again speaking colloquially, *What you see may not be what is*.

How does one model such a process? This idea intrigued applied mathematicians and statisticians in the early-1960s, who were studying the problem of characterizing random processes with incomplete observations. They eventually modeled the problem as a doubly embedded stochastic process (i.e., matrix row and columns marginals sum to 1) with an underlying stochastic process that is not directly observable but is known only through another set of stochastic processes that produce the sequence of observations (Rabiner & Juang, 1993). Mathematicians referred to this conceptualization of a process as the Hidden Markov Model (HMM) because the generating process is not observable.[3]

HIDDEN MARKOV MODEL

Despite the mathematical complexity underlying an HMM, it is conceptually easy to understand: the observed phenomena, observation sequence $O = \{o_1 o_2 ... o_T\}$, represents the stochastically generated manifestation of a non-observed process, which itself is stochastically generated, and both are modeled using only the observed sequence.

For example, if we assume a pure Markov model, then any given affect state will produce a specific and predictable internal or external response (e.g., negative comment or reported negative affect expression = negative state) that always corresponds in a deterministic, non-random, manner to the underlying state. It can be understood intuitively that such invariant correspondence does not occur in social, especially intimate, relationships. An isolated observation of a particular affect (e.g., positive) does not indicate the state of the individual. Modeling complex processes requires more realism. It is therefore preferable to allow each state to be characterized by a probability distribution of affect categories and allow the transitions between states to be characterized by a state-transition matrix. Ambiguity about the process generating the characteristics of a complex system necessitates using a modeling technique, such as an HMM, that allows the measured features to be characterized as a stochastic process.

Components of an HMM

Several elements are needed to create an HMM. In the following, I briefly introduce these elements, and describe how they combine to form an HMM that, in turn, can be used to classify sequential emotional or behavioral response sets in human interaction. An HMM is characterized by the following.

States (N). These are the number of states in the model. They are hidden, and may or may not correspond to some physical feature of the phenomena they represent. For example, in speech recognition, a state may represent a phoneme (i.e., the smallest phonetic unit), and when strung together, they form a word. For the model presented in this paper, no correspondence to a delineated affect state is considered, although I think that with enough data, a state representative of an affect cluster could be constructed. These individual states are denoted as $S = \{S_1, S_2, \ldots, S_N\}$, and the state at time t as q_t.

There is not a consensus about the appropriate number of states an HMM should have. Unless the investigator has an idea of how he or she wants the model to map onto a physical or theoretical detail of the process (see Rabiner, 1989), this is usually determined empirically by examining the percentage of classification errors produced by a sweep of *state × symbol* combinations and selecting the model that produces the fewest errors (Deller et al., 1993; Rabiner & Juang, 1993). Although not ideal scientifically, the method is effective in developing initial models.

Observation symbols (M). These are the number of distinct observation symbols per state, where each symbol represents the observable feature of the modeled system. They represent the corpus of what a system can be observed to be doing. These can range, depending on the field of study, from the faces on a coin, to the phonemes of a word, to protein sequences in a strand of DNA, or to *affect* expressed during a conversation. Irrespective of what measured feature(s) of the process is selected, its generated sequence should be an accurate estimate of the process. Obviously, a poorly selected or poorly measured observable produces an inaccurate model. If an investigator, for example, were coding behavioral interactions, the code system being used represents the limit of what can be observed and how one conveys a sequence of behavior produced by the interaction process. In the data presented herein, the observables are male affect rating, female affect rating, and joint rating duration. Collectively, the three values form a vector score (i.e., the symbol) characterizing the affect configuration at time t until t_{+1}; each couple produces a string of these symbols that represent the interaction process. The individual symbols are denoted as $V = \{v_1, v_2, \ldots, v_M\}$. To illustrate, let affect be expressed as 5 discrete categories: extreme negative, negative, neutral, positive, extreme positive; denoted as $\{en, ng, nu, po, ep\}$, respectively, and arbitrarily let duration range from 2-20. An observed sequence for couple Y, $O_Y = \{o_1 o_2 \ldots o_T\}$, would be shown as $O_Y = \{ng, en, 7_1; ng, ng, 12_2; nu, ng, 4_3; \ldots ; po, ep, 15_T\}$. Replacing the discrete affect category symbols with integers, and allow extreme negative to equal 1 though extreme positive equaling 5, we have a complete accounting of the affect structure during the interaction of couple Y, denoted as $O_Y = \{2,1,7_1; 2,2,12_2; 3,2,4_3; \ldots ; 4,5,15_T\}$.

State transition probability distribution $(A = \{a_{ij}\})$. This matrix determines the distribution of transitions among states, where

$$a_{ij} = P[q_t = S_j | q_{t-1} = S_i], \quad 1 \leq i, j \leq N. \tag{0.2}$$

In the current analysis, only self-transitions or a transition to the next indexed state were allowed to occur; that is; $a_{ij} = 0$ where $j > i + 1$.[4] No transitions are allowed to states whose indices are lower than the current state,

$$a_{ij} = 0, \quad j < i. \tag{0.3}$$

Distribution of observations (B). This is the observation symbol (i.e., codes, ratings) probability distribution in state j, such that $B = \{b_j(k)\}$ where,

$$b_j(k) = P[v_k \text{ at } t \mid q_t = S_j], \quad \begin{aligned} 1 &\leq j \leq N \\ 1 &\leq k \leq M. \end{aligned} \tag{0.4}$$

For example, assuming four symbols, state j might be characterized by the following symbol distribution, $j = \{v_1 = .2, v_2 = .3, v_3 = .07, v_4 = .43\}$ whereas symbols in state s might be distributed as $s = \{v_1 = .16, v_2 = .16, v_3 = .56, v_4 = .12\}$.

Initial state distribution (π). To initiate a model, a state is selected, $\pi = \{\pi i\}$ where

$$\pi i = P[q_1 = S_i], \quad 1 \leq i \leq N. \tag{0.5}$$

For left-to-right models, as used for this analysis, the initial state probabilities have the property

$$\pi = \begin{cases} 0, & i \neq 1 \\ 1, & i = 1, \end{cases} \tag{0.6}$$

because the state sequence must begin in state 1 (and end in state N).

All of the primary HMM components have been defined and now we describe how they combine to model a process. To briefly summarize HMMs using the elements defined above, we first consider the mechanisms used by an HMM to recognize patterns. There are N discrete states, usually derived empirically. An initial state is selected ($q_1 = S_i$) according to initial state distribution (π). At some time point t, either occurring in a natural length or some specified interval, a state transition occurs in accordance with the transition probability distribution (A). The specific transition depends on the previous state (i.e., a_{ij}). As the new state is entered, an observation output symbol (v_k) is emitted according to a probability distribution (B) that depends on the current state (i.e., $b_i(k)$). The probability distribution is invariant for the state, irrespective of when and how the state was entered. Combined, these elements produce N such observation probability distributions, each representing a stochastic process.

The above discussion shows that a completely specified HMM requires the specification of two model parameters (N [# of states], M [# of symbols]), the specification of observation symbols, and the specification of three probability measures A, B, and π. Allowing λ to represent the specified model, the complete parameter set can be expressed as

$$\lambda = (A, B, \pi). \tag{0.7}$$

This set is important because all estimates of model appropriateness and fit derive from the parameter configuration λ. Thus, altering the model occurs by modifying λ.

SOCIO-AFFECTIVE PROCESSES AND HMMS

Next, we show how HMMs, as described above, can be applied to the recognition of socio-affective processes. Our objective is to discriminate distressed from nondistressed couples using only their self-reported affect. Our observable data consists of a sequence of affect ratings by the husband and wife during their lab discussion (see Methods below for details). As noted, in these data we have three observed, continuously measured, features of the interaction forming a vector score comprised of his rating, her rating, and the duration of the joint ratings. If either spouse changes affect rating (e.g., moves from neutral to negative), then the current affect configuration unit terminates, and a new unit is added to the sequence; this continues until the last unit, o_T, terminates at end of the experimental procedure. If we assume that an affect rating configuration does not correspond directly to an affect state, but instead allowing the configuration to be characterized by a stochastic process, then the HMM is appropriate for modeling this type of socio-affective interaction. Specifically, the observation probability distribution (B) would be collections of symbols representing affect configurations generated from the vector scores where each state has a different distribution of the symbols. It follows then that recognizing a typical sequence, $O = \{o_1 o_2 \ldots o_T\}$ as being associated with one level of distress or the other, consists of determining the probability of the observed sequence given the model (i.e., $\lambda(0.7)$); more formally,

$$P(O|\lambda). \tag{0.8}$$

This is the first, and considered the simplest, problem associated with describing a process with HMMs. It is usually solved using a technique called the *forward algorithm*, which simply estimates the likelihood of moving forward through a sequence of states (Jelinek, 1997; Juang & Rabiner, 1991).

Next, comes the difficult step of determining the hidden part of the model–the state sequence. This is the estimation problem where one seeks to find an optimal state sequence ($Q = q_1 q_2 L\ q_T$) that best explains the observation. Solving this provides information about the structure of the model, and generates average statistics for individual states. A technique referred to as the *Viterbi* algorithm (Viterbi, 1967) is used to find the "best" state sequence–although, no true "best" state sequence can be found because the criteria for optimality varies by investigator needs, and with it, the solution changes (Jelinek, 1997; Rabiner & Juang, 1993).

Finally, the third and most difficult problem: finding the optimal model parameters $\lambda = (A, B, \pi)$ to maximize $P(O\backslash\lambda)$. This operation attempts to optimize the model parameters so as to best describe how the observed sequence comes about. This is where the model is trained to data. To solve this problem, an HMM specific Expectation-Maximization (EM) procedure, known as the Baum-Welch (B-W) method iteratively seeks to locally maximize $P(O\backslash\lambda)$ Fortunately, each of the aforementioned problems associated with parameterizing an HMM has a coupled solution (e.g., Viterbi, Baum-Welch).[5]

There are, however, several additional features of the HMM that need to be introduced before reviewing results from the current data. First, as noted above, the observables are measurements, possibly discrete but typically continuous, of the process at each t and in a discrete HMM, the possible number of vector configurations is obviously very large. Consequently, the vector configurations are reduced to a reasonable number of symbols using a technique called *vector quantization* (Linde, Buzo, & Gray, 1980). The resulting symbols become the *codebook*, i.e., the size of the codebook equals the number of symbols.

In practice, vector quantization occurs by first dividing the training (data) vectors into M sets or clusters, where M equals the desired number of symbols. Each training vector (i.e., couple affect configuration unit in these data) is assigned a location on an n-dimensional map, where n is the vector size. The algorithm then assigns a prototypic vector to each mth set, and then iteratively optimizes the partition and the codebook until each prototypic vector is a centroid for the assigned mth region (i.e., Voronoi tessellation) (Rabiner, 1989). (See Author's notes about available HMM software.)

HMMs are typically used to recognize discrete classifications of elements ranging from small vocabularies of less than 100 words to in excess of 100,000 words; similar ranges in human gene sequencing are found in the bioinformatics literature (Deller et al., 1993). Good classification in these fields typically requires very large codebooks (e.g., 512-1024 symbols), although the number of states is usually low, ranging from 4 to 20. Simple processes or short sequences usually require few states whereas some very complex processes can require many states. By comparison, the classification of human interaction is relatively simple. Usually only a few categories are needed to classify the behavior into meaningful subtypes and the variety of behavior assessed is limited (i.e., experimental situation or coding structure delimits the types of behavior culled). This limitation is usually evident in the smaller number of symbols needed to represent the behavior. Although there are usually only a few classification categories, the complexity inherent in human interaction, especially as it unfolds over time, may require a large number of states to provide an accurate characterization of the interaction. In effect, the variability in behavior can be represented in a few symbols, but the distribution of those behaviors during a complex interaction may require a large number of states. Estimating the appropriate number of states and symbols requires ample training data.

Training data is the second feature that needs introducing before discussing the HMM results. Obviously, to create models, an HMM needs the process to be characterized probabilistically and this is done using training data. Sequences of data must be sufficiently long and varied to allow adequate estimates of the stochastic properties inherent in the process. Without training data the HMM cannot estimate the model parameters $\lambda = (A, B, \pi)$ to maximize $P(O\vert\lambda)$.

METHOD

Subjects

Thirty married couples from the Phoenix, Arizona metropolitan area responded to newspaper advertisements offering twenty-five dollars for participation in a study on marital communication. Couples in the study were typical of those found in marital interaction studies: relatively young and moderately educated lower-middle-class couples with one child at home. A series of t-tests found that, other than the number of children in the home ($t(28) = 2.10$, $p < .05$, df = 28), the groups were not statistically significantly different on these salient demographic features. Eighty percent (24) of the couples were Caucasian, 16 percent (5) were mixed ethnically, and one was African-American. See Griffin (1993) for additional recruitment and demographic information.

Marital Satisfaction

Marital Satisfaction was assessed using the Locke-Wallace Marital Adjustment Test (MAT) (Locke & Wallace, 1959). Widely used, the MAT has the greatest number of reliability and validity studies of all self-report marital adjustment measures. Although an older instrument, it correlates highly with newer instruments (approximately $r = .90$), and it permits comparisons to the majority of other marital interaction studies and their samples (Crane, Allgood, Larson, & Griffin, 1990). Possible scores can range from 2 to 158; a couple mean of ≥ 101 is considered nondistressed, below this value couples are considered maritally distressed. As expected, distressed couples had statistically significantly lower MAT scores ($t(28) = 7.87$, $p < .000$); this group difference was also found for husbands ($t(28) = 7.06$, $p < .000$) and wives ($t(28) = 5.8$, $p < .000$). Within group gender differences were not significant.

Procedure

Couples were seated in a room constructed to resemble a small living area with two chairs in the center of the room. Two unobtrusive, partially concealed, remotely controlled cameras were mounted on the walls at head level behind each chair. All audio-visual and mixing equipment was controlled from a room adjacent to the interaction. Video signals were combined producing a split screen image with audio being obtained from lavaliere microphones worn by each spouse.

Interaction Task

Each couple engaged in a 12-minute conversation focusing on problem areas in their relationship. Couples were asked to rank problem areas using the Areas of Disagreement Inventory (Gottman, 1979). Using a list of common problems areas in a relationship, each spouse ranked the areas. Three areas were selected, and the couple was instructed to discuss and attempt to resolve the issue(s). This is a common task used to evoke negative interaction in married dyads (Weiss & Heyman, 1990).

Affect Ratings

Spouses were separated immediately after each conversation, and then simultaneously reviewed the videotaped splitscreen playback, and rated his or her own affect during the interaction. The videotape was played back through a specially configured microcomputer using software that overlays a 9-level, color-coded, vertical bar on the 19" color video monitor. This overlay was positioned beside the face on the monitor of the individual reviewing the tape. The affect rating ranges from extreme negative (red), through neutral (gray) to extreme positive (blue), and is controlled by a pc mouse. Extreme negative is at the monitor bottom, neutral is at mid-monitor, and positive is at the top of the monitor. The width of the bar varies at each affect level (5 pixel increments) corresponding to the intensity of the affect, neutral being the thinnest. The widest affect level is 28 pixels wide (1.5 cm). As the reviewer moves the mouse, the affect bar is high-lighted corresponding to the degree and direction of the affect. During the review of the tape, each spouse was asked to move the mouse to reflect affect experience during the interaction (i.e., "How were you feeling at each moment?"). Software recorded the location of the bar position every second, providing a continuous measure of affect throughout the interaction. Prior to the first interaction task each couple was taught how to use the rating system. Additional information about this data acquisition technique and assumptions about validity is in Griffin (1993).

During the 12-minute interaction each couple produced approximately 720 seconds of affect recording ($M = 717$; variation due to equipment error). General descriptive data show the expected tendencies: distressed couples expressed more negative affect ($M = 4.79$, $SD = 1.05$) than the nondistressed couples ($M = 3.76$, $SD = 1.37$), $t(28) = 3.27$, $p < .000$ (one-tailed) and within gender across group ratings were also significantly different; males (distressed $M = 4.56$, $SD = .91$, nondistressed $M = 3.7$, $SD = 1.41$): $t(28) = 1.98$, $p < .02$ (one-tailed); females (distressed $M = 5.03$, $SD = .1.16$, nondistressed $M = 3.82$, $SD = 1.38$): $t(28) = 2.59$, $p < .001$. Within group across gender differences were not significant. To aid interpretation, average ratings are referenced to a 5-point scale (i.e., from the original 9 point scale -9 or $8 = 1$, 7

or 6 = 2, etc.) where: 1 = extreme negative, 2 = negative, 3 = neutral, 4 = positive, and 5 = extreme positive.

The individual rating data were then collapsed to an affect configuration (i.e., affect state.[6]) Determining and measuring the relevant process features is the critical first step in developing an HMM. It is necessary that the selected features be sensitive to the condition of the system, such that their sequencing accurately tracks changes in the system dynamics over time (see MacDonald & Zucchini, 1997). With couple or family data, either expressed overtly (i.e., behavioral coding) or internally (e.g., physiological responses), there are numerous ways that behaviors or ratings can be meaningfully combined to capture relevant features of an interaction (see Griffin, 2000, for detailed discussion). In the current data, as noted above, the affective features of the interaction were assembled as an affect configuration unit consisting of male rating, female rating, and joint duration. It was assumed these three features characterize the affect structure of the couple during the conversation. Moreover, the values used to construct the configuration are sensitive to process changes that occur during the interaction and that the generated sequences are patterned as a function of marital satisfaction.

In these data, distressed couples produced an average of 79 discrete units per interaction sequence compared to 65 units among the nondistressed couples. Consequently, the average duration per unit was shorter (M = 9.05s, SD = 10.29s) for distressed than nondistressed couples (M = 11.08s, SD = 15.82s), this difference was significant, $t(2137) = 3.52$, $p < .000$. Units were treated as independent because only 4 of the 30 couples has significant autocorrelation functions at lag 1 and 2, thus the duration of the state being exited did not predict the duration of the forthcoming unit. Most ($\geq$* 90%) of the affect configuration units lasted less than 20 seconds irrespective of distress level. Finally, the affect rating and joint duration values were normalized (i.e., $\frac{affect\ rating}{5}$; $\frac{joint\ duration}{720}$) to allow a common metric and ease interpretation (Williams, 1997).

RESULTS

First, it was necessary to determine the appropriate number of *states* and *symbols*. Initially, 25 datasets were created: each contained training data from 27 couples and test data from 3 couples. Couple classification (i.e., distressed or nondistressed) is placed in the data string, hence allowing for an estimate of classification error. Each dataset was used for a single trial. In jackknife fashion,[7] the 3 couples used per trial to test the HMM were randomly selected at each trial from the complete set of 30 couples. Next, each trial consisted of a series of runs that used a parameter sweep of *states* by *symbols*. States per run ranged from 3 to 15, and symbols (codebook size) varied across increments of 2, 4, 8, and 16. (These doubling codebook sizes are typical in HMM software.) Ranges for the states (3-15) and symbols (2-16) were selected because only two conditions are being examined (i.e., distressed, nondistressed) and it was thought that these ranges were sufficient to create adequate HMMs. Each trial produced 52 *state*-by-*symbol* combinations (i.e., 13 states × 4 codebook sizes), each associated with a correct classification percentage. For example, for each dataset {1,2,3,K,25}, the trial began with *state* = 3 (S_3) and *symbol* = 2 (v_2), and an HMM was constructed, run, and the percent of couples correctly classified was obtained (i.e., % = 0,33,66,100). This was repeated with the same dataset until all possible *state*-by-*symbol* combinations were run and their classification errors recorded. A new dataset was then selected and the procedure was repeated. With 25 datasets generating 52 *state* × *symbol* combinations, these data produced 1300 estimates of classification error.

Across all trials, the best classification combination was a 10-state model using 4 symbols, producing an average of 20% errors. Stated differently, this 10-state, 4-symbol HMM correctly classified distressed from non-distressed couples about 80% of the time. Although 80% correct classification appears moderately good, but certainly not overwhelmingly successful, several features of the data and the model aid in the interpretation of the significance of this finding. First, the data contain couples across an extended range of marital satisfaction including many that had marital satisfaction scores in the middle range (either as a couple, or separate his and hers on either side of the 100 points cutoff); for example, approximately 25% of the couples had mean MAT scores between 90 and 110, making marital satisfaction classification for this group somewhat arbitrary (Filsinger, 1983). Classifying continuous scores as nominal categorical increases the likelihood of classification error. It could also be argued that with an appropriately trained model, even ambiguous mid-range behavior that contains features of each category can be classified correctly. This can occur by simply increasing the amount and variety of training data, which provides better estimations of the two-group model, or with additional data a third, middle-tier, group can be created and modeled. To investigate this idea, additional trials were run with the 3 highest ($M = 137$, Range: 136-138) and 3 lowest ($M = 54.6$, Range: 44-64) scoring (MAT) couples; each couple was tested against a re-estimated 10-state, 4-symbol model using the other 29 couples as training data. In each trial, the couple was classified correctly–100% for the 6 trials. It appears that the combination of two additional couples in the training data and testing against clearly classified couples produces a highly accurate model.

To determine whether it was the additional training or ambiguous classification having the greater influence on classification accuracy, 5 additional trials were run where one randomly selected couple was tested against the 10-state, 4-symbol HMM generated from the other 29 couples. In these runs, 4 of the 5 had correct classification; the one misclassified couple had a combined MAT score of 95, he reported a 111 and she a 76. Of the 4 couples that were correctly classified, 2 were clearly distressed (MAT: 77, 76), and 1 had a combined MAT of 100 with the male reporting a MAT of 68 and female a score of 132. Finally, comparing data from the two seemingly similar mid-range couples indicated that the misclassified couple with the lower MAT (95) had a higher average affect rating than did the correctly classified couple with the slightly higher MAT (100); the former averaged a neutral rating whereas the latter averaged a negative rating. It appears that the model was sensitive to this disparity from expectation.

Irrespective of the reason for the one misclassification, the additional trials using 29 couples indicated that, on average, whether testing either extreme cases or random cases, the 10-state 4-symbol HMM could classify distressed from non-distressed couples with an accuracy rate of 91% (10 of 11).[8] This value would probably be higher with fewer indeterminate distress status couples, or more data and the creation of a third classification group. Another possible factor that might suppress the classification rate is that both models were estimated using the same number of states; although common, this is not necessary, but was done to illustrate the method and allow comparison across distress level models. To maximize sensitivity to category differences, it is preferable to have a separate N-state model for each category.

Another factor that should enter into the appreciation of this high classification rate is that it contained no investigator manipulation or bias, other than selecting the process features. Four symbols (i.e., $V = \{v_1, v_2, v_3, v_4\}$) were sufficient to generate the final 91% classification rate (these are detailed below). As was noted in the previous section describing codebook size, each symbol represents a centroid for its assigned region of vector scores. The fit to any specific couple may not be exact but the stochastic characterization provides a sufficiently accurate description for the purposes of classification. In the present model, it is easy to crudely but meaningfully classify the four symbols. Symbol 1 (v_1), with a vector score of, {1.64,1.72,11.54},[9] has a moderate negative rating for the husband and the wife for nearly 12 seconds. Symbol 2 (v_2), {2.37,3.69,8.63}, has a husband rating between negative and neutral–but closer to negative–and the wife is neutral to positive, and they maintain the ratings for 8 to 9 seconds. A near opposite configuration occurs for v_3, {3.53,1.59,8.63}, the husband is neutral to positive but the wife is very negative. Finally, v_4, {4.29,3.83,12.03}, has husband and wife ratings near or at positive for 12 seconds. In effect, v_1 and v_4 represent negative and positive configurations, respectively; whereas, v_3 shows a male negative relative to a female positive and v_4 a near opposite pattern with a clear and meaningful exception–the female negative in v_4 is substantially greater than the comparable husband score in v_3. This captures the propensity of wife ratings to be, on average, more negative–especially in distressed couples.

Once an HMM is constructed, depending on its eventual use, the internal structure may or may not be important to the investigator beyond its ability to correctly classify a process. However, for some processes, the internal structure of the final model contains important information about the system that generates the observables (MacDonald & Zucchini, 1997). To illustrate, Figures 1 and 2 show the complete HMMs for distressed and nondistressed couples, respectively. Before describing the differences between models, there are several features common to both models that help interpretation. States (S_i) are shown as circles and observables (i.e., symbols; v_k) as squares; within each square is the symbol probability distribution associated with the state transition. The probability distribution shown in each square characterizes the likelihood of each of the symbols being emitted during the transition back to self or to the next state. A legend at the bottom of each figure references the specific symbol and its affect configuration.

As expected, two features within each model provide much of the information: state transitions and symbol probability distributions. For state transitions, one compares the likelihoods for self-transition versus next-state transitions, and then, how these likelihoods change over time. Next, one looks within each state to determine how the symbol probability distribution shifts. Looking at the distress couple model in Figure

FIGURE 1. Discrete HMM for distressed married couples (n = 14) showing state transition probabilities (α) and symbol probability distributions (b).

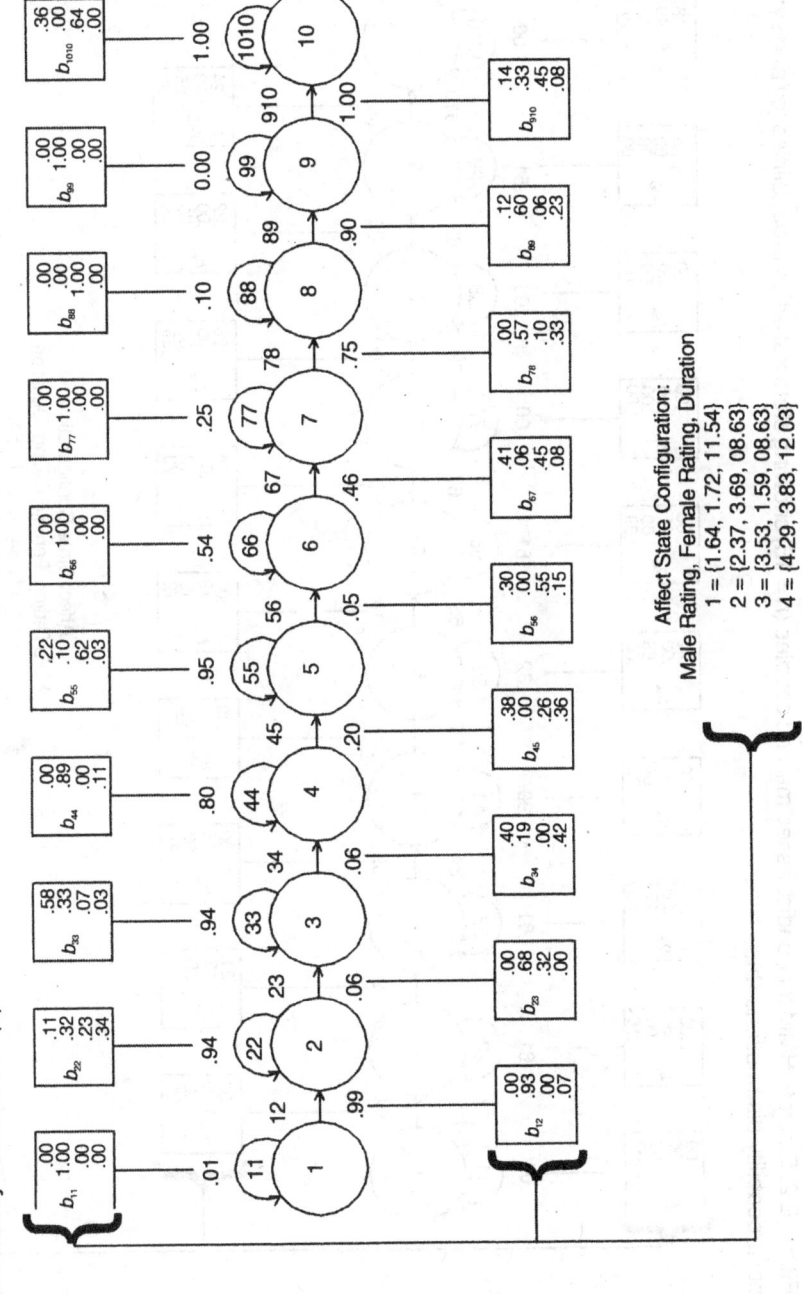

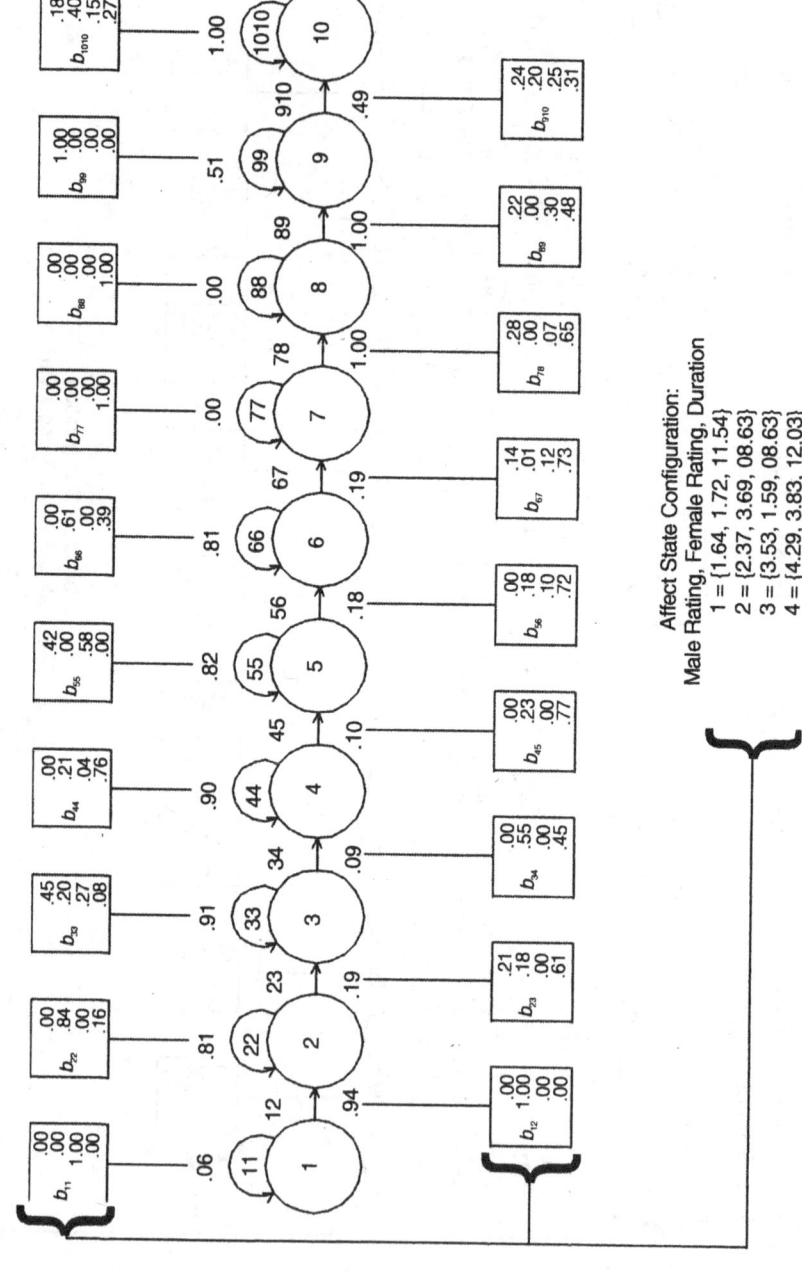

FIGURE 2. Discrete HMM for nondistressed married couples (n = 16) showing state transition probabilities (α) and symbol probability distributions (b).

1, couples tended to move immediately from S_1 to S_2 ($\alpha_{12} = .99$) and show v_2 ($b_{12} = .93$), and settle down in S_2-S_5 ($\alpha_{22} = .94$; $\alpha_{33} = .94$; $\alpha_{44} = .8$; $\alpha_{55} = .95$). A shift in observables occurs starting in S_4 and S_5–symbols characterized by negative affect, especially for females (v_1, v_3), increase their likelihood (v_3: $\alpha_{55} = .95$ with $b_{55} = .62$ and $b_{56} = .55$). A decidedly different distribution is evident in the observables for self-transitions and states transitions for nondistressed couples (see Figure 2). There is a shift toward showing greater v_4 (mutual positive affect) after S_3 (e.g., $b_{45} = .45, b_{56} = .77, b_{67} = .72, b_{78} = .73$), especially through the middle of the sequence.

DISCUSSION

These two stochastic models shown in Figures 1 and 2 provide a nice summary of the affective proclivities of distressed and nondistressed couples, which–it should be noted–accurately map on to known, empirically derived, behavioral propensities found in marital interaction laboratories during the last thirty years (see Gottman & Notarius, 2000; Weiss & Heyman, 1990; 1997). Even though the models constrained the number of couple states to be equivalent across couple types (for purposes of illustration), the processes demarcating differences between groups was clearly evident–distressed couples quickly settled into a pattern of experiencing negative affect and then spent more there. It was not that the nondistressed group did not also express negative affect (see Figure 2, Symbol 1) but their pattern of expressing the affect was different. These models indicate that much of the interaction that defines (i.e., discriminates) each group is evident in the states 2-6; among distressed couples, the propensity was to move via Symbols 1 or 3–higher negative affect for the wife–whereas the nondistressed couples tended to transition with Symbol 4–greater joint positive.

There also appears, at least among the distressed couples during the middle states, to be a tendency for self-transitions to be lower when husbands report greater negativity (i.e., Symbol 2). Compare, for example, the self-transitions of States 3 ($\alpha_{33} = .94$) or 5 ($\alpha_{55} = .95$) where Symbol 2 = .33 and .10 respectively, to States 4 ($\alpha_{44} = .80$) or 6 ($\alpha_{66} = .54$) where Symbol 2 = .89 and 1.00 respectively (see Figure 1). The pattern is less evident among the nondistressed couples, probably due to the couple's general tendency to report joint positive affect. During those intervals where the husband tended to be more negative than the wife, the HMM ferreted out the periods as unique and thus constructed them as discrete states. Stated differently, when the husband was more negative, the distribution of the symbols formed unique clusters during the interaction. This differential expression of emotion by gender in married couples is consistent with existing literature; however, the HMM models also provide evidence that the processes characterizing the interaction vary systematically as a function of which gender is experiencing greater negativity at that cross-section in time. In effect, when the male is more negative the interaction has different characteristics than when the female is more negative, at least during some small window of time. The ability to successfully discriminate distressed from nondistressed couples using only their sequences of affect during a conversation is testament to the utility of the Hidden Markov Model as a potential tool for the microanalysis of human behavior. Such analytic strength has numerous implications for the study of couples and families—at least two are immediately evident. First, HMMs should be useful in discriminating, or failing to discriminate, between two or more sub-types of behavioral classifications. For example, we assumed that distressed and nondistressed couples were different in their internal affect structure, this assumption was validated through the HMM. Second, HMMs generate stochastic parameters characterizing the behavioral tendencies that may or may not discriminate between classifiable groups, as shown in Figures 1 and 2.

Together these two benefits offer the social scientist the opportunity to validate many of the behavioral classifications used in the social and behavioral sciences. In the area of child development, for example, different attachment styles are assumed to produce distinct patterns of behavioral sequences in response to experimental conditions (Ainsworth, Blehar, Waters, & Wall, 1978); such assumptions are clearly testable using HMMs. Similarly, the most ubiquitous behavioral classification system for humans, and one in desperate need of validating, is the DSM (Carson, 1997). The *Diagnostic and Statistical Manual of Mental Disorders IV* (APA, 1994) states that, "each of the mental disorders is conceptualized as a clinically significant behavioral or psychological syndrome or pattern that occurs in an individual . . . " (APA, 1994, pp. xxi-xxii).

Such statements clearly posit behavioral differences between individuals classified in one diagnostic category versus another. Each major and minor classification, assumed to reflect conjunctive entities, contains diagnostic criteria that could be easily converted to quantifiable discrete behaviors or affective patterns. These, in turn, could become the measured observables in an HMM. Of course, the model may not successfully discriminate between some categories–and I would argue that is an additional strength of a well constructed HMM. Any failure to validate a diagnostic category because of an HMM's inability to differentiate could be due the inadequacy of the model (e.g., as articulated above–number of states or symbols may be wrong, or inadequate measurement of the important features); on the other hand, maybe the model is good but the putative categorical distinctions are not warranted (Carson, 1997).

Of course, the classification accuracy shown by these analyses should be viewed within the framework of several obvious limitations. First, the specified HMM is derived from data drawn from only 30 couples and may not generalize beyond the Marital Interaction Lab at Arizona State or the method used to collect the affect rating. Second, additional data may alter the final HMM parameters–although the model seems capable of distinguishing at a classification rate of approximately 90%, which is acceptable at this stage of model development (and permits a confident wager on the couple distress level). The eventual goal would be to construct a model with accuracy rates in excess of 95-97%, a rate well within the capacity of the HMM. Despite these limitations, the effectiveness of the method is evident, and any additional modifications in the model or additional data should only enhance classification accuracy.

AUTHOR NOTE

Numerous footnotes are cited throughout the paper. Although none are essential to understanding the presented material, each provides additional clarification about the subject or adds relevant historical information. To conserve printed space, these footnotes are posted electronically at the author's Website.

REFERENCES

Ainsworth, M. D. S., Blehar, M. C., Waters, E., & Walls, S. (1978). *Patterns of attachment: A psychological study of the strange situation.* Hillsdale, N.J.: Erlbaum.

American Psychiatric Association. (1994). *Diagnostic and statistical manual of mental disorders* (4th ed.). Washington, D.C.: Author.

Applebaum, D. (1996). *Probability and information: An integrated approach.* New York: Cambridge University Press.

Auyang, S. Y. (1998). *Foundations of complex-system theories: In economics, evolutionary biology, and statistical physics*. New York: Cambridge University Press.
Bakeman, R., & Gottman, J. M. (1997). *Observing interaction: An introduction to sequential analysis*. New York: Cambridge University Press. 2nd edition.
Bakeman, R., & Quera, V. (1995). *Analyzing interaction: Sequential analysis with SDIS and GSEQ*. New York: Cambridge University Press
Bar-Yam, Y. (1997). *Dynamics of complex systems*. Reading, MA: Addison-Wesley.
Bradbury, T. N., Fincham, F. D., & Beach, S. R. (2000). Research on the nature and determinants of marital satisfaction: A decade in review. *Journal of Marriage and the Family, 62*, 964-980.
Carson, R. C. (1997). Costly Compromises: A critique of the diagnostic and statistical manual of mental disorders. In S. Fisher & R. P. Greenberg (Eds.), *From placebo to panacea: Putting psychiatric drugs to the test* (pp. 98-112). NY: Wiley.
Charniak, E. (1993). *Statistical language learning*. Cambridge, MA: MIT Press.
Crane, R., Allgood, S., Larson, J., & Griffin, W. (1990). Assessing marital quality with distressed and nondistressed couples: A comparison and equivalency table for three frequently used measures. *Journal of Marriage and the Family, 52*, 87-93.
Deller, J. R., Jr., Proakis, J. G., & Hansen, J. H. L. (1993). *Discrete-time processing of speech signals*. New York: MacMillan.
Durbin, R., Eddy, S., Krogh, A., & Mitchison, G. (1998). *Biological sequence analysis*. New York: Cambridge University Press.
Ferguson, J. D. (1980). Hidden Markov analysis: An introduction, in *Hidden Markov models for speech*. Princeton, NJ: Institute for Defense Analysis.
Filsinger, E. E. (1983). Assessment: What is it and why it is important. In E. E. Filsinger (Ed.), *Marriage and family assessment* (pp. 9-11). Beverly Hills, CA: Sage.
Gottman, J. M. (1994). *What predicts divorce?* New Jersey: Lawrence Erlbaum.
Gottman, J. M. (1979). *Marital Interaction: Experimental investigations*. New York: Academic Press.
Gottman, J. M., & Levenson, R. W. (1985). A valid procedure for obtaining self-report of affect in marital interaction. *Journal of Consulting and Clinical Psychology, 53*, 151-160.
Gottman, J. M., & Notarius, C. I. (2000). Decade review: Observing marital interaction. *Journal of Marriage and the Family, 62*, 927-947.
Griffin, W. A. (1993). Transitions from negative affect during marital interaction: Husband and wife differences. *Journal of Family Psychology, 6*, 3, 230-244.
Griffin, W. A. (1995). Assessing state changes in micro-social interaction: An introduction to event history analysis. In J. M. Gottman (Ed.), *Analysis of change*. Hillsdale, NJ: Erlbaum.
Griffin, W. A. (2000). A conceptual and graphical method for converging multi-subject behavioral observational data into a single process indicator. *Behavior Research Methods, Instruments, and Computers, 32* (1), 120-133.
Griffin, W. A., & Gottman, J. M. (1990). Statistical methods for analyzing family interaction. In G. R. Patterson (Ed.), *Family social interaction: Content and methodological issues in the study of aggression and depression* (pp. 131-168). Hillsdale, NJ: Erlbaum.

Jelinek, F. (1997). *Statistical methods for speech recognition.* Cambridge, Massachusetts: MIT Press.
Juang, B. H., & Rabiner, L. R. (1991). Hidden markov models for speech recognition. *Technometrics, 33*, 251-272.
Linde, Y., Buzo, A., & Gray, R. M. (1980). An algorithm for vector quantizer design. *IEEE Trans. Comm, 20*, 84-95.
Locke, H., & Wallace, K. (1959). Short marital adjustment and prediction tests: Their reliability and validity. *Journal of Marriage and the Family, 36*, 57-63.
MacDonald, I. L., & Zucchini, W. (1997). *Hidden Markov and other models for discrete-valued time series.* London: Chapman & Hall.
Olinick, M. (1978). *An introduction to mathematical models in the social and life sciences.* Reading, MA: Addison-Wesley Publishing.
Rabiner, L. R. (1989). A tutorial on hidden Markov models selected applications in speech recognition. *Proceedings of the IEEE. 77*, 257-286.
Rabiner, L. R., & Juang, B. H. (1993). *Fundamentals of speech recognition.* New York: Prentice Hall
Rabiner, L. R., & Juang, B. H. (1986). An introduction to hidden Markov models. *IEEE ASSP Magazine*, January, 4-15.
Viterbi, A. J. (1967). Error bounds for convolutional codes and an asymptotically optimal decoding algorithm. *IEEE Trans. Informational Theory, 13*, 260-269.
Watts, D. J. (1999). *Small worlds: The dynamics of networks between order and randomness.* Princeton, NJ: Princeton University Press.
Weiss, R. L., & Heyman, R. E. (1990). Observation in marital interaction. In F. D. Fincham & T. N. Bradbury (Eds.), *The psychology of marriage* (pp. 87-117). New York: Guilford.
Weiss, R. L., & Heyman, R. E. (1997). A clinical-research overview of couples interactions. In W. K. Halford & H. J. Markman (Eds.), *Clinical handbook of marriage and couples intervention* (pp. 13-41). New York: Wiley.
Williams, G. P. (1997). *Chaos theory tamed.* Washington, DC: John Henry Press.

The Role of Emotions in Marriage and Family Therapy: Past, Present, and Future

Debra A. Madden-Derdich

SUMMARY. As the traditional perspective of viewing emotions from an intrapsychic perspective has shifted to a more relational stance, the interpersonal functions of emotions within the family system have been underscored. As a result, the role of emotions in therapeutic interventions designed to assist distressed couples and families requires attention. The purpose of the current paper is to trace the role that emotions have played in marriage and family therapy (MFT) interventions both historically and currently. Towards this end, a brief overview of the historical role of emotions in MFT is presented followed by a review of research and therapeutic approaches that have integrated emotion into systemically based therapies. Future directions for incorporating emotions into MFT research, theory, and intervention are addressed. *[Article copies available for a fee from The Haworth Document Delivery Service: 1-800-HAWORTH. E-mail address: <docdelivery@haworthpress.com> Website: <http://www.HaworthPress.com> © 2002 by The Haworth Press, Inc. All rights reserved.]*

KEYWORDS. Family emotions, family systems, marital interaction

---

Debra A. Madden-Derdich is affiliated with Arizona State University.

[Haworth co-indexing entry note]: "The Role of Emotions in Marriage and Family Therapy: Past, Present, and Future." Madden-Derdich, Debra A. Co-published simultaneously in *Marriage & Family Review* (The Haworth Press, Inc.) Vol. 34, No. 1/2, 2002, pp. 165-179; and: *Emotions and the Family* (ed: Richard A. Fabes) The Haworth Press, Inc., 2002, pp. 165-179. Single or multiple copies of this article are available for a fee from The Haworth Document Delivery Service [1-800-HAWORTH, 9:00 a.m. - 5:00 p.m. (EST). E-mail address: docdelivery@haworthpress.com].

Over the past two decades, the traditional perspective of viewing emotions as intrapsychic phenomena has been supplanted with a relational perspective that emphasizes the central role that emotions play in organizing, maintaining, and motivating interpersonal interactions (Bretherton, Fritz, Zahn-Waxler, & Ridgeway, 1986; Campos, Campos, & Barrett, 1989). As is illustrated in the empirical and theoretical work presented in this volume, in no other realm are the interpersonal functions of emotions more apparent than in the family system. It is within the family system that marital relationships are established and fostered, children are nurtured and socialized, and sibling relationships are formed and shaped. It also is within the context of family relationships that individuals are victimized, mistreated, and neglected. Thus, within this complex web of interactional positions, emotions play a key role in determining how individual family members respond to one another, how they attach meaning to each other's behavior, and the degree to which they remain connected.

Given the principal functions that emotions serve within the family system, it is logical to expect that emotions would be an integral part of therapeutic interventions designed to assist distressed couples and families. Unfortunately, the previously longstanding conceptualization of emotions as intrapsychic processes significantly delayed the integration of emotion into systemically based clinical interventions in marriage and family therapy (MFT). The purpose of the current paper is threefold: (1) to offer a brief historical overview of the role of emotions in the field of marriage and family therapy, (2) to present a review of the research and therapeutic approaches that have integrated emotion and systemic principles, and (3) to highlight future directions for MFT research, theory, and intervention in this area.

A HISTORICAL OVERVIEW

The family systems therapies that emerged within the field of MFT during the 1960s and 1970s advanced a novel approach to the conceptualization of problematic behavior and pathology. Rooted in the tenets of general systems theory (Von Bertalanffy, 1968) and cybernetics (Werner, 1948), the most significant departure of these MFT approaches was the assertion that pathology, rather than being an intrapsychic phenomenon, was the product of the individual's interactional context. [It is noteworthy that this reconceptualization is very similar to the reconceptualization of emotions noted in the introduction to this article; see Fabes, Valiente, & Leonard, this volume]. In particular, maladaptive family interaction patterns were posited to be the etiological source of individual pathology and problematic behavior. Consistent with this interactional perspective, the primary focus of intervention in the early models of MFT (i.e., structural and strategic models) was the assessment and modification of behavior patterns and cognitions that supported and maintained these behaviors. Hence, most interventions were designed to highlight dysfunctional family interaction patterns and, in turn, to alter behavioral functioning.

A defining characteristic of the field of MFT during these formative decades was its steadfast rejection of psychoanalytic principles and literature. The foundation of this resolute rejection was derived in part from the original leaders' enthusiasm for viewing family interaction patterns as the primary source of individual pathology and their commitment to treating the family as a unit, as well as from the firm resistance they encountered from the psychoanalytic field (Nichols & Schwartz, 1995).

The notable outcome of this opposition to intrapsychic speculation was an almost unmitigated inattention to individual motivation and emotional functioning in early family systems approaches. Consistent with the psychological perspective at the time that emotions were intrapsychic processes that were secondary to cognition, emotions were marginalized as intrapsychic phenomena that were outside the domain of interactional interest (Krause, 1993). If emotions were addressed, it was likely to be in terms of how they could be either bypassed or subdued (Greenberg & Johnson, 1998). Even in the case of Bowenian Family Systems Theory (Bowen, 1966; Kerr & Bowen, 1988), which addressed the family emotional system as a core theoretical construct and viewed emotional attachment to one's family as a key source of symptomatology, the primary goal of therapy was an intellectual awareness and transcendence of family emotional processes. From this theoretical perspective, a well-adjusted individual was one who was rational and objective with a solid sense of individuality. Hence, the focus of therapeutic intervention was cognitive insight as opposed to emotional expression. Perhaps the one exception to this marginalized approach to emotions was Virginia Satir's (e.g., 1967) efforts to get family members to express their emotions openly to one another in her therapeutic work, but this empathic style with an emphasis on emotional expression was not embraced by the key systemic figures of the time (Schwartz & Johnson, 2000). As a result, at the end of the 1970s, the role of emotion in family systems therapies was theoretically underdeveloped and all but ignored in the domain of intervention (Diamond & Siqueland, 1998; Johnson & Greenberg, 1994).

Although still a relatively young discipline, the field of MFT entered the decade of the 1980s as a well-established and respected psychotherapeutic approach. With this recognition came a confidence that permitted the field to relax its staunch reactionary position against psychoanalytic and intrapersonal approaches. For the first time, some scholars in the field began to suggest that the field's exclusive focus on the interpersonal realm may be a bit limiting (e.g., Nichols, 1987), proposing that it may be important to consider the inner experiences that motivate individuals to interact in specific ways. This proposition was consistent with the paradigm shift being witnessed in the field of psychology at the time acknowledging the relational aspects of emotions. In addition, empirical research emerged that underscored the salient role that emotions play in marital interaction (Gottman & Levenson, 1986). Finally, with the introduction of emotion-focused therapy for couples, this decade witnessed a systemically based couple intervention in which emotional expression was viewed as a central component of the therapeutic change process (Greenberg & Johnson, 1986a, 1986b; Johnson & Greenberg, 1987). In combination, all of these factors (i.e., theoretical challenges, emerging research, and the introduction of an emotion-focused systemic intervention) led to the realization that the emotional aspects of relationship systems may play a significant role in systemically oriented approaches to therapeutic change.

RESEARCH INVESTIGATING EMOTION IN THE CONTEXT OF MARITAL INTERACTION

The research conducted by John Gottman (e.g., Gottman, 1994; Gottman & Krokoff, 1989; Gottman & Levenson, 1986) highlights the key role that emotions play in marital satisfaction and stability. Early research on marital interaction indicated that three characteristics of emotional engagement in couples distinguished satisfied from dissatisfied couples (summarized in Gottman, 1979; Schaap, 1982). First, dissatisfied couples expressed more negative affect in their interactions than did satisfied couples. Second, dissatisfied couples demonstrated a higher degree of negative reciprocity in their interactions than did satisfied couples. Finally, for dissatisfied couples, it was easier to predict the behavior of one spouse based on the other spouse's behavior than it was for satisfied couples.

Gottman's research expanded our understanding of these patterns by establishing a multimeasure, multimethod (i.e., observational, physiological, and self-report) database. Moreover, his work utilized a longitudinal methodology that permitted him not only to determine which factors distinguished martially satisfied and dissatisfied couples but also provided insight into which factors distinguished marriages that became more or less satisfying over time.

The results of these studies clearly located emotion within the interpersonal realm, contradicting the notion that affect and emotion could be sidestepped in systemic therapies designed to enhance marital relationships. In particular, it appeared that the degree and type of emotional engagement in a marital relationship were more important than the overall amount of conflict that occurred in determining the stability of marital satisfaction over time. More specifically, interactions that were indicative of criticizing, contempt, defensiveness, and withdrawal were problematic. Gottman (1994) suggested that evidence of these four behaviors in a couple's interaction pattern was rooted in a sense that the marriage was not an emotionally safe place. Taken together, these findings suggested that interventions for couples needed to target these emotional responses and the related interaction patterns that were identified in distressed marriages.

THE INTEGRATION OF EMOTION INTO CLINICAL APPROACHES WITH COUPLES

As previously discussed, early models of marital therapy conceptualized emotion as a secondary outcome that could be managed by changing behavior and/or cognition. The omission of emotion from these early models of clinical intervention, however, was theoretically rather than empirically determined. Hence, with the theoretical position regarding emotions shifting to a more relational stance, and with the building empirical data supporting the key role of emotional engagement in marital relationships, the development of systemically based couples therapy that emphasized the organizing role of emotion in marital interaction was the logical outcome.

Emotion-Focused Couples Therapy. Concurrent with the publication of Gottman's research, the introduction of Emotion-Focused Couples Therapy (EFT) marked the development of the first systemically based model of marital intervention to integrate emotion as a core aspect of the treatment approach (Greenberg & Johnson, 1986a, 1988; Johnson & Greenberg, 1985,1987). Grounded in attachment theory (Greenberg &

Marques, 1998; Johnson & Greenberg, 1995), this model represented a synthesis of experiential and systemic perspectives that offered a novel intervention modality. Rather than viewing the organizing forces behind interactional positions to be strictly cognitive (as the majority of systemic therapies had done), this approach placed emotion in a central role. Emotions were conceptualized to be an integral part of the couple system, serving to motivate action, to provide meaning to the relationship between an individual's internal state and their external environment, and to connect individuals with others in their social environment (Greenberg & Johnson, 1990). In other words, emotions were an integrating force between the intrapsychic and interpersonal domains.

This approach assumed that the negative interaction patterns within the couple system (such as those identified in Gottman's research) were rooted in unmet primary attachment needs–that is, the individually based vulnerabilities, fears, anxieties, and insecurities of each spouse were believed to play a key role in organizing and maintaining the interactional positions taken by each partner. A primary goal of EFT was the disclosure of these inner vulnerabilities and emotions to the partner, in the hope that these revelations would allow the spouses to interpret each other's actions in a new way. This process was thought to facilitate the creation of new and different behavioral responses (Greenberg & Marques, 1998). Such a strategy allowed the therapist to alternate between the intrapsychic and interpersonal domains, permitting each domain to extend and redefine the other (Johnson & Greenberg, 1987). As a result, rather than being conceptualized as strictly intrapersonal processes, emotions were seen as occurring at the interface between self and system.

Integrative Behavioral Couples Therapy. The other theoretically and empirically based approach to couple intervention that addressed the central role of emotions in couple interactions was Integrative Behavioral Couple Therapy (IBCT; Christensen, Jacobson, & Babcock, 1995; Jacobson & Christensen, 1996a). Empirical outcome research conducted on traditional behavioral couple therapy (Jacobson et al., 1984; Jacobson, Schmaling, & Holtzworth-Munroe, 1987) indicated that only 50% of the couples treated with this approach could be expected to maintain any long term (i.e., beyond 2 years) improvement. A review of the empirical and clinical data available on the more "difficult" couples who did not demonstrate improvement revealed a common set of couple characteristics that included lower levels of commitment to the relationship, increased age of the partners, less emotional engagement, more traditional marital roles, and lower convergence of marital goals. Taken together, these factors were believed to interfere with the couple's ability to interact in a collaborative and compromising manner, a prerequisite in behavioral approaches that require accommodation on the part of each partner (Cordova, Jacobson, & Christensen, 1998).

IBCT was developed in response to the realization that for many of these couples, traditional behavioral techniques alone were not sufficient to achieve long term behavioral change. Rather, the crux of this model rested on the belief that some behaviors cannot be changed and that the better approach under these circumstances was to change the context that made the behavior problematic. In particular, the goal, rather than being a change in the problematic behavior, was what the developers of the model referred to as emotional acceptance.

More specifically, emotional acceptance requires a change in the emotional reaction that the complainant has to the problematic behavior. This change is achieved by creating a new view of the problem as an understandable difficulty that is rooted in the polarized positions the partners have assumed (see Jacobson & Christensen, 1996b for a more detailed discussion of this polarization process). The goal of this process is similar to that of the emotional reframe used in EFT, that is, to offer a new interpretation of the problem that allows for a new response to the problematic behavior. In particular, the model is designed to foster responses to the problem that are compassionate and understanding rather than blaming and defensive.

Although IBCT encourages the use of "softer" emotions (i.e., sadness, hurt), an important distinction between EFT and IBCT is the degree of emphasis each approach places on the intrapsychic emotional processes of the partners. In IBCT, the expression of feelings is viewed primarily as an interpersonal process, with no attention given to the intrapersonal exploration of the emotional experience (Koerner & Jacobson, 1994). Although the attention to emotion in IBCT does not provide for an interface between the intrapsychic and interpersonal domains like that provided in EFT, the integration of emotion into the interpersonal domain represents a key distinction of IBCT as compared to traditional models of behavioral couples therapy. Rather than viewing emotion as an outcome of cognition and overt behavior, IBCT recognizes the important role that the emotional context plays in defining a behavior as problematic.

THE INTEGRATION OF EMOTION INTO FAMILY INTERVENTION MODELS

The two models of couple intervention detailed above represent important advances in the movement to integrate emotional processes into systemically based interventions for couples. Moreover, it is encouraging that the empirical outcome data for these two models support their clinical effectiveness (see Alexander, Holtzworth-Munroe, & Jameson, 1991 for a summary of these studies). Unfortunately, the advances in the domain of family-level interventions are more limited. A review of the family intervention literature reveals one family-based model that addresses the role of emotions. Multidimensional Family Therapy (MDFT; Liddle, 1994), developed to treat adolescent drug abuse and behavior problems, utilizes a multidimensional assessment and intervention framework that considers the interdependence of the emotional, cognitive, and behavioral domains as part of the treatment process. Consistent with its conceptualization of emotions as action tendencies, one facet of this model focuses on clarifying the affective factors that motivate parent-child interactions. In turn, one goal of the intervention process is the strengthening of the attachment relationship between the parent and the adolescent. Towards this goal, the behavior of the parent and adolescent are viewed within the historical emotional context of the family. In particular, actions are considered in relation to the parent's commitment and love and to the adolescent's hurt feelings. Like with EFT and IBCT, the problematic interactional processes are reframed in an emotional context in the hope that behavioral changes will result. The important distinction in this case is that the primary focus is on the emotional nature of the parent-child subsystem rather than on the marital subsystem.

MDFT's acknowledgement of the interdependence of cognition, behavior, and emotion and its subsequent clinical consideration of the emotional nature of the parent-child subsystem represents an important first step towards the incorporation of emotion into the clinical domain of family intervention. As Cummings, Goeke-Morey, and Papp (this volume) note, however, the availability of research and theory that investigates the role of emotions from a family-wide perspective (rather than at the level of dyadic subsystems) is not very extensive. The theoretical and research limitations in this realm are reflected further in the lack of family interventions in the clinical domain addressing the role of emotions in the broader family system. Although this gap can be explained in part by the relatively recent paradigmatic shift conceptualizing emotions from a relational rather than an intrapsychic perspective, the complex nature of family interaction and development also make the evolution of a family systems-based theory of emotion that is comprehensive enough to be applied to clinical intervention a challenging task.

Structural and Developmental Complexities. From a family systems perspective, the marital subsystem represents only one key relationship system in the complex web of interrelationships that constitute the family system. To gain a true understanding of the emotional processes of the family, not only the marital, but the parental, parent-child, and sibling relationship systems also must be considered. To complicate matters further, the interrelationships amongst these subsystems, as well as the triadic nature of some relationship systems (e.g., mother-father-child), must be considered. For example, the degree of negative affect and conflict present in marital and parental interactions is surmised to impact parent-child interactions in notable ways. In particular, high levels of negative affect and conflict in the marital and parental subsystems are hypothesized to increase the likelihood of parent-child coalitions (i.e., the child is asked to align with one parent in opposition to the other parent) (Minuchin, 1974; Minuchin & Fishman, 1981), reduce the consistency and effectiveness of discipline practices (Fauber, Forehand, Thomas, & Weirson, 1990), and diminish the amount of warmth displayed in parent-child interactions (Engfer, 1988; Fauber et al., 1990). Moreover, these destructive patterns are hypothesized to jeopardize the child's sense of emotional security in the family system (Davies & Cummings, 1994, 1998). In turn, these interaction processes are posited to threaten child adjustment.

In addition to the complexities that emerge from the interrelationships amongst the various subsystems, the emotional relationships of parents and children are intricately interwoven with the developmental age of the child. As is reflected in the extensive literature on emotion, the factors that are salient in the parent-child emotional system vary as a function of the child's developmental status (see Denham, 1998; Saarni, Mumme, & Campos, 1998). No one assumes, for instance, that the emotional system will be the same across early childhood, middle childhood, and adolescence. Rather each of these time periods is investigated independently with attention given to the developmental tasks that are prominent for each period (e.g., control and autonomy are more salient issues influencing the emotional nature of the parent-child relationship during adolescence than they are during early and middle childhood).

Finally, family systems in the current United States society reflect extensive heterogeneity. A multitude of family structures, values, and goals are represented including, but not limited to, households headed by married parents, households headed by single divorced parents, households headed by single parents who have never been married, households headed by grandparents, households headed by biological parents married to stepparents, and households headed by teen-aged single parents. The parental and parent-child emotional systems that emerge from each of these structures are somewhat unique. Consequently, theoreticians, researchers, and clinicians are faced with the challenging task of identifying commonalities that can be applied across diverse family forms as well as identifying the unique aspects of each family type.

Family systems approaches to intervention, with their detailed attention to the contextual embeddedness of individuals and subsystems (as well as their recognition of the interdependent and reciprocal nature of family interactions), offer a prime starting point for considering the role of emotions in family-level interventions. With the growing body of empirical evidence supporting the interdependence of cognition, behavior, and emotion, inattention to the emotional domain in family systems interventions is contradictory to the tenet of wholism that is central to systems approaches. Hence, the task facing the field of MFT is to determine how best to integrate emotions into the clinical domain of family intervention. Such an integration will require a focus not only on dyadic subsystems within the family, but on the reciprocity and interrelatedness of dyadic emotional subsystems, on the triadic nature of emotional relationships, and on the overall family emotional system. Thus, the challenge is to determine how best to accomplish this task.

A THEORETICAL ASSESSMENT OF FAMILY-SYSTEMS-BASED MODELS OF INTERVENTION

Despite their tendency to view emotions as secondary outcomes of cognition and behavior, systems-based models of family intervention (e.g., structural and strategic approaches) have much to contribute theoretically to the type of comprehensive integration delineated above. Systems-based models of clinical intervention have addressed the theoretical interrelationships between individuals and subsystems by discussing such constructs as family hierarchy, parent-child alliances, parent-child coalitions, and triangulation. From a theoretical and clinical perspective, it frequently has been thought that children's problems are often closely interrelated with problems in the marital and/or parental subsystem (Haley, 1987; Minuchin, 1974). For example, when the parental subsystem is not functioning in a collaborative and cohesive manner, children are more likely to be pressured to form a coalition with one parent in opposition to the other parent (Minuchin, 1974). The formation of such a coalition then impacts the nature of the child's relationship with both parents as well as the child's adjustment. Thus, these models provide a solid framework for considering the complex relationships that emerge between individuals and subsystems when a family-wide emotion-related perspective is taken. The limitation of these models has been their tendency to view emotions as secondary outcomes that result from cognitions and behavior.

As was the case with the integration of emotion into the intervention approaches outlined above (i.e., EFT, IBCT, MDFT), the merging of emotional processes into family-focused interventions does not necessarily require the development of a novel clinical approach. Rather, based on the available empirical and theoretical literature, existing models can be modified in a fashion that affords emotional processes an integral role. In the case of EFT, empirical and theoretical knowledge regarding emotional processes was combined with established experiential and systemic perspectives on intervention. Likewise, IBCT incorporated the available knowledge on emotional processes into a firmly established model of behavioral couples therapy. Finally, MDFT utilizes an ecologically oriented, developmental psychopathology framework to address the interrelationship between cognition, behavior, and emotion in the treatment of adolescent drug abuse and behavior problems.

A similar parallel can be seen in the realm of therapeutic technique. EFT, IBCT, and MDFT incorporated a modified version of the therapeutic reframe that was developed and utilized in the structural and strategic models of MFT (Minuchin, 1974; Selvini Palazzoli, Boxcolo, Cecchin, & Prata, 1978; Watzlawick, Weakland, & Fisch, 1974). The goal of reframing in all of these approaches was the same–to get the individual or couple to view the problem differently in an effort to elicit new behavioral responses. Rather than utilizing a cognitive reinterpretation of the problem behavior as the structural and strategic approaches did, however, these models utilized the reframing technique to place the problem behavior within an emotional context. The parallel use of the reframing technique across both cognitive and emotional approaches offers a prime example of how emotions, once integrated into the theoretical conceptualization of a clinical model, can be translated to the level of intervention.

CONCLUSIONS

Acknowledgement of the relational nature of emotional processes and the growing body of empirical evidence supporting this position has required that the role of emotion in clinical interventions for couples and families be revisited. Although advances in the area of couple interventions are notable (e.g., EFT and IBCT), progress in the realm of family intervention has been more limited. The paucity of applied models linking empirical knowledge to clinical practice that is apparent in the literature as a whole (Liddle, 1994) appears to be exaggerated in the case of emotionally focused family intervention. It appears that the complex nature of family relationships that makes empirical investigations of family-wide emotional processes difficult also precludes advancement of emotionally based theoretical models of family intervention. As our empirical knowledge base regarding family-wide emotional processes and their relationship to individual and family adjustment expands, our ability to design informed family-level interventions also will be enhanced. Likewise, clinical observations of family emotional processes can be used to offer direction for future research.

A review of the commonalities that exist across current emotionally focused models (i.e., EFT, IBCT, and MDFT), however, suggests that integrative, multidimensional models offer promise in regard to the integration of emotional processes. In addition, it is noteworthy that the MFT models that are rooted in constructivist and social constructivist thought (i.e., solution-focused therapy and narrative therapy) also have been identified in the literature as offering the necessary theoretical flexibility to address the relational role of emotion (Kiser, Piercy, & Lipchik, 1993; Parry, 1998; Schwartz, 1999; Turnell & Lipchik, 1999), although specific intervention strategies remain to be identified. Given the resurgence of emotion-related research and conceptualizations that have taken place over the past decade, it is critical that MFT researchers and clinicians give greater attention to the role of emotions in MFT processes. Doing so would allow the field to "keep pace" with the growing field of emotion research and the importance of this work to our understanding of the various components and models of couple and family functioning.

REFERENCES

Alexander, J. F., Holtzworth-Munroe, A., & Jameson, P. (1991). The process and outcome of marital and family therapy: Research review and evaluation. In A. S. Gurman & D. P. Kniskern (Eds.), *Handbook of Family Therapy* (pp. 595-629). New York: Brunner/Mazel.

Bowen, M. (1966). The use of family theory in clinical practice. *Comprehensive Psychiatry, 7*, 345-374.

Bretherton, I., Fritz, J., Zahn-Waxler, C., & Ridgeway, D. (1986). Learning to talk about emotions: A functionalist perspective. *Child Development, 57*, 529-548.

Campos, J. J., Campos, R. G., & Barrett, K. C. (1989). Emergent themes in the study of emotional development and emotion regulation. *Developmental Psychology, 25*, 394-402.

Christensen, A., Jacobson, N. S., & Babcock, J. C. (1995). Integrative behavioral couples therapy. In N. S. Jacobson & A. S. Gurman (Eds.), *Clinical handbook of marital therapy* (2nd ed.) (pp. 31-64). New York: Guilford Press.

Cordova, J. V., Jacobson, N. S., & Christensen, A. (1998). Acceptance versus change interventions in behavioral couple therapy: Impact on couples' in-session communication. *Journal of Marital and Family Therapy, 4*, 437-455.

Davies, P. T., & Cummings, E. M. (1994). Marital conflict and child adjustment: An emotional security hypothesis. *Psychological Bulletin, 116*, 387-411.

Davies, P. T., & Cummings, E. M. (1998). Exploring children's emotional security as a mediator of the link between marital relations and child adjustment. *Child Development, 69*, 124-139.

Denham, S. A. (1998). *Emotional development in young children*. New York: Guilford.

Diamond, G., & Siqueland, L. (1998). Emotions, attachment, and the relational reframe: The first session. *Journal of Systemic Therapies, 17*, 36-50.

Engfer, A. (1988). The interrelatedness of marriage and the mother-child relationship. In R. A. Hinde & J. Stevenson-Hinde (Eds.), *Relationships within families: Mutual influences* (pp. 104-118). Oxford: Clarendon Press.

Fauber, R., Forehand, R., Thomas, A. M., & Wierson, M. (1990). A mediational model of the impact of marital conflict on adolescent adjustment in intact and divorced families: The role of disrupted parenting. *Child Development, 61*, 1112-1123.

Gottman, J. M. (1979). *Marital interaction: Experimental investigations*. New York: Academic Press.

Gottman, J. M. (1994). An agenda for marital therapy. In S. M. Johnson & L. S. Greenberg (Eds.), *The heart of the matter: Perspectives on emotion in marital therapy* (pp. 256-293). New York: Brunner/Mazel.

Gottman, J. M., & Krokoff, L. J. (1989). Marital interaction and satisfaction: A longitudinal view. *Journal of Consulting and Clinical Psychology, 57*, 47-52.

Gottman, J. M., & Levenson, R. W. (1986). Assessing the role of emotion in marriage. *Behavioral Assessment, 8*, 31-48.

Greenberg, L. S., & Johnson, S. M. (1986a). Emotionally focused couples therapy: An affective systemic approach. In N. S. Jacobson & A. S. Gurman (Eds.), *Handbook of clinical and marital therapy* (pp. 253-276). New York: Guilford Press.

Greenberg, L. S., & Johnson, S. M. (1986b). Affect in marital therapy. *Journal of Marital and Family Therapy, 12*, 1-10.

Greenberg, L. S., & Johnson, S. M. (1988). *Emotionally focused therapy for couples*. New York: Guilford Press.

Greenberg, L. S., & Johnson, S. M. (1990). Emotional change processes in couples therapy. In E. A. Blechman (Ed.), *Emotions and the family: For better or worse* (pp. 137-153). Hillsdale, NJ: Laurence Erlbaum.

Greenberg, L. S., & Johnson, S. M. (1998). Emotion in systemic therapies: Commentary. *Journal of Systemic Therapies, 17*, 126-133.

Greenberg, L. S., & Marques, C. M. (1998). Emotions in couples systems. *Journal of Systemic Therapies, 17*, 93-107.

Haley, J. (1987). *Problem-solving therapy* (2nd ed.). San Francisco: Jossey-Bass.

Jacobson, N. S., & Christensen, A. (1996a). *Acceptance and change in couple therapy: A therapist's guide to transforming relationships.* New York: Norton.

Jacobson, N. S., & Christensen, A. (1996b). *Integrative couple therapy: Promoting acceptance and change.* New York: Norton.

Jacobson, N. S., Follette, W. C., Revenstorf, D., Baucom, D. H., Hahlweg, K., & Margolin, G. (1984). Variability in outcome in clinical significance of behavioral marital therapy: A reanalysis of outcome data. *Journal of Consulting and Clinical Psychology, 52*, 497-564.

Jacobson, N. S., Schmaling, K. B., & Holtzworth-Munroe, A. (1987). Component analysis of behavioral marital therapy: Two-year follow-up and prediction of relapse. *Journal of Marital and Family Therapy, 13*, 187-195.

Johnson, S. M., & Greenberg, L. S. (1985). Emotionally focused couples therapy: An outcome study. *The Journal of Marital and Family Therapy, 11*, 313-317.

Johnson, S. M., & Greenberg, L. S. (1987). Emotionally focused marital therapy: An overview. *Psychotherapy, 24*, 552-560.

Johnson, S. M., & Greenberg, L. S. (1994). Emotion in intimate relationships: Theory and implications for therapy. In S. M. Johnson & L. S. Greenberg (Eds.), *The heart of the matter: Perspectives on emotion in marital therapy* (pp. 3-22). New York: Brunner/Mazel.

Johnson, S. M., & Greenberg, L. S. (1995). The emotionally focused approach to problems in adult attachment. In N. S. Jacobson & A. S. Gurman (Eds.), *Clinical Handbook of Couple Therapy* (pp. 121-141). New York: Guilford Press.

Kerr, M. & Bowen, M. (1988). *Family Evaluation.* New York: Norton.

Kiser, D. J., Piercy, F. P., & Lipchik, E. (1993). The integration of emotion in solution-focused therapy. *Journal of Marital and Family Therapy, 19*, 233-242.

Koerner, K., & Jacobson, N. S. (1994). Emotion and behavioral couple therapy. In S. M. Johnson & L. S. Greenberg (Eds.), *The heart of the matter: Perspectives on emotion in marital therapy* (pp. 207-226). New York: Brunner/Mazel.

Krause, I. (1993). Family therapy and anthropology: A case for emotions. *Journal of Family Therapy, 15*, 35-56.

Liddle, H. A. (1994). The anatomy of emotions in family therapy with adolescents. *Journal of Adolescent Research, 9*, 120-157.

Minuchin, S. (1974). *Families and family therapy.* Cambridge, MA: Harvard University Press.

Minuchin, S., & Fishman, H. C. (1981). *Family therapy techniques.* Cambridge, MA: Harvard University Press.

Nichols, M. P. (1987). *The self in the system: Expanding the limits of family therapy.* New York: Brunner/Mazel.

Nichols, M. P., & Schwartz, R. C. (1995). *Family therapy: Concepts and methods* (3rd ed.). Needham Heights, MA: Allyn & Bacon.

Parry, T. A. (1998). Reasons of the heart: The narrative construction of emotions. *Journal of Systemic Therapies, 17*, 65-79.

Saarni, C., Mumme, D. L., & Campos, J. J. (1998). Emotional development: Action, communication, and understanding. In W. Damon & N. Eisenberg (Eds.), *Handbook of child psychology* (Vol. 3, pp. 237-310). New York: Wiley.

Satir, V. (1967). *Conjoint family therapy* (revised edition). Palo Alto, CA: Science and Behavior Books, Inc.

Schaap, C. (1982). *Communication and adjustment in marriage.* The Netherlands: Swets & Feitlinger.

Schwartz, R. C. (1999). Narrative therapy expands and contracts family therapy's horizons. *Journal of Marital and Family Therapy, 25,* 263-267.

Schwartz, R. C., & Johnson, S. M. (2000). Does couple and family therapy have emotional intelligence? *Family Process, 39,* 29-33.

Selvini Palazzoli, M., Boxcolo, L., Cecchin, G., & Prata, G. (1978). *Paradox and counterparadox.* New York: Jason Aronson.

Turnell, A., & Lipchik, E. (1999). The role of empathy in brief therapy: The overlooked but vital context. *Australia New Zealand Journal of Family Therapy, 20,* 177-182.

Von Bertalanffy, L. (1968). *General Systems Theory.* New York: Braziller.

Watzlawick, P., Weakland, J. H., & Fisch, R. (1974). *Change: Principles of problem formation and problem resolution.* New York: W. W. Norton.

Werner, N. (1948). *Cybernetics, or control and communication in the animal and the machine.* Cambridge, MA: Technology.

PART II:
DEVELOPMENTAL AND PARENT/CHILD PROCESSES

The Contribution of Older Siblings' Reactions to Emotions to Preschoolers' Emotional and Social Competence

Katharine Strandberg Sawyer
Susanne Denham
Elizabeth DeMulder
Kimberly Blair
Sharon Auerbach-Major
Jennifer Levitas

SUMMARY. According to Tompkins' (1991) theory on the socialization of emotion, young children's emotional and social competence are influenced by others' reactions to the children's emotions. Patterns of

---

Katharine Strandberg Sawyer, Susanne Denham, Elizabeth DeMulder, Kimberly Blair, Sharon Auerbach-Major, and Jennifer Levitas are all affiliated with George Mason University.

Address correspondence to: Susanne Denham, George Mason University, Department of Psychology, MS 3F5, 4400 University Drive, Fairfax, VA 22030-4444.

This investigation was supported by R01MH54019, granted by the National Institutes of Mental Health.

The authors wish to thank the many children and their families, as well as nursery school and daycare teachers, who gave so much time and good will so that the authors could learn about emotional competence, as well as Kathleen Aux, Krysti Batt, Bettye Changizi, Alvin Malesky, Patrick Queenan, and Meredith Vickery, who assisted in gathering the data presented here.

[Haworth co-indexing entry note]: "The Contribution of Older Siblings' Reactions to Emotions to Preschoolers' Emotional and Social Competence." Sawyer, Katharine Strandberg et al. Co-published simultaneously in *Marriage & Family Review* (The Haworth Press, Inc.) Vol. 34, No. 3/4, 2002, pp. 183-212; and: *Emotions and the Family* (ed: Richard A. Fabes) The Haworth Press, Inc., 2002, pp. 183-212. Single or multiple copies of this article are available for a fee from The Haworth Document Delivery Service [1-800-HAWORTH, 9:00 a.m. - 5:00 p.m. (EST). E-mail address: docdelivery@haworthpress.com].

© 2002 by The Haworth Press, Inc. All rights reserved.

parental reactions to emotions have been shown to account for significant variance in preschoolers' emotion and social competence. However, the impact of others significant in the preschooler's life has been largely ignored. To help fill this gap, associations were examined between older siblings' reactions to 41 preschoolers' emotions and the preschoolers' social-emotional competence (i.e., affective balance, emotion knowledge, positive, prosocial, and provocative responding to peers' emotions, sociometric likability, and teacher-rated social competence). Using a multiple regression strategy, the contributions of sibling reactions and moderating demographic variables to preschooler emotional and social competence were evaluated. Certain sibling reactions, especially positive emotional responsiveness, were shown to play important roles. Many predictions were moderated by age of child, sex of one dyad member, or age interval between siblings. *[Article copies available for a fee from The Haworth Document Delivery Service: 1-800-HAWORTH. E-mail address: <docdelivery@haworthpress.com> Website: <http://www.HaworthPress.com> © 2002 by The Haworth Press, Inc. All rights reserved.]*

KEYWORDS. Siblings, preschoolers, emotion

Attaining developmentally appropriate emotional and social competence is a complex task of the preschool period. Although this early development is no doubt facilitated by a number of interacting influences, socialization by people from whom the child learns is central. For example, parental emotional and social behaviors and beliefs are related to their children's emotional and social competence (Denham, 1993; Denham & Grout, 1993; Denham, Mitchell-Copeland, Strandberg, Auerbach, & Blair, 1997; Lamb, 1982). Parental influences have been studied more often than other socializers', but it follows that teachers, day care providers, grandparents, aunts, uncles, peers, siblings, and others significant in the child's life also play a role in the socialization of emotional and social competence. Children's involvement with these people is often emotionally laden, replete with a variety of both positive and negative interactions.

In particular, the mutual interests, equality, and reciprocity of the peer relationship forces children to think of the feelings of others, rather than simply attempting to meet their own needs exclusively as they do with adults (Piaget, 1965; Sullivan, 1953). Children learn about emotions, social rules, and others' points of view through cooperative play.

If peers play such a formative role in each others' lives, then a similar and perhaps even stronger argument could be made for siblings (Dunn, 1983; 1988b). The emotional intensity and intimacy of the sibling relationship and the amount of time siblings spend together make sibling interaction a prime arena for mutually significant influences (Bank & Kahn, 1975; Brown & Dunn, 1992; Dunn & Kendrick, 1982). The affective quality of sibling interactions ranges from prosocial behaviors and obvious affection to hostility and mutual physical aggression (Abramovitch, Corter, & Lando, 1979; Abramovitch, Pepler, & Corter, 1982; Dunn & Kendrick, 1982). This breadth and depth of emotions suggests that the sibling relationship is fertile ground for emotion socialization.

Thus, both theoretical and empirical evidence support the notion that siblings, particularly older upon younger, play this major role in each others' social and emotional development. But how? Siblings are believed to create different environments for each other (Dunn & Plomin, 1991; Scarr & Grajek, 1982). That is, by simply being there and interacting with each other, they influence each others' development.

More specifically, links exist between the interaction of two siblings and the children's emotional competence (Dunn, 1992). For example, young children who maintained a cooperative and friendly relationship with their older sibling, and whose older sibling had been affectionate toward them, performed significantly better on an affective perspective-taking task than children whose sibling relationships did not possess these qualities, seven months later (Dunn, Brown, Slomkowski, Tesla, & Youngblade, 1991; see also Dunn & Dale, 1984). The direction of effect in this correlational research is tantalizing: It could be that children who are better at understanding the emotions of others have more positive relationships with their siblings, analogous to findings with peers (Denham, McKinley, Couchoud, & Holt, 1990). However, it could also be that positive relationships with siblings provide children with an optimal environment in which to learn about emotions. Children with supportive siblings may be less preoccupied with their own distress, so that they are more able to learn about or understand the feelings of others (Eisenberg, Fabes, Miller, Shell, Shea, & May-Plumlee, 1990; Smiley & Huttenlocher, 1989). Although the direction of effect remains a thorny issue, the present study attempts to take these possibilities a step further by documenting a possible avenue of sibling influence.

A closer look at the specific interactions within sibling relationships reveals that various aspects of emotional competence demonstrated by children are related to the manner in which the older sibling treats the younger (Dunn & Munn, 1986a). For example, the quality of sibling caretaking (e.g., nurturance, discipline, encouragement of autonomy) during middle childhood is related to the child's social-emotional functioning (e.g., empathy, perspective taking; Bryant, 1989).

Negative interactions between siblings also can play a positive role in the child's emotional and social competence. When siblings are engaged in negative interactions, they are provided with important exposure to the views of others (Dunn & Munn, 1987; Dunn & Herrera, 1997). Social understanding is promoted, as well as demonstrated, during these sibling conflict situations (Dunn, 1983; Dunn & Munn, 1985; Dunn, Slomkowski, Donelan, & Herrera, 1995). For example, the teasing and pestering behaviors of very young siblings actually indicate these youngsters' sophisticated knowledge of precisely the behavior that will "get" their older sibling. Thus, preschoolers come to understand the emotions of their siblings and act accordingly, and this understanding may contribute to their overall understanding of emotions.

Are these important sibling contributions distinct from either parental or peer contributions? Many theoretical and empirical viewpoints do impart an important and exclusive role to the older sibling in the development of the younger sibling's social and emotional competence. There are unique factors present in the sibling relationship that do not appear in peer relationships (Dunn & McGuire, 1992). First, siblings do not choose each other as friends do (Dunn, 1992). Second, the frequency of interaction is extremely high between young siblings (Bank & Kahn, 1975; Buhrmester & Furman, 1990), with an emotional range of far greater breadth and intensity than that observed in the peer group (Dunn, 1983; Dunn & Kendrick, 1982). Third, older siblings possess a fair amount of power, suggesting that the sibling relationship may be less symmetrical than the peer relationship (Dunn & Munn, 1986b). The older sibling's combination of greater power and knowledge may allow the sibling to teach the younger child directly about social and emotional functioning. In addition, the child may be a better "student" of the older sibling, more captivated and watchful than with agemates. Fourth, Dunn (1992) suggests that the conflict present in many sibling relationships is qualitatively different from that present in peer relationships. Siblings frequently do not like each other. Moreover, they often engage in competition for parental attention and approval. Consequently, the quality of their conflict is quite different than peers'. Fifth, it is highly unlikely that there is a one-to-one correspondence between children's behavior with peers and with siblings (Abramovitch, Corter, Pepler, & Stanhope, 1986; Berndt & Bulleit, 1985; Patterson, 1984; Stocker &

Dunn, 1990). Therefore, it is important to consider the two relationships as separate but influential upon each other in their contributions to competence.

What of the unique role of siblings as compared to parents? Although the parental relationship with both the sibling and the child undoubtedly influences the sibling relationship (Brody & Stoneman, 1987; Brody, Stoneman, & Burke, 1987), siblings may exert influence on each other that is independent from parental factors (Bank & Kahn, 1975; Scarr & Grajek, 1982). First, siblings are not as accommodating as parents, and are as demanding as the child is to get their needs met. Within the context of the sibling relationship, children are forced to learn and think about the needs of another individual, because siblings will not be as forgiving or understanding as their parents (Watson-Gegeo & Gegeo, 1989). Second, the majority of play between siblings appears to be complementary (i.e., both are equally engaged in interactive roles), whereas mothers more often merely watch rather than engage their young children in interactive play (Dunn, 1988; Dunn & Dale, 1984).

Third, Baskett and Johnson (1982) found that siblings respond to each others' emotions less positively and more negatively than their parents do (see also Dunn, Creps, & Brown, 1996). Parents serve as reinforcers of positive social behaviors, whereas siblings more often use coercion in an attempt to control the child. Children may learn more from their parents about how to maintain positive social interaction; but with siblings, they become knowledgeable about how to be controlling, as well as what to do when being controlled.

Fourth, preschool age is a particularly ripe time for sibling influence on social and emotional development. During the child's third year, the older sibling becomes significantly more interested in the child, and begins communicating and interacting with the child with greater frequency (Brown & Dunn, 1991; Brown & Dunn, 1992). The child, in turn, initiates more interaction with the older sibling (Munn & Dunn, 1989), and begins to interact less with the mother (Brown & Dunn, 1992).

Fifth, more positive and negative affect is displayed during child-sibling interaction than during child-parent interaction (Dunn et al., 1996). Siblings may elicit more negative emotions from each other than parent-child dyads because of the ubiquity of conflict in their relationship, and also because anger, for example, would be more tolerated than when expressed toward a parent. Dunn et al. also found that young children play more with older siblings than with their mothers, and this activity may pull for high intensity emotion, whether positive or negative.

Regardless of its cause and specific parameters, this greater proportion of emotions between siblings suggests that the sibling relationship is a key area where a child can learn about emotions. In addition, mothers talk about the child's emotions much more than siblings do; siblings concentrate more on themselves when talking about emotions. Again, siblings almost force the child to at least listen to the feelings of another, whereas parents allow their younger children to think predominantly about their own needs and emotions. This differential response of siblings may facilitate the child's emerging appreciation for the emotions of others.

Along with these clear differences between interacting with siblings versus parents or peers, siblings also provide very specific functions for each other (e.g., Bank & Kahn, 1975; Buhrmester, 1992). Bank and Kahn (1975) suggest that siblings fulfill four main purposes: (1) identification and differentiation, (2) mutual regulation, (3) direct services, and (4) dealing with parents. Briefly, identification and differentiation refer to siblings' taking on or rejecting certain characteristics based on what they do or do not like about each other. Mutual regulation indicates that siblings are regulators of each other's behaviors and learning experiences; they try out new behaviors on each other before using them in the outside world. Direct services encompass the straightforward functions that siblings serve, such as offering advice, fixing a broken toy, or introducing new friends. Dealing with parents refers to the important role siblings have in each other's lives based on the relationship they each have with the parents. For example, siblings can protect each other from parents discovering their misdeeds, or they can tattle and get each other into trouble.

The first three of these functions appear to be the most relevant to the impact of siblings on the socialization of emotional and social competence. Accordingly, we use these functions in the present study as a framework for discussion and assessing the specific avenues via which older siblings contribute to young children's developing social and emotional competencies. In fact, these functions fit well with the terminology we used in earlier work on parental socialization of emotional and social competence (e.g., Denham et al., 1997). Identification and differentiation are equivalent to modeling, mutually regulatory influences are similar to our contingency pathways, and coaching can be seen as a direct service.

Modeling. Siblings can identify with each other more readily than they can with their parents–they are closer in age and often maintain common interests. Based on what they do and do not like about their siblings, they can take on or reject certain characteristics of their older sibling (Bank & Kahn, 1975). Children learn about emotions, when and where to display them, by watching others' emotional displays (Denham & Grout, 1993; Denham, Zoller, & Couchoud, 1994). Children frequently imitate their older siblings, regardless of age interval or gender composition of the dyad (Abramovitch et al., 1979; Abramovitch et al., 1982; Dunn, 1983; Pepler, Corter, & Abramovitch, 1982). These findings suggest that children are paying attention to the older siblings' actions. This attention is a possible source of great influence. It may be that the child learns about emotions and emotional behavior by watching an older sibling, and then applying the same strategies, even generalizing these behaviors to other relationships outside the family.

Contingency. Children learn a great deal about emotions from how others' react both verbally and nonverbally to their own emotional displays (Denham et al., 1994; Malatesta & Haviland, 1982, 1985). Tomkins' (1991) theory regarding the socialization of emotions suggests that there are rewarding as well as punitive contingencies that contribute to emotion socialization in children. Through rewarding experiences, as in positive reactions from the sibling, the child may learn that self-experienced emotions are to be tolerated (see Bryant & Crockenberg, 1980, for analogous findings with mothers and preschoolers).

However, when the response is punitive, the child may learn to minimize emotional displays, perhaps in fear of further parental reprisal (Tomkins, 1991). In these situations, the child may be in a difficult position to learn about and understand emotions in the self and others, especially when they must deal with their own emotions alone. In support of these theoretical predictions, children whose mothers responded negatively during parent-child interaction were found to be more emotionally self-focused and negative with peers (Putallaz, 1987). Moreover, if positive reinforcement stops when the emotion becomes too intense, the child may learn that the emotion is also to be controlled.

Consequently, through others' reactions, children are not only learning how to react verbally and nonverbally to others' emotional displays, but they are also learning about where and when to display their own emotions. For example, when a child's laughter is responded to with laughter, he or she learns something very different than if that laughter is returned with anger. If his or her laughter is repeatedly met with anger, the child may learn to suppress this positive emotional expression and develop an alternative behavior (Denham, 1993; Denham et al., 1994).

Older siblings' contingent reactions to young children are probably very powerful. Siblings tend to be honest and uninhibited with each other, so that they criticize, reinforce, and influence each other's behavior both directly and indirectly. In fact, older siblings tend to respond less positively and more negatively than parents to the behavioral and emotional displays of the younger child (Dunn et al., 1996; Wahl, Johnson, Johansson, & Martin, 1974). Based on how each sibling reacts to the behavior of the other, behaviors and emotions are either positively or negatively reinforced (Dunn et al., 1995, Dunn & Herrera, 1997).

Even more specifically, it should be noted that across families, siblings evidence much greater variability in responsiveness than parents. This variability may account for some of the individual differences that occur in young children's emotional and social competence. Moreover, a substantial proportion of emotional interactions between siblings are mismatches, that is, when one is happy, the other might be angry or sad (Dunn, 1983; Dunn & Kendrick, 1982; Dunn & Munn, 1986a). These mismatches may be important for the child, teaching something different about emotions than when the emotion is matched.

It is important to note that contingency, as well as modeling, may operate over substantial periods of time. Several researchers have noted that the pattern of sibling interaction is relatively stable, even over a 4-year period (Brown & Dunn, 1992; Dunn & Kendrick, 1982; Patterson, 1986; Stillwell & Dunn, 1985). For example, siblings who were positive and nurturing at time one were also positive and nurturing at time two. This consistency of behavior, compounded with the unique qualities of the sibling relationship, adds further credibility to the notion that children learn a great deal about emotions from their older brother's or sister's reactions to their own emotions.

Coaching. The direct services that siblings employ can make each other's lives either easier or more difficult. These services include offering advice and giving or taking things away (Bank & Kahn, 1975). The older sibling also is often a teacher of his or her younger brother or sister (Brody, Stoneman, MacKinnon, & MacKinnon, 1985; Dunn, 1983). When compared with unrelated older children, for example, target children learned more on a structured learning task from their older siblings, perhaps because they already have an established pattern of interaction, through which communication and the conveyance of knowledge is made easier (Cicirelli, 1972, 1975).

Children can learn about emotion in conversations with others (Denham, Cook, & Zoller, 1992). Talking about emotions not only provides the child with direct instruction about emotions, but also may teach the child that a way of controlling and expressing them is through talking about them (Dunn & Munn, 1985; Kopp, 1989). Preschoolers who engage in more affective discussion with their mothers tend to perform better on measures of affective perspective-taking than preschoolers who do not (Dunn, Brown, & Beardsall, 1991; Dunn, Brown, Slomkowski et al., 1991). Because discourse about feelings increases between siblings during the preschool years (Brown & Dunn, 1992), its contribution to emotional competence should be assessed.

Thus, siblings, like parents, contribute to socialization of emotional and social competence via three specific pathways: modeling, contingency, and coaching (Denham et al., 1994). In the present study, it was predicted that older siblings' contingent reactions to their younger siblings' emotions play an important role in the development of a child's emotional, and ultimately social, competence. It was hypothesized that: (1) older siblings' reactions to the preschool-aged child's emotions would predict the child's emotional competence–their ability to label emotions, articulate the situational causes of emotions, and take another's emotional perspective, as well as their positive and negative emotions in the preschool classroom; and (2) these reactions also would predict, both directly and through emotional competence, peer and teacher ratings of likability and social competence.

Sex, age of child, and age interval between siblings also were selected as potential moderators for the following reasons: (1) documented sex differences in prediction of social and emotional development (e.g., Denham et al., 1997), (2) the preschool period is a time of such emotional and social growth, with much age-related change, (3) the age difference between siblings has been associated with patterns of sibling interaction (Buhrmester & Furman, 1990). For example, it might be most sensible for certain aspects of preschoolers' emotional and social competence, such as emotion knowledge, to be associated with sibling behavior most significantly during the beginning of the period, when they are most actively changing.

METHOD

Participants

The participants, a subsample from the first cohort of a larger, longitudinal study, consisted of 41 preschool-age children (23 boys) who had older siblings under 10 years old. Volunteer families were recruited through local preschool and daycare centers to participate in a study of preschoolers' behavior at home and in preschool. The average age of the preschoolers was 45.65 months (SD = 5.12 mos, range = 35 to 58 mos) at the time of the observation in the home. The average age of the older siblings (22 boys) was 79.02 mos (SD = 15.84 mos, range = 53 to 115 mos). The average age interval between the child under study and the older sibling was 33.37 months (s.d. = 15.17, range = 12 to 74 mos). There were 12 younger brother/older brother pairs, 11 young brother/older sister pairs, 10 young sister/older brother pairs, and 8 younger sister/older sister pairs.

A majority of children under study had either one or two siblings ($N = 37$) and most were second born ($N = 29$). The modal level of education for mothers was graduation from college ($N = 16$), and for fathers was the completion of a master's degree ($N = 15$). Most children were described as Caucasian ($N = 32$), and the annual income for a large majority of the families was over $50,000 ($N = 28$). Almost all of the children lived in two-parent homes ($N = 36$).

Procedures

Sibling interaction was observed during a visit to each family's home. The children were observed in a free play situation with their siblings for a total of 60 minutes by an experimenter with whom the child and the sibling were familiar.

For the next four measures, each child left his or her classroom with an experimenter with whom he or she was familiar. With the experimenter the child engaged in an emotional expression identification task, an interpretation of emotional situations, and an affective perspective task using puppets with differing emotional expressions. The next measure consisted of a sociometric rating scale where *every* child in each classroom participated in an adaptation of Asher, Singleton, Tinsley, and Hymel's (1979) sociometric task. For each measure, children worked with a familiar adult, outside the classroom, for 20 to 30 minutes. The children's emotions and reactions to peers' emotions also were observed in the classroom (see Denham et al., 1997). Last, each child's teacher completed a rating scale of social competence.

Predictors

Sibling reactions to child emotions. During the 60 minutes of sibling free play, software created by Roberts (1993) was used to code child emotions and sibling reaction to emotion data. The process of coding was as follows: Observers entered the child's emotion's code at its onset, observed the sibling's reactions, entered them as they occurred, and then looked back to the child; if the same emotion continued, reactions were again searched for, but if no emotion was being displayed, the observer re-entered the neutral code. We have standardized training to use this coding system and laptop technology.

Frequencies of the following sibling reactions to children's emotions were coded: Matching positive or negative emotions, inappropriate affective reaction (e.g., smiles when child is hurt), hurt feelings, positive reinforcement (e.g., touches, complies, praises, acknowledges, approaches), negative reinforcement (e.g., verbal discouragement of emotional display, distracting, punishment, leaving to get away from the emotion), help or concern, looking, ignoring, hurt feelings/sad, or antisocial reactions (e.g., exacerbation of the emotion by physical, verbal, or behavioral means) (see also Denham, 1986). These reactions were considered mutually exclusive, but could be coded successively. Kappas for coding reactions to emotions in the home averaged .82. Frequency of each reaction was divided by number of emotions emitted by the child.

For purposes of analyses, these reaction proportions were aggregated into three predictor variables. First, sibling positive responsiveness, consisted of the z score of positive affect match minus the z-score of ignoring, which were inversely correlated, $r(39) = -.66, p < .001$. Second, the sibling prosocial responding was created by summing z scores for the reactions of helping and concern minus the z score for hurt feelings/sad reaction. The creation of this aggregate is justified by the following: (1) the helping and comforting proportions were correlated, $r(39) = .34, p < .05$; (2) both emotional and behavioral indices of prosocial responsiveness are included; and (3) removing the hurt feelings/sad reactions more closely embodies other-oriented, as opposed to self-directed, empathy (see Eisenberg, McCreath, & Ahn, 1988). Third, sibling provocative responding, consisted of the sum of z scores for opposite affect match and antisocial reactions, which were correlated, $r(39) = .42, p < .05$. Complementing the first aggregate, this one embodies the concept of both behavioral and emotional responses that serve to exacerbate or create emotional suffering.

Criteria

Previously developed observational methodologies were used to examine the emotions expressed by children in the preschool classroom, and their peers' reactions to these emotions. Semi-structured interviews were used to assess children's knowledge about their emotions. Care was taken for assistants familiar to the children (but not those who observed them in the home) to administer all measures in the classroom.

Children's emotions and reactions to peers' emotions. Children's emotions and their reactions to peers' emotions were assessed in their preschool or daycare, by observers using the computer technology described above. Observers obtained 24 5-minute observations for each child (12 with the child as focal, counting his/her emotions, and 12 with the child as target, counting his/her reactions to peers' emotions). During each 5-minute period, occurrence of discrete emotions of the focal participant was tallied. Happy, sad, angry, afraid/tense, tender, neutral, and "other" emotional displays of the focal participant were coded, using facial, vocal, postural and behavioral indicators of emotion (for details regarding operational definitions, see Denham, 1986; Denham & Grout, 1993). Kappas for interrater reliability of coding emotions averaged .80.

Robust negative correlations have been previously found between percentage happy and percentage angry scores in our research (e.g., Denham, McKinley et al., 1990; Denham & Grout, 1993). Accordingly, affective balance aggregates, which equaled standard scores for percentage of happy displays minus percentage of angry displays, were created. Next, the same reaction codes, as already described for the sibling play sessions, were created–prosocial responding to peers' emotions, provocative responding to peer's emotions, and positive responsiveness to peers' emotions. Kappas for interrater reliabilities of coding reactions to emotions in the classroom averaged .78 (range = .68 to .87).

Understanding of emotion. Children's understanding of emotion (nonverbal recognition and verbal labeling of emotional expressions, identification of emotions unequivocally appropriate to certain situations, and inferences of emotions in equivocal situations) was first assessed using puppets with detachable faces that depict happy, sad, angry, and afraid expressions. Because these measures have been described in detail elsewhere (Denham, 1986; Denham & Couchoud, 1990a, 1990b; Denham et al., 1994), they will be summarized as follows.

Children were first asked to identify happy, sad, angry, and afraid facial expressions verbally, by naming them, and then non-verbally, by pointing. In the next two emotional situation identification tasks, the puppeteer made standard facial and vocal expressions of emotions while enacting an emotion-laden story. The child was asked to place on the puppet the face that depicted the puppet's feeling in the situation.

The first emotional situation identification task explored how well children know others' feelings in eight common situations that elicit unequivocal emotional reactions, such as happiness at being given an ice cream cone, or fear at having a nightmare (Denham, 1986). The second emotional situation identification task measures how well children identify others' feelings in situations where the other feels differently than the child. All situations could elicit one of two emotions, as in feeling happy or afraid to get into a swimming pool (Denham, 1986; Denham & Couchoud, 1990b). Children's mothers had reported, via forced-choice questionnaire, how their children would feel in twelve such vignettes. For each vignette, their response determined the emotion expressed by the puppet. Standard scores for each item of these tasks were summed for the emotion knowledge aggregate. Alpha for the aggregate equaled .90.

Peer-rated sociometric likability. Each child in the classroom was taken out of the classroom by a familiar adult and presented with a set of pictures of all his or her classmates (Asher, Singleton, Tinsley, & Hymel, 1979). To model the task, the researcher placed one Fisher Price "person" in each of three small boxes marked with sketched drawings. The "Like-a-Lot" box was marked with a smiling face; the "Kinda Like" box with a flat-mouthed face; and the "Do Not Like" box with a frowning face. After this demonstration, each child who participated was asked to place each of his or her peers' pictures into the happy face, neutral face, or unhappy face boxes, according to how much he or she likes to play with each peer. At the completion of picture placement, each child chose a sticker reward, and was asked to make up his or her own stories with puppets. Concluding with this neutral, constructive activity ensured that the peer rating had no negative impact on the child's social interactions upon return to the classroom (see Bell-Dolan & Wessler, 1994).

Based on the sociometric component of the task, each child in the study received scores for both the number of positive ratings and the number of negative ratings. One-year test-retest reliabilities for these scores were .38 and .34, $ps < .01$. A peer likability score for each child was computed by subtracting the number of negative nominations from the number of positive nominations/over the total number of ratings (see also Denham, McKinley et al., 1990; Denham et al., 1997).

Social competence: Teacher ratings. Teachers/daycare providers completed the Social Competence and Behavior Evaluation–Short

Form (SCBE-30: LaFreniere & Dumas, 1996), which assesses the teacher's perceptions of the child's behavior in the classroom. This 30-item measure is rated on a Likert-type scale of 1 (not at all like this child) to 6 (very much like this child). Three scales are obtained: angry/aggressive (e.g., forces other children to do things; hits teacher when angry); anxious/withdrawn (e.g., inhibited or uneasy in a group; timid, afraid, avoids new situations); and social competence (e.g., negotiates solutions to conflicts; comforts or assists children in difficulty).

Test-retest reliabilities over a one-year period were as follows: .43 for the Angry-Aggressive Factor, .33 for the Isolated Factor, and .30 for the Sensitive-Cooperative Factor, all $ps < .001$. Cronbach's α was .87 for the Angry-Aggressive Factor, .88 for the Isolated Factor, and .90 for the Sensitive-Cooperative Factor. This measure also has been well validated; comparison with the Child Behavior Checklist Teacher Rating Form has demonstrated that it distinguishes between clinical samples of aggressive and withdrawn children.

In the present study, then, each child received total scores for these three factors. These scores were then converted into z scores. Because of their substantial intercorrelation, a teacher-rated social competence aggregate score was then determined for each subject by subtracting the Isolated and Aggressive Factor z-scores from the Cooperative-Sensitive Factor z score ($\alpha = 66$).

RESULTS

Analytic Strategy

Prior to multiple regression analyses, analyses of variance and Pearson correlations were conducted to examine the relationship between the individual demographic variables (as well as the interaction of sex of child and sex of sibling) and each of the predictor and criterion variables. These analyses were examined to elucidate any demographic patterns in the predictor and criterion variables. Next, Pearson correlation coefficients between predictor and criterion variables were obtained to aid in the interpretation of the overall analyses. Pearson correlation coefficients among criterion variables also were examined to determine if any could be aggregated for the overall multiple regression analyses.

We then formulated a multiple regression strategy to predict children's emotional and social competence in the preschool. Given the relatively small sample size, and relatively large number of independent variables, spurious inflation of R^2 was a concern. We chose to reduce the large number of independent variables available by considering for inclusion, for the first step of the regressions, only those demographic variables whose zero-order correlations with the criterion variables were significant at the $p < .10$ level or better. Next, the aggregates of sibling reactions were considered for entry simultaneously at the second step (or the first step if there were no demographic variables to enter).

Moderator effects were also assessed via Baron and Kenny's (1986) methodology. The moderating effects of sex of child, sex of older sibling, age of child, and age interval between siblings on six criterion variables were examined using hierarchical regression equations. Accordingly, in separate equations, the sex of child, sex of older sibling, age of child or age interval between siblings, and *each* predictor were entered on the first step, and their interaction term was entered on the second step. If the interaction term's contribution to R^2 was significant in this equation ($p < .05$), separate regression equations for girls and boys, brothers and sisters, young and old (as divided at the 45-month age median), or small or large age interval groups (as divided at the 30-month median) were used to assess differences in the uniqueness of each predictor of social and emotional competence. A total of 72 moderation analyses were run (3 predictors × 6 dependent measures × 4 moderator variables), with 15 reaching significance.

Relations between demographic variables and predictor and criterion variables. One- and two-way ANOVAs and Pearson correlations were performed to examine the effects of sex and age of both the child and the sibling and the age interval between siblings, on both predictor and criterion variables.

Older sisters engaged in significantly more sibling prosocial responding then did older brothers, $F(1, 39) = 6.50, p < .05$. Older sisters were also more likely to engage in positive responsiveness than were older brothers, $F(1, 39) = 4.14, p < .05$. Older brothers engaged in more provocative responding than older sisters, $F(1, 39) = 4.82, p < .05$. None of the predictor variables varied according to the child's sex, however, nor was the interaction of sex of child and sibling significant in any analysis.

Age of older sibling and the predictor variables were significantly related only for positive responsiveness, $r(39) = .35, p < .05$. The age interval between siblings also was significant for this aggregate, $r(39) =$

.32, $p < .05$. There was a trend between age interval and peer-rated likability, $r(39) = .28, p < .10$. The age of the child under study was marginally related to sibling prosocial responding, $r(39) = .29, p < .10$. Older children also engaged in more provocative responding to peer, $r(39) = .45, p < .01$).

Zero-order correlations of predictors and criteria. Nine of the 21 correlations yielded results that were either significant or approaching significance (see Table 1). Siblings' prosocial responding met this standard with five of the criterion variables: teacher-rated social competence, peer-rated likability, affective balance, emotion knowledge, and provocative responding to peers. Sibling positive responsiveness was significantly correlated with four criterion variables: emotion knowledge, prosocial responding to peer, positive responsiveness to peer emotions, and provocative responding to peer. Siblings' provocative responding was not significantly associated with any of the criterion variables. Correlation coefficients' significance in all tables is evaluated with respect to two-tailed probabilities.

There were no significant correlations among the predictors. Surprisingly, only four significant correlations emerged among criterion variables (see Table 2): Affective balance was positively correlated with peer-rated likability. Provocative responding to peer was correlated negatively with both affective balance, and peer-rated likability. In addition, emotion knowledge and positive responsiveness to peers' emotions were positively associated. Despite these associations, the lack of

TABLE 1. Zero-order Correlations Between Predictor and Criterion Variables

Child Criterion Variable	Sibling Predictor Variables		
	Prosocial Responding	Positive Responsiveness to Child's Emotions	Provocative Responding
Emotion knowledge	−.22+	.27*	.06
Affective balance	−.22+	−.15	−.08
Prosocial responding to peers	−.04	.28*	.02
Positive responsiveness to peers' emotions	−.19	.37**	−.14
Provocative responding to peers	−.32*	.30*	−.15
Peer-rated sociometric likeability	.23+	−.17	.07
Teacher-rated social competence	.39**	.19	.02

+ $p < .10$, * $p < .05$, ** $p < .01$.

TABLE 2. Zero-order Correlations Among Criterion Variables

	1	2	3	4	5	6	7
1 Emotion knowledge	...						
2 Affective balance	−.15	...					
3 Prosocial responses to peers	−.07	.00	...				
4 Positive responsiveness to peers' emotions	.30*	.12	.15	...			
5 Provocative responses to peers	.03	−.36**	−.17	.02	...		
6 Peer-rated sociometric likeability	.00	.32*	−.02	−.15	−.40**	...	
7 Teacher-rated social competence	.06	−.03	.14	−.13	−.10	−.09	...

* $p < .05$, ** $p < .01$.

compelling theoretical support persuaded us to keep them separate in the overall analyses.

Initial multiple regression analyses and moderation. Siblings' positive responsiveness did approach significant in predicting emotion knowledge (see Table 3). This finding was moderated by age, with significant prediction only for younger children (see Table 4).

Regarding social competence, children's positive responsiveness to peers' emotions was predicted by the same behavior of siblings. This finding was moderated by age interval, with significant prediction only for siblings closer in age than 30 months. This apparent modeling of contingent reactions was also moderated by sex, with boys more likely than girls to show this pattern, and by age, with younger children more likely than older children to show the pattern. Children's positive responsiveness to peers' emotions also was predicted by less sibling provocative responding for siblings close in age.

Children's provocative responding to peers' emotions was predicted by age, with older children more often showing this reaction, and modestly by siblings' positive responsiveness. Siblings' less provocative responding and less prosocial responding also predicted this aspect of social competence for boys only. Children's prosocial responding to peers' emotions was predicted by the same behavior in siblings. Moreover, the contribution of sibling negative responsiveness to prosocial responding to peers' emotions was also moderated by sex and age of child. For boys and older children, less sibling negative responsiveness predicted prosocial responding; no such prediction held for girls and younger children.

TABLE 3. Prediction of Emotional and Social Competence

Step	Predictor	B	R^2_{ch}
	Criterion: Emotion Knowledge Aggregate		
1	Sibling positive responsiveness	.261+	.068+
	Sibling provocative responding	.120	
	Sibling prosocial responding	−.120	
	Criterion: Prosocial responses to peers' emotions		
1	Sibling positive responsiveness	.280*	.077+
	Sibling provocative responding	.083	
	Sibling prosocial responding	−.025	
	Criterion: Positive responsiveness to peers' emotions		
1	Sibling positive responsiveness	.37**	.133*
	Sibling provocative responding	−.064	
	Sibling prosocial responding	−.161	
	Criterion: Provocative responses to peers' emotions		
1	Age of child	.450**	.203**
2	Sibling positive responsiveness	.242+	.260**
	Sibling provocative responding	−.090	
	Sibling prosocial responding	−.120	
	Criterion: Peer-rated sociometric likeability		
1	Age interval	.273+	.075+
2	Sibling positive responsiveness	−.271+	.140+
	Sibling provocative responding	.053	
	Sibling prosocial responding	.156	
	Criterion: Teacher-rated social competence		
1	Sex of child	.333*	.111*
2	Sibling positive responsiveness	.212	.223**
	Sibling provocative responding	.021	
	Sibling prosocial responding	.338*	

+ $p < .10$, * $p < .05$, ** $p < .01$.

Greater difference in siblings' ages, as well as lack of sibling positive responsiveness, each modestly predicted peer-rated likability. As for moderation, provocative responding predicted likability for boys, and when siblings were close in age. For siblings close in age, lower levels of sibling positive responsiveness also predicted peer-rated likability.

Child sex (with girls more likely to be rated higher) and sibling prosocial responding each predicted teacher-rated social competence. Sibling prosocial responding predicted teacher-rated social competence only when siblings were close in age.

TABLE 4. Moderation by Sex of Child, Sex of Sibling, Age of Child, Age of Sibling, and Age Interval

Criterion	Predictor	Moderator	$\beta_{interaction}$	$R^2_{ch\ interaction}$	Simple Effects' βs	
Emotion Knowledge	Sibling Positive Responsiveness	Age of Child	-3.400+	-.081	Older = .179	Younger = .547***
Positive Responsiveness	Sibling Positive Responsiveness	Sex of Sibling	-1.356*	.115	Sisters = .223	Brothers = .571*
	Sibling Positive Responsiveness	Age of Child	.543*	.099	Older = .173	Younger = .477*
	Sibling Negative Responsiveness	Age Interval	-.653*	.120	Larger = .048	Smaller = .495**
	Sibling Negative Responsiveness	Age Interval	1.061*	.156	Larger = .323	Smaller = .426*
Prosocial Responses	Sibling Negative Responsiveness	Sex of Child	1.104*	.114	Girls = .249	Boys = -.492*
	Sibling Negative Responsiveness	Age of Child	-4.715**	.185	Older = -.572**	Younger = -.059
Provocative Responses	Sibling Prosocial Responsiveness	Sex of Child	1.216*	.122	Girls = .008	Boys = -.657***
	Sibling Negative Responsiveness	Sex of Child	1.243*	.062	Girls = .161	Boys = -.378+
Peer-Rated Likeability	Sibling Positive Responsiveness	Age Interval	.727*	.064	Larger = .008	Smaller = .578**
	Sibling Negative Responsiveness	Sex of Child	-1.056*	.104	Girls = -.262	Boys = .372+
	Sibling Negative Responsiveness	Age Interval	.442*	.069	Larger = .130	Smaller = .442*
Teacher-Rated Social Competence	Sibling Prosocial Responsiveness	Age Interval	.485*	.064	Larger = .485*	Smaller = .238

+ p < .10, * p < .05, ** p < .01, *** p < .001

DISCUSSION

According to our contingency theory, young children can acquire emotional and social competence from the way others react to their emotions. For example, patterns of parental reactions to emotions have been shown to account for significant variance in preschoolers' emotion and social competence (Denham et al., 1997). However, the impact of others significant in the preschooler's life has been largely ignored. In an attempt to help fill this gap, the association between older siblings' reactions to preschoolers' emotions were examined in the present study. Using a multiple regression strategy, the predictive power of sibling reactions and moderating demographic variables on preschooler emotional and social competence was evaluated. Certain sibling reactions, as follows, were shown to play important roles in children's developing social and emotion competence. Moreover, the contributions of such sibling reactions were often moderated by age, sex, and age interval.

Siblings' Positive Emotional Responsiveness

Our findings suggest that the degree of sibling positive responsiveness may be a contributor to the social and emotional competence of preschoolers. Sibling positive responsiveness was in some way related to six of the eight variables of emotional and social competence examined in the present study. A sibling's act of being positively responsive, not ignoring or disregarding any of the emotions of the child, is associated with the child's emotional and social growth.

Sibling positive responsiveness was positively related to emotion knowledge. These positive responses from siblings during emotional interchanges may assist preschoolers in understanding emotions via decreased self-focus (Denham, 1986). A similar link has been found between parental reactions and children's emotion knowledge (Denham et al., 1997). In the preliminary correlations, sibling prosocial responding also was associated at a borderline level with the emotion knowledge aggregate. This trend lends further credence to the supposition that positive responses from siblings enhance preschoolers' abilities to focus on the emotional needs of others.

The association between sibling positive responsiveness and preschoolers' emotion knowledge was moderated by age. By 40 months, children are generally able to label emotional expressions (Denham et al., 1994) and are beginning to master the causes of emotions. Emotion knowledge may be most influenced by many factors, including sibling socialization, earlier in preschool period. This age trend also has been found in parental socialization of emotion knowledge (Denham et al., 1997).

The overall association between sibling responsiveness and child positive responding in the preschool classroom may exist for several reasons. The older sibling may be serving as a model, as youngsters are often quite entranced by the behavior of their older brother or sister, and children have been shown to learn much simply from watching others in their dealings with emotions (Denham & Grout, 1993). Therefore, children's positive responsiveness in the classroom may be simply a factor of direct behavioral imitation and affective contagion: The child sees what the sibling does and does it, especially when the older sibling is positive towards the child (Dunn & Kendrick, 1982).

Also, young children's imitation of older siblings' positively responsive actions may become intrinsically motivating–these actions "feel good" (Bryant & Crockenberg, 1980). Then, in a process of "identification" (Bank & Kahn, 1975) with the older sibling, the young child may actually choose to adopt that particular behavior of the sibling and incorporate it into his or her repertoire of behaviors. Therefore, instead of simply mimicking, the child is actively choosing the behavior.

The association between child responsiveness and sibling positive responsiveness was moderated by three variables: age of child, age interval between the siblings, and the gender of the older sibling. For children who were less than 45 months old, had siblings who were less than 30 months older, and/or whose older siblings were boys, older sibling positive responsiveness was predictive of child positive responsiveness in the classroom. The younger the child, the greater are imitation and identification (Abramovitch et al., 1979). As a final point, there are direction of effect issues here: it may be that siblings are more positively responsive to children who are more positive themselves.

Although age interval and sex have been found to have no impact on imitation of other behaviors (Abramovitch et al., 1979), in this study positive responsiveness may have had an impact on boys because of its rarity and salience (see also Abramovitch et al., 1982). The same argument could possibly be made for age interval: Because siblings closer in age tend to have a more negative relationship than siblings further apart (Buhrmester & Furman, 1990), when the younger older sibling is positively responsive, it may be more salient and thus have more of an impact.

Finally, both child age and siblings' positive responsiveness were positively associated with preschoolers' provocative responding to peer emotions. At first glance these findings were surprising. First, most research reports that older preschoolers tend to be generally more positive than younger ones (Abramovitch et al., 1979). Second, we usually consider provocative responding to be a detriment rather than strength. But, could provocative responding to peers be a sign of older preschoolers' using emotions to meet their needs and desires? Children whose siblings are positively responsive may be more emotionally able to understand and manipulate others' emotion. For example, Ben smiles as he plays happily with a puzzle. Sarah wants to play with the puzzle. Sarah knows that if she cries, the teacher may come and make Ben share the puzzle with her, thereby accomplishing her goal. In our coding system we would have captured Sarah's behavior as provocative responding. Therefore, it is possible that responsiveness by the sibling permits the child to learn a wide variety of emotional responses, including provocative ones, which may be used to advantage in certain situations; in this case, Sarah got what she wanted, but in such a way that the teacher did not notice her provocativeness. Considering bi-directional influences, it could also be that older siblings treat their more difficult younger siblings with "kid gloves," a point we will return to later. Further microanalytic research is needed to examine thoroughly these possible connections.

The negative relation between sibling responsiveness and likability with peers is the most surprising finding here. The other associations of child emotional and social competence with sibling positive responsiveness would lead one to believe that the child whose sibling is more responsive will be more skilled socially and emotionally, including being viewed more favorably by peers. How can this contrary finding be explained?

First, age interval was correlated significantly with older sibling positive responsiveness: Older siblings tended to be more positively responsive, a finding supported in recent literature (e.g., Buhrmester & Furman, 1990). Second, greater sibling positive responsiveness was associated with lower ratings of likability particularly when the age interval between the siblings was small (less than 30 months). When the age interval is smaller, there is usually a preponderance of conflict, which may serve to educate and render the child more effective in social interactions (Dunn & Munn, 1987). But, when the older sibling closer in age to the child is more accommodating and responsive, important social learning may be prevented because the child is not forced to take others' feelings into consideration. Therefore, positive responsiveness in siblings closer together in age may fail to teach the child important social rules, with negative consequences for the preschoolers' likability. Finally, if sibling positive responsiveness is associated with increased provocative responding with peers as has been demonstrated in the present study, then it follows that sibling responsiveness could be negatively related to peer-rated likability.

Again, as conjectured above, it may be that older siblings show greater levels of positive responsiveness to younger siblings who are just as difficult to like at home as in preschool, in an effort to appease them and make interaction run more smoothly. Similarly, as surmised above, these not-so-likable behaviors on the younger sibling's part may prompt an older sibling to make things better, whereas peers would not be as forgiving and teachers might be none the wiser (note that sociometric likability and teacher-rated social competence are not correlated in this study).

Siblings' Prosocial Responding to Preschoolers' Emotions

Although sibling prosocial responding correlated with five criterion variables in the zero-order analyses, these hints of association did not carry over into the findings for overall regression analyses. For children with siblings more than 30 months older, however, sibling prosocial responding was positively related to teacher ratings of social competence. When children's own emotional experience is overly negative, they may be so wrapped up in their own negative experiences that they are less able to understand the situation and respond appropriately with peers (Denham et al., 1994; Smiley & Huttenlocher, 1989). Having an older sibling who helps them with their negative emotions, they are essentially relieved of their negative feelings, and freer to learn about and focus on the emotions of others. This ability may influence how the teacher perceives the child's social competence.

What is the moderating effect of age interval here? When older siblings behave normatively (i.e., behave more prosocially the greater the age interval between siblings, but quarrel when the lower the age interval; Buhrmester & Furman, 1990), then children are more likely to be rated as more socially competent or likable. However, if the older sibling responds contrary to their developmentally appropriate role, there may be negative consequences for the child's social competence.

Siblings' Provocative Responding to Preschoolers' Emotions

Provocative responding by the older sibling was not significantly related to any emotional or social competence variable in either zero-order correlations or regression analyses. As was the case with prosocial responding, the opportunity for provocative responding may have been limited because of the preponderance of positive emotion displayed by the younger child during the observed sibling interaction. Some interesting moderating effects did, however, emerge.

Provocative responding by the sibling was, however, negatively related to children's positive responsiveness in the classroom when siblings were closer together in age. This finding fits within Tomkins' theory (1991), in which punitive reactions to emotions serve to increase emotional negativity in the child, leading to increased self-preoccupation and fewer opportunities for social-emotional learning.

In contrast, for dyads with younger siblings, sibling provocativeness was positively related to children's likability. Dunn (e.g., 1983) has repeatedly argued that at least some sibling conflict is important–it teaches children how to negotiate, forces them to think about the views of others, and may actually demonstrate a level of sophistication. The current findings support Dunn's contention, and again hint at the importance of considering the developmental appropriateness of each sibling's behavior.

For boys, provocative responding by the sibling approached a negative relation with provocative responding to peers. Although few studies have found a significant relation between behavior with siblings and behavior with peers (e.g., Berndt & Bulleit, 1985), it may be that sibling conflict promotes the development of social and emotional skills. Boys who are responded to provocatively may learn about the points of view of others, and increased social understanding may promote less negative behavior. Although this interpretation slightly contradicts our ideas that provocativeness with peers may reflect social acuity, it is likely that there are two types of provocative responding to peers: (1) provocative responding due to ignorance and/or irritable temperament, or (2) provocativeness due to skill at manipulation or dominance. At this point we have no way to code the difference between the two.

Taken together, our findings on sibling provocative responding connote a possibly valuable avenue of influence. For boys, and when the age interval between siblings is small, provocative responding by the sibling can have positive consequences.

No relation was found between any of the predictor or demographic variables and children's affective balance in the classroom. It is possible that these specific types of sibling reactions do not influence a child's degree of happiness in the classroom. However, that is not to say that siblings do not influence each other's emotionality in other ways. Affective balance was, however, positively related with peer-rated likability and negatively with provocative responding.

Limitations and Directions for Future Research

The most important limitation is the small number of participants. Although approximately 40 participants was considered sufficient for power to detect the direct regression analyses, the inclusion of moderation analyses due to the apparent complexity of relations between sibling reactions and social/emotional competence warranted more elaborate and numerous analyses. A larger study with many more participants would better delineate these complex pathways. Importantly, greater statistical power also would enable investigators to examine an avenue of influence that we were not able to with our small sample: the contribution of gender constellation on the outcomes studied here, along with three-way moderations of sibling reactions to emotions, sex of child, and sex of sibling (McHale, Updegraff, Jackson-Newsom, Tuck, & Crouter, 2000). Along with a large participant sample, a prospective, longitudinal project would verify the pathways discussed here even more conclusively.

Moreover, the participant sample in this study was quite homogeneous. The relative lack of variability in levels of income, parental education, and race limits the generalizability of the present findings, as well as preventing understanding of whether and how socioeconomic status and race play a role in siblings' influence on children's social and emotional development.

A mere 60 minutes of observation during sibling free play also may have been insufficient to index the sibling relationship. However, Dunn and Kendrick (1982) compared data obtained from two one-hour observations made one week apart, and found behavior to be generally stable over time. For most children these were relatively placid and happy intervals, as well. In retrospect, it may be advisable in future research to create an ethical, believable conflict situation in which the child would display more negative emotion in order to get a better sampling of siblings' reactions. Another methodological refinement possible with a larger sample of participants would be disaggregating sibling predictors. With a larger sample, Denham and colleagues (1997) found individual parental reactions, not the aggregates used here, to powerfully predict emotional and social competence.

The focus of the present study was purposely narrow, but in future research it may be useful to include other important predictors of children's social and emotional competence. First, sibling modeling of emotions and possible sibling coaching should be studied. Second, the relationship between siblings may be moderated by a multitude of other factors (Brody, Stoneman, & McCoy, 1994; Munn & Dunn, 1989; Stocker, Dunn, & Plomin, 1989).

For example, when temperaments of child and sibling do not fit, or when older siblings are quite irritable, young children may avoid their siblings and not learn from them about social and emotional issues. As well, the degree to which the child shows temperamental cues of distress may influence sibling prosocial behavior, especially for siblings who are best able to take the perspective of others (Garner, Jones, & Palmer, 1994). Thus, temperament may be a moderating influence requiring further study.

The quality of the attachment relationship between children and their mothers, as well as between siblings, has a significant impact on siblings' behavior (Stewart, 1983; Teti & Ablard, 1989). In particular, attachment may have an impact upon how a given sibling reaction is perceived by the child. For example, a child who is securely attached to his or her older sibling, or to parents, may react to provocative interactions very differently from a child who is not securely attached. Therefore, future research should examine how attachment may moderate the influence of sibling reactions upon children's social and emotional competence.

In summary, it is important to acknowledge that older siblings' reactions play a role in development of emotional and social competence in preschoolers. The degree of older sibling positive responsiveness appears to be especially important. Further, the time between the ages of 3 and 4 years is a ripe one for the development of social and emotional skills, and the preschool sibling relationship lends itself to centrality. But these influences are quite complex—what might be true for children with older brothers, might not be true for children with older sisters; what might be true for siblings close in age might not be true for those more separated in age. As usual, the closer we get to uncovering intricacies of human behavior and relationships, the more intricate they turn out to be.

REFERENCES

Abramovitch, R., Corter, C., & Lando, B. (1979). Sibling interaction in the home. *Child Development, 50*, 997-1003.

Abramovitch, R., Corter, C., Pepler, D., & Stanhope, I. (1986). Sibling and peer interaction: A final follow-up and a comparison. *Child Development, 57*, 217-229.

Abramovitch, R., Pepler, D., & Corter, C. (1982). Patterns of sibling interaction among preschool-aged children. In M. Lamb & B. Sutton-Smith (Eds.), *Sibling relationships: Their nature and significance across the lifespan* (pp. 61-86). Hillsdale, NJ: Erlbaum.

Asher, S., Singleton, L., Tinsley, B., & Hymel, S. (1979). A reliable sociometric measure for preschool children. *Developmental Psychology, 15*, 443-444.

Bank, S. & Kahn, M. (1975). Sisterhood-brotherhood is powerful: Sibling sub-systems and family therapy. *Family Process, 14*, 311-337.

Baron, R. & Kenny, D. (1986). The moderator-mediator variable distinction in social psychological research: Conceptual, strategic, and statistical consideration. *Journal of Personality and Social Psychology, 51*, 1173-1182.

Baskett, L. & Johnson, S. (1982). The young child's interactions with parents versus siblings: A behavioral analysis. *Child Development, 53*, 643-659.

Bell-Dolan, D. & Wessler, A. (1994). Ethical administration of sociometric measures: Procedures in use and suggestions for improvement. *Professional Psychology: Research and Practice, 25*.

Berndt, T. & Bulleit, T. (1985). Effects of sibling relationships on preschoolers' behavior at home and at school. *Developmental Psychology, 21*, 761-767.

Brody, G. & Stoneman, Z. (1987). Sibling conflict: Siblings themselves, the parent-sibling relationship, and the broader family system. *Journal of Children in Contemporary Society, 19*, 39-53.

Brody, G., Stoneman, Z., & Burke, M. (1987). Child temperaments, maternal differential behavior, and sibling relationships. *Developmental Psychology, 23*, 354-362.

Brody, G., Stoneman, Z., MacKinnon C., & MacKinnon, R. (1985). Role relationships and behavior among preschool-aged sibling pairs. *Developmental Psychology, 21*, 124-129.

Brody, G., Stoneman, Z., & McCoy, J. (1994). Forecasting sibling relationship in early adolescence for child temperaments and family processes in middle childhood. *Child Development, 65*, 771-884.

Brown, J. & Dunn, J. (1991). "You can cry, mum": The social and developmental implications of talk about internal states. *British Journal of Developmental Psychology, 9*, 237-256.

Brown, J. & Dunn, J. (1992). Talk with your mother or your sibling? Developmental changes in early family conversations about feelings. *Child Development, 63*, 336-349.

Bryant, B. (1989). The child's perspective of sibling caretaking and its relevance to understanding social-emotional functioning and development. In P. G. Zukow (Ed.), *Sibling interaction across cultures* (pp. 143-164). Springer-Verlag: New York.

Bryant, B., & Crockenberg, S. (1980). Correlations and dimensions of prosocial behavior: A study of female siblings and their mothers. *Child Development, 51,* 529-544.

Buhrmester, D. (1992). The developmental courses of sibling and peer relationships. In F. Boer & J. Dunn (Eds.), *Children's sibling relationships* (pp. 19-40). Hillsdale, New Jersey: Lawrence Erlbaum Associates.

Buhrmester, D., & Furman, W. (1990). Perceptions of sibling relationships during middle childhood and adolescence. *Child Development, 61,* 1387-1398.

Cicirelli, V. (1972). The effects of the sibling relationship concept learning of young children taught by child teachers. *Child Development, 43,* 282-287.

Cicirelli, V. (1975). Effects of mother and older sibling on the problem-solving behavior of the younger child. *Developmental Psychology, 11,* 749-756.

Denham, S. (1986). Social cognition, social behavior, and emotion in preschoolers: Contextual validation. *Child Development, 57,* 194-201.

Denham, S. (1993). Maternal emotional responsiveness and toddlers' social-emotional competence. *Journal of Child Psychology and Psychiatry, 34,* 715-728.

Denham, S., Cook, M., & Zoller, D. (1992). "Baby looks very sad": Implications of conversations about feelings between mother and preschooler. *British Journal of Developmental Psychology, 10,* 301-315.

Denham, S. & Couchoud, E. (1990a). Young preschoolers' ability to identify emotions in equivocal situations. *Child Study Journal, 20,* 153-169.

Denham, S. & Couchoud, E. (1990b). Young preschoolers' understanding of emotions. *Child Study Journal, 20,* 171-192.

Denham, S. & Grout, L. (1993). Socialization of emotion: Pathway to preschoolers' emotional and social competence. *Journal of Nonverbal Behavior, 17,* 205-227.

Denham, S., McKinley, M., Couchoud, E., & Holt, R. (1990). Emotional and behavioral predictors of preschool peer ratings. *Child Development, 61,* 1145-1152.

Denham, S. A., Mitchell-Copeland, J., Strandberg, K., Auerbach, S., & Blair, K. (1997). Parental contributions to preschoolers' emotional competence: Direct and indirect effects. *Motivation & Emotion, 21,* 65-86.

Denham, S. A., Zoller, D., & Couchoud, E. A. (1994). Socialization of preschoolers' understanding of emotion. *Developmental Psychology, 30,* 928-936.

Dunn, J. (1983). Sibling relationships in early childhood. *Child Development, 54,* 787-811.

Dunn, J. (1988). Connections between relationships: Implications of research on mothers and siblings. In R.A. Hinde & J. Stevenson-Hinde (Eds.), *Relationships within families* (pp. 168-180). Oxford: Clarendon.

Dunn, J. (1992). Sisters and brothers: Current issues in developmental research. In F. Boer & J. Dunn (Eds.), *Children's sibling relationships* (pp. 1-17). Hillsdale, New Jersey: Lawrence Erlbaum Associates.

Dunn, J., Brown, J., & Beardsall, L. (1991). Family talk about feeling states and children's later understanding of others' emotions. *Developmental Psychology, 27,* 448-455.

Dunn, J., Brown, J., Slomkowski, C., Tesla, C., & Youngblade, L. (1991). Young children's understanding of other people's feelings and beliefs: Individual difference and their antecedents. *Child Development, 62,* 1352-1366.

Dunn, J., Creps, C., & Brown, J. (1996). Children's family relationships between two and five: Developmental changes and individual differences. *Social Development*, *5*, 230-250.

Dunn, J. & Dale, N. (1984). "I a daddy": 2 year-olds' collaboration in joint pretend with sibling and mother. In I Bretherton (Ed.), *Symbolic Play: The development of social understanding* (pp. 131-158). San Diego, CA: Academic Press.

Dunn, J., & Herrera, C. (1997). Conflict resolution with friends, siblings, and mothers: A developmental perspective. *Aggressive Behavior*, *23*, 343-357.

Dunn, J. & Kendrick, C. (1982). *Siblings: Love, envy, and understanding*. Cambridge, Mass.: Harvard University Press.

Dunn, J. & McGuire, S. (1992). Sibling and peer relationships in childhood. *Journal of Child Psychology and Psychiatry*, *33*, 67-105.

Dunn, J. & Munn, P. (1985). Becoming a family member: Family conflict and the development of social understanding in the second year. *Child Development*, *56*, 480-492.

Dunn, J. & Munn, P. (1986a). Siblings and the development of prosocial behavior. *International Journal of Behavioral Development*, *9*, 265-284.

Dunn, J. & Munn, P. (1986b). Sibling quarrels and maternal intervention: Individual differences in understanding and aggression. *Journal of Child Psychology and Psychiatry*, *27*, 583-595.

Dunn, J. & Munn, P. (1987). Developmental justification in disputes with mother and sibling. *Developmental Psychology*, *23*, 791-798.

Dunn, J. & Plomin, R. (1991). Why are siblings so different? The significance of differences in sibling experiences within the family. *Family Process*, *30*, 271-283.

Dunn, J., Slomkowski, C., Donelan, N., & Herrera, C. (1995). Conflict, understanding, and relationships: Developments and differences in the preschool years. *Early Education and Development*, *6*, 303-316.

Eisenberg, N., Fabes, R., Miller, P., Shell, R., Shea, C., & May-Plumlee, T. (1990). Preschoolers' vicarious emotional responding and situational and dispositional prosocial behavior. *Merrill-Palmer Quarterly*, *36*, 507-529.

Eisenberg, N., McCreath, H., & Ahn, R. (1988). Vicarious emotional responsiveness and prosocial behavior. *Personality and Social Psychology*, *14*, 298-311.

Garner, P. W., Jones, D. C., & Palmer, D. J. (1994). Social cognitive correlates of preschool children's sibling caregiving behavior. *Developmental Psychology*, *30*, 905-911.

Kopp, C. (1989). Regulation of distress and negative emotions: A developmental review. *Developmental Psychology*, *25*, 343-354.

LaFreniere, P., & Dumas, J. E. (1996). Social competence and behavior evaluation in children ages 3 to 6 years: The short form. *Psychological Assessment*, *8*, 369-377.

Lamb, M. (1982). Sibling relationships across the lifespan: An overview and introduction. In M. Lamb & B. Sutton-Smith (Eds.), *Sibling relationships: Their nature and significance across the lifespan* (pp. 1-11). Hillsdale, NJ: Erlbaum.

Malatesta, C. & Haviland, J. (1982). Learning display rules: The socialization of emotion expression in infancy. *Child Development*, *53*, 991-1003.

McHale, S. M., Updegraff, K. A., Jackson-Newsom, J., Tucker, C. J., & Crouter, A. C. (2000). When does parents' differential treatment have negative implications for siblings? *Social Development*, *9*, 149-172.

Munn, P., & Dunn, J. (1989). Temperament and the developing relationship between siblings. *International Journal of Behavioral Development, 12*, 433-451.

Patterson, G. (1984). Siblings: Fellow travelers in coercive family processes. *Advances in the Study of Aggression, 1*, 173-215.

Patterson, G. (1986). The contribution of siblings to training for fighting: A microsocial analysis. In D. Olweus, J. Block, & M. Radke-Yarrow (Eds.). *Development of antisocial and prosocial behavior: Research, theories and issues* (pp. 235-261). New York: Academic Press.

Pepler, D., Corter, C., & Abramovitch, R. (1982). Social relations among children: Siblings and peers. In K. Rubin & H. Ross (Eds.), *Peer relationships and social skills in childhood* (pp. 211-227). New York: Springer-Verlag.

Piaget, J. (1965). *The moral judgment of the child*. New York: Free Press.

Putallaz, M. (1987). Maternal behavior and children's sociometric status. *Child Development, 54*, 1417-1426.

Roberts, W. (1993). *Programs for the field collection and analysis of observational data: A manual*. Unpublished, Cariboo College, Canada.

Scarr, S. & Grajek, S. (1982). Similarities and differences among siblings. In M. Lamb & B. Sutton-Smith (Eds.), *Sibling relationships: Their nature and significance across the lifespan* (pp. 357-381). Hillsdale, NJ: Erlbaum.

Smiley, P., & Huttenlocher, J. (1989). Young children's acquisition of emotional concepts. In C. Saarni & P. L. Harris (Eds.), *Children's Understanding of Emotions* (pp. 27-49). Cambridge: Cambridge University Press.

Stewart, R. (1983). Sibling attachment relationships: Child input interaction in the Strange Situation. *Developmental Psychology, 19*, 192-199.

Stillwell, R., & Dunn, J. (1985). Continuities in sibling relationships patterns of aggression and friendliness. *Journal of Child Psychology and Psychiatry, 26*, 627-637.

Stocker, C. & Dunn, J. (1990). Sibling relationships in childhood: Links with friendships and peer relationships. *British Journal of Developmental Psychology, 8*, 227-244.

Stocker, C., Dunn, J., & Plomin, R. (1989). Sibling relationships: Links with child temperament, maternal behavior, and family structure. *Child Development, 60*, 715-727.

Sullivan, H. (1953). *The interpersonal theory of psychiatry*. New York: Norton.

Sutton-Smith, B. & Rosenberg, B. (1970). *The sibling*. New York: Holt, Rinehart, & Winston.

Teti, D., & Ablard, K. (1989). Security of attachment and infant-sibling relationships: A laboratory study. *Child Development, 60*, 1519-1528.

Tomkins, S. (1991). *Affect, imagery, & consciousness, Vol. III. The negative affects: Anger and fear*. NY: Springer-Verlag.

Wahl, G., Johnson, S., Johansson, S., & Martin, S. (1974). An operant analysis of child-family interaction. *Behavior Therapy, 5*, 64-78.

Watson-Gegeo, K. & Gegeo, D. (1989). The role of sibling interaction is child socialization. In P. G. Zukow (Ed.), *Sibling interaction across cultures* (pp. 54-76). Springer-Verlag: New York.

Children's Understanding of Emotion Communication in Families

Carolyn Saarni
Maureen Buckley

SUMMARY. There is a paucity of research on children's awareness of how emotion communication varies within relationships. Indeed, we operate on the assumption that a very significant function of emotion is to regulate interpersonal interaction. In this essay we discuss how children come to understand such phenomena as: (a) emotional-expressive behavior can have powerful interpersonal consequences; (b) relationship dimensions such as degree of power and closeness interact with intensity of emotion in how emotion is communicated; and (c) maintenance of relationship quality (e.g., equilibrium, attenuation, or deepening) requires different strategies of emotion communication. Among the constructs that we address are several that are useful for understanding the dynamics of interpersonal communication; they have also proven their utility over a considerable period of time. However, these constructs derive from social psychology and family systems; they have not been systematically investigated from a developmental perspective. *[Article copies available for a fee from The Haworth Document Delivery Service: 1-800-HAWORTH. E-mail address: <docdelivery@haworthpress.com> Website: <http://www.HaworthPress.com> © 2002 by The Haworth Press, Inc. All rights reserved.]*

Carolyn Saarni and Maureen Buckley are affiliated with Sonoma State University, California.

Address correspondence to: C. Saarni, Department of Counseling, Sonoma State University, Rohnert Park, CA 94928 (E-mail: saarni@sonoma.edu).

[Haworth co-indexing entry note]: "Children's Understanding of Emotion Communication in Families." Saarni, Carolyn, and Maureen Buckley. Co-published simultaneously in *Marriage & Family Review* (The Haworth Press, Inc.) Vol. 34, No. 3/4, 2002, pp. 213-242; and: *Emotions and the Family* (ed: Richard A. Fabes) The Haworth Press, Inc., 2002, pp. 213-242. Single or multiple copies of this article are available for a fee from The Haworth Document Delivery Service [1-800-HAWORTH, 9:00 a.m. - 5:00 p.m. (EST). E-mail address: docdelivery@haworthpress.com].

KEYWORDS. Emotion communication, family relationships, children's emotionality

A guiding assumption that will be evident in our theoretical views is that emotion communication occurs within a social system, which means that children's understanding of emotion communication is embedded in a system of interpersonal relationships and social transactions. We also see emotion communication as multi-channel: both verbal and nonverbal behaviors are vehicles for communicating emotion. Furthermore, our perspective on emotional phenomena borrows from both functional and social constructivist theoretical platforms (e.g., Campos, Mumme, Kermoian, & Campos, 1994; Lerner, 1998; Saarni, 1999). More specifically, we shall apply to our analysis of children's understanding of emotion communication within families *metacommunication* (Satir, 1967), *report and command* (Watzlawick, Beavin, & Jackson, 1967), and *interpersonal negotiation and intersubjectivity* (e.g., Selman, Beardslee, Schultz, Krupa, & Podorefsky, 1986). We shall also address the McMaster model of family functioning (Epstein, Bishop, & Baldwin, 1981), which seems especially relevant to the transmission of emotional patterns within families.

EMOTION AS A REGULATOR OF INTERPERSONAL RELATIONSHIPS

Consequences of Emotional-Expressive Behavior

Perhaps among the most significant ways that we communicate with others is through our emotional-expressive behavior; for example, a smile accompanied by eye contact will typically be interpreted quite differently than a smile with gaze averted. Yet this difference in attributed meaning will be further qualified by the culture of origin of the 'sender' as well as by the 'receiver.' Culturally determined meanings, family-based beliefs, and idiosyncratic assumptions about what some instance of emotional-expressive behavior might imply fall under the larger rubric of *metacommunication*, namely, a message about a message. When we are interacting with another, our verbal exchanges have a lexical content, but it is our nonverbal behavior that carries our metacommunicative intentions. Parallel to metacommunication is *metaperception* (Patterson, 1999), which refers to our perception of how we think another is perceiving us. Stated differently, when we are closely monitoring and managing the impression we are making on another, we pay close attention to how the target might be judging us. It is these expressive, often emotionally loaded nonverbal behaviors that regulate the back and forth of interpersonal negotiations, almost in a dove-tailing fashion (see, for example, Patterson's [1999] comments on parallel process in nonverbal communication exchanges).

Reciprocity of expressive behavior and compensation for anticipated (especially negative) responses characterize the dynamics of interpersonal interaction (Ickes, Patterson, Rajecki, & Tanford, 1982). We argue that it is metacommunication and metaperception that carry the weight of interpersonal consequences in emotional-expressive behavior, and families constitute the first and perhaps primary forum for these exchanges (see also Gottman, Katz, & Hooven, 1997; also this volume). Research on the socialization of emotion also suggests that parents are likely to respond to their children's emotional behavior in light of their perceptions of their children's emotional reactivity (e.g., Fabes, Eisenberg, Karbon, Bernzweig, Speer, & Carlo, 1994), and, in turn, children respond to their parents' emotional-expressive behavior and responsiveness (e.g., Roberts & Strayer, 1987).

Verbal behavior is obviously a significant component of children's understanding of emotion communication, and we will later address the significance of early conversations and the power of narratives for promoting children's emotion communication understanding. We concur with Bloom (1998) that language acquisition has as its most significant function the task of communicating beliefs, desires, feelings, and intentions. Language (or any symbolic system such as signing or artistic expression) allows for the expression of what would otherwise be inaccessible, namely, one's representations of meaning. When we share our meanings with others, we also transform them, for interpersonal exchanges of meaning invariably have recursive influence on our states of mind (i.e., another's response to one's own expression of a belief, desire, and so forth redounds to one's attribution of meaning). When verbal and nonverbal expressions of emotion are seen as working together as an efficient system for the communication of emotion, then we can also see how one expression component, for example, nonverbal expressive behavior, can be used to qualify or add emphasis or nuance to the other component, namely, linguistic expression–and vice versa (Mehrabian, 1972).

Early theorizing by the family therapist Virginia Satir (1967) reflected her appreciation of this systemic functioning of language and emotional-expressive behavior. She was interested in people's feelings about themselves and their interactants, and she contended that these feelings profoundly affected the dynamics of the resulting interaction. She maintained that metacommunicative behavior conveyed three messages: (a) the person's attitude toward the verbal explicit message (e.g., "I intend this message to be a caring one."); (b) the person's emotionally nuanced attitude toward her- or himself (e.g., "I am a good parent."); and very importantly, (c) the person's emotion-laden attitudes and intentions toward the interactant (e.g., "I care about you and want to protect you."). Illustrative of the power of Satir's theorizing was an investigation undertaken by Noller, Feeney, Peterson, and Sheehan (1995) with adolescent twins and their parents (see also Feeney, Noller, Sheehan, & Peterson, 1999). Their results showed that fathers were particularly influential, and those fathers who expressed 'unpleasant vocalics' (rejecting, anxious, controlling tone of voice), negatively toned facial expressive behavior (glaring, rolling eyes), and sarcastic, blaming, disapproving verbal behavior while engaged in conflict with their adolescent twins had, not surprisingly, problematic relationships with their children. But what is particularly noteworthy in this research is that the relationship *between* the siblings was also more hostile than those pairs of twins whose fathers engaged in supportive and pleasant expressive exchanges with them. Although Feeney et al. (1999) did not use Satir's metacommunication ideas, it is our speculation that what may have occurred in these hostile, non-supportive families is that the adolescent pairs of twins developed an understanding of the metacommunicative rules of emotion-laden communications within their families as characterized by hostile intentions, one-upmanship, and disapproval toward family members.

A complementary study on adolescents and parents' emotion communication patterns was carried out by Cook, Kenny, and Goldstein (1991) with families seeking counseling. They examined reciprocal communication patterns in these families in order to shed light on how dysfunctional interaction comes about. What they determined was that adolescents, and to some extent fathers, bore much of the responsibility for both initiating and reciprocating the interpersonal expression of emotional negativity. Mothers were more apt to reciprocate their adolescents' negativity. But the major outcome was the statistically robust feedback loop or vicious cycle that these families *as a whole* were caught in: Adolescents communicated negatively with their parents, who in turn reciprocated with negativity, thus eliciting still more affective negativity from their sons and daughters, and so forth. The emotion-laden milieu of such families suggests that metacommunicative styles can be quite destructive for both the individuals involved as well as for the family as a *systemic* whole.

Functions of Emotion-Laden Messages

Satir was not alone in thinking about how metacommunication affected social relationships. Earlier Bühler (1934) had also speculated that emotion-laden messages could have several functions: a symbolic function as in what the message implies about the relationship (illustrated by Feeney et al., 1999 and Cook et al., 1991); a 'symptomatic' function as in the manifestation of the sender's emotional state; and thirdly, an appeal function, which was intended to reflect likelihood of action (e.g., motivated behavior, much like Satir's third supposition). From the standpoint of what children learn about emotion communication within their families, they learn that nonverbal expressive displays (especially facial expressions, but vocal quality, posture, gestures, and gaze pattern are included here as well) can refer to emotional states in the person displaying them. Perhaps more importantly, however, these emotional-expressive displays have consequences for the *relationship* between the sender and the recipient of the display (for supporting research, see assorted review chapters in Philippot, Feldman, & Coats, 1999; also Saarni, Mumme, & Campos, 1998).

Children learn within their families, from peers, and from media what the 'symptomatic' referents of emotional-expressive behavior may include as emotional states. Early research has shown that 4-year-olds can nominate the sorts of situations that are likely to elicit common emotional responses (i.e., emotional states) in North American culture (Barden, Zelko, Duncan, & Masters, 1980), and their accuracy in decoding posed facial expressions is reasonably good by age 6 (Gross & Bailif, 1991). However, some children, specifically those who have been maltreated, develop along a different trajectory of learning what emotional-expressive behaviors might mean (e.g., Camras, Sachs-Alter, & Ribordy, 1996). These investigators found that abused/neglected children were less accurate than non-abused children in decoding the facial expressions of photos of child subjects.

In another intriguing study (Barth & Bastiani, 1997), *biases* in children's labeling of facial expressions were found among those 4- and 5-year-olds who were more likely to have adjustment problems and difficult peer relations (as judged by their teachers). These young children were more likely "to see" angry facial expressions on their classmates' photos, even when the target child was not displaying such an expression in the photo. This research is consistent with studies with older children who use a hostile attribution bias in their peer relationships (e.g., Dodge, 1995). The implication here for emotion communication is that some young children may already have well-established patterns of bias in what expressions they believe their peers are displaying; when their bias is toward "seeing" angry expressions, they may engage in more socially distancing behaviors, resulting in less peer acceptance. This study is also illustrative of how the theoretical construct metaperception might operate, with the result that perception errors in what is decoded as an affective response from another can translate into an escalation of conflict and pre-emptive aggression.

Social referencing as a strategy for determining likely action. Bühler's notion that emotion communication also addressed what was the likely action to ensue has been indirectly examined in the now extensive literature on social referencing in infants and toddlers. Infants as young as 10-12 months look to their parents' emotional-expressive behavior when faced with an emotionally ambiguous situation as a guide to developing their own emotional reaction and subsequent adaptive action (e.g., Mumme, Fernald, & Herrera, 1996). In her review of social referencing and emotion regulation, Walden (1991) suggests that infants of about 1 year of age may already have some functional notion of what is an appropriate action or response to a situation, because they are less likely to use their mothers' *in*appropriate emotional expressions as a guide for their behavior when her reaction does not fit the eliciting situation.

By age 2, many normally developing toddlers are able to verbalize simple feeling states and can describe anticipatory affective states such as liking or wanting something. Walden (1991) notes that by this time they often negotiate with their parents around 'what to feel' in different situations and may choose not to use their parents' emotional expression as a guide to how to behave in some situation. On the other hand, in a genuinely new and uncertainty-filled situation, a 2- to 3-year-old will still look to others to see how to emotionally make sense of the situation.

Emotion communication and domestic violence. Under "the tyranny of dread," some of our most vulnerable and at-risk children learn very different sorts of emotion meanings and accompanying actions via social referencing and modeling (e.g., McCloskey, Figueredo, & Koss, 1995). Investigators have determined that children pay close attention indeed to the cues that tell them to expect parental anger and aggression

(Cummings & Davies, 1994; see also this volume). Literature reviews on the effects of family violence on children indicate that children learn some sad lessons about emotion communication (Fantuzzo & Mohr, 1999): one's home is not a safe haven (depression, anxiety, hyper-vigilance, suicidal behaviors, low self-esteem are common among children witnessing domestic violence); one's parents or caregivers do not protect their children from harm (many children witnessing domestic violence are also physically abused); and aggression is 'the norm' (externalizing behavior is common among children from violent homes). Tragically, the lessons in emotion communication that are learned by many of the children exposed to family violence prove to be maladaptive for these children in their experiences at school, with peers, and with the larger community. However, their responses to these repeated traumatic incidents may be appropriate responses *in the short run* to the circumstances of emotional turmoil and powerlessness in which these children find themselves. Studies of resilient children indicate that the personal resources and temperament of an individual child may help a child to overcome the adversity of growing up in a violent home or community (e.g., Masten, Hubbard, & Gest, 1999), but family, school, and community support are just as important in helping children to overcome these traumatic experiences (e.g., D'Imperio, Dubow, & Ippolito, 2000; Klein & Forehand, 2000).

RELATIONSHIP DIMENSIONS AND EMOTION COMMUNICATION

The Effects of Power

Haley's early work (1963) addressed structural features in dyadic relationships that affected metacommunicative outcomes. He proposed that the relationships could be *symmetrical*, such that influence was mutual and equally reciprocated, or *complementary*, in which case members of a relationship exercised differential influence toward one another as in superordinate and subordinate relations. Mehrabian's (1972) subsequently extended this into consideration of what parts of nonverbal behavior carry messages of power and social control. Early work on children's nonverbal behavior when interacting with their peers indicated that children do indeed make use of specific expressive gestures that convey power or dominance to influence the outcomes of dyadic interaction. For example, Camras (1980) examined the facial and postural behaviors of pairs of kindergarten children who were engaged in a competitive game as to who would get to hold a pet gerbil. Those children who succeeded more often in holding onto the box containing the gerbil tended to use a combination of expressive behaviors such as lowered brows, lips pressed together, and the lower jaw thrust forward. The effect may have intimidated the other child, who tended to use supplicating expressive behavior. No actual aggressive behavior ensued, but the children's expressive behaviors clearly influenced their interaction together.

Report and command features. These are further applications of metacommunication theory (Satir, 1967; Watzlawick, Beavin, & Jackson, 1967). They interpreted report features to be more often the content of what was expressed verbally. But of greater interest to them was the command feature of communication, which referred to what the sender wanted from the receiver. This would be the point at which we would also see issues of social control and attempts at dominance over the interactant as in Camras' work. The command feature may also simply be a request to be validated or heard out by the interactant. The popular press suggests that such validation has become difficult for many children and youth to obtain within their families (e.g., *Time* magazine, 2000).

Peers and emotion communication. Peers increasingly become the source for such validation in middle childhood as suggested by the growing body of research on children's friendships (e.g., Asher & Rose, 1997). Friendships are symmetrical relationships, and according to Haley's definition, attempts at dominance by one friend over the other would be expected to be balanced with attempts to restore mutuality and equilibrium of power. For example, von Salisch (1991) compared the interactive and expressive behavior of preadolescent pairs of "best" friends with pairs of children who were casual acquaintances as they played a computer game that had been rigged so that it would appear as though one member of the pair was at fault for losing the game. With close friends, children smiled much more frequently, even as they uttered reproaches or expressed contempt for their friend's failure in the game. Their smiling was reciprocated, and the dance of smiles functioned as a mutual reassurance that the relationship between the children was maintained and not threatened, in spite of the occasional reproaches and expressions of contempt. The children's smiles not only expressed positive feelings, they also contained important social messages about relationship durability (or equilibrium) and about how the interactants defined their relationship by their style of emotional communication.

Related results from younger children also suggest that friendship tends to elicit compromise or attempts to resolve conflicts (e.g., Hartup, Laursen, Stewart, & Eastenson, 1988) and that reactions to well-liked "provocateurs" are more controlled (Fabes, Eisenberg, Smith, & Murphy, 1996). Not surprisingly, child friends also have more disagreements and conflicts and may even criticize one another more (e.g., Gottman, 1983): If friendship is also characterized by children as a relationship in which genuine feelings are more likely to be expressed, then that also includes negative reactions as well as positive ones.

An area needing more systematic investigation is how children's emotional communication within relationships changes with transition into adolescence. Among the few studies available is one by Zeman and Shipman (1997), who examined fifth-, eighth-, and 11th-grade children and youth. These authors found that it was the eighth-graders (13-14 years old) who demonstrated emotional distancing from their mothers and tended to expect more negative consequences to their sad or angry emotional behavior. By 11th grade (16-17 years), these older adolescents seemed to be more accepting of their emotional experiences and anticipated more support and acceptance from others, although they were very clear that expressing anger toward their mothers was not likely to be acceptable. In sum, these teens managed their emotional experience (sadness and anger) relative to social context (peers and family), but it was done in light of their own developmental needs and goals.

The Effects of Closeness of Relationship

As suggested by the preceding research, closeness of relationship has the effect of facilitating genuine emotion communication, which includes disclosures of vulnerable information. How children come to understand this contextual influence of relationship quality on their emotion-laden discourse is well illustrated by research on disclosure of secrets. Watson and Valtin's (1997) study on school-age children's willingness to disclose secrets of varying content to friends versus to mothers found that younger children were more willing to disclose to their mothers but older children were more likely to disclose secrets to their friends, in part as a testimony to the friendship. Research has also examined children's understanding of how their expressive behavior has different effects on different audiences and therefore entails variable consequences for them (e.g., Underwood, Coie, & Herbsman, 1992).

Perhaps one of the most significant effects of relationship closeness on emotion communication that children learn has to do with disclosure of vulnerable information about the self. Such disclosures interact with social roles associated with gender and age status, and few studies have examined the processes that characterize developmental changes in children's emotionally vulnerable disclosures. Research on shame and embarrassment touch on this topic as well, but we will not address these studies here (Ferguson & Stegge, 1995; Lewis, 1992). The research we have found to be most useful for thinking about this topic was conducted by Harter and her colleagues (Harter, Marold, Whitesell, & Cobbs, 1996) on adolescents' beliefs about how they evaluated "true" or "false" selves within different kinds of relationships: mother, father, romantic partner, and friends. In the earlier study, the teens responded that they generally did not like their false self when interacting with someone about whom they cared a great deal: such interaction violated the assumptions of a close *trusting* relationship. However, if the teens felt that their relationship with their mothers, for example, was conditional, then they felt greater ambivalence about revealing their true selves, meaning that they were less likely to disclose genuine and vulnerable information about themselves for fear of disapproval. In the latter study, Harter et al. (1996) found that those teens who reported conditional relationships with parents or peers felt devalued; they also presented the most distressed psychological health profiles, and they reported using more often a false portrayal of themselves within close relationships.

Children also report that if an emotion is experienced as very intense, they are likely to express it, regardless of the context of relationship (e.g., Saarni, 1988; Saarni & Weber, 1999). However, it should be emphasized that this is the viewpoint of North American children, and in other societies, this is not necessarily the expectation at all. Indian girls report at young ages the importance of managing their emotional-expressive behavior with family members out of fear of severe punishment (Joshi & MacLean, 1994), and Chinese child-rearing values emphasize restraint and temperance in emotional expressiveness (e.g., Chen, Hastings, Rubin, Chen, Cen, & Stewart, 1998).

RELATIONSHIP QUALITY AND EMOTION COMMUNICATION

Intersubjectivity

Our application of the construct "intersubjectivity" emphasizes how family members mutually influence one another's emotional responses.

When people have close relationships with one another over time, their joint attention to emotion-laden events provides a shared history, which in turn is thought to influence their representations accompanying *current* emotional responses (e.g., Bloom, 1998). For example, if a child feels hurt but has a parent who has typically minimized or even ridiculed the child's hurt feelings, that child is more likely to represent "hurtness" as a state that should be repressed, avoided, or disavowed. It is in this sense that mental representations are essentially causal relationships that have meaning for the self in relation to one's environment. When representations are then linked together into networks, we can talk about scripts and event schemas (Nelson, 1996) that provide us with expectancies for both action and anticipated outcomes.

Intersubjectivity manifests itself in attachment relations when children use their caregivers as beacons of emotional meaningfulness. Depending on whether the attachment is secure, avoidant, or ambivalent, one would expect children's representations of emotion meaning to be influenced by the caregiver's own reactivity to the emotion in question; for example, "sadness is weakness, so get over it," "only babies cry," or "being scared is for cowards" might be associated with more avoidant attachment relationships, and the child in question would embed vulnerable emotions (fear, distress, sadness) in a representational network of minimization, expectation of parental disapproval, and defensiveness. In contrast, examples such as "let me hold you when you're upset" or "you have good reason to be hurt and angry" would presumably characterize parental emotional-laden responses that promote a secure attachment relationship for the child and a representational network that entails expectations of comfort and support when experiencing aversive emotions (see relevant reviews in Cassidy & Shaver, 1999). Research linking emotion socialization, attachment, and children's understanding of emotion communication is fragmented at present, but theorists are linking children's theory of mind (i.e., understanding others' thoughts and feelings and recursive understanding as in "I know that you know that I know . . . ") with internal working models (Harris, 1997; Thompson, 2000). Thompson in particular emphasizes that during periods of significant cognitive growth, as during the preschool years and again during early adolescence, that the developing ability to represent complex relationships may also be periods of time when internal working models are revised and elaborated. We return later to this topic as part of our discussion of narratives and discourse.

From a different vantage point, emphasizing parental goals and ethno-theories of emotion, the anthropologist, Catherine Lutz (1983) has suggested that emotion is both the medium and the message in emotion socialization. Thus, parents' feelings about a targeted emotion are "packaged" together in their socializing efforts directed at their children's experience of this particular emotion–as illustrated in the preceding quotes. A similar view is held by Gottman et al. (1997) with regard to the significance of parental philosophy (or meta-emotion) in children's subsequent development of emotion regulation from the preschool years to middle childhood. Other relevant research includes a study conducted by Steinberg and Laird (1989) who found that mothers who used primarily situational information for determining what they thought children were feeling tended to have children who also relied more on situational information for figuring out what they were feeling. Mothers who relied more on children's expressive behavior for inferring their emotions had children who similarly were more responsive to their expressive behavior. We do not know here who influenced whom, but of note is the mutuality of how emotion understanding was construed.

Additional research on parental disciplinary style suggests that intersubjectivity may play a role in how reciprocity and compensation play out in parents' and children's reactions to one another's negative emotional behavior. For example, Eisenberg, Fabes, Shepard, Guthrie, Murphy, and Reiser (1999) found in their longitudinal research of school-age children (from age 6-12) that cycles of children's externalizing emotional behavior at ages 6-8 predicted parental punishing responses 2 years later, which in turn predicted further externalizing behavior at ages 10-12. Parental distress was also correlated with their children's internalizing emotional behavior across time periods. The intersubjective shared history of negative emotional exchanges between the children and their parents appeared to elicit reciprocity of emotional negativity, as well as compensatory reactions: some parents appeared to disengage from their children as a result of their children's negative emotional behavior.

In contrast, empathic and sympathetic parents appear to promote children's empathic, prosocial, and sympathetic behavior toward others (Eisenberg, Fabes, Carlo, & Karbon, 1992; Koestner, Franz, & Weinberger, 1990). Individual differences in parental empathy may well prove related to the attachment representations of the parents themselves, which in turn are hypothesized to influence their own parenting practices that facilitate or impede their infants' degree of secure attachment. Psychiatric disorder, depression, and highly conflicted marital relationships also take their toll on parental resources, including empathic responsiveness to one's children (Cummings & Davies, 1994; Zahn-Waxler, 1991; Zahn-Waxler & Robinson, 1995).

An important reservation to bear in mind in examining parent-child mutual influence is that just as children obviously change, so do parents. The implication for mutual influence becomes even more complex: parents understandably modify how they respond to their children *because* their children are maturing, and those parental modifications may in fact elicit further variability in their children's response. Parents may also function more effectively with their children at one age but less so when confronted with the challenging behavior at a later age (e.g., dealing with defiant 2-year-olds may be a lot easier than dealing with defiant 12-year-olds). A recent review on child-rearing (Holden & Miller, 1999) concluded that parenting is simultaneously variable and stable: At more general levels of analysis, greater stability was found (e.g., global beliefs, propensity to monitor a child's safety) but when examined contextually, parenting responses to children were highly variable. Relative to parents' emotionality (positive or negative affect), Holden and Miller determined from their meta-analysis that maternal emotionality was more stable over time than particular kinds of behaviors emitted by the mother in response to her child's needs at the moment. However, this is not to say that emotionality in a parent is a trait that stems only from the parent: Dix (1992) has persuasively argued that parental emotion is intimately tied to immediate (and therefore variable) goals and appraisals that are much influenced by the events occurring at a particular point in time, and these events are *often generated by the child herself.*

Interpersonal Negotiation

Interpersonal negotiation has typically been examined for what sort of strategies interactants use when they have to solve a problem in which each has a stake in the outcome (Selman et al.,1986). The fact that the interactants have a stake in the outcome guarantees that the interaction will be accompanied by assorted emotions, which means that interpersonal negotiation simultaneously involves emotion communication. When the problem resolution appears to entail mutually exclusive outcomes for the interactants, there is a conflict. Selman et al. suggest that the degree to which power assertion versus striving for equitability of outcome is one of the most elementary ways of looking at interpersonal negotiation strategies. The former are characterized by one-sided, often disrespectful metacommunication and the latter by more mutual, flexible, and open-ended metacommunication.

Negotiation in the family. Families engage in interpersonal negotiation seemingly non-stop: conflicting wants and expectations at times seem to be more the rule than the exception, especially if there are numerous siblings. Relevant research on negotiation and emotion communication includes the study conducted by Dunn, Brown, and Beardsall (1991) on naturally occurring conversations in the home. They investigated how mothers and their young children used "feeling talk" in the home and found that conflicts and disputes elicited about 22% of the total amount of emotion-laden discourse (ranging from 0-75% across households). When disputes were negotiated, about 67% of the conversations included reference to causes of feelings, whereas conversations that did not focus on conflicts referred to causes of feelings only 45% of the time. As Dunn et al. point out, when children are feeling badly, they are motivated to express, verbally and otherwise, their feelings in order to get their needs attended to. In order for them to attain that goal, they need to learn to communicate their feelings in ways that not only regulate their own behavior but also influence the behavior of others. Learning to express affection to a parent is also a highly effective way to elicit positive attention, and children desire pleasurable interaction, not just attention to their distress or pain.

Another study by Dunn and Brown (1994) sheds further light on the effects of family emotional expression on children's acquisition of emotion-descriptive language. Again they found that occasions of negative feeling on the part of the child were when most emotion-related discourse occurred between mother and child. What this study also documented was that if families were characterized as high in frequency of anger and distress, the children were *less* likely to be engaged in discourse about feelings. But if the families were low in frequency of negative emotional expression, then when a negative emotional event did occur for the child, there was a greater likelihood of an emotion-related conversation to ensue between child and parent. Their findings suggest that children's acquisition of emotion-descriptive language is anchored in relationship contexts: If everyone is angry or distressed a lot of the time, then an episode of distress on the part of a child may be viewed as trivial. What may be meta-communicated in such families is that a child's feelings are not very important.

The Role of Scripts and Narratives in Negotiation

Families, peers, and media provide "short-cuts," so to speak, about consensually accepted ways for making sense of events, relations with others, one's own and others' behavior, and subjective experience (feeling states as well as physiological states). When faced with interpersonal negotiation, we need to use conventionally understood strategies for dealing with others in order to reach our goals. We refer to these strategies as scripts, and we propose that they are typically embedded in narratives both produced by and heard by children. We define these terms below.

Definition of scripts. Scripts are essentially representational guides (schemes) for how to infer what happens next; they entail sequential expectancies or beliefs about predictable sequences of events (Abelson, 1981). We learn that antecedent and consequence are meaningfully linked; thus, when an antecedent event occurs, we are likely to follow our expectancy and embark on a course of action that follows the script. Children learn social scripts early, and many of these social scripts are overlaid with emotional implications; the research by Dunn and her associates is only one example among other similarly descriptively rich research. One of us has also examined coping scripts in school-age children; 6-year-olds were as knowledgeable as 11-year-olds in terms of knowing what were the "best" and "worst" ways of coping with assorted negative emotions (Saarni, 1997).

Definition of narratives. Narratives are somewhat similar to scripts in that they represent symbolic schemes for how situations are thought to unfold (e.g., an expectancy for a sequence of events). Narratives are usually understood to have a more unique construction than scripts, for they reflect the individual's attempts to attribute meaning to his or her particular experience (e.g., Neisser & Fivush, 1994), yet they also have commonality, for we all grow up in a cultural context with access to some degree of shared meaning systems. Without access to shared meaning, we could neither communicate our experience to others nor expect them to understand us. Investigators concerned with narratives and the construction of meaning tend to emphasize language and its role in the stories that we tell about ourselves (e.g., Nelson, 1996). In addition, Fivush (1991) found that the narratives that are both told *to* children and *by* children typically involve an organization that sets the contextual stage (orientation), describes the crucial event, and provides a way for how to think about or evaluate the event. From our perspective, narrative practices facilitate children's acquisition of script understanding, for it is through narratives, essentially orally transmitted stories, that meaning is ascribed to experience for the young child. To quote Nelson: "Narrative ... provides the organization of the whole that makes the content memorable" (1996, p. 218).

Narratives and scripts coalesce in interpersonal negotiation. This topic is presented strictly as a theoretical speculation and as a platform for systematic developmental research. A few observational studies exist that look at how children deal with peer conflict in a naturalistic setting (e.g., Underwood, Hurley, Johanson, & Mosley, 1999; von Salisch, 1991), but these studies were not designed to examine children's use of scripts and narratives as a way to resolve the conflict. We are not aware of any observational studies of children that include analyses of *both* verbal and nonverbal behavior and which have been designed specifically to look at what scripts are used and how they are transmitted via the use of narrative when the child is faced with family conflict. Suggestive possibilities appear in research by Dunn et al. (1991), and Hudson and Shapiro (1991), and in clinical cases such as that described by Weingarten (1997; see case summary below).

We turn next to a discussion of the McMaster model of family functioning, a systemic view that proposes a number of dimensions that appear to be crucial to families' emotional health. This model has more often been used pragmatically by family therapists to make sense of the communication patterns they witness in the families that they counsel rather than as a theoretical model for empirical studies. Yet we find again that many empirical studies do indeed fit this model very well; we include a number of cases to illustrate the model.

FAMILY SYSTEMS AND EMOTIONAL UNDERSTANDING

The family systems paradigm informs our understanding of emotional development. The family context plays a unique and crucial role in shaping an individual's emotional life, as well as a person's understanding of emotion communication. According to the systems model, the functioning of the family system, and the behavior of its members, is determined by rules, particularly rules of communication. Such emotional communication rules are especially salient in the organization of the child's affective life insofar as patterns of family communication contain tacit messages conveying beliefs about emotions, including what emotions are acceptable, appropriate ways to express feelings, methods for dealing with emotions, and what to expect from others emotionally.

The McMaster Model of Family Functioning

We singled out the McMaster model of family functioning (Epstein et al., 1981) because of its emphasis on the emotional dynamics in families. This model invokes six distinct but interdependent dimensions of family functioning: communication, affective responsiveness, affective involvement, roles, problem solving, and behavior control. Each dimension ranges from most effective, that is, fostering physical and emotional health, to ineffective. Each dimension also has relevance for understanding how emotion communication works in families, and how children's own emotion understanding develops. What follows is an overview of the utility of each dimension for explaining the development of children's understanding of emotion. The dimension of behavior control is excluded from this overview because its relevant impact is subsumed under the other dimensions.

Communication. Families differ markedly in their emotional communication, both verbal and nonverbal, and this variability is mirrored in the affective discourse of their children, which in turn, influences their understanding of emotion as discussed above (e.g., Dunn & Brown, 1994). Effectively functioning families send clear messages, communicated unequivocally to the appropriate target. Such clear and direct communication is considered the most effective, since it allows family members to receive corrective feedback, including information about emotion communication. Difficulties occur when messages are vague or disguised, or conveyed indirectly through other family members. For example, for families in which one or more members have an eating disorder, meals are not merely about sharing food together. The act of eating or not eating can become a communication in and of itself and may function as an attempt to cope with intense feelings (Bloom, 1999). The anorexic daughter who cannot directly express her feelings of disempowerment within the confines of her rigid family system may nevertheless be able to send a "you can't control me" message via the refusal to eat.

Given that familial patterns of communication also affect children's representations of feeling states in themselves and others, it comes as no surprise that children who are raised with a person-centered communication style are more adept at utilizing peers' perspectives for offering comfort as well as for formulating persuasive arguments (Applegate, Burleson, & Delia, 1992). Children use their knowledge of feeling states to influence relationships, whether it be to comfort another or to alter a situation to their own advantage (Dunn et al., 1991). In contrast, some children grow up in families where emotions are not shared openly, and the children are left to make sense of their own affective experiences as well as the feeling states of others.

In her discussion of therapy with mothers and their adolescent daughters, Weingarten (1997) provides an excellent example of how family emotional communication influences the emotional life of children. Weingarten adopts a postmodern approach, attending to discourse analysis and narratives, yet, her example is equally amenable to a systems analysis. In one particular therapy session, Weingarten described her meeting with two mothers and their residentially placed daughters. As the daughters lamented their respective mothers' lack of caring, both mothers asserted that they cared deeply about their daughters. A discussion ensued in which the two daughters acknowledged that significant portions of their hearts were "cold," that is, blocked from feeling. In pondering how the "feeling part" of the heart may be encouraged to grow, one mother offered the need for caring. She also shared the insight that, due to the emotional climate of her own family of origin, she learned "cold caring," inhibiting her ability to share affectively with her daughter. She linked her own experience with familial emotional expression to her daughter's behavior by stating, "I think they feel nobody cares, then that's where not feeling comes in" (Weingarten, 1997, p. 326). In effect, this mother described a family of origin system in which inhibited expression of caring was the norm. These patterns of emotion communication extended into her interactions with her daughter, creating an environment that, to the daughter, seemed emotionally unresponsive. The daughter adapted by disconnecting her own affective life, leaving both mother and daughter feeling alienated and cut-off.

Affective responsiveness. Closely related to affective communication are the dimensions of affective responsiveness and affective involvement (Epstein et al., 1981). Affective responsiveness reflects the capacity of family members to respond to a particular affect eliciting event with a suitable emotion. Such responsiveness is considered in terms of (1) whether the particular emotion(s) expressed are appropriate to the situation at hand, (2) whether family members can utilize the full range of possible emotional responses, and (3) the strength of the emotional response (on a continuum from absent to excessive). Effectively functioning families have a range of emotional responses at their disposal, utilize these affective responses appropriately, and respond with suitable affective intensity.

The dimension of affective responsiveness is intimately linked to the children's understanding and appreciation for the feelings of others, that is, their ability to empathize. Applegate and his colleagues (1992) explored the role of parents' "reflection-enhancing messages" in children's social cognitive and communication development (Applegate et al., 1992). They proposed that parents who elaborate on the causes and consequences of feeling facilitate the expression of an array of emotions, validate their children's feelings, and encourage their children's reflection on their own emotional states. Although these messages promote in children an understanding of their own feelings, they also encourage reflection about the impact of one's emotional behavior on others, thus propelling the child toward more mature levels of social-cognitive functioning.

In contrast, children growing up in households characterized by lack of parental responsiveness learn different messages about emotion. Deficits in parental responsiveness occur for a variety of reasons, ranging from abuse or neglect to maternal depression. For example, responsiveness and an ability to discern children's needs is often compromised with depressed mothers (e.g., Downey & Coyne, 1990; NICHD, 1999.) Families struggling with substance abuse often adopt affective repression as a coping strategy (e.g., Copans, 1989). Maltreating parents spend less time interacting with their children in a child-centered manner, infrequently invoking responsive strategies such as request and reasoning (e.g., Trickett & Kuczynski, 1986) and more often exhibiting controlling behaviors and directives (e.g., Oldershaw, Walters, & Hall, 1986).

In each of these familial situations, children's emotional understanding unfolds in environments where their feelings are not validated. In effect, they are cut off from their own emotional experience, which yields deficits in the ability to feel, experience, and regulate emotions. Thus, children of alcoholics appear less adept at identifying emotions, regulating feelings and expressing emotions in a suitable manner (El-Sheikh & Cummings, 1997) and are often at-risk for cognitive and behavioral difficulties (Dix, 1992). Likewise, maltreated children demonstrate deficits in social responsivity, and neglected children, specifically, spend less time relating mutually with both parents and peers (Iverson & Segal, 1992). Even in non-maltreating families, children who grow up to be aggressive and oppositional often have parents who are emotionally unavailable (Edmister, 1999).

It is likely that family learning and modeling influences the engagement style developed by children (Iverson & Segal, 1992). Dix (1992) contends that children whose parents are not responsive learn that the parent is not available to meet their needs and, accordingly, adopt coercive methods for getting their interests met. He proposes that such coercive methods are not needed by children of empathic parents, because these parents understand their child's needs and wishes. Similarly, the attachment process is markedly influenced by the degree of parental sensitivity shown in response to a child's feelings (Dunn & Hughes, 1998). The development and elaboration of children's relationships is closely tied with the empathic understanding of the feelings, interests and needs of others (e.g., Asher & Rose, 1997). Without the opportunity to form secure attachments, children develop deficits in understanding their own feelings and those of others, which impacts their ability to experience empathy for others (see relevant reviews in Cassidy & Shaver, 1999).

An illustration of the impact of parental emotional responsiveness is found in the case of 13-year-old Nicholas. His already marginal academic performance declined further, and he garnered frequent detentions for disrespectful behavior towards his teacher and peers. Greatly frustrated, his mother, Crystal, brought him to therapy. Crystal spent most of Nicholas's early years addicted to alcohol. Now in recovery, the process of maintaining sobriety consumed most of her energy. Despite her recent involvement in Nicholas's behavior at home and at school, Crystal had extreme difficulty responding to Nicholas on an emotional level. During one session, when Nicholas, in a rare display of emotion, shared his deep pain and sadness about not knowing his father, his mother responded, "The guy was a jerk. A total loser. He's gone, thank God. Deal with it. Anyway, that was years ago."

Crystal herself faced the difficult challenge of dealing with her own intense affect that, in prior years, alcohol had numbed. To respond to her son's feelings empathically would potentially overwhelm her coping resources. As a consequence, Nicholas himself grew up in a family situation in which his emotional needs were inadequately recognized. His mother's abuse of alcohol had impeded her ability to attend and respond to her young son's feelings. Consequently, Nicholas missed opportunities to receive feedback and guidance regarding his emotional experience. This family interaction pattern led Nicholas to develop deficits in understanding the feelings, interests, and needs of himself and others. It is likely also that he came to doubt that the world would respond to his needs. Given such early learning experiences, Nicholas's coercive style of interaction with teachers and peers represented an affective response style learned in adaptation to his family environment.

Affective involvement. Affective involvement concerns the degree and quality of family members' investment in the welfare of one another and may range from the absence of involvement to symbiotic involvement (Epstein et al., 1981). The extremes of over- and under-engagement present challenges to effective functioning, whereas empathic involvement is the most effective form of connection (Epstein et al., 1981). Empathically involved parents engage with their children not out of motives for personal gain but because they have a genuine understanding of their children's needs. They validate the feelings of their children, which allows children to possess and take responsibility for their own feelings, thereby aiding as well their process of individuation.

In contrast, symbiotic or enmeshed involvement has been implicated in the development of eating disorders (Bruch, 1978). The family systems of anorexic individuals may entail intense involvement, but this involvement does not stem from an understanding of the child as a unique individual. Such parents may not even be able to appreciate that their child might have an entirely different perspective. The parents may also offer conditional love and investment based on how well the child fulfills parental expectations. What looks like parental dedication may, in fact, be efforts extended to meet their own needs rather than their child's needs. Threatened by their child's attempts at separation, some parents of children struggling with anorexia may react with intense over-control.

Roles. Family members adopt roles pertaining to family functions, support, and sustenance of family members. For healthy family functioning, these roles need to be clearly assigned to individuals capable of carrying out the associated responsibilities, and mechanisms must be in place which permit monitoring of the degree to which functions are accomplished (Epstein et al., 1981).

Gender socialization practices provide a useful example for how the roles dictated by the family system influence the developing child's understanding of emotions. Young boys in our society are socialized to disconnect from relationships and sever emotional ties in favor of gender role traits such as autonomy, self-sufficient coping and emotional control. This conceptualization of the male role is closely linked to the domain of affective responsiveness, since young boys are often not encouraged by family members to experience or express the entire spectrum of potential emotions (e.g., Pollack, 1998). Indeed, research indicates that, even in infancy, mothers foster more affective communication with girls than boys, and, in general, parents tend to express more emotion with girls as compared to boys (Halberstadt, 1991). Messages, subtle and not-so-subtle, are given that certain feelings, such as sadness and anger, are not appropriate. The young boy thus comes to understand that "weak" emotions must be kept in check, and that affective responsiveness on his part, particularly in areas involving comfort and nurturance, is not appropriate.

As an illustration, 7-year-old Michael presented with multiple behavioral difficulties at home and at school, picking fights and displaying chronic opposition to both his mother and female teacher. Although distressed by Michael's behavior, his mother commented, "but I guess boys will be boys." His father, in contrast, argued that his wife was too soft with their son. He reasoned that Michael's noncompliance reflected the fact that his mother spoiled him, adding that he himself had no trouble handling Michael. His mother countered by stating that she tried to be firm, but that Michael was "just too sensitive." Michael's father expressed a belief that his son had to learn to "take care of himself," adding that, at times, physical aggression is a necessary evil for young boys. In the course of the interview, his parents observed that Michael's behavioral difficulties escalated following the death of his grandmother 6 months earlier. His grandmother lived with the family, and both Michael and his sister were very close to her. However, Michael's father reported that his son did not seem upset, whereas both parents reported spending a great deal of time with their daughter discussing the loss, due to her visible distress after her grandmother's death.

In this example, a pattern of reinforcing certain emotional states and discounting others is evident. Michael receives support and validation for feelings of anger. His parents' beliefs about the inherent nature of boys include attributions of aggression and disruptiveness. Likewise, parental beliefs about young males' emotional comportment suggest the need for self-sufficiency. While Michael's emotional sensitivity is deemed excessive, his sister's distress is met with compassion.

Problem solving. Families must effectively overcome the obstacles facing the family and its members. Beyond solving basic problems of daily living, such as the provision of food and shelter, families must adequately address affective challenges (Epstein et al., 1981). In families coping with alcohol abuse, children learn specific roles that allow them to function within the anxiety and turmoil of the alcoholic system, which may include taking on responsibility for both instrumental and affective problem solving. In this case, the child may become the nurturer, providing emotional comfort to the parent. Similarly, the child may assume responsibility for regulating family affective intensity, taking action to decrease the emotional upheaval present in the family (e.g., El-Sheikh & Cummings, 1997). In the case of the alcoholic family system, emotional attunement may actually contribute to the codependent and enabling behaviors characteristic of adult children of alcoholics (e.g., Copans, 1989).

CONTEXT AND EMOTION UNDERSTANDING

The preceding review of relevant dimensions of family functioning illustrates how children's emotional development is greatly influenced by the family context. Families provide children with a model for the expression of emotion and coping with emotional issues. They influence children's familiarity with and understanding of their own emotions and give children a sense of whether or not the world will provide a safe context for experiencing feelings. It is in this sense that families are central to the idea that emotions are socially constructed, particularly due to the influence of early relationships with significant others. Similarly, family therapists operating within the narrative model postulate that all knowledge is socially constructed and is contextually bound. More specifically, such therapists explore the process of shared meaning-making in families (e.g., Smith & Nylund, 1997), whereby families construct narratives that pattern their experiences. Part of the organizing influence of such stories is the determination of admissible behaviors, including emotional conduct. Through family interactions, children learn emotion scripts, or interpretive schemes, that help them understand their emotional experiences (Saarni, 1999; see also preceding discussion).

Such schema, or narratives, may explain what Malatesta (1990) terms "emotional biases," or the proclivity to experience certain emotional experiences more than others. Dunsmore and Halberstadt (1997) propose that growing up in a family with a particular style of emotional expressiveness creates in the child a template for normative emotional experiences and expressions. According to this model, children evaluate how their own emotional attributes compare with their family's expressive style and attributions about emotions, as well as cultural standards for emotional articulation. This, in turn, influences the development of the child's self- and world-schemas. These interconnected factors contribute to the construction of meaning regarding emotion. Thus, depending on the expressive style of the family, the child may conceptualize the world as empathic and demonstrative or emotionally inhibited.

Furthermore, the meaning attributed to emotional experiences influences emotion-related behavior. For example, children growing up in conflict-ridden homes may develop unique appraisal of family occurrences which, in turn, influence their feelings of emotional security (El-Sheikh & Cummings, 1997). Such children have learned hard lessons: Their behavior outside the family may well reflect what Dodge (1995) and others have observed as a hostile attributional bias; yet these children also demonstrate internalizing behavior (e.g., McCloskey et al., 1995), perhaps implying a false sense of self and devaluation (Harter et al., 1996).

CONCLUSION

In conclusion, what we intentionally or unintentionally express in our nonverbal channels of behavior has powerful effects on what others think and feel. Indeed, what we may be communicating to others will be taken by them as *reflected appraisals* of their own worth and acceptability (Leary, 1999; see also Patterson's concept of metaperception 1999). This has critical implications for children's beliefs about their own self-worth if they have the misfortune of living with emotionally abusive or unavailable parents. Such children grow up understanding themselves as devalued within their family, which they may generalize to their peer relationships. In fact, the problem lies in the system of emotion communication within the family, not within these children's self-esteem. Leary suggests that effective therapeutic interventions in such cases would include helping the children and youth learn to develop social skills of inclusion and enhanced coping strategies such that they come to experience more positive reflected appraisals from others outside their family (perhaps analogous to "earned" secure attachment; see relevant chapters in Cassidy & Shaver, 1999). In effect, learning such social skills and coping behaviors is tantamount to altering one's emotion communication with others.

REFERENCES

Abelson, R. (1981). Psychological status of the script concept. *American Psychologist*, 36, 715-729.

Applegate, J. L., Burleson, B., & Delia, J. (1992). Reflection-enhancing parenting as an antecedent to children's social-cognitive and communicative development. In I. E. Sigel, A. McGillicuddy-DeLisi & J. J. Goodnow (Eds.), *Parental belief systems:*

The psychological consequences for children (2nd ed., pp. 3-39). Hillsdale, NJ: Erlbaum.

Asher, S., & Rose, A. (1997). Promoting children's social-emotional adjustment with peers. In P. Salovey & D. Sluyter (Eds.), *Emotional development and emotional intelligence* (pp. 196-224). New York: Basic Books.

Barden, R. C., Zelko, F., Duncan, S. W., & Masters, J. C. (1980). Children's consensual knowledge about the experiential determinants of emotion. *Journal of Personality and Social Psychology, 39,* 968-976.

Barth, J., & Bastiani, A. (1997). A longitudinal study of emotion regulation and preschool children's social behavior. *Merrill-Palmer Quarterly, 43,* 107-128.

Bloom, E. T. (1999). Combined effects of family systems and societal influences on eating behaviors. *Progress: Family Systems Research and Therapy, 8,* 35-46.

Bloom, L. (1998). Language acquisition in its developmental context. In D. Kuhn & R. S. Siegler (Eds.), W. Damon (Series Ed.), *Handbook of child psychology: Vol. 2. Cognition, perception, and language* (5th ed., pp. 309-370). New York: Wiley.

Bruch, H. (1978). *The golden cage.* Cambridge, MA: Harvard University Press.

Bühler, K. (1934). *Sprachtheorie.* Jena, Germany: Fischer.

Campos, J. J., Mumme, D., Kermoian, R., & Campos, R. G. (1994). A functionalist perspective on the nature of emotion. In N. Fox (Ed.), *The development of emotion regulation. Monographs of the Society for Research in Child Development* (Vol. 59, pp. 284-303).

Camras, L. (1980). Children's understanding of facial expressions used during conflict encounters. *Child Development, 51,* 879-885.

Camras, L., Sachs-Alter, E., & Ribordy, S. (1996). Emotion understanding in maltreated children: Recognition of facial expressions and integration with other emotion cues. In M. Lewis & M. W. Sullivan (Eds.), *Emotional development in atypical children* (pp. 203-225). Mahwah, NJ: Erlbaum.

Cassidy, J., & Shaver, P. L. (Eds.) (1999). *Handbook of attachment.* New York: Guilford Press.

Chen, X., Hastings, P., Rubin, K., Chen, H., Cen, G., & Stewart, S. (1998). Child-rearing attitudes and behavioral inhibition in Chinese and Canadian toddlers: A cross-cultural study. *Developmental Psychology, 34,* 677-686.

Cook, W., Kenny, D., & Goldstein, M. (1991). Parental affective style risk and the family system: A social relations model analysis. *Journal of Abnormal Psychology, 100,* 492-501.

Copans, S. (1989). The invisible family member: Children in families with alcohol abuse. In L. Combrinck-Graham (Ed.), *Children in family contexts: Perspectives on treatment* (pp. 277-298). New York: Guilford.

Cummings, E. M., & Davies, P. (1994). *Children and marital conflict.* New York: Guilford Press.

D'Imperio, R., Dubow, E., & Ippolito, M. (2000). Resilient and stress-affected adolescents in an urban setting. *Journal of Clinical Child Psychology, 29,* 129-142.

Dix, T. (1992). Parenting on behalf of the child: Empathic goals in the regulation of responsive parenting. In I. E. Sigel, A. McGillicuddy-DeLisi & J. J. Goodnow (Eds.), *Parental belief systems: The psychological consequences for children* (2nd ed., pp. 319-346). Hillsdale, NJ: Erlbaum.

Dodge, K. A. (1995). Attributional bias in aggressive children. In P. C. Kendall (Ed.), *Advances in cognitive behavioral research and therapy* (Vol. 4, pp. 73-110). Orlando, FL: Academic.

Downey, G., & Coyne, J. C. (1990). Children of depressed parents: An integrative review. *Psychological Bulletin, 108*, 50-76.

Dunn, J., & Brown, J. (1994). Affect expression in the family, children's understanding of emotions, and their interactions with others. *Merrill-Palmer Quarterly, 40*, 120-137.

Dunn, J., Brown, J., & Beardsall, L. (1991). Family talk about feeling states and children's later understanding of others' emotions. *Developmental Psychology, 27*, 448-455.

Dunn, J., & Hughes, C. (1998). Young children's understanding of emotions within close relationships. *Cognition and Emotion, 12*, 171-190.

Dunsmore, J. C., & Halberstadt, A. (1997). How does family expressiveness affect children's schemas? In K. C. Barrett (Ed.), *The communication of emotion* (pp. 45-68). San Francisco, CA: Jossey-Bass.

Dupont, H. (1994). *Emotional development, theory, and application.* New York: Praeger.

During, S., & McMahon, R. (1991). Recognition of emotional facial expressions by abusive mothers and their children. *Journal of Clinical Child Psychology, 20*, 132-139.

Edmister, P. (1999). School violence: Causes and prevention. *Progress: Family Systems Research and Therapy, 8*, 19-34.

Eisenberg, N., Fabes, R. A., Shepard, S., Guthrie, I., Murphy, B., & Reiser, M. (1999). Parental reactions to children's negative emotions: Longitudinal relations to quality of children's social functioning. *Child Development, 70*, 513-534.

Eisenberg, N., Fabes, R. A., Carlo, G., & Karbon, M. (1992). Emotional responsivity to others: Behavioral correlates and socialization antecedents. *New Directions for Child Development, 55*, 57-73.

El-Sheikh, M., & Cummings, E. M. (1997). Marital conflict, emotional regulation and the adjustment of children of alcoholics. In K. C. Barrett (Ed.), *The communication of emotion: Current research from diverse perspectives* (pp. 25-44). San Francisco, CA: Jossey-Bass.

Epstein, N.B., Bishop, D.S., & Baldwin, L. M. (1981). The McMaster Model of Family Functioning: A view of the normal family. In F. Walsh (Ed). *Normal family process* (pp. 115-141). New York: Guilford Press.

Fabes, R. A., Eisenberg, N., Smith, M., & Murphy, B. (1996). Getting angry at peers: Associations with liking of the provocateur. *Child Development, 67*, 942-956.

Fabes, R. A., Eisenberg, N., Karbon, M., Bernzweig, J., Speer, A., & Carlo, G. (1994). Socialization of children's vicarious emotional responding and prosocial behavior with mothers' perceptions of children's emotional reactivity. *Developmental Psychology, 30*, 44-55.

Fantuzzo, J., & Mohr, W. K. (1999). Prevalence and effects of child exposure to domestic violence. *The Future of Children, 9*, 21-32.

Feeney, J. A., Noller, P., Sheehan, G., & Peterson, C. (1999). Conflict issues and conflict strategies as contexts for nonverbal behavior in close relationships. In R. S. F. P.

Philippot, & E. J. Coats (Eds.), *The social context of nonverbal behavior* (pp. 348-371). Cambridge, UK: Cambridge University Press.

Ferguson, T., & Stegge, H. (1995). Emotional states and traits in children: The case of guilt and shame. In J. Tangney & K. Fischer (Eds.), *Self-conscious emotions: The psychology of shame, guilt, embarrassment, and pride* (pp. 174-197). New York: Guilford.

Fivush, R. (1991). The social construction of personal narratives. *Merrill-Palmer Quarterly, 37,* 59-82.

Gottman, J. (1983). How children become friends. *Monograph of the Society for Research in Child Development, 44* (3, Serial No. 201).

Gottman, J., Katz, L. F., & Hooven, C. (1997). *Meta-emotion.* Hillsdale, NJ: Erlbaum.

Gross, A. L., & Bailif, B. (1991). Children's understanding of emotion from facial expressions and situations: A review. *Developmental Review, 11,* 368-398.

Gurian, M. (1998). *A fine young man: What parents, mentors, and educators can do to shape adolescent boys into exceptional men.* New York: Tarcher/Putnam.

Halberstadt, A. G. (1991). Toward an ecology of expressiveness: Family socialization in particular and a model in general. In R. S. Feldman and B. Rimé (Eds.), *Fundamentals of nonverbal behavior* (106-160). New York: Cambridge University Press.

Haley, J. (1963). *Strategies of psychotherapy.* New York: Grune & Stratton.

Harris, P. L. (1997). Between strange situations and false beliefs: Working models and theories of mind. In W. Koops, J. Hoeksma & D. V. D. Boom (Eds.), *Early mother-child interaction and attachment: Old and new approaches* (pp. 187-199). Amsterdam: Royal Netherlands Academy of Arts and Sciences.

Harter, S., Marold, D., Whitesell, N., & Cobbs, G. (1996). A model of the effect of parent and peer support on adolescent false self-behavior. *Child Development, 67,* 360-374.

Hartup, W., Laursen, B., Stewart, M. I., & Eastenson, A. (1988). Conflict and the friendship relations of young children. *Child Development, 59,* 1590-1600.

Holden, G., & Miller, P. C. (1999). Enduring and different: A meta-analysis of the similarity in parents' child rearing. *Psychological Bulletin, 125,* 223-254.

Hudson, J. A., & Shapiro, L. R. (1991). From knowing to telling: The development of children's scripts, stories, and personal narratives. In A. McCabe & C. Peterson (Eds.), *Developing narrative structure* (pp. 89-136). Hillsdale, NJ: Erlbaum.

Ickes, W., Patterson, M. L., Rajecki, D., & Tanford, S. (1982). Behavioral and cognitive consequences of reciprocal versus compensatory responses to preinteraction expectancies. *Social Cognition, 1,* 160-190.

Iverson, T. J., & Segal, M. (1992). Social behavior of maltreated children: Exploring links to parent behavior and beliefs. In I. E. Sigel, A. McGillicuddy & J. J. Goodnow (Eds.), *Parental belief systems: The psychological consequences for children* (2nd ed., pp. 267-289). Hillsdale, NJ: Erlbaum.

Joshi, M. S., & MacLean, M. (1994). Indian and English children's understanding of the distinction between real and apparent emotion. *Child Development, 65,* 1372-1384.

Klein, K., & Forehand, R. (2000). Family processes as resources for African American children exposed to a constellation of sociodemographic risk factors. *Journal of Clinical Child Psychology, 29,* 53-65.

Koestner, R., Franz, C., & Weinberger, J. (1990). The family origins of empathic concern: A 26-year longitudinal study. *Journal of Personality and Social Psychology, 58*, 709-717.

Leary, M. R. (1999). The social and psychological importance of self-esteem. In R. Kowalski & M. R. Leary (Eds.), *The social psychology of emotional and behavioral problems* (pp. 197-221). Washington, D.C.: American Psychological Association.

Lerner, R. M. (1998). Theories of human development: Contemporary perspectives. In R. M. Lerner (Ed.), W. Damon (Series Ed.), *Handbook of child psychology: Vol. 1. Theoretical models of human development* (5th ed., pp. 1-24). New York: Wiley.

Lewis, M. (1992). *Shame: The exposed self.* New York: Free Press.

Lutz, C. (1983). Parental goals, ethnopsychology, and the development of emotional meaning. *Ethos, 11*, 246-262.

Malatesta, C. (1990). The role of emotions in the development and organization of personality. In R. Thompson (Ed.), *Socioemotional development. Nebraska Symposium on Motivation* (Vol. 36, pp. 1-56). Lincoln, NB: University of Nebraska Press.

Masten, A., Hubbard, J., & Gest, S. (1999). Competence in the context of adversity: Pathways to resilience and maladaptation from childhood to late adolescence. *Developmental Psychology, 35*, 143-170.

McCloskey, L. A., Figueredo, A. J., & Koss, M. P. (1995). The effects of systemic family violence on children's mental health. *Child Development, 66*, 1239-1261.

Mehrabian, A. (1972). *Nonverbal communication.* New York: Aldeno Atherton.

Mumme, D. L., Fernald, A., & Herrera, C. (1996). Infants' responses to facial and vocal emotional signals in a social referencing paradigm. *Child Development, 67*, 3219-3237.

Neisser, U., & Fivush, R. (1994). *The remembering self: Construction and accuracy in the self-narrative.* New York: Cambridge University Press.

Nelson, K. (1996). *Language in cognitive development: Emergence of the mediated mind.* New York: Cambridge University Press.

NICHD. (1999). Chronicity of maternal depressive symptoms, maternal sensitivity and child functioning at 36 months. *Developmental Psychology, 35*, 1297-1310.

Noller, P., Feeney, J., A., Peterson, C., & Sheehan, G. (1995). Learning conflict patterns in the family: Links between marital, parental, and sibling relationships. In T. Socha & G. Stamp (Eds.), *Parents, children and communication: Frontiers of theory and research* (pp. 273-298). Hillsdale, NJ: Erlbaum.

Oldershaw, C., Walters, G. C., & Hall, D. K. (1986). Control strategies and noncompliance in abusive mother-child dyads: An observational study. *Child Development, 57*, 722-730.

Patterson, M. L. (1999). The evolution of a parallel process model of nonverbal communication. In P. Philippot, R. S. Feldman & E. J. Coats (Eds.), *The social context of nonverbal behavior* (pp. 317-347). Cambridge, UK: Cambridge University Press.

Philippot, P., Feldman, R. S., & Coats, E. (Eds.). (1999). *The social context of nonverbal behavior.* Cambridge, UK: Cambridge University Press.

Pollack, W. S. (1998). *Real boys: Rescuing our sons from the myths of boyhood.* New York: Random House.

Roberts, W. L., & Strayer, J. (1987). Parents' responses to the emotional distress of their children: Relations with children's competence. *Developmental Psychology, 23,* 415-422.

Saarni, C. (1988). Children's understanding of the interpersonal consequences of dissemblance of nonverbal emotional-expressive behavior. Special issue: Deception. *Journal of Nonverbal Behavior, 12 (4, Pt. 2),* 275-294.

Saarni, C. (1997). Coping with aversive feelings. *Motivation and Emotion, 21,* 45-63.

Saarni, C. (1999). *The development of emotional competence.* New York: Guilford Press.

Saarni, C., Mumme, D., & Campos, J. (1998). Emotional development: Action, communication, and understanding. In N. Eisenberg (Ed.), W. Damon (Series Ed.), *Handbook of child psychology: Vol. 3. Social, emotional, and personality development.* (5th ed., pp. 237-309). New York: Wiley.

Saarni, C., & Weber, H. (1999). Emotional displays and dissemblance in childhood: Implications for self-presentation. In P. Philippot, R. S. Feldman & E. Coats (Eds.), *The social context of nonverbal behavior* (pp. 71-105). Cambridge, UK: Cambridge University Press.

Satir, V. (1967). *Conjoint family therapy* (rev. ed.). Palo Alto, CA: Science and Behavior Books.

Selman, R., Beardslee, W., Schultz, L., Krupa, M., & Podorefsky, D. (1986). Assessing adolescent interpersonal negotiation strategies: Toward the integration of structural and functional models. *Developmental Psychology, 22,* 450-459.

Smith, C. & Nylund, D. (Eds.) (1997). *Narrative therapies with children and adolescents.* New York: Guilford Press.

Steinberg, S., & Laird, J. (1989). Parent attributions of emotion to their children and the cues children use in perceiving their own emotions. *Motivation and Emotion, 13,* 179-191.

Thompson, R. A. (2000). The legacy of early attachments. *Child Development, 71,* 145-152.

Time. (2000, 7/3/00). Paging all parents. *Time, 156,* 47.

Trickett, P., & Kuczynski, L. (1986). Children's misbehaviors and parental discipline strategies in abusive and nonabusive families. *Developmental Psychology, 22,* 115-123.

Underwood, M., Hurley, J., Johanson, C., & Mosley, J. (1999). An experimental, observational investigation of children's responses to peer provocation: Developmental and gender differences in middle childhood. *Child Development,* 1428-1446.

Underwood, M. K., Coie, J., & Herbsman, C. (1992). Display rules for anger and aggression in school-age children. *Child Development, 63,* 366-380.

von Salisch, M. (1991, April). *Emotional expressions in peer negotiations.* Paper presented at the Biennial meeting of the Society for Research in Child Development, Seattle, WA.

Walden, T. (1991). Infant social referencing. In J. Garber & K. Dodge (Eds.), *The development of emotion regulation and dysregulation* (pp. 69-88). Cambridge, UK: Cambridge University Press.

Watson, A. J., & Valtin, R. (1997). Secrecy in middle childhood. *International Journal of Behavioral Development, 21*(431-452).

Watzlawick, P., Beavin, J., & Jackson, D. (1967). *Pragmatics of human communication: A study of interactional patterns, pathologies, and paradoxes.* New York: Norton.

Weingarten, K. (1997). From "cold care" to "warm care": Challenging the discourses of mothers and adolescents. In C. Smith & D. Nylund (Eds.), *Narrative therapies with children and adolescents* (pp. 307-337). New York: Guilford Press.

Zahn-Waxler, C. (1991). The case for empathy: A developmental review. *Psychological Inquiry, 2,* 155-158.

Zahn-Waxler, C., & Robinson, J. (1995). Empathy and guilt: Early origins of feelings of responsibility. In J. Tangney & K. Fischer (Eds.), *Self-conscious emotions: The psychology of shame, guilt, embarrassment, and pride* (pp. 143-173). New York: Guilford.

Zeman, J., & Shipman, K. (1997). Social-contextual influences on expectancies for managing anger and sadness: The transition from middle childhood to adolescence. *Developmental Psychology, 33,* 917-924.

Maternal Sensitivity and Infant Emotional Reactivity: Concurrent and Longitudinal Relations

Tracy L. Spinrad
Cynthia A. Stifter

SUMMARY. Although the construct of infant reactivity is thought to be a temperamental dimension, investigators have been interested in the relation between emotional reactivity and maternal behaviors. In this study, infants' emotional reactivity to frustrating stimuli and maternal sensitivity and intrusiveness were observed at 5 and 10 months of age. Cluster analysis of infants' emotional expressions revealed three patterns of expressive behavior emerged at both ages: (1) frequent anger and negative (distress) expressions, (2) intense anger expressions, and (3) frequent happy expressions. Results demonstrated that patterns of emotional reactivity at 5 and 10 months differed by maternal interactive style. In addition, patterns of emotional reactivity at 10 months of age could be predicted by differences in maternal caregiving, and conversely, 5-month infant reactivity was predictive of 10-month maternal behavior. Conclusions are made regarding

---

Tracy L. Spinrad is affiliated with the Arizona State University and Cynthia A. Stifter is affiliated with The Pennsylvania State University.

Address correspondence to: Tracy L. Spinrad, Department of Family and Human Development, Arizona State University, Tempe, AZ 85287-2502.

Support for this paper was provided by a grant from the National Institute of Mental Health (#MH44324) to the second author. The authors' appreciation is extended to the families who participated in the study and to Craig Edelbrock for helpful comments on this manuscript.

[Haworth co-indexing entry note]: "Maternal Sensitivity and Infant Emotional Reactivity: Concurrent and Longitudinal Relations." Spinrad, Tracy L., and Cynthia A. Stifter. Co-published simultaneously in *Marriage & Family Review* (The Haworth Press, Inc.) Vol. 34, No. 3/4, 2002, pp. 243-263; and: *Emotions and the Family* (ed: Richard A. Fabes) The Haworth Press, Inc., 2002, pp. 243-263. Single or multiple copies of this article are available for a fee from The Haworth Document Delivery Service [1-800-HAWORTH, 9:00 a.m. - 5:00 p.m. (EST). E-mail address: docdelivery@haworthpress.com].

© 2002 by The Haworth Press, Inc. All rights reserved.

ways that mothers socialize emotions and the bi-directional nature of mother-infant interactions. *[Article copies available for a fee from The Haworth Document Delivery Service: 1-800-HAWORTH. E-mail address: <docdelivery@haworthpress.com> Website: <http://www.HaworthPress.com> © 2002 by The Haworth Press, Inc. All rights reserved.]*

KEYWORDS. Infant temperament, emotional reactivity, maternal sensitivity

Recent approaches to the study of emotions during infancy have focused on the constructs of emotional reactivity and regulation (Rothbart & Bates, 1998). Developmentalists generally agree that these dimensions reflect important aspects of temperament. Despite this emphasis, there also is work to suggest that environmental factors, particularly caregiving behaviors, play an important role in infants' emotional behaviors. The direction of effects, however, has long been debated. The general consensus appears to be that the effects are bi-directional, but little research has confirmed this conclusion. The goal of this investigation was to examine infant emotional reactivity and its relation to maternal caregiving behaviors during the first year of life.

Rothbart and others have proposed that emotional reactivity is one of the basic dimensions of temperament (Rothbart & Bates, 1998; Rothbart & Derryberry, 1981). Consistent with this view, researchers have shown clear individual variation in infants' emotional reactivity from birth and have linked these differences to measures reflecting physiological processes such as vagal and adrenocorticol activity (Gunnar, Malone, Vance, & Fisch, 1985; Stifter & Fox, 1990; Tennes & Carter, 1973). There also is evidence of stability in emotional reactivity over time (Axia, Bonichini, & Benini, 1999; Malatesta, Culver, Tesman, & Shepard, 1989; Riese, 1987; Stifter & Fox, 1990; Sullivan, Lewis & Alessandri, 1992), although this pattern is not always found in early infancy (Fish, Stifter, & Belsky, 1991; St. James-Robert & Plewis, 1996).

Research on infants' emotional reactivity generally has focused on the intensity and duration of negative reactions to stimuli measured globally. Few investigations have considered individual differences in the expression of specific emotions (i.e., anger, distress, fear) during stressful situations. In one study, Izard and associates (1995) found that infants' expressions of interest, joy, sadness and anger were present by

2.5 months of age and their rate of occurrence was relatively stable over the first 9 months. Izard, Hembree and Huebner (1987) also demonstrated individual variation in emotional expression in response to inoculations as well as changes in emotional expression to the same stimuli over time. Whereas the predominant response to inoculation in young infants was pain/distress, by 19 months of age, the primary expression had changed to anger. Infant responses to less aversive stimuli (such as frustration) also have been investigated (Lewis, Alessandri, & Sullivan, 1990; Stenberg, Campos, & Emde, 1983). Lewis, Sullivan, Ramsay, and Alessandri (1992) examined facial expressions during a contingency task and observed differential outcomes for anger and sad expressions to extinction. Studies also have shown that individual differences in the patterning of responses to negative stimuli appear to have important consequences for children's development (Cole, Zahn-Waxler & Smith, 1994; Eisenberg, Fabes, Nyman, Bernzweig, & Pinuelas, 1994; Fabes & Eisenberg, 1992; Stifter, Spinrad, & Braungart-Rieker, 1999). Taken together, the evidence suggests that it is important to consider specific indices of emotional reactivity (such as facial expressions) rather than rely on more global measures. In the present study, infants' facial expressions of emotion in response to mildly frustrating stimuli were observed longitudinally at 5 and 10 months of age with the goal of examining patterns in their responses to frustration over time.

Although emotional reactivity is often thought of as stemming from temperamental differences, maternal behavior has been identified as a contributor to differences in infants' emotional behaviors (Eisenberg, Cumberland & Spinrad, 1998; Kopp, 1989; Thompson, 1990). Maternal sensitivity, or the mother's ability to respond appropriately to her infant's cues and to modify her behavior to maintain the infant's optimal level of arousal, has received considerable research attention (Ainsworth, Bell & Stayton, 1974; Thompson, 1998; van den Boom, 1994). In the early years of life, sensitive caregiving is believed to impact infants' emotional development by providing a context for maintaining positive affect and regulating negative affect. Indeed, researchers have found that higher levels of maternal contingent responding or appropriate responsivity has been linked with infants' expressed positivity and low levels of negative reactivity (Capatides & Bloom, 1993; Cohn & Tronic, 1983; Field, 1981; Malatesta et al., 1989).

Alternatively, when mothers lack sensitivity by ignoring their infants' signals or by providing too much stimulation, infants tend to respond with distress (Gable & Isabella, 1992; Gianino & Tronick, 1988). For example, Stifter and Moyer (1991) found that mothers who provided too much or too little stimulation during a peek-a-boo interaction had infants who displayed less frequent and less intense smiles than did infants whose mothers were moderately active (reflecting an optimal level of stimulation). And, at extreme levels, as when mothers are depressed or simulate depression (i.e., are unresponsive to their infants during face-to-face interactions), their infants show a reduction in positive affect and an increase in negative affect (Cohn & Tronick, 1983; Pickens & Field, 1994).

Over time, it is expected that maternal sensitivity influences infants' subsequent emotional development. Mothers who are more responsive to their infants' negative emotions may influence their infants' experience of negative emotions and foster the infants' development of emotion regulation strategies. Consistent with this argument, maternal sensitivity has been related to a decrease in negative reactivity over the first year of life (Bell & Ainsworth, 1979; Fish et al., 1991; van den Boom, 1994). Fish et al. (1991) found that infants who exhibited an increase in negative reactivity from birth to 5 months had less responsive mothers than did infants who remained stable or became less negative over time. Thus, early maternal caregiving appears to be related to changes in infant emotional behavior over time.

Associations between maternal sensitivity and infants' emotional reactivity generally have been studied from the position that parents influence infants' emotional behavior; however, researchers agree that this relation is undoubtably bi-directional (Bell, 1968). Little is known regarding the ways that infants' emotional reactivity influences subsequent maternal sensitivity. Using maternal reports of temperament, Klein (1984) found an association between infant temperament and later maternal caregiving behaviors. That is, infants who were rated by their mothers as more intense received more stimulation from their mothers. Few studies have examined the relation between infants' observed behaviors and mothers' caregiving interactions (Crockenberg & Smith, 1982; van den Boom, 1994).

In the present study, we examined the relation between patterns of infants' emotional reactivity and maternal sensitivity when infants were 5 and 10 months of age. Although one would expect that mothers who are more sensitive to their infants' cues would maximize their infants' positive arousal and reduce expressions of negative emotion during face-to-face play, it is less clear how these constructs will be related when infants are observed during a frustrating situation. It is possible that, similar to face-to-face play, infants with more sensitive mothers will be less reactive to frustration than will infants with less sensitive mothers. Because sensitive mothers are more accepting of the range of infants' emotions (Malatesta et al., 1989), the alternative also is possible. That is, infants of sensitive mothers may display more negative affect, particularly anger, in response to frustration, as this reaction would be considered an appropriate and adaptive response.

In terms of longitudinal relations, it was expected that more sensitive and less intrusive parenting over time would serve to change a highly negative infant's responses to frustration by fostering the development of self-regulatory strategies. In addition, it was hypothesized that infants' emotional reactivity would predict later caregiving behaviors. Infants who are extremely negative at an early age were expected to elicit more stimulation (perhaps over-stimulation or intrusive caregiving) and less sensitive caregiving from their mothers.

The present study is noteworthy for several reasons. First, we examined infants' facial expressions of emotion in response to mildly aversive stimuli rather than rely on more global measures of negative affect. Second, rather than measuring reactivity in response to pain-eliciting or startling stimuli, we examined infant emotional responses during a less-aversive frustration task that we anticipated would elicit varying levels of negative facial expressions as well as positive expressions of emotion. In one study by Lewis et al. (1990), both positive and negative responses to frustration were coded in a cross-sectional sample of infants 2-6 months of age. In the present study, we extended Lewis et al.'s (1990) research by examining longitudinally the positive and negative facial expressions exhibited during frustrating tasks at 5 and 10 months of age. Finally, we addressed the issue of the relation between patterns of infants' emotional reactivity and maternal behavior in the first year of life. Because of the longitudinal nature of this study, we were able to determine same-age and cross-age relations between these two factors.

METHOD

Sample

The participants for this investigation included 87 mother-infant pairs who were part of a longitudinal study of infant temperament. Mothers and infants were recruited from the maternity ward of a community hospital in Central Pennsylvania. The sample consisted of healthy, full-term infants from predominantly white, middle-class backgrounds. All infants were tested within 2 weeks of their 5- and 10-

month birthdays. Whereas all 87 pairs were present for the 5-month assessment (45 males), fewer infants were seen at the 10-month visit ($N = 76$; 40 males) due to relocation out of the area. Those infants who were dropped from the study did not systematically differ on any demographic or study indices from those infants who remained in the investigation.

Procedures and Measures

This study included laboratory assessments when the infants were 5 and 10 months of age and were designed to evaluate infant positive and negative reactivity. Although the tasks designed to elicit frustration were different at both ages, they were selected because of their age-appropriateness. Maternal behavior (i.e., sensitivity, intrusiveness) was measured independent of infant reactivity during a free-play procedure.

Negative reactivity tasks. To elicit frustration in the 5-month-old infants, an arm restraint procedure was administered. In this task, infants were placed in an infant seat at eye-level across from their mothers. Mothers were instructed to maintain an expressionless face while gently holding down their infants' arms. If infants began to cry, mothers were instructed to release the infants' arms after 20 seconds of hard crying. Otherwise, the arm restraint continued for 2 minutes. One minute after the infants' arms were released, mothers were instructed to soothe the infants in any manner.

At 10 months of age, a toy-withdrawal procedure was administered to elicit frustration. During this task, infants were seated in a high-chair across from their mothers. Mothers and infants played with an attractive toy for 90 seconds, after which mothers were instructed to remove the toy from the infants' reach but to hold it within sight. After 2 minutes, or 20 seconds of hard crying, the mothers returned the toy to the infants. Mothers were instructed to maintain a neutral posture during the toy withdrawal. If the infants continued to cry/fuss one minute after the toy was returned, mothers were permitted to soothe the infants. Although the tasks were different at each age, they elicited similar levels of reactivity based on a 5-point scale (0 = none, 4 = high) of the intensity of negative vocalizations (5 months, $M = 1.83$; 10 months, $M = 1.83$).

Infant facial affect. Infant facial affect during the frustration tasks was coded using Emotion Facial Action Coding System (EMFACS; Ekman & Friesen, 1983), which is an anatomically-based affect coding system. EMFACS is a technique designed to score emotion-related facial activity. Based on the microanalytic system, FACS (Ekman &

Friesen, 1978), EMFACS identifies the combinations of facial configurations resembling universal facial expressions for certain emotions. For example, an anger expression involves lowering and drawing together of the brows, the narrowing of the eyes, and the raising of the upper lip. EMFACS also is designed to code the duration of each emotion as well as the intensity of the emotional expression. Because the young infant's face has an excess of fatty tissue, FACS has been adapted for use with infants (BABYFACS; Oster & Rosenstein, in press). Thus, prior to coding infants' expressions, coders were trained to reliability (above .75) on the FACS system. Then, coders were trained on EMFACS as well as the BABYFACS adaptations for those facial expressions used in EMFACS.

In addition to coding the presence of facial configurations, some of the facial expressions were scored for intensity. The intensity of an expression, which was based on the degree of muscle contraction, was scored on a scale of 1 to 5. In cases where the emotion expression had more than one intensity rating, the score was averaged.

Facial expressions of emotion were coded for the most frustrating portion of the tasks. Thus, data were obtained for the arm restraint portion of the 5-month task and the toy removal portion of the 10-month task. Reliabilities for the present study were done for 10% of the cases on the timing of an emotion expression, the intensity of the facial configurations, and the emotion translations and ranged from 74% to 82% (percent agreement). Any discrepancies between the two coders on the subjects coded for reliability were corrected in conference.

Although all of the 10-month-olds completed the entire frustration task, 29% of the 5-month-old infants completed only a portion of the arm restraint ($M = 105$ seconds; $SD = 24$). Thus, proportion variables were used in the current study. Based on the distributions of the coded expressions as well as their intensities, four emotion variables were included in this study: (1) proportion of time infants displayed anger expressions, (2) mean intensity of anger expressions, (3) proportion of time infants displayed negative affect (distress) expressions,[1] and (4) proportion of time infants displayed happy expressions. The intensity of distress and happy expressions were not included in the study analyses because they were highly correlated with their respective frequencies (and thus could not be considered distinct from the emotion frequencies) at each age all rs (85, 74) > .63 and .68, ps < .0001 for 5- and 10-month variables respectively. Further, duration of anger, distress, and positive affect were not included in the study because they were moderately correlated with their respective intensities, all rs (85, 74) > .65 and .55, ps < .0001 at 5 and 10 months, respectively.

Maternal responsivity. Maternal responsivity was assessed from a 5-minute free-play laboratory session when the infants were 5 and 10 months of age. The procedure took place in a large carpeted area. Mothers were presented with a basket of toys and instructed to play with their infants as they normally would at home. The free-play task was video-taped, and mothers were rated for sensitivity and intrusiveness on a 4-point scale (0 = none; 3 = high) every 30 seconds for the duration of the free-play session.

Maternal sensitivity scores were based on contingent, infant-centered interactions. A high score on sensitivity reflected baby-centered, synchronous interactions that had an appropriate level of response/stimulation. Maternal sensitivity scores were summed over the 5-minute free play. Inter-rater reliabilities (Cohen's Kappa) for maternal sensitivity were calculated on 10% of the sample and were .63 and .68 for the 5- and 10-month scores, respectively.

Maternal intrusiveness also was evaluated during the free-play interaction. Intrusiveness was based on overcontrolling and ill-timed behaviors. High scores for intrusiveness reflected making overly stimulating responses, ignoring infant signals (e.g., failing to modulate behavior that infant turns away from or expresses negative affect to, taking away objects while the infant still appears interested, not allowing the infant to handle toys he or she reaches for), and making developmentally inappropriate demands on the infant. Maternal intrusiveness scores were summed over the 5-minute free play. Inter-rater reliabilities (Cohen's Kappa) were calculated on 10% of the sample and were .72 and .71 for the 5- and 10-month scores, respectively.

RESULTS

Descriptive Analyses

The means for infant expressions and maternal interactive behaviors at 5 and 10 months of age can be found in Table 1.

We first examined whether there were differences in infant emotion expressions and maternal interactive style as a function of infant sex. *T*-tests revealed no significant differences between boys and girls on emotion expressions, and mothers' behaviors did not significantly dif-

TABLE 1. Means and Standard Deviations for Infant Emotion Variables (proportion scores) and Maternal Interactive Style

	Mean	SD
Infant Variables		
5 Month (N = 87)		
Anger Frequency	.35	.27
Anger Intensity	.22	.17
Negative/Distress Frequency	.10	.18
Positive Frequency	.06	.12
10 Month (N = 76)		
Anger Frequency	.38	.22
Anger Intensity	.18	.06
Negative/Distress Frequency	.05	.08
Positive Frequency	.07	.11
Mother Variables		
5 Month (N = 75)		
Sensitivity	12.45	4.92
Intrusiveness	5.55	4.46
10 Month (N = 73)		
Sensitivity	15.34	4.87
Intrusiveness	4.67	3.70

fer for sons versus daughters. Thus, the primary analyses were conducted with males and females combined.

Intercorrelations of the emotion variables indicated that infants who expressed more frequent anger also expressed more distress expressions, $r(85) = .28, p < .009$ and less happy expressions, $r(85) = -.26, p < .015$. In addition, anger intensity was negatively related to the frequency of happy expressions, $r(85) = -.25, p < .02$. At 10 months, the frequency of anger expressions was positively related to anger intensity, $r(74) = .30, p < .009$ and negatively related to the frequency of happy expressions, $r(74) = -.26, p < .021$. In addition, anger intensity was marginally negatively related to the frequency of happy expressions, $r(74) = -.19, p < .086$.

Correlations for mothers' interactive behaviors revealed a negative relation between maternal sensitivity and intrusiveness at both 5 and 10 months of age, $rs(73, 71) = -.62$ and $-.24, ps < .0001$ and $.042$ respectively. Longitudinal correlations showed that maternal sensitivity was moderately stable from 5 to 10 months, $r(61) = .32, p < .012$. On the other hand, maternal intrusiveness was not significantly correlated across the 5- and 10-month visits, $r(61) = .18, p < .15$.

Cluster Analyses

To examine whether maternal interactive behaviors were associated with individual differences in infants' emotional expressions during frustration, we chose to categorize infants based on their patterns of emotional reactivity. Cluster analysis (a multivariate technique used to group individuals according to the similarity of their profiles on specified variables) was conducted on the infant expression variables at 5 and 10 months to identify patterns of emotional reactivity.

Variables were standardized prior to running cluster analysis to ensure that all variables were scaled equivalently. A hierarchical clustering method was applied to the data such that individuals who were most similar were linked first and were successively linked until all entities were grouped together. Specifically, the average-linkage method of clustering was chosen because it is widely used and outperforms most other clustering methods (Aldenderfer & Blashfield, 1984; Everett, 1993). To detect similarity in pattern, as opposed to elevation, the cosine similarity measure was selected to detect pattern differences across the four variables (Skinner, 1978).

It should be noted that cluster analysis is an exploratory technique used to group individuals, and the number of subgroups chosen was based on inspection of the hierarchical tree of groups and subgroups. The decision to choose a particular cluster solution was based on two rules. First, it was required that the number of clusters chosen significantly differentiated all variables. Second, after examination of higher cluster solutions, increasing the number of subgroups would not change significant differences between variables.

When cluster analysis was conducted on the 5- and 10-month data, three similar patterns of reactivity were identified at both ages. Standardized cluster means (see Table 2 for unstandardized means) revealed an "angry-distressed" cluster, characterized by high frequencies of both anger and distress expressions, moderate anger intensity, and low frequencies of happy expressions (n-35 for 5 months; $n = 31$ for 10 months). In the second cluster, labeled "anger-intense," infants displayed moderate anger expressions, had very high intensity anger expressions, and low frequencies of distress and happy expressions ($n = 22$ for 5 months; $n = 15$ for 10 months). The third group of infants, la-

TABLE 2. Unstandardized Means and Standard Deviations in Facial Expressions for 5- and 10-Month Cluster Groups

Facial Expression	5-Month Clusters			F-Values
	Angry-Distressed ($n = 35$)	Anger-Intense ($n = 22$)	Positive Affect ($n = 30$)	
Anger Frequency	.58 (.23)[a]	.27 (.09)[b]	.11 (.13)[c]	62.32***
Anger Intensity	.21 (.07)[a]	.40 (.20)[b]	.09 (.08)[c]	39.97***
Distress Frequency	.20 (.24)[a]	.06 (.07)[b]	.02 (.05)[b]	11.08***
Happy Frequency	.03 (.12)[a]	.01 (.04)[a]	.14 (.14)[b]	9.68***
Facial Expression	10-Month Clusters			F-Values
	Angry-Distressed ($n = 30$)	Anger-Intense ($n = 15$)	Positive Affect ($n = 30$)	
Anger Frequency	.59 (.15)[a]	.30 (.12)[b]	.21 (.13)[b]	58.19***
Anger Intensity	.18 (.03)[a]	.24 (.04)[b]	.14 (.07)[c]	18.51***
Distress Frequency	.09 (.11)[a]	.03 (.04)[b]	.03 (.06)[b]	4.67**
Happy Frequency	.05 (.07)[a]	.00 (.00)[a]	.13 (.14)[b]	11.00***

Note. Different superscripts indicate that means are significantly different from each other.

beled "positive-affect" was characterized by low anger frequency and intensity, low distress expressions, and high frequency of happy expressions ($n = 30$ at 5 months; $n = 30$ at 10 months).

Stability of Reactivity

To determine the stability of cluster group membership, a chi-square analysis was conducted. Results of this analysis indicated that there was little stability in cluster membership between 5 and 10 months, $\chi^2 = 3.570$, $p < .467$. As can be seen in Table 3, 40% of the infants who exhibited high levels of anger/distress were grouped into the positive affect cluster by 10 months of age. Similarly, over one-half of the infants showing high levels of positive affect at 5 months were classified into one of the negative affect clusters at 10 months.

TABLE 3. Frequency and Percent of Infants Classified by 5- and 10-Month Cluster Groups

	10-Month Clusters		
5-Month Clusters	Angry-Distressed ($n = 31$)	Anger-Intense ($n = 15$)	Positive Affect ($n = 30$)
Angry-Distressed ($n = 30$)	15 (19.74%)	3 (3.95%)	12 (15.79%)
Anger-Intense ($n = 19$)	6 (7.89%)	5 (6.58%)	8 (10.53%)
Positive Affect ($n = 27$)	10 (13.16%)	7 (9.21%)	10 (13.16%)

Relations Between Patterns of Reactivity and Maternal Sensitivity and Intrusiveness

Concurrent relations. To test the hypothesis that maternal behaviors would distinguish between patterns of infant reactivity, one-way analysis of variance and planned comparisons were conducted. The results indicated a significant effect of cluster membership at 5 months of age, $F(2, 72) = 3.51, p < .035$. Planned comparisons revealed that mothers of "anger-intense" infants were less sensitive compared to mothers of infants in the "positive affect" group, $F(1, 72) = 5.14, p < .026$ and infants in the "angry-distressed" group, $F(1, 72) = 6.19, p < .015$. Thus, it appears that mothers of infants who expressed positive affect or high frequency anger and distress in response to the arm restraint procedure at 5 months were more responsive to their infants' cues during a free-play interaction than were mothers of infants who reacted with intense anger. There were no significant associations between 10-month cluster membership and 10-month maternal sensitivity and intrusiveness (see top and bottom quarters of Table 4 for means and standard deviations for these analyses).

Predicting infant reactivity from maternal behavior. Because parental behaviors are believed to contribute to children's emotionality and regulation, we examined the extent to which early maternal behavior predicted later infant emotional reactivity. There is reason to believe that mothers who were more sensitive to their infants' cues would help reduce infants' negative emotions and foster infants' self-regulation strategies. Thus, infants of mothers who were more sensitive and less intrusive at an early age would be expected to respond with fewer anger

TABLE 4. Means and Standard Deviations in Maternal Interactive Behaviors by Infant Reactivity Groups

Maternal Variable	5-Month Clusters		
	Angry-Distressed ($n = 35$)	Anger-Intense ($n = 22$)	Positive Affect ($n = 30$)
5 Month			
Sensitivity	13.30 (4.74)	9.76 (4.01)	13.16 (5.23)
Intrusiveness	5.36 (4.29)	7.35 (5.54)	4.56 (3.59)
10 Month			
Sensitivity	16.35 (4.17)	14.32 (5.91)	15.68 (4.70)
Intrusiveness	5.71 (4.38)	4.23 (3.26)	3.36 (2.77)
	10-Month Clusters		
	Angry-Distressed ($n = 31$)	Anger-Intense ($n = 15$)	Positive Affect ($n = 30$)
5 Month			
Sensitivity	14.34 (5.63)	11.50 (4.58)	10.96 (4.12)
Intrusiveness	5.07 (5.15)	5.50 (4.72)	6.37 (4.01)
10 Month			
Sensitivity	16.13 (3.92)	14.47 (6.67)	14.96 (4.73)
Intrusiveness	4.00 (3.43)	4.93 (4.61)	5.25 (3.46)

and distress expressions 5 months later. Results indicated a significant effect for 10-month cluster groups, $F(2, 63) = 3.58$, $p < .034$. Contrary to prediction, however, planned comparisons indicated that infants in the "angry distressed" group at 10 months of age had mothers who were more sensitive at 5 months compared to infants who were classified in the "positive affect" group, $F(1, 63) = 6.65$, $p < .012$. There were no predictions from 5 month maternal intrusiveness (see third quarter of Table 4).

Predicting maternal behavior from infant reactivity. Not only may mothers' interactive behavior influence infants' emotional reactivity, but it also is believed that infants may elicit particular types of behavior from their mothers. Infants who are particularly negative at an early age may elicit more intrusive and less sensitive caregiving, whereas infants who tend to respond to frustration with little or no negative affect (or positive affect) may elicit fewer caregiving behaviors altogether from their mothers. Consistent with these hypotheses, there was a significant effect of 5-month clusters, $F(2, 75) = 3.02$, $p = .05$. Planned comparisons revealed that mothers of infants who were classified as "angry-distressed" at 5 months were more intrusive during a free play at 10 months of age than mothers of "positive affect" infants, $F(1, 75) = 5.82$, $p < .018$. Cluster membership at 5 months did not predict later maternal sensitivity (see second quarter of Table 4). [2,3]

DISCUSSION

Although emotional reactivity has been considered to be a temperamental construct, we reasoned that infants' emotional reactivity would be related to differences in maternal behavior. Mothers' sensitive interactions were thought to promote their infants' positive emotional expressiveness and optimal emotion regulation (Gianino & Tronick, 1988). In contrast, mothers' intrusive or insensitive behaviors were expected to be linked with infants' distress reactions.

In the present study, 5-month-old infants who responded to frustration with intense anger expressions had mothers who were less sensitive to their cues than were infants who expressed either positive expressions or frequent anger/distress expressions. These findings support our hypothesis that low sensitivity may elicit more negative reactivity. A mother who is unresponsive or inconsistent may heighten her infant's existing levels of anger reactivity. In addition, her inability to respond appropriately to her infant's cues would not support the development of the ability to regulate emotions. In the present study, although anger in response to a frustrating task, particularly at 5 months, might be interpreted as appropriate, a highly intense anger response would be neither adaptive nor healthy.

Two findings that seem contradictory at first glance may actually be explained by considering infants' interactions with their mothers (Malatesta et al., 1989). The first of these findings is that mothers who were more sensitive at 5 months had infants who reacted with frequent anger and distress expressions to a frustrating task at 10 months. Secondly, high positivity in infants at 10 months was predicted by low maternal sensitivity at 5 months. Thus, the present study indicates that mothers were the agents of their infants' frustration (i.e., they held down their infants' arms and removed the toy) and were asked to maintain a neutral expression during the tasks. Previous work has demonstrated that infants make associations between their distress and the intervention of caregivers at a very young age (Lamb & Malkin, 1986; Stenberg et al., 1983). Lamb and Malkin (1986) found that some infants, at the sight or sound of the caregiver, would soothe *before* being picked up by an adult and that infants between 4 and 5 months of age protested (cried more loudly) when their expectations were violated (i.e., the mother did not pick them up). Thus, it may be that infants who had experienced a history of sensitive caregiving would have developed expectations that their mothers would comfort them immediately when frustrated. However, when the mother instigates and continues frustrating the infant, as she was requested to do in the present study, the infant may express more frequent anger and distress.

Why would low maternal sensitivity predict greater infant positive affect to frustration? It may be that these infants are minimizing, or suppressing, their negative emotions. Although it is appropriate for the infant to become upset during the frustration tasks, some infants may have learned, through inconsistent parenting, not to share their distress with their caregiver. Cassidy (1994) proposed that infants who experience consistent rejection by their parents (particularly in times of distress) develop a strategy of minimizing their negative emotions, and such a regulation strategy is adaptive for these infants. This strategy is adaptive because minimizing anger, distress, or sadness protects the infant from further rejection and alienation from the caregiver, and as a consequence, maintains the parent-child relationship. Maintaining the relationship is an important goal for the infant, as he or she depends on the caregiver for survival. Thus, infants who have less sensitive mothers may display less negative affect and more positive affect in response to frustration in order to maintain the mother-infant relationship.

Interesting relationships also exist between maternal intrusiveness and infants' emotional reactivity. In terms of predictive relations, infants who responded with frequent anger or distress at 5 months of age tended to have mothers who were more intrusive 5 months later. Correlational analyses also indicated that maternal intrusiveness at 10 months was positively related to infant positive affect concurrently. One interpretation of these findings is that mothers who have infants who are at extreme levels of reactivity (i.e., high or low) may engage in more contact with their infants. For example, to prevent future negativity, mothers of highly reactive infants may continually stimulate their infants. The ways that mothers attempt to prevent their infants from becoming negative have received less attention by researchers, though it is likely that protection from negative affect is an important parental strategy, particularly when infants are prone to negative reactivity. Maternal behavior, such as introducing a new toy, would have been interpreted by our present coding system as intrusive, because it does not follow the child's agenda. The very same behavior, however, could have been used to distract the child from getting distressed. Future research would benefit, therefore, from taking a closer look at the type of behavior that mothers use with dispositionally negative infants.

In contrast to the negatively reactive infant, infants who express positive emotion in response to frustration may be viewed as under-reactive to aversive events. In these cases, mothers may feel the need to increase their stimulation for the purpose of inducing reactivity in their infants. An alternate explanation for these findings is that mothers who are intrusive with their infants are disapproving of their infants' displays of negative emotion. Thus, these infants may have learned, through interactions with their mothers, that expressions of negativity in response to frustration are not acceptable. Because most research has focused on negative rather than positive expressivity in response to aversive stimuli, it is clear that more work is needed in this area.

A notable aspect of this investigation is that, despite the fact that the frustration tasks were different at 5 and 10 months of age (arm restraint and toy removal), the same patterns of emotional reactivity were elicited. However, infants did not exhibit stability in facial patterns between 5 and 10 months of age. In fact, infants who were classified as negatively reactive at 5 months of age were not necessarily grouped similarly at 10 months of age.

This absence of stability, therefore, is interesting in light of the developmental tasks of this period. By around 7 to 9 months of age, infants are proposed to progress through a second biobehavioral shift (the first occurring at 3 months of age) during which the infant is believed to reorganize both physiologically and behaviorally (Emde, Gaensbauer, & Harmon, 1976). Behaviorally, this second shift is characterized by self-initiated mobility, a heightened awareness of strangers, and separation protest (Sroufe, 1979). Thus, the lack of stability found in the present study between 5 and 10 months may be a consequence of this dynamic period of development.

Although the present investigation focused on individual differences in infants' facial responses to frustration, it is important to note that there has been considerable debate about whether infants are capable of displaying discrete expressions of negative affect (Malatesta, Izard, & Camras, 1991). Some studies have called into question whether infants' negative facial expressions can be interpreted as discrete negative emotions such as anger, fear and sadness (Camras, Oster, Campos, Miyake, & Bradshaw, 1992; Oster, Hegley, & Nagel, 1992). Contrary to these views, other coding systems have discriminated between negative expressions in infants (Izard et al., 1987, 1995; Izard, Hembree, Dougherty, & Spizzirri, 1983). The results of this study do not address this debate, per se, but should promote further inquiries regarding infants' emotional responses to frustration stimuli. Future studies should examine infant facial expressions across a wide variety of negative situations to further explain the emotional experiences of infants.

The present study serves as a step in studying the role of maternal socialization on emotional reactivity in infancy. Future research should examine the processes by which emotional socialization occurs. Because maternal sensitivity and intrusiveness were observed during a free-play situation, it is uncertain how the mothers in this investigation responded to their infants' distress. Mothers' soothing behaviors in response to distress likely have important consequences for the development of infants' emotional reactivity and regulation (Cassidy, 1994; Kopp, 1989; Lewis & Ramsay, 1999). In addition, it is important to keep in mind that there are other important socializers of emotion in the family, particularly fathers (Parke & Buriel, 1998). Different patterns of relations between infants' emotional reactivity and fathers' interactive behaviors are likely to occur. Relatively little information exists, however, on the role of fathers in the development of infants' emotional reactivity.

Although beyond the scope of this study, our findings on the relations between infants' emotional reactivity and mothers' concurrent and later interactive styles lead us to speculate about the role that infant emotions play in family functioning. Using the ecological perspective (Bronfenbrenner, 1989), we can speculate that infants' negative emotionality would not only influence infants' interactions with their parents, but that negative emotions might be transmitted into other family relationships (i.e., the marital relationship, other parent-sibling interactions). Perhaps mothers who deal with an extremely reactive infant become frustrated or feel overwhelmed during their interactions with their babies. As a result, they may approach their subsequent interactions by conveying other family members with more negative emotion. Consistent with this notion, there is recent evidence that tension spillover occurs between parent-child dyads and marital dyads (Almeida, Wethington, & Chandler, 1999). Likewise, parental conflict has been linked with children's emotional functioning (Cummings & Davies, 1992), in the sense that frequent expression of anger between parents could influence infants' emotional reactivity in response to frustration. Future research in this area should consider how parental conflict contributes to the emotional development of infants.

Nonetheless, the findings of this study indicate that maternal responsivity is an important feature in the study of infants' emotional reactivity. Indeed, results are consistent with the notion that the development of emotional reactivity is a transactional process, reflecting relations among maternal socialization behaviors and the infants' temperamental characteristics. Whereas it is clear that maternal interactive behaviors play a role in infants' emotional reactivity, the present study also provides evidence for the claim that infants elicit particular types of behavior from their mothers.

NOTES

1. EMFACS has a "negative affect" translation but not a "distress" translation. "Negative affect" is used to designate nonspecific expressions of negative emotion. To avoid confusion around this terminology, we use "distress" to represent those expressions translated as "negative affect" by EMFACS.

2. In addition, a one-way analysis of covariance was conducted (controlling for 5-month maternal behaviors). Similar to the ANOVA, there was a marginally significant effect of 5-month clusters, $F(2, 64) = 2.79$, $p = .069$. Planned comparisons revealed that mothers of infants who were classified as "angry-distressed" at 5-months were at least marginally more intrusive during a free play at 10 months of age than mothers of "positive affect" and "anger intense" infants, $Fs(1, 64) = 4.45$, and 3.09, $ps < .039$ and $.084$, respectively. Cluster membership at 5 months did not predict later maternal sensitivity.

3. Because cluster analysis is an exploratory procedure used to classify infants, Pearson correlations were conducted to determine if there was a relation between individual emotional expressions and maternal behavior. Results were consistent with findings for infant cluster groups with two exceptions. There was a positive relation between the frequency of negative expressions at 10 months and 10-month maternal sensitivity, $r(71) = .24$, $p < .041$. In addition, infants who expressed more frequent positive emotions at 10 months had mothers who were more intrusive at 10 months, $r(71) = .29$, $p < .014$.

REFERENCES

Ainsworth, M. D., Bell, S. M., & Stayton, D. J. (1974). Infant-mother attachment and social development: Socialization as a product of reciprocal responsiveness to signals. In M. P. M Richards (Ed.), *The integration of the child into a social world* (pp. 99-135). Cambridge, England: Cambridge University Press.

Aldenderfer, M. S. & Blashfield, R. K. (1984). *Cluster Analysis*. Sage University Paper series on Quantitative Applications in the Social Sciences, series no. 07-044. Beverly Hills and London: Sage Publications.

Almeida, D. M., Wiethington, E., & Chandler, A. L. (1999). Daily transmission of tensions between marital dyads and parent-child dyads. *Journal of Marriage and the Family, 61*, 49-61.

Axia, G., Bonichini, S., & Benini, F. (1999). Attention and reaction to distress in infancy: A longitudinal study. *Developmental Psychology, 35*, 500-504.

Bell, R. Q. (1968). A reinterpretation of the direction of effects in studies of socialization. *Psychological Review, 75*, 81-95.

Bell, S. M., & Ainsworth, M. D. S. (1979). Infant crying and maternal responsiveness. *Child Development, 43*, 1171-1190.

Bronfenbrenner, U. (1989). Ecological systems theory. *Annals of Child Development, 6*, 187-249.

Camras, L. A., Oster, H., Campos, J. J., Miyake, K., & Bradshaw, D. (1992). Japanese and American infants' responses to arm restraint. *Developmental Psychology, 28*, 578-583.

Capatides, J. B., & Bloom, L. (1993). Underlying process in the socialization of emotion. In C. Rovee-Collier & L. P. Lipsitt (Eds.). *Advances in infancy research* (Vol. 8., pp. 99-135). Norwood, NJ: Ablex.

Cassidy, J. (1994). Emotion regulation: Influences of attachment relationships. *Monographs of the Society for Research in Child Development, 59* (2-3, Serial No. 240).

Cohn, J. F., & Tronick, E. Z. (1983). Three-month-old infants' reaction to simulated maternal depression. *Child Development, 54*, 185-193.

Cole, P. M., Zahn-Waxler, C., & Smith, K. D. (1994). Expressive control during a disappointment: Variations related to preschoolers' behavior problems. *Developmental Psychology, 30*, 835-846.

Crockenberg, S. & Smith, P. (1982). Antecedents of mother-infant interaction and infant irritability in the first three months of life. *Infant Behavior and Development, 4*, 69-81.

Cummings, E. M. & Davies, P. T. (1992). Parental depression, family functioning and child adjustment: Risk factors, processes, and pathways. In D. Cicchetti & S. L. Toth (Eds.) Developmental perspectives on depression. *Rochester Symposium on Developmental Psychopathology* (Vol. 4, pp. 283-322). Rochester, NY: University of Rochester Press.

Eisenberg, N., Cumberland, A., & Spinrad, T. L. (1998). Parental socialization of emotion. *Psychological Inquiry, 9*, 241-273.

Eisenberg, N., Fabes, R. A., Nyman, M., Bernzweig, J., & Pinuelas, A. (1994). The relations of emotionality and regulation to children's anger-related reactions. *Child Development, 65*, 109-128.

Ekman, P., & Friesen, W. V. (1978). *Facial Action Coding System.* Palo Alto, CA; Consulting Psychologists Press.

Ekman, P., & Friesen, W. V. (1983). *EMFACS Facial Coding Manual.* San Francisco, CA.

Emde, R. N., Gaensbauer, T. J., & Harmon, R. J. (1976). *Emotional expressions in infancy: A biobehavioral study* (Psychological Issues Monograph, Vol.10, No. 37). New York: International Universities Press.

Everett, B. S. (1993). *Cluster Analysis.* New York, NY: John Wiley & Sons, Inc.

Fabes, R. A. & Eisenberg, N. (1992). Young children's coping with interpersonal anger. *Child Development, 63*, 116-128.

Field, T. M. (1981). Infant gaze aversion and heart rate during face-to-face interactions. *Infant Behavior and Development, 4*, 307-315.

Fish, M., Stifter, C. A., & Belsky, J. (1991). Conditions of continuity and discontinuity of infant negative emotionality: Newborn to five months. *Child Development, 62*, 1525-1537.

Gable, S. & Isabella, R. A. (1992). Maternal contributions to infants regulation of arousal. *Infant Behavior and Development, 15*, 95-107.

Gianino, A., & Tronick, E. Z. (1988). The mutual regulation model: The infant's self and interactive regulation, coping, and defense. In T. Field, P. McCabe, & N. Schneiderman (Eds.) *Stress and coping* (pp. 47-68). Hillsdale, NJ: Laurence Erlbaum Associates, Inc.

Gunner, M., Malone, S. Vance, G. & Fisch, R. (1985). Coping with aversive stimulation in the neonatal period: Quiet sleep and plasma cortisol during recovery from circumcision. *Child Development, 53*, 571-600.

Izard, C. E., Fantauzzo, C. A., Castle, J. M., Haynes, M., Rayias, M. F., & Putnam, P. H. (1995). The ontogeny and significance of infants' facial expressions in the first 9 months of life. *Developmental Psychology, 31*, 997-1031.

Izard, C. E., Hembree, E. A., Dougherty, L. M., & Spizzirri, C. C. (1983). Changes in facial expressions of 2- to 19-month-old infants following acute pain. *Developmental Psychology, 19*, 418-426.

Izard, C. E., Hembree, E. A., & Huebner, R. R. (1987). Infants' emotion expressions to acute pain: Developmental change and stability of individual differences. *Developmental Psychology, 23*, 105-113.

Klein, P. S. (1984). Behavior of Israeli mothers toward infants in relation to infants' perceived temperament. *Child Development, 55*, 1212-1218.

Kopp, C. B. (1989). Regulation of distress and negative emotions: A developmental view. *Developmental Psychology, 25*, 343-354.

Lamb, M. E., & Malkin, C. M. (1986). The development of social expectancies in distress-relief sequences. A longitudinal study. *International Journal of Behavioral Development, 9*, 235-249

Lewis, M., Alessandri, S. M., & Sullivan, M. W. (1990). Violation of expectancy, loss of control, and anger expressions in young infants. *Developmental Psychology, 26*, 745-751.

Lewis, M., & Ramsay, D. (1999). Environments and stress reduction. In M. Lewis & D. Ramsay (Eds.), *Soothing and stress* (pp. 171-191). Mahwah, NJ: Lawrence Erlbaum Associates.

Lewis, M., Sullivan, M., Ramsay, D. & Alessandri, S. (1992). Individual differences in anger and sad expressions during extinction: Antecedents and consequences. *Infant Behavior and Development, 15*, 443-452.

Malatesta, C. Z., Culver, C., Tesman, J. R., & Shepard, B. (1989). The development of emotion expression during the first two years of life. *Monographs of the Society for Research in Child Development, 54* (1-2, Serial No. 219).

Malatesta-Magai, C. Z., Izard, C. E., & Camras, L. A. (1991). Conceptualizing early infant affect: Emotions as fact, fiction or artifact? In K. Strongman (Ed.) *International Review of Studies on Emotion* (pp. 1-36). New York: Wiley.

Oster, H., Hegley, D., & Nagel, L. (1992). Adult judgements and fine-grained analysis of infant facial expressions: Testing the validity of a priori coding formulas. *Developmental Psychology, 28*, 1115-1131.

Oster, H. & Rosenstein, D. (in press). *Baby FACS: Analysis of facial movement in infants.* Palo Alto, CA: Psychologist Press.

Parke, R. S. & Buriel, R. (1998). Socialization in the family: Ethnic and ecological perspectives. In W. Daman (Series Ed.) and N. Eisenberg (Vol. Ed.), *Social, emotional and personality development: Vol. 3. Handbook of child psychology* (pp. 463-552). New York: Wiley.

Pickens, J., & Field, T. (1994). Facial expressivity in infants of depressed mothers. *Developmental Psychology, 29,* 986-988.

Riese, M. L. (1987). Temperament stability between the neonatal period and 24 months. *Developmental Psychology, 23,* 216-222.

Rothbart, M. K. & Bates, J. E. (1998). Temperament. In W. Damon (Series Ed.) and N. Eisenberg (Vol. Ed.), *Handbook of child psychology. Vol. 3. Social, emotional and personality development* (5th ed., pp. 105-176). New York: Wiley.

Rothbart, M. K., & Derryberry, D. (1981). Development of individual differences in temperament. In M. E. Lamb & A. L. Brown (Eds.), *Advances in developmental psychology* (Vol. 1, pp. 37-86). Hillsdale, NJ: Erlbaum.

St. James-Roberts, I., & Plewis, I. (1996). Individual differences, daily fluctuations, and developmental changes in amounts of infant waking, fussing, crying, feeding, and sleeping. *Child Development, 67,* 2527-2540.

Skinner, H. A. (1978). Differentiating the contribution of elevation, scatter, and shape in profile similarity. *Educational and Psychological Measurement, 38,* 297-308.

Sroufe, L. A. (1979). Socioemotional development. In J. Osofsy (Ed.). *Handbook of infant development* (pp. 462-516). New York: Wiley & Sons, Inc.

Stenberg, C. R., Campos, J. J., & Emde, R. N. (1983). The facial expression of anger in seven-month-old infants. *Child Development, 54,* 178-184.

Stifter, C. A., & Fox, N. A. (1990). Infant reactivity: Physiological correlates of newborn and 5-month temperament. *Developmental Psychology, 26,* 582-588.

Stifter, C. A., & Moyer, D. (1991). The regulation of positive affect: Gaze aversion activity during mother-infant interaction. *Infant Behavior and Development, 14,* 111-123.

Stifter, C. A., Spinrad, T. L., & Braungart-Rieker, J. M. (1999). Toward a developmental model of child compliance: The role of emotion regulation in infancy. *Child Development, 70,* 21-32.

Sullivan, M. W., Lewis, M., & Alessandri, S. M. (1992). Cross-age stability in emotional expressions during learning and extinction. *Developmental Psychology, 28,* 58-63.

Tennes, K., & Carter, D. (1973). Plasmal cortisol levels and behavioral states in early infancy. *Psychosomatic Medicine, 35,* 121-128.

Thompson, R. A. (1990). Emotion and self-regulation. In R. A. Thompson (Ed.), *Socioemotional development. Nebraska Symposium on Motivation* (Vol. 36, pp. 383-483). Lincoln: University of Nebraska Press.

Thompson, R. A. (1998). Early sociopersonality development. In W. Damon (Series Ed.) and N. Eisenberg (Vol. Ed.), *Handbook of child psychology. Vol. 3. Social, emotional and personality development* (5th ed., pp. 25-104). New York: Wiley.

van den Boom, D. C. (1994). The influence of temperament and mothering on attachment and exploration: An experimental manipulation of sensitive responsiveness among lower-class mothers with irritable infants. *Child Development, 65,* 1457-1477.

Children's Emotional Reactions to Stressful Parent-Child Interactions: The Link Between Emotion Regulation and Vagal Tone

John Mordechai Gottman
Lynn Fainsilber Katz

SUMMARY. This paper examines children's physiological reactions to stressful parent-child interactions and tests the notion that vagal tone is a physiological index of the ability to regulate emotion. Basal vagal tone and the suppression of vagal tone at age 4-5 were examined as predictors of mother ratings of child's emotion regulation ability at age 8. Two hypotheses about the mechanism by which vagal tone predicts emotion regulation were examined: a stress inoculation hypothesis and a recovery from arousal hypothesis. Path analyses showed that age 4-5 regulatory physiology predicted child emotion regulation scores at age 8, and that this was partially mediated by the 4- to 5-year-old child's ability to maintain a low heart rate during stressful parent-child interactions. Interrupted time-series analyses of these events as a function of the child's basal vagal tone showed that children with higher basal vagal tone have both a larger heart rate increase to these events as well as faster recovery than children with lower vagal tone. *[Article copies available for a fee from The Haworth Document Delivery Service: 1-800-HAWORTH. E-mail address:*

John Mordechai Gottman and Lynn Fainsilber Katz are affiliated with the University of Washington.

[Haworth co-indexing entry note]: "Children's Emotional Reactions to Stressful Parent-Child Interactions: The Link Between Emotion Regulation and Vagal Tone." Gottman, John Mordechai, and Lynn Fainsilber Katz. Co-published simultaneously in *Marriage & Family Review* (The Haworth Press, Inc.) Vol. 34, No. 3/4, 2002, pp. 265-283; and: *Emotions and the Family* (ed: Richard A. Fabes) The Haworth Press, Inc., 2002, pp. 265-283. Single or multiple copies of this article are available for a fee from The Haworth Document Delivery Service [1-800-HAWORTH, 9:00 a.m. - 5:00 p.m. (EST). E-mail address: docdelivery@haworthpress.com].

© 2002 by The Haworth Press, Inc. All rights reserved.

<docdelivery@haworthpress.com> Website: <http://www.HaworthPress.com> © 2002 by The Haworth Press, Inc. All rights reserved.]

KEYWORDS. Emotional regulation, vagal tone, parent-child interactions

There has been a great deal of interest in the developing child's ability to regulate emotion (e.g., Fox, 1994; Garber & Dodge, 1991). It has been suggested that the ability to regulate emotion underlies the development of other competencies, such as children's peer social skills (Gottman & Katz, 1989; Katz & Gottman, 1991) and cognitive performance in tasks involving delay or inhibition (e.g., Mischel & Mischel, 1983). Central peer social competencies include the ability to resolve conflict, to find a sustained common ground play activity, and to empathize with a peer in distress (e.g., see Asher & Coie, 1990; Gottman, 1983; Gottman & Parker, 1986).

Despite widespread differences in the definition of emotion regulation, most researchers agree that parents play a powerful role in the socialization of emotion and in the development of emotion regulation abilities (Denham, 1998; Eisenberg, Cumberland & Spinrad, 1998; Parke & McDowell, 1998). Most theorists have suggested that it is through parent-child interaction that children learn how to modulate emotional expression. Thus, it appears that parental direction and coaching function to promote the development of emotion regulation skills. It is also the case that the family is a prime context for children to exercise their emerging regulatory abilities. Family interactions are replete with both positive and negative emotion, and the ability to regulate emotion, particularly during conflictual moments, is necessary for the successful navigation of many familial relationships, including the sibling relationship (Stocker & Youngblade, 1999), the parent-child relationship (Gottman, Katz & Hooven, 1997; Katz & Gottman, 1996), and the marital relationship (Gottman, 1994). In this paper, we focus particularly on how children regulate emotion within the context of stressful parent-child interactions.

Another area of agreement among researchers interested in emotion regulation is the idea that what is regulated involves physiological arousal, cognitive processes (e.g., attentional processes, interpretation of events, expectations), and behavioral tendencies (Calkins, 1994). Attention to individual differences in the ability to regulate emotion has been important in efforts to distinguish factors that predict adaptive and maladaptive child outcomes. One fruitful approach has been in the examination of individual differences in children's physiological reactivity to emotional events. Individual differences in the reactivity of particular physiological systems have been linked to differences in children's behavioral reactivity to specific emotion-eliciting events (Fox, 1989b; Kagan, Reznick & Snidman, 1989). For example, Kagan and colleagues (e.g., Kagan et al., 1989) have found that children with high and stable heart rates are more inhibited in the face of novelty than children with low and more variable heart rates.

Porges (1984) suggested that the physiological basis for the ability to regulate emotion lies in the functioning of the vagus nerve, the main nerve of the parasympathetic nervous system (PNS). The tonic firing of the vagus nerve slows many physiological processes down, such as heart rate. Research by Porges and his colleagues on the PNS indicates a strong association between high vagal tone and good attentional abilities, and he has speculated that these processes are also related to emotion regulation abilities. Porges (1984) reviewed evidence that suggests that a child's *baseline vagal tone* is related to the child's capacity to react to environmental stimuli. There is a substantial body of literature that shows that basal vagal tone is related to greater behavioral reactivity, but also to greater soothability, greater ability to focus attention, and greater ability to self-soothe and explore novel stimuli (DiPietro & Porges, 1991; Fox, 1989a; Hofheimer & Lawson, 1988; Linnemeyer & Porges, 1986; Porter, Porges, & Marshall, 1988; Richards, 1987; Stifter & Fox, 1990; Stifter, Fox & Porges, 1989). There is also preliminary evidence that vagal tone is related to the regulation of emotion in social situations. Fox (1989a) found that 14-month-old infants with high vagal tone showed a shorter latency to approach a stranger and less proximity to mother while the stranger was present than infants with low vagal tone. Fox and Field (1989) found children with that high vagal tone, high activity level and low distractibility exhibited a faster shift from solitary to group play during the transition to a new preschool environment. Thus, there is preliminary evidence that individual differences in vagal tone predict reliable differences in behavioral reactivity and regulation to emotion-eliciting situations.

There is another dimension of vagal tone that needs to be considered, namely, the ability to suppress vagal tone. In general, vagal tone is suppressed during states that require focused or sustained attention, mental effort, focusing on relevant information, emotional interaction, and organized responses to stress. Thus, the child's ability to perform a transitory suppression of vagal tone in response to environmental, and particularly emotional demands, is another index that needs to be added to the child regulatory physiology construct.[1] It relates to the likelihood of approach rather than withdrawal; some infants with a high vagal tone who were unable to suppress vagal tone in attention-demanding tasks exhibited other regulatory disorders (e.g., sleep disorders) (Huffman, Bryan, Pederson, & Porges, 1992). Porges, Doussard-Roosevelt, Portales- Lourdes and Suess (1994) found that 9-month-old infants who had lower baseline vagal tone and less vagal tone suppression during the Bailey examination had the greatest behavioral problems at 3 years of age, as measured by the Child Behavior Checklist (Achenbach & Edelbrock, 1986). Measures of infant temperament derived from maternal reports (Bates, 1980) were not related to the 3-year outcome measures.

In this paper, we further explore Porges' suggestions that basal vagal tone and the ability to suppress vagal tone may be related to children's emotion regulation ability within the context of stressful parent-child interactions. To date, studies of individual differences in children's physiological reactivity have largely examined emotion regulation in infants and toddlers. Furthermore, we know little about the degree to which variation in physiological reactivity is useful in predicting long-term behavioral adjustment (i.e., Fox, 1989a; Porges et al., 1994). In our research, we examine whether individual differences in vagal tone at the preschool-age predicts children's emotion regulation abilities during middle childhood. The child's emotion regulation ability was measured with the Katz-Gottman Emotion Regulation Questionnaire that asked parents to report how much they have to "down-regulate" their 8-year-old child's negative emotions; that is, how much they think that their child is emotionally out of control.

A second goal of this research was to understand *how* the vagal tone variables might work to predict emotion regulation. How does the child with higher vagal tone and greater ability to suppress vagal tone manage to regulate emotions? We suggest two possible hypotheses of how a higher vagal tone might function. One is a "stress inoculation" hypothesis and the second is a "recovery hypothesis." According to a "stress inoculation" hypothesis, having high vagal tone protects the child from having a strong physiological reaction to stressful life events. If the stress inoculation hypothesis were true, the child should maintain a high vagal tone and lowered heart rate during normally stressful interactions. However, according to a "recovery" hypothesis, having high vagal tone would enable a child to recover quickly from strong physiological arousal during stress. If the recovery hypothesis were true, then a child with high vagal tone might be quite physiologically reactive during stressful interactions but should still recover more quickly. In this paper we explore these two hypotheses.

Children's physiological reactivity is examined in response to what was hypothesized to be a particularly potent interpersonal stressor, that of parental rejection. Parental rejection has been associated with depression, alcohol use, delinquency, truancy and runaway behavior, disruptive classroom behavior, and physical aggression in children (Gray & Ray, 1990; Peretti, Clark & Johnson, 1984; Simons, Robertson & Downs, 1989; Williams, 1989). Parental rejection during childhood has also been found to predict a variety of adjustment problems in adulthood, including poor relationships between adult children and their parents, alcohol abuse, depression, the intergenerational transmission of depressed mood, and Type A behavior (Whitbeck, Hoyt, & Huck, 1994; Whitbeck, Hoyt, Simons, & Conger, 1992; Wright, 1983). We indexed parental rejection by assessing three types of negative parenting behaviors during a parent-child teaching interaction: mockery, criticism and intrusiveness. Children's physiological reactivity to these stressful negative parenting events which may tax children's emotion regulation abilities was hypothesized to be a good context in which to explore how vagal tone is related to emotion regulation.

METHODS

Participants

Fifty-six families were recruited from a small Midwestern university town for this study; 32 families had a male and 24 had a female child. The average age of the children was 67.45 months (SD = 6.3 months). Ninety-six percent of the parents were Caucasian. The mean age of husbands and wives were 33.5 and 32.9, respectively. Number of years of education for husbands and wives averaged 14.1 and 13.7, respectively. Approximately two-thirds of the families were classified as white-collar workers and the remaining families were classified as blue-collar workers (see Krokoff, 1984, for classification criteria). Three years later 53 of the 56 families were recontacted (94.6% of the original sample).

Procedures

Procedures consisted of laboratory sessions and home interviews for both parents and children. A combination of naturalistic interaction, highly structured tasks, and semi-structured interviews were used. Home and laboratory visits consisted of two home visits, one with the marital couple and one with the child, and three laboratory visits, one with the couple only, one with the couple and their 4-5-year-old child, and one with the child alone. Only procedures directly relevant to the conceptual question addressed in this paper will be described.

Time-1 Assessments

Parent-child interaction. The parent-child interaction session consisted of a modification of two procedures used by Cowan and Cowan (1987). In the first task parents were asked to obtain information from their 4-5-year-old child. The parents were informed that the child had heard a story and they were to find out what the story was. The story that the children heard did not follow normal story grammar and was read in a monotone voice, and so the story was only mildly interesting for the children and hard for most children to recall. This made the parents' inquiry potentially stressful. The second task involved teaching the child how to play an Atari game that the parents had learned to play while the child was hearing the story. The interaction lasted 10 minutes. Videotaped data was collected from all three family members but physiological data was obtained only from the child.

Children's film viewing. To obtain an assessment of child's baseline vagal tone and ability to suppress vagal tone outside of the parent-child interaction context, children were shown segments of a neutral and an emotion-eliciting film. The neutral film was an instructional film about fly-fishing. The emotion-eliciting film was a clip from the flying monkey scene in *The Wizard of Oz* in which the monkeys take Dorothy to the witch's castle. This film clip was preceded by a neutral story and an emotion induction film clip of an actress who acted out the emotions of the protagonist in the upcoming story. The function of the emotion induction was to direct the child to identify with the protagonist and to experience the specific emotion in question.

Child's physiological functioning. The child's cardiac interbeat interval (IBI) was assessed continuously by measuring the time between successive R-waves of the electrocardiogram (EKG). Miniature Beckman silver-silver chloride electrodes were applied to either side of the child's chest after lightly abrading the area with Omni-prep solution. Bechman's electrolyte was used to facilitate conductivity of electrical signals. IBI was averaged into 1-second intervals and synchronized in time with observational data.

Time-1 Measures/Coding

Observational coding of parent-child interaction. Parental rejection was coded using the Kahen Engagement Coding System (KECS) and the Kahen Affect Coding Systems (KACS) (Kahen, 1995). The KECS consists of seven parental engagement codes: Engaged, Positive Directiveness, Responds to Child's Needs, Disengaged, Negative Directiveness, Intrusiveness, and neutral. The KACS also consists of seven parental affect codes: Affection, Enthusiasm, Humor, Criticism, Anger, Mockery, and Neutral. Given our interest in parental rejection, only the Criticism, Intrusiveness and Mockery codes were examined in the analyses. Intrusiveness involved physical interference with the child's actions (e.g., grabbing the joy stick). Criticism involved direct disparaging comments or put-downs of the child's behavior or performance. Mockery occurred when parents used humor in a derisive way, at the child's expense (e.g., through sarcasm or by making fun of the child).

Parent-child interactions were coded continuously in real-time with coding synchronized to the original parent-child interaction. The total number of times each variable occurred in the 10-minute parent-child interaction session was recorded and totals across time were calculated for each of the 14 parent-child interaction variables. This index represents an estimate of the frequency of the parenting behavior within a 10-minute period. Mothers and fathers were coded by independent observers. Engagement and affect dimensions were also coded by independent observers. Reliability was calculated across coders using a correlation coefficient. Because total number of seconds within each parent code was the variable computed and used in all data analyses, the appropriate reliability statistic is a correlation coefficient rather than Cohen's kappa or percent agreement. For the KECS, the mean inter-coder correlation was .96, with a range of .86 to .99, and for the KACS the mean correlation was .93, with a range of .84 to .97.

Child regulatory physiology. For our physiological variables we selected as an estimate of the child's baseline vagal tone the vagal tone when the child was listening to a neutral story about fly fishing, a variable we will call "BASAL VAGAL." This story was presented before any of the emotion-eliciting films were shown. The child's ability to withdraw vagal tone was estimated as a difference between this estimate of basal vagal tone and the child's vagal tone during the flying monkeys scene in *The Wizard of Oz*, a clip designed to elicit a strong emotional response. We expect vagal tone to be withdrawn and heart rate to increase when the child is emotionally engaged with the fearful stimuli in this second film clip. We call this second variable "DELTA VAGAL." This second variable indexes the child's ability to suppress vagal tone when engaging with a strong emotional stimulus which includes an environmental demand for changing attentional focus, or regulating emotion; in our case the engagement with the environment involves the demands for an emotional response being elicited by the emotional film, as well as the demands to focus attention on the Atari video game the child played immediately after each film clip standing for a difference in vagal tone from the baseline film to the exciting film conditions. However, the order of the films was randomized; hence DELTA VAGAL represents the difference between two vagal tones, the child's vagal tone while viewing the neutral story about fly fishing minus the child's vagal tone while viewing the emotion-eliciting film from *The Wizard of Oz*. We computed our index of "vagal tone" as the amount of variance in the interbeat interval (related to the heart rate: Heart rate = 60000/interbeat-interval) spectrum that was within the child's respiratory range using spectral time-series analysis. This measures respiratory sinus arrhythmia, a measure of parasympathetic nervous system tonus, which has been found to index attentional processes and emotion regulation abilities (Porges, 1984). For our computations, we used the program SPEC from the Gottman-Williams computer program time-series package (Williams & Gottman, 1981). We also computed mean levels of interbeat interval during parent-child interaction to examine the stress inoculation and reactivity hypotheses.

Time-2 Assessments

Families were re-contacted 3 years later for follow-up assessments of child outcomes. Children were on average 8 years old (M = 96.9 months; Range = 82-110). Ninety-five percent (53 out of 56) of the families in the initial sample agreed to participate in the Time-2 assessments.

Mothers filled out a 45-item questionnaire about the degree to which their child requires external regulation of emotion (Katz & Gottman, 1986). This questionnaire includes items that reflect instances within the past week when the parent needed to "down regulate" the child. Sample items include: "How often did you tell your child to simmer down? How often did you tell your child to get to bed when he/she was too excited to go to sleep? How often did you tell your child to stop interrupting?" The alpha coefficient for the scale was .74.

RESULTS

Table 1 summarizes the means and standard deviations for the major variables used in our analyses. We now turn to the questions explored in this study.

Does Vagal Tone at Age 4-5 Predict Emotion Regulation at Age 8?

The program EQS was used for the path analyses (Bentler, 1992). A *non-significant* chi-square is sought as evidence that the model fits the data. Figure 1 is a summary of a path analytic model from the vagal tone variables at age 4-5 and emotion regulation at age 8. The model fit the data well, with a non-significant $\chi^2(1) = .007$, $p = .935$, Bentler-Bonett Normed Index of fit (BBN) = 1.00, with multiple correlation coefficient $R^2 = .52$ for emotion regulation at age 8. The path coefficient from basal vagal tone to the suppression of vagal tone at age 4-5 was statistically

TABLE 1. Means and Standard Deviations for Key Variables in the Analyses

Variable	Mean	Standard Deviation
Basal Vagal Tone	15.57	1.66
Delta Vagal Tone	.98	2.73
Down Regulation	1.91	.47
Child IBI* during paternal criticism	340.28	293.97
Child IBI during paternal mockery	222.57	241.80
Child IBI during paternal intrusiveness	450.81	343.04

* IBIs are in milliseconds

FIGURE 1. Vagal Tone Variables at Age 4-5 Predict Emotion Regulation at Age 8

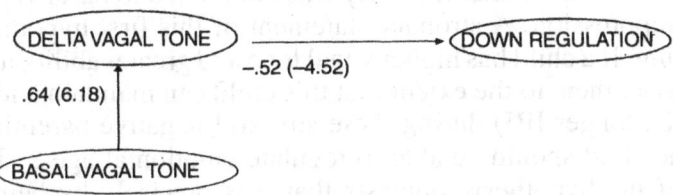

significant (.64, $z = 6.18$), and the path coefficient from the suppression of vagal tone variable at age 4-5 to the down regulation variable at age 8 was significant ($-.52$, $z = -4.52$).

How Might Vagal Tone Variables Work to Predict Emotion Regulation at Age 8?

The relational data base. To begin examining a stress inoculation and a recovery hypothesis, we first asked whether it was the case that to the extent that the child's vagal tone was being used to keep heart rate low during stressful parent-child moments at age 5, the child would be higher in emotion regulation ability at age 8. To find a mechanism that might provide an answer to this question, we constructed a relational data base that time-locked the parent's most negative and potentially stressful behaviors (Intrusiveness, Mockery, and Criticism) to the child's physiology during the parent-child interaction in our laboratory. We then correlated the child's cardiac interbeat interval during these specific moments with our emotion regulation variable and with our two vagal tone variables, the child's basal vagal tone and the child's ability to suppress vagal tone.

Stress Inoculation Hypothesis

Table 2 provides support for the stress inoculation hypothesis that the child's vagal tone was being used to keep heart rate low during stressful parent-child moments with the father. For example, for father mockery, those children higher in basal vagal tone and higher in the ability to suppress vagal tone were able to keep their heart rates low (i.e., had longer IBIs). The children lower in heart rate during moments of father mockery also required less down regulation at age 8. The child who maintained a lower heart rate during moments of mockery by the mother also required less down regulation at age 8. However, judging by the pattern of correlations, the effect was not mediated by the vagal tone variables since IBI during mother mockery was not related to basal vagal tone or vagal suppression. A stronger statement of this first hypothesis is the following: If a child has higher vagal tone and greater ability to suppress vagal tone, then, to the extent that this child can maintain a lower heart rate (i.e., longer IBI) during these stressful negative parenting behaviors, the child should be able to regulate emotion at age 8. This statement of the hypothesis suggests that it is precisely by being able to

TABLE 2. Relationship Between the Child's Cardiac Interbeat Interval and Basal Vagal Tone, the Suppression of Vagal Tone at Age 5, and Emotion Regulation Ability at Age 8

Variable IBI During	Basal Vagal Tone	Suppression of Vagal Tone	Parents need to down regulate Child at age 8
Father Mockery	.46*	.70**	−.46*
Mother Mockery	.05	−.02	−.69*
Father Criticism	.31*	.38*	−.32*
Mother Criticism	.19	.10	−.19
Father Intrusiv.	.23	.35ª	−.59**
Mother Intrusiv.	.43ª	.47ª	−.40

ª $p < .10$; * $p < .05$; ** $p < .01$; *** $p < .001$; Intrusiv. = Intrusiveness

maintain a lowered heart rate during stressful moments that a high vagal tone child is able to regulate negative affect.

To test this strong form of the first hypothesis, we took the father's mockery, which seemed to best fit the weak form of the hypothesis in terms of its pattern of correlations, and we then fit a path analytic model, attempting to place the child's interbeat interval during the father's mockery between DELTA VAGAL and DOWN REGULATION in the model in Figure 1.

Figure 2a shows that the new model fit the data well ($\chi^2(3) = 4.92, p = .178$, BBN = .992), and the path coefficients significant between the DELTA VAGAL and the child's interbeat interval when the father used mockery, and between the child's interbeat interval when the father used mockery and DOWN REGULATION. Hence, the old path between DELTA VAGAL and DOWN REGULATION was successfully replaced with an intervening variable, making the direct pathway an indirect pathway through our theoretical variable. Figure 2b adds a path to this model suggested by Baron and Kenny (1986). This model fit the data, with $\chi^2(2) = .03, p = .986$, BBN = .999. Consistent with the Baron and Kenny's suggested analysis, one compares the path coefficient of Figure 1 of −.52 with the same path coefficient in Figure 2b of −.35 between DELTA VAGAL tone and DOWN REGULATION. Since the path coefficient of −.35 is significant, but smaller in absolute value than the path coefficient of −.52, we have the conditions for partial mediation.

FIGURE 2a. Child's IBI During Father Mockery as a Mediating Variable Between Vagal Tone at Age 5 and Down Regulation at Age 8

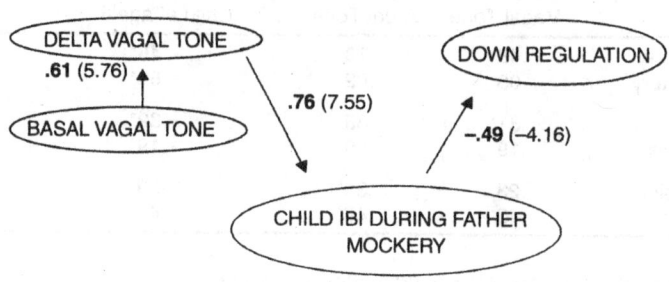

FIGURE 2b. Model Demonstrating Partial Mediation

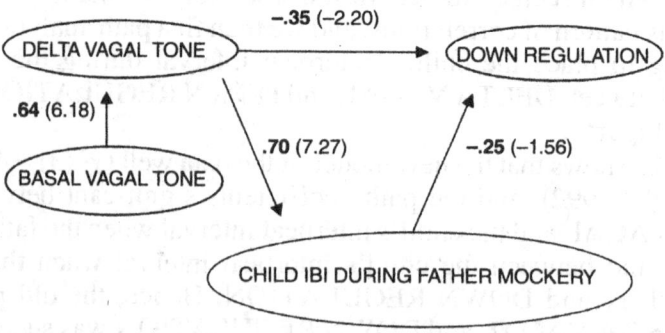

We also fit identical models as in Figure 2a (new model) for father criticism and father intrusiveness. For father criticism, the model did not fit, with $\chi^2(3) = 9.84$, $p = .020$, BBN = .975. However, the path coefficient from the child's interbeat interval when the father used criticism to DOWN REGULATION was $-.33$, $z = -2.54$, $p < .05$, and the path coefficient from DELTA VAGAL to the child's interbeat interval when the father used criticism was .54, $z = 3.30$, $p < .01$. For father intrusiveness, the model also did not fit, with $\chi^2 (3) = 8.07$, $p = .045$, BBN = .983. However, the path coefficient from the child's interbeat interval when the father used criticism to DOWN REGULATION was $-.59$, $z = -5.41$, $p < .001$, and the path coefficient from DELTA VAGAL to the child's interbeat interval when the father used criticism was .47, $z = 2.88$, $p < .05$. Hence, in these two cases, although the overall model did not fit the data, the relevant paths for judging whether the variable of the child being able to keep his or her heart rate down mediated significantly between DELTA VAGAL and DOWN REGULATION in both instances.

The Recovery Hypothesis: Interrupted Time-Series Analyses

A problem with the path modeling analyses is that, although they support the inoculation hypothesis, they do not rule out the recovery hypothesis because they do not tell us how the child maintains a lowered heart rate. The child could maintain a lowered heart rate by reacting more but still recovering more quickly. This would be an unusual state of affairs in physiology in which greater reactivity is typically associated with slower recovery (Martin & Venables, 1980). However, Porges has noted that children higher in vagal tone are more emotionally responsive, and this observation was supported by Fox (1989a).

Therefore, we used interrupted time-series analysis to continue testing the recovery hypothesis by studying the immediate effects on the child's heart rate of parental mockery, criticism, or intrusiveness, as well as the amount of the child's recovery from heart rate increases within a 5-second window (i.e., 5 seconds before and 5 seconds after the parental stressor). For our analyses we used the Crosbie (1993) interrupted time-series analysis computer program (see Figure 3; see also Crosbie & Sharpley, 1989). In this analysis, straight lines (each with an intercept and a slope) are fit to the pre-moment and post-moment IBI data (the moments are parental mockery, intrusiveness, or criticism), after controlling for autocorrelation in the data. The change in the intercept (post minus pre) is an index of the size of the heart rate response, whereas the change in the slope (post minus pre) is an index of the amount of heart rate recovery. To study physiological recovery, we selected all moments in which the child's interbeat interval intercept (IBI) decreased (i.e., the level of the child's heart rate increased) after the parental behavior, and then computed the change in slope from pre-moment to post-moment. We split the children at the median on their baseline vagal tone and conducted the time-series analyses.

FIGURE 3. Interrupted Time-Series Analyses Effects of Parental Criticism on Children's Heart Rate as a Function of Whether the Children Were High or Low on Basal Vagal Tone, Showing a Greater Response and a Greater Recovery of Children High in Basal Vagal Tone

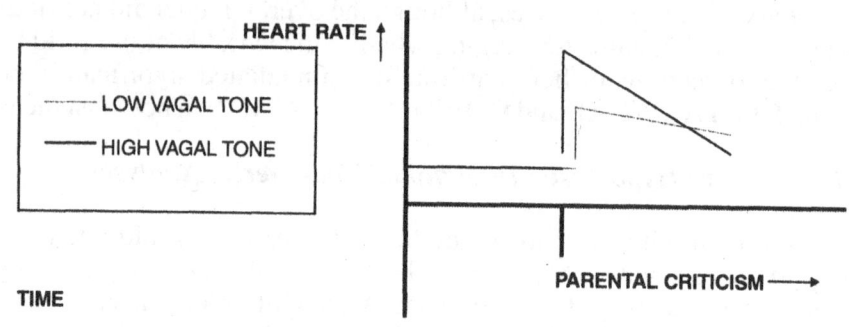

Amount of heart rate increase. Because there were many more moments of criticism than either mockery or intrusiveness, we compared the extent of the child's heart rate increase in response to parental criticism as a function of whether the children were high or low in basal vagal tone. For mother criticism, children with high vagal tone showed larger decrease in IBI (i.e., greater increase in heart rate) than children with low vagal tone, $F(1,85) = 6.25$, $p = .014$; the low vagal tone group decreased 42.43 msec and the high basal vagal tone group decreased 73.35 msec. Results for father criticism showed a similar pattern but did not approach significance $F(1,68) = 0.20$, ns; the low basal vagal tone group decreased 46.63 msec and the high basal vagal tone group decreased 51.24 msec. Thus, children high in basal vagal tone whose heart rate increased in response to parental criticism had a greater heart rate increase in response to maternal criticism increase and a faster recovery than children low in basal vagal tone.

Recovery from heart rate increase. In examining the slope change, for mockery and intrusiveness there were no significant differences between groups $F(1, 23) = 0.04$, and $F(1,35) = 1.25$, respectively, but for criticism there was a significant effect, $F(1,155) = 8.58$, $p < .01$ (low basal vagal tone group: slope change = 8.45, high group: slope change = 15.94); hence, the high basal vagal tone group recovered significantly more quickly than the low basal vagal tone group. The basal vagal heart rate recovery effect for criticism did vary depending on whether the mother or father did the criticizing, for mother, $F(1,85) = 5.88, p = .017$; for father, $F(1,68) = 2.69$, ns. Splitting children on the suppression of vagal tone variable yielded no significant effects.

Thus, children high in basal vagal tone had a *greater heart rate increase in response to maternal criticism and a faster recovery* (for both paternal and maternal criticism) than children low in basal vagal tone. These results support the recovery hypothesis rather than the stress inoculation hypothesis. Thus, the path modeling data supported a stress inoculation hypothesis for children's response to the father's stress-inducing behavior, while the interrupted time series analyses supported a recovery hypothesis, for mother's stress-inducing behavior.

DISCUSSION

This paper provides further support for Porges' (1984) suggestion that children's vagal tone is related to their emotion regulation abilities. We found that children's vagal tone at age 4-5 predicted mother ratings of emotion down-regulation ability at age 8. This provides an extension of studies with infants and toddlers, indicating that basal vagal tone is related to greater ability to self-soothe.

The mechanism by which vagal tone works to predict emotion regulation was also investigated in this paper. The hypothesis that the child's maintaining a relatively lowered heart rate during stressful parent-child interaction could be a mediating variable that could explain this prediction was supported. However, this path model did not specify the process by which this effect occurred, via an inoculation against stress model (in which children high in vagal tone do not react very much physiologically to parental negativity), or a recovery model (in which children high in vagal tone do react, but recover quickly). From the interrupted time-series analyses we learned that the basal vagal tone variable was related to a recovery model and not to an inoculation against stress model. Children with high vagal tone are not avoiding situations that lead to stress, nor are they non-reactive. Instead we found that they are both more highly reactive and able to recover more quickly than children low in basal vagal tone. This combination is quite unusual physiologically.

It is interesting that children's physiological reactions vary with fathers and mothers. With fathers, the patterns in the data supported a stress inoculation hypothesis. When fathers were mocking, those children with high vagal tone and greater ability to suppress vagal tone were better able to maintain a lower heart rate and were better able to regulate emotion at age 8. This may partly reflect the father's role in the development of emotion regulation skills. Consistent with evidence of gender differences in overt expression of emotion between men and women (see, for example, Hall, 1984), fathers may discourage the expression of strong negative emotion in their children, and may instead encourage children to take a more "level-headed" approach to negative events. This may be reflected in children exhibiting less autonomic reactivity to stress when with their fathers. In response to mother's negativity, children with high basal vagal tone had a greater heart rate increase and faster recovery than children low in vagal tone. The greater heart rate increase to mother's criticism may reflect children's greater emotional reaction to mother's negativity. An examination of children's behavioral reactions to fathers' and mothers' negativity would be useful in addressing these possibilities.

NOTE

1. Porges points out that we must be cautious about expecting the suppression of vagal tone to always be the appropriate vagal response to external demands. In the neonatal intensive care unit the appropriate response to gavage feeding turned out to be increases in vagal tone, consistent with the support of digestive processes (DiPietro & Porges, 1991). Premature infants who increased vagal tone during gavage feeding had significantly shorter hospitalizations.

REFERENCES

Achenbach, T. M. & Edelbrock, C. (1986). *Manual for the Teacher's Report Form and Teacher Version of the Child Behavior Profile.* Burlington, VT: University of Vermont Department of Psychiatry.

Asher, S. R., & Coie, J. D. (1990). *Peer rejection in childhood.* New York: Cambridge University Press.

Baron, R. M., & Kenny, D. A. (1986). The moderator-mediator variable distinction in social psychological research: Conceptual, strategic and statistical considerations. *Journal of Personality and Social Psychology, 51,* 1173-1182.

Bates, J. E. (1980). The concept of difficult temperament. *Merrill-Palmer Quarterly, 26,* 299-319.

Bentler, P. M. (1992). *EQS: Structural equations program manual.* Los Angeles: BMDP Statistical Software.

Calkins, S. D. (1994). Origins and outcomes of individual differences in emotion regulation. *Monographs of the Society for Research in Child Development, 59*, 53-72.
Cowan, P. A., & Cowan, C. P. (1987, April). Couple's relationships, parenting styles and the child's development at three. Paper presented at the Society for Research in Child Development. Baltimore, MD.
Crosbie, J. (1993). Interrupted time-series analysis with brief single-subject data. *Journal of Consulting and Clinical Psychology, 61*, 966-974.
Crosbie, J., & Sharpley, C. F. (1989). DMITSA: A simplified interrupted time-series analysis program. *Behavior Research Methods Instruments and Computers, 21*, 639-642.
Denham, S. (1998). *Emotional development in young children.* New York, NY: Guilford Press.
DiPietro, J. A., & Porges, S. W. (1991). Relations between neonatal states and 8-month developmental outcome in preterm infants. *Infant Behavior & Development, 14*, 441-450.
Eisenberg, N., Cumberland, A., & Spinrad, T. L. (1998). Parental socialization of emotion. *Psychological Inquiry, 9*, 241-273.
Fox, N. A. (Ed.) (1994). The development of emotion regulation. *Monographs of the Society for Research in Child Development, 59* (2-3).
Fox, N. A. (1989a). The psychophysiological correlates of emotional reactivity during the first year of life. *Developmental Psychology, 25*, 364-372.
Fox, N. A. (1989b). Infant response to frustrating and mildly stressful events: A positive look at the first year. *New Directions in Child Development, 45*, 47-64.
Fox, N. A., & Field, T. M. (1989). Individual differences in preschool entry behavior. *Journal of Applied Developmental Psychology, 10*, 527-540.
Garber, J., & Dodge, K. A. (Eds.) (1991). *The development of emotion regulation and dysregulation.* New York: Cambridge University Press.
Gottman, J.M. (1994). *What predicts divorce?* Hillsdale, NJ: Erlbaum.
Gottman, J. M. (1983). How children become friends. *Monographs of the Society for Research in Child Development, 48* (2, Serial No. 201).
Gottman, J. M., & Parker, J. (Eds.) (1986). *Conversations of friends.* New York: Cambridge University Press.
Gottman, J. M., & Katz, L. F. (1989). The effects of marital discord on young children's peer interaction and health. *Developmental Psychology, 25*, 373-381.
Gottman, J. M., Katz, L. F., & Hooven, C. (1997). *Meta-emotion: How families communicate emotionally.* Mahwah, NJ: Lawrence Erlbaum.
Hall, J. A. (1984). *Nonverbal sex differences.* Baltimore, MD: The Johns Hopkins University Press.
Hofheimer, J.A. & Lawson, S. (1988). Neurophysiological correlates of interactive behavior in preterm newborns. *Infant Behavior and Development, 11*, 143.
Huffman, L. C., Bryan, Y. E., Pederson, F. A., & Porges, S. W. (1992). *Autonomic correlates of reactivity and self-regulation at twelve weeks of age.* Unpublished manuscript, National Institute of Mental Health, Rockville, MD.
Kagan, J., Reznick, J. S., & Snidman, N. (1989). The constructs of inhibition and lack of inhibition to unfamiliarity. In D. S. Palermo (Ed.), *Coping with uncertainty: Be-*

havioral and developmental perspectives (pp. 131-149). Hillsdale, NJ: Lawrence Erlbaum.

Kahen, V. (1995). *The Kahen Engagement and Affect Coding Systems*. Unpublished manuscript. University of Washington. Seattle, WA.

Katz, L. F., & Gottman, J. M. (1986). *The Emotion Regulation Questionnaire*. Unpublished manuscript. University of Washington. Seattle, WA.

Katz, L. F., & Gottman, J. M. (1991). Marital discord and child outcomes: A social psychophysiological approach. In J. Garber & K. A. Dodge (Eds.), *The development of emotion regulation and dysregulation* (pp. 129-155). New York, NY: Cambridge University Press.

Katz, L. F., & Gottman, J. M. (1996). Spillover effects of marital conflict: In search of parenting and co-parenting mechanisms. *New Directions for Child Development, 74*, 57-76.

Linnemeyer, S. A., & Porges, S. W. (1986). Recognition memory and cardiac vagal tone in 6-month-old infants. *Infant Behavior and Development, 9*, 43-56.

Martin, I., & Venables, P. H. (1980). *Techniques in psychophysiology*. New York: John Wiley & Sons.

Mischel, H. N., & Mischel, W. (1983). The development of children's knowledge of self-control strategies. *Child Development, 54*, 603-619.

Parke, R. D., & McDowell, D. J. (1998). Toward an expanded model of emotion socialization: New people, new pathways. *Psychological Inquiry, 9*, 303-307.

Porges, S. W., Walter, G. F., Korb, R. J., & Sprague, R. L. (1975). The influence of methylphenidate on heart rate and behavioral measures of attention in hyperactive children. *Child Development, 46*, 727-733.

Porges, S. W. (1984). Heart rate oscillation: An index of neural mediation. In M. G. H. Coles, J. R. Jennings, & J. A. Stern (Eds.), *Psychophysiological perspectives: Festschrift for Beatrice and John Lacey*. New York: Van Nostrand Reinhold.

Porter, F. L., Porges, S. W., & Marshall, R. E. (1988). Newborn pain cries and vagal tone: Parallel changes in response to circumcision. *Child Development, 59*, 495-505.

Richards, J. E. (1987). Infant visual sustained attention and respiratory sinus arrhythmia. *Child Development, 58*, 488-496.

Simons, R. L., Robertson, J. F., & Downs, W. R. (1989). The nature of the association between parental rejection and delinquent behavior. *Journal of Youth and Adolescence, 18*, 297-310.

Stifter, C. A., & Fox, N. A. (1990). Infant reactivity: Physiological correlates of newborn and 5-month temperament. *Developmental Psychology, 26*, 582-588.

Stifter, C. A., Fox, N. A., & Porges, S. W. (1989). Facial expressivity and vagal tone in 5- and 10-month-old infants. *Infant Behavior and Development, 12*, 127-137.

Stocker, C. M., & Youngblade, L. (1999). Marital conflict and parental hostility: Links with children's sibling and peer relationships. *Journal of Family Psychology, 13*, 598-609.

Whitbeck, L. B., Hoyt, D. R., & Huck, S. M. (1994). Early family relationships, intergenerational solidarity and support provided to parents by their adult children. *Journal of Gerontology, 49*, 585-594.

Whitbeck, L. B., Hoyt, D. R., Simons, R. L., & Conger, R. D. (1992). Intergenerational continuity of parental rejection and depressed affect. *Journal of Personality and Social Psychology, 63,* 1036-1045.

Williams, R. C. (1989). The relationship of parental alcoholism, psychological separation and parental rejection to depression in college students. *Dissertation Abstracts International, 49 (12-A, Pt 1):* 3672.

Williams, E., & Gottman, J. M. (1981). *A user's guide to the Gottman-Williams time-series programs.* New York: Cambridge University Press.

Wright, L. S. (1983). Correlates of reported drinking problems among male and female college students. *Journal of Alcohol and Drug Education, 28,* 47-57.

The Coping with Children's Negative Emotions Scale (CCNES): Psychometric Properties and Relations with Children's Emotional Competence

Richard A. Fabes
Richard E. Poulin
Nancy Eisenberg
Debra A. Madden-Derdich

SUMMARY. The *Coping with Children's Negative Emotions Scale* (CCNES) is an increasingly used self-report instrument consisting of six subscales that reflect different ways parents respond to their young children's negative emotions. However, psychometric testing of this scale has not been conducted. In two studies, we examine its psychometric properties. In the first study, 101 parents (mostly mothers) completed the CCNES and a variety of other scales. The results reveal that the CCNES is internally reliable and has sound test-retest reliability and construct va-

---

Richard A. Fabes, Richard E. Poulin, Nancy Eisenberg, and Debra A. Madden-Derdich are affiliated with Arizona State University.

Address correspondence to: Richard A. Fabes, Department of Family & Human Development, Arizona State University, Tempe, AZ 85287-2502 (E-mail: rfabes@asu.edu).

Richard A. Fabes and Nancy Eisenberg were funded in part by a grant from the National Institute of Mental Health (1 R01 HH55052). Parts of this manuscript are based on the Master's thesis of the second author. The authors express their appreciation to all of the parents and children who contributed to this project.

[Haworth co-indexing entry note]: "The Coping with Children's Negative Emotions Scale (CCNES): Psychometric Properties and Relations with Children's Emotional Competence." Fabes, Richard A. et al. Co-published simultaneously in *Marriage & Family Review* (The Haworth Press, Inc.) Vol. 34, No. 3/4, 2002, pp. 285-310; and: *Emotions and the Family* (ed: Richard A. Fabes) The Haworth Press, Inc., 2002, pp. 285-310. Single or multiple copies of this article are available for a fee from The Haworth Document Delivery Service [1-800-HAWORTH, 9:00 a.m. - 5:00 p.m. (EST). E-mail address: docdelivery@haworthpress.com].

© 2002 by The Haworth Press, Inc. All rights reserved.

lidity. Factor analysis of the structure of the CCNES suggests that there may be only four rather than six subscales. In the second study, we examined the predictive validity of the CCNES to 36 children's emotional competence (decoding and expressiveness). The supportive subscales (positively) and parental distress (negatively) predicted children's decoding, whereas emotional encouragement (positively) and nonsupportive parenting (negatively) predicted children's expressiveness. It was concluded that the CCNES is a reliable and valid instrument and that further research and refinement of its use is needed. *[Article copies available for a fee from The Haworth Document Delivery Service: 1-800-HAWORTH. E-mail address: <docdelivery@haworthpress.com> Website: <http://www.HaworthPress.com> © 2002 by The Haworth Press, Inc. All rights reserved.]*

KEYWORDS. Parental coping, negative emotions, socialization of emotion

Although a number of researchers (Baumrind, 1989; Greenberger & Goldberg, 1989), theorists (Dix, 1991; Patterson, 1982; Wahler & Dumas, 1987), and clinicians (Anastopoulos & Barkley, 1989; Barkley, 1985) have been interested in how parents respond to their children's negative behaviors, relatively little focus has been placed on parental responses to children's negative emotional displays (Fabes, Leonard, Kupanoff, & Martin, 2001). Even when there has been interest, most of the interest has been limited to whether children's emotions should be encouraged or restricted. For example, Tomkins (Tomkins, 1962, 1963) hypothesized that parental acceptance rather than suppression of children's negative emotions would be beneficial to children. Likewise, Leavitt and Power (1989) observed day care workers and parents and noted how the emotional expressions of preschoolers often were minimized. They postulated that this lack of emotional encouragement leads to decreased emotional understanding. Similarly, Buck (1984) hypothesized that children punished for affect expressions learn to hide their outward expression of emotions but become physically aroused in situations that involve emotion. Halberstadt and colleagues (Halberstadt, 1983; Halberstadt, 1986; Halberstadt, Cassidy, Stifter, Parke, & Fox, 1995) argued that greater parental emotional expressiveness would lead to greater expressiveness in children. Beyond acceptance and restrictiveness of children's emotions, however, we know relatively little about how parents respond to children's negative emotions and the consequences of these responses for children's socio-emotional outcomes. The purpose of the present paper is to examine the psychometric properties of a scale designed to fill the gap in this literature–namely, the *Coping with Children's Negative Emotions Scale* (CCNES; Fabes, Eisenberg, & Bernzweig, 1990a).

Studying parents' reactions to children's negative emotions is important because it is in the family that children first express their needs and desires, and where socialization of this communication first takes place (Eisenberg, Cumberland, & Spinrad, 1998; Fabes et al., 2001). For example, Malatesta and Haviland (Malatesta & Haviland, 1982) found that parents' emotional responses to their children were related to affect expression in children as young as 3 to 6 months of age. Moreover, Dunn and colleagues (Dunn, Bretherton, & Munn, 1987) found that mothers' references to feeling states when children were 18-months-old were positively correlated with children's references to feeling states at 24 months. These results suggest that how parents' respond to children's negative emotions influences children's abilities to cope with their own (and others') emotional states.

Children's expressions of negative emotion provide an important context in which the effects of emotion socialization on social and emotional competence can be examined. Due to the aversive nature of negative emotions, parents often are motivated to react to them using negative control strategies (such as punishment). This may be due, in part, to a belief that children's expressions of negative emotions are used for manipulation, are reflective of poor character, and are harmful to children. For example, Gottman (1997) suggests that parents who perceive children's negative emotions to be aversive tend to punish children or trivialize the negative emotion in order to quickly put a stop to their expressions. Putting a stop to children's negative emotions, in turn, removes the aversiveness of the negative emotional reactions.

MEASUREMENT OF PARENT RESPONSES TO CHILDREN'S NEGATIVE EMOTIONS

Currently, there are very few measures available to measure emotion socialization and/or how parents respond to children's negative emotions. Halberstadt (1986) developed the *Family Expressive Questionnaire* (FEQ) that is an inventory designed to assess the emotions expressed by one's family. A second instrument, the *Parent Attitude Toward Children's Expressiveness Scale* (PACES) (Saarni, 1985) examines the degree to which parents are permissive or restrictive towards children's emotional expressiveness. In both cases, these measures focus primarily on whether or not a parent is encouraging or restrictive of negative emotional expressions (either through their own emotions or through their responses to children's emotions). However, neither of these scales provide information regarding the various ways that parents go about encouraging or discouraging children's negative emotional expressions. Moreover, these measures do not allow parents to describe the variety of behaviors they may use when responding to children's negative emotional states.

THE COPING WITH CHILDREN'S NEGATIVE EMOTIONS SCALE

In response to these issues, Fabes and colleagues developed the *Coping with Children's Negative Emotions Scale* (CCNES) (Fabes et al., 1990a) that is designed to assess how parents typically respond to young children's (preschool or early elementary school) negative emotions. This self-report scale presents parents with 12 hypothetical scenarios in which their child is upset or angry (the CCNES and its scoring is available on-line at *http://www.public.asu.edu/~rafabes/GUEST. HTM#ccnes*). These hypothetical situations represent common emotionally evocative events that young children are exposed to. Parents are asked to rate the likelihood of responding to the scenario in each of six possible ways–with each of the six responses representing theoretically different ways of responding to children's negative emotions.

These six subscales delineate different responses that a parent might engage in when exposed to their young children's negative emotions. *Problem-focused responses* reflect the degree to which parents help the child solve the problem that caused the child's distress. In contrast, *emotion-focused responses* reflect the degree to which parents respond with strategies that help the child feel better (i.e., comfort or distract the child). These two types of coping responses reflect the basic distinction made by stress and coping theorists (Folkman & Lazarus, 1990; Lazarus & Folkman, 1991) between coping responses designed to address the source of stress (problem-focused coping) versus those designed to address the emotional distress (emotion-focused coping). Evidence suggests that parents who cope with children's negative emotions in supportive ways contribute positively to the development of children's social and emotional competence (Eisenberg, Fabes, Schaller, Carlo, &

Miller, 1991; MacDonald & Parke, 1984; Roberts & Strayer, 1987). Although both problem-focused and emotion-focused responses to children's negative emotions contribute to children's outcomes in similar ways, we distinguish between the two because parents indicate that they do not use these two responses to the same extent. For example, parents are considerably more likely to utilize problem-solving strategies in response to children's distress than they are to use comforting or distracting (Roberts & Strayer, 1987). Moreover, problem- and emotion-focused strategies have been found to vary in their effectiveness depending on the degree of control present in the situation. In situations where there is some degree of control, problem-focused strategies generally are more effective, whereas emotion-focused coping responses are more effective when the situation involves low degrees of control (Altshuler & Ruble, 1989).

Actively encouraging children's expression of negative emotions is reflected in the *Expressive Encouragement* subscale. This subscale reflects the degree to which parents are accepting of children's negative emotional displays. Parental encouragement of children's expression of negative emotions has been found to be related to children's perspective-taking and empathy (Bryant, 1987), complex thinking about emotionally expressive behavior (Saarni, 1989), and the ability to decode other's emotions (Halberstadt, 1986).

Two subscales focusing on nonsupportive coping responses also are included on the CCNES. The first, the *Minimization Reactions* subscale, reflects the degree to which parents discount the seriousness of their children's emotional reactions or devalue their problem or distressed responses. As such, it represents one of the ways in which a parent may attempt to restrict or limit children's expression of negative emotions. The second nonsupportive subscale, the *Punitive Reactions* subscale, represents the degree to which parents use verbal or physical punishment to control children's negative emotional display. Minimization responses represent the more subtle and less overtly controlling methods of attempting to limit children's negative emotional displays. Both types of nonsupportive coping responses have been found to be related to children's non-optimal outcomes, such as lower levels of empathic and social responsiveness (Eisenberg et al., 1991; Fabes et al., 2001; Roberts & Strayer, 1987) and increased anxiety (Buck, 1984). Although parents report using these nonsupportive responses relatively infrequently, their use generally undermines children's social and emotional competence (but perhaps not to the same degree).

Thus, current research and theory suggest that parents who use negative control strategies when their children express negative emotions have children who do not regulate their emotions or behaviors effectively (Denham, Mitchell-Copeland, Strandberg, Auerbach, & Blair, 1997; Fabes et al., 2001). Additionally, the use of nonsupportive strategies to control children's negative emotions teaches children to suppress negative emotions, which in turn, increases their negative emotional arousal and anxiety (Gross & Levenson, 1993). When parents succeed at suppression, the child tends to "store" the negative emotion until a time when a similar circumstance arises. Thus, a pattern of stored and released negative emotion is created over time and is thought to result in more intense expressions that children have difficulty regulating (Buck, 1984).

A final possible response that parents have to children's expression of negative emotions is that parents may become distressed themselves. The amount of distress a parent experiences is important because of its effects on their socializing behaviors. Those parents who become distressed when their children express negative emotions are likely to focus on their own discomfort rather than on the needs and conditions of their children (Fabes, Eisenberg, & Miller, 1990b; Fabes et al., 2001). When parents feel such distress, they may have trouble calming down, may feel emotionally disorganized, and may "fly off the handle" when faced with children's negative emotional displays (Gottman, 1997). These parents are unlikely or unable to support their children through a negative emotional experience and, instead, are more likely to intensify their efforts to control their children's negative emotional expressions by punishing or minimizing them. In turn, children who are punished for expressions of negative emotion tend to suppress that emotion until they lose control. Thus, parents who become emotionally overaroused due to children's negative affectivity and rely on punishing and minimizing responses to achieve relief from the aversive exposure do so at the cost of socializing children to suppress emotion until it is released in highly intense and dysregulated ways (Buck, 1984; Tomkins, 1962). As a result, the child may display decreased social and emotional competence.

The CCNES is a self-report instrument that allows researchers to examine these issues. Evidence from studies that have included the CCNES generally support these theoretical assumptions (Eisenberg & Fabes, 1994; Eisenberg, Fabes, Carlo, & Karbon, 1992; Eisenberg et al., 1992b; Eisenberg, Fabes, Shepard, Guthrie, Murphy, & Reiser, 1999; Fabes et al., 2001; Smith & Walden, 1996). Although these studies have found adequate internal reliability of the subscales of the CCNES, to date there has not been any attempt to assess the broader psychometric properties of the CCNES. The primary purpose of this paper is to examine the general psychometric properties. We conducted two studies in which we addressed the reliability and validity of the CCNES. In the first study, we examined the internal consistency, test-retest reliability, factor analytic structure, and concurrent and construct validity of the CCNES. In the second study, we examined the differential predictions of the subscales of the CCNES to young children's emotional decoding and expressiveness.

STUDY 1

In the first study, we examined the reliability and validity of the CCNES. We did this by recruiting parents (mostly mothers) of young children to fill out a variety of questionnaires (see below). A subset of these parents completed the CCNES twice (for test-retest assessment).

METHODOLOGY

Sample

The sample consisted of 101 parents, primarily mothers (96 mothers and 5 fathers) of 3- to 6-year-old (mean age = 56.4 months) children enrolled in 27 private preschools in the east valley of the Phoenix metropolitan area. The sample consisted of primarily middle-class Caucasian mothers who had an average of 2.05 children. Of these participants, 86% were Caucasian, 9% Hispanic, 3% Black, 1% of Asian heritage, and 1% of mixed origin. Family income ranged from $4,000 to $140,000 (mean income = $47,000). Mean level of parental education was 15 years (range = 11 to 20 years $SD = 2.1$).

Procedures

Parents' participation entailed completing a survey battery that consisted of the CCNES (Fabes et al., 1990a), a demographics questionnaire, the *Parent Attitude Toward Children's Expressiveness Scale* (PACES) (Saarni, 1985), the *Parental Control Scale* (PCS) (Greenberger, 1988), the *Parent Affect Test-Anger* (PATa) (Linehan, Paul, & Egan, 1983), and the *Interpersonal Reactivity Index* (IRI) (Davis, 1983). Because responses on any self-report inventory may be influenced by the degree to which a respondent answers in a socially desirable fashion, an index of social desirability (Crowne & Marlowe, 1964) also was included.

Twenty-seven preschools were randomly selected from those listed in the telephone directory. After receiving permission from each participating school, a letter introducing the study was distributed to all parents at the preschools. This letter contained an informed consent form for interested parents to sign and return. One hundred and eighty parents provided initial permission and were subsequently given the packet of questionnaires (randomly ordered) to be completed and returned via collection boxes at each school. From these 180 parents, 101 useable forms were returned (56%). Forty-four of these 101 parents were chosen at random, contacted by telephone, and sent a copy of the CCNES to complete a second time approximately four months after the original administration. Data from 35 parents (75%; 7 did not return the survey and 2 were unusable) were available to establish test-retest reliability. Retest parents were similar in overall characteristics to the larger sample (i.e., no significant differences in child's age, parent's education, or parent's annual income were found).

Measures

In addition to the CCNES, several measures were included in the current study to determine concurrent and construct validity. A brief synopsis of each of the scales used in the current investigation for these purposes follows.

Coping with Children's Negative Emotions Scale (CCNES; Fabes et al., 1990a). The CCNES consists of six 12-item subscales that assess separate parental coping responses in response to young children's negative emotions. For each question, a hypothetical scenario is presented in which the respondent's child feels upset (i.e., "If my child is panicky and can't go to sleep after watching a scary TV show, I would . . ."). Six possible responses that could be made by the parent are provided (i.e., "Remain calm and not let myself get anxious," "Talk to my child about ways to make it hurt less.") Utilizing a 7-point scale ranging from "very unlikely" (1) to "very likely" (7), the parent was asked to rate the likelihood of responding to the scenario in each of the six possible ways. These subscales (corresponding to the six previously discussed) reflect six qualitatively different responses to children's negative emotional expressions: Problem-Focused Reactions (PRF), Emotion-Focused Reactions (EFR), Expressive Encouragement (EE), Minimization Reactions (MR), Punitive Reactions PR), and Distress Reactions (DR).

Parent Attitude Toward Children's Expressiveness Scale (Saarni, 1985; PACES). The PACES provides a measure of how accepting or controlling a parent is regarding their child's emotional expressions. PACES is a 20-item, multiple choice scale (i.e., "If my school age child starts to giggle during a funeral, I would . . . "). For each item, parents select one response from four options ranging in degree from permissive to controlling (i.e., "smile understandingly at my child," "ignore it," "frown at my child," "frown and also tell my child to be quiet"). The options are treated as a 4-point scale in which high scores reflect a more controlling attitude towards children's expression of emotions. PACES was designed for use with parents of children between the preschool and older adolescent ages. Modifications to the original format changed "my school age child" to "my preschooler." Positive relations between the PACES (reflecting restrictive/controlling responses) and the nonsupportive subscales of the CCNES (PR, MR, and DR) were expected. The reverse was expected for the supportive subscales (EE, EFR, PFR).

Parental Control Scale (Greenberger, 1988; PCS). This measure is used to identify the amount of disciplinary control a parent exerts over a child. The PCS is a 39-item scale in which parents respond to each item on a 7-point Likert scale ranging from "strongly disagree" to "strongly agree" (i.e., "I have to keep my child's natural curiosity firmly in check," "I don't set limits on what my child can eat," "A well-raised child is one who doesn't have to be told twice to do something.") Three subscales consisting of 13 items each assess Harsh, Firm/Responsive, and Lax Control. Harsh parenting on the PCS was expected to be positively related to PR and MR and inversely related to EE, EFR, and PFR. Because the supportive responses of EFR and PFR reflect an authoritative style of parenting (Baumrind, 1989), we expected EFR and PFR (and perhaps EE) to be positively related to Firm parenting. MR and PR were considered to be reflective of authoritarian parenting and thus expected to be positively related to Harsh parenting.

Parental Anger. Parents' angry responses to children's behavior were assessed through the use of the Parental Anger subscale of the Parent Affect Test (PATa) (Linehan et al., 1983). The PATa assesses a parent's tendency to become angry and express angry emotions. For each item (i.e., "If my child starts crying when I punish him/her, I would . . . ," "If I ask my child to do something and he/she gets really angry, I would . . . ," "If my child talks back to me, I would . . . "), a 7-point scale ranging from "very unlikely" to "very likely" is used for parents to rate the likelihood that they respond in each of four different ways. Parents respond with the degree to which they "feel angry," "feel tense," "want to yell at child," and "want to send child to room." Higher scores reflect greater anger. Once again, we expected the nonsupportive responses (DR and PR) to be positively related to PATa and the supportive indexes (EFR, PFR, EE) to be negatively related.

Interpersonal Reactivity Index (Davis, 1983; IRI). The IRI is a 28-item scale used to measure four separate aspects of empathy (seven items each). The three scales most relevant to the present investigation were used (the Fantasy Empathy scale–which assesses the degree to which individuals respond empathically to the emotions or actions of fictitious characters–was not used). The Perspective-Taking (PT) subscale assesses the tendency to adopt the point of view of another (i.e., "I sometimes try to understand my friends better by imagining how things look from their perspective."). The Empathic Concern (EC) subscale assesses the tendency to experience "other oriented" feelings of warmth, compassion, and concern for another (i.e., sympathy–"I often have tender concerned feelings for people less fortunate than me.") In contrast, the Personal Distress (PD) subscale measures "self-oriented" feelings of personal unease and discomfort in reaction to the emotions of others (i.e., "When I see someone who badly needs help in an emergency, I go to pieces."). We expected a positive relation between PD on the IRI and DR on the CCNES. Moreover, we expected perspective-taking and empathic responding to be positively related to the supportive CCNES subscales and negatively related to the nonsupportive subscales.

Social Desirability. A subset of 25 items from Crowne and Marlowe's (1964) Social Desirability true-false questionnaire was used to identify the degree to which individuals conform to societal norms in their responses (i.e., "No matter who I'm talking to, I'm always a good listener," "I never hesitate to go out of my way to help someone in trouble," "I never resent being asked to return a favor."). One point is scored for each response in the socially desirable direction. The higher the score received, the greater the tendency to describe oneself in favorable terms.

RESULTS

Analysis of the psychometric properties of the CCNES consisted of first examining the internal consistency of the subscales of the CCNES (and the other scales). We next examined the test-retest reliability. Following this, we examined the relations among the subscales of the CCNES and the degree to which the subscales were related to social desirability. Next, relations of scores on the CCNES to demographic and child characteristics were examined. Finally, we explored the concurrent and construct validity of the subscales of the CCNES by examining the relations of the subscales to theoretically similar measures.

Assessment of Internal and Test-Retest Reliability of the CCNES

Table 1 presents the means, standard deviations, ranges, and the internal reliability alphas for the CCNES and the other measures used in this study. The internal reliability for the scales of the CCNES were within acceptable limits. The reliability estimates ranged from .69 for the Punitive Reactions subscale to .85 for the Expressive Encouragement subscale. Reliability estimates for the other study indexes were comparable, with the Parental Control and PACES indexes showing the lowest levels of internal reliability (see Table 1).

TABLE 1. Means and Standard Deviations for Measures Used in Study 1

Measure	Mean	SD	Range	α
CCNES				
Distress Reactions	2.41	.79	1.00-4.18	.70
Punitive Responses	2.01	.60	1.00-4.08	.69
Minimization Responses	2.24	.70	1.00-4.75	.78
Expressive Encouragement	5.32	.79	3.50-6.92	.85
Emotion-Focused Responses	5.48	.74	3.75-6.92	.80
Problem-Focused Responses	6.01	.66	4.36-7.00	.78
Interpersonal Reactivity Index				
Empathic Concern	4.10	.52	3.86-5.00	.69
Perspective Taking	3.73	.70	1.71-4.57	.83
Personal Distress	2.33	.77	1.14-4.57	.82
Social Desirability	13.45	4.85	3-23	.83
Parent Affect Test–Anger	3.08	.95	1.02-5.75	.94
Parental Control				
Harsh	31.61	7.86	17-52	.68
Firm	69.85	7.22	52-90	.59
Lax	39.10	8.10	16-57	.63
PACES	32.27	4.82	17-40	.60

Test-retest reliability for the 35 participants who completed the CCNES twice (separated by four months) revealed that respondents' answers on the CCNES were significantly correlated from Time 1 to Time 2, $rs(33) = .62, .83, .77, .56, .57$, and $.77$, all $ps < .01$ for the distress, punitive, minimization, expressive, emotion-focused, and problem-focused subscales, respectively. Tests of mean differences from Time 1 to Time 2 revealed significant differences only for the punitive and problem-focused subscales. Specifically, scores on PR were significantly lower at Time 2 than they were at Time 1 ($Ms = 2.10$ and 1.95, $SDs = .66$ and $.65$ for Time 1 and Time 2 PR scores, respectively; paired $t(34) = 2.24, p < .05$). A similar pattern was found for the PRF subscale ($Ms = 6.05$ and 5.83, $SDs = .64$ and $.63$ for Time 1 and Time 2 PR scores, respectively; paired $t(34) = 2.88, p < .01$).

Relations with Social Desirability

To determine the degree to which parents' CCNES scores were influenced by social desirability, the relations of the subscales of the CCNES to the index of social desirability were computed. As can be seen in Table 2, social desirability was significantly related only to the DR subscale of the CCNES. Specifically, mothers whose responses tended to reflect greater levels of social desirability also tended to report lower distress when exposed to their children's negative emotions. Thus, only one of the six subscales of the CCNES was related to social desirability. In contrast, four of the eight correlations of the other study indexes were related to social desirability (see Table 2). Similar to the CCNES, the index of personal distress on the IRI was significantly inversely related to social desirability. Additionally, social desirability was significantly positively correlated with empathic concern, perspective taking, and harsh parental control.

Relation of CCNES to Parent and Child Demographics

To examine the degree to which the subscales of the CCNES varied as a function of the characteristics of our sample, we conducted correlations and tests of mean differences. For the parent demographic indexes, only maternal education was significantly correlated with subscales of the CCNES (paternal education, family income, maternal and paternal age, and family size were not significantly correlated with any CCNES subscale). Specifically, maternal education was positively correlated with DR and EE, $rs(99) = .21$ and $.24$, $ps < .05$, respectively.

TABLE 2. Relations with Social Desirability

Measure	Correlation with Social Desirability
CCNES	
Distress Reactions	−.52**
Punitive Responses	−.15
Minimization Responses	−.19
Expressive Encouragement	.07
Emotion-Focused Responses	.01
Problem-Focused Responses	.15
Interpersonal Reactivity Index	
Empathic Concern	.25*
Perspective Taking	.37**
Personal Distress	−.39**
Parent Affect Test–Anger	−.20
Parental Control	
Harsh	.11
Firm	.32**
Lax	−.16
PACES	.06

Note. $dfs = 100$. * $p < .05$; ** $p < .01$.

Thus, mothers who were more educated tended to report experiencing more distress when exposed to their children's negative emotions and to be more encouraging of children's expressions of emotions than were mothers who were less educated. Given the number of correlations computed, however, these relations may be due to chance. Examination of the relation of scores on the CCNES to children's age, gender, ethnicity, and family structure (single-parent, dual-parent, etc.) did not reveal any significant differences.

Interrelations of Parent Measures

Subscales of the CCNES. Table 3 presents the interrelations among the six subscales of the CCNES. As can be seen in Table 3, the supportive parental responses of Emotion-Focused Reactions (EFR), Problem-Focused Reactions (PFR), and Expressive Encouragement (EE) were significantly, positively correlated with one another. Likewise, the

TABLE 3. Relations Among CCNES Subscales

	DR	PR	MR	EE	EFR	PFR
Distress Reactions (DR)		.32**	.32**	.02	−.01	−.14
Punitive Responses (PR)			.64***	−.15	−.18	−.24*
Minimization Responses (MR)				−.16	.12	−.01
Expressive Encouragement (EE)					.36**	.54***
Emotion-Focused Responses (EFR)						.65***
Problem-Focused Responses (PFR)						

Note. dfs = 100. * $p < .05$; ** $p < .01$, *** $p < .001$

nonsupportive parental reactions of Minimization Reactions (MR), Punitive Reactions (PR), and Distress Reactions (DR) were significantly, positively related with each other.

Interestingly, the positive subscales of the CCNES generally were not significantly, inversely related with the negative subscales of the CCNES. Thus, the positive and negative subscales do not appear to represent a linear continuum from positive to negative parental reactions. Instead, they appear to represent distinct factors. Moreover, the strength of the interrelations among positive and negative subscales varied. To examine the distinctive qualities of the subscales, we conducted a principal components factor analysis (with Varimax rotation) using each parent's six subscale scores as the variables in the analysis. The analysis revealed four factors with Eigenvalues greater than .5 (accounting for a total of 90% of the variance). A .5 Eigenvalue was used because the scree plot fit better using that level (and because it was a conceptually better fit as well). The first factor accounted for 37% of the variance and consisted of MR and PR. The first factor appears to reflect a pattern of harsh negative and nonsupportive responses to children's negative emotions. The second factor accounted for an additional 26% of the variance and consisted of EFR and PFR. This factor reflects supportive responses focused on helping the child cope with the negative emotional response and its cause. The third factor accounted for 17% of the variance and was made up of EE. The final factor accounted for another 10% of the variance and was made up of DR.

Relations of the CCNES to other parent indexes. The interrelations of the CCNES to the other parent indexes are presented in Table 4. Inspection of this table reveals patterns that generally provide construct validity for the subscales of the CCNES. For the *Interpersonal Reactivity Index*

(IRI), self-reported empathic concern and perspective taking were significantly, positively related to EFR, PRF, and EE (see Table 4). In contrast, empathic concern was inversely related to MR and PR. Moreover, perspective taking was inversely related to MR. Thus, parents who are empathic, sympathetic, and relatively better perspective takers tend to respond more supportively and less harshly when their children express negative emotions. Consistent with our prediction, the DR subscale of the CCNES was positively related to the distress scale of the IRI.

Parental anger, as indexed by the PATa, was significantly positively related to the three negative response subscales of the CCNES (MR, PR, DR). As such, parents who reported feeling more anger when children do something wrong or are annoying also reported responding harshly and with distress when exposed to children's negative emotions.

Relations of the subscales of the CCNES with the Harsh, Firm, and Lax subscales of the *Parental Control Scale* revealed several significant correlations. Specifically, Harsh parenting was significantly positively correlated with PR and MR. Additionally, Harsh parenting was inversely related to EE. Thus, parents who tend to report harsh parenting practices also tend to report harsh responses to their children when their children express negative emotions. Lax parenting was positively related to DR and MR. Parents who perceived themselves as Lax in control also tended to be higher in DR and MR. Firm parental control was significantly positively related to the supportive parenting subscales of EFR, PFR, and EE. Moreover, Firm parenting was inversely related to DR. These results suggest that the subscales of the CCNES are related to parents' general perceptions of their level of parental control and responsiveness.

There also were two significant findings for the relations of the CCNES with the *Parent Attitude Toward Children's Expressiveness Scale* (PACES; see Table 4). Higher parental control of children's expressiveness (i.e., high scores on the PACES) was related to greater punitive and minimization responses on the CCNES.

DISCUSSION

The results of Study 1 confirmed that the CCNES has good internal and test-retest consistency. Moreover, the interrelations of the subscales of the CCNES with other parent-related indexes also confirmed that the CCNES is generally a valid instrument that relates to theoretically simi-

TABLE 4. Relations of CCNES Subscales to Parent-Report Indexes

	Interpersonal Reactivity Index				Parental Control			
CCNES	Empathic Concern	Perspective Taking	Personal Distress	Parent Affect Test–Anger	Harsh	Firm	Lax	PACES
Distress Reactions	-.09	-.17	.38**	.32**	-.12	-.32**	.22*	-.19
Punitive Responses	-.30**	-.17	.07	.42***	.34**	-.12	.08	.26**
Minimization Responses	-.32**	-.26**	.24*	.29**	.37***	-.03	.22*	.23*
Expressive Encouragement	.45***	.22*	-.06	-.02	-.32***	.23*	.04	-.17
Emotion-Focused Responses	.23*	.22*	.01	-.06	-.10	.26**	.07	.07
Problem-Focused Responses	.43***	.25*	.15	-.06	-.15	.25*	-.08	.18

Note. dfs = 100. * p < .05; ** p < .01, *** p < .001

lar constructs. The issue that remains unresolved is the degree to which the CCNES consists of six or four relatively distinct subscales. The interrelations among the subscales and the factor analysis revealed that the subscales reflecting supportive parental coping responses (PFR and EFR) may reflect a singular subscale. Similarly, the subscales reflecting nonsupportive parental coping with children's negative emotions (MR and PR) also may reflect a singular subscale. Although the subscales of the CCNES reflect theoretically different aspects of parental coping with children's negative emotions, parents may not necessarily distinguish among these. It may be that these distinctions are too subtle for parents to make, or that parents in fact distinguish these but when they occur they tend to co-occur such that the subscales are relatively difficult to distinguish. Certainly more research is necessary, particularly in the prediction of outcomes for children. Thus, our next step was to conduct a study to determine if the subscales of the CCNES differentially predict children's emotion-related outcomes.

STUDY 2

The purpose of this study was to examine the degree to which parents' scores on the CCNES predicted children's emotional competence at decoding (i.e., interpreting) and expressing emotional states. This study addressed the validity of the CCNES in differentially predicting these two important aspects of children's emotional competence. Based on the literature previously reviewed, we expected that children whose parents respond in generally supportive ways to their negative emotional states and conditions would be better at correctly interpreting and identifying emotions than children whose parents respond in nonsupportive or distressed ways. We expected this relation to be stronger for EFR than PFR responses because of the theoretical and empirical link between emotionally supportive parenting and children's empathy, sympathy, and perspective taking (Denham & Grout, 1993; Denham, Zoller, & Couchoud, 1994; Fabes et al., 1990b). Moreover, because harsh parental coping responses are thought to teach children the need to suppress emotional states, children's emotional expressiveness is expected to be inversely related to the nonsupportive parenting subscales of the CCNES, but positively associated with parental encouragement of emotional states.

METHODOLOGY

Sample

The sample consisted of 36 mothers of preschool children enrolled to two classrooms at a university-affiliated child care center. None of the participants was involved in Study 1 and the sample consisted of primarily middle-class Caucasian mothers; 87% were Caucasian, 9% Hispanic, 3% Black, and 1% Asian. Family income ranged from $10,000 to $200,000 (median income = $55,000). Mean levels of maternal and paternal education were 17.5 and 17.8 years (SDs = 2.4 and 2.5 years), respectively (range = 12 to 22 years). The children (16 boys and 20 girls) ranged in age from 48 to 76 months (mean age = 58.9 months, SD = 8.6 months).

Procedures

Decoding task. Based on the procedures used by Denham and colleagues (Denham, McKinley, Couchoud, & Holt, 1990), cloth puppets with neutral facial expressions were used to enact 8 vignettes. The vignettes involved common everyday situations that elicit emotions (e.g., getting a present, having a nightmare, having someone break a favorite toy, etc.). Each vignette was accompanied by standardized vocal and visual affective cues emitted by the puppet/experimenter. After seeing each vignette, children were asked to pick the proper face for the puppet from the available choices (happy, sad, angry, afraid, surprised, or nothing–children had been tested prior to beginning to make certain they understood how to use the faces). Faces were selected in answer to the question, "How does the puppet feel?" Decoding scores were created by giving the child 2 points for each correct choice, 1 point for identifying the correct positive/negative affective valence of the emotion but not actually identifying the correct emotion (e.g., selecting the sad instead of the angry face), and 0 for a totally incorrect choice.

Expressiveness. During the time the child was engaged in the decoding task, two observers watched the child's facial expressions and rated the child's expressiveness using a scale from 1 (none) to 7 (very high). The observers were instructed to base their ratings on the degree to which children expressed both positive and negative emotions. The observers were trained to use both the frequency and the intensity of the children's emotional expressions. These observations were made from behind a one-way mirror and the observers could not hear what the child said. Thus, the ratings were based primarily on the facial expressions of the child. The coders independently rated each child and the interrater reliability correlation for the two observers was quite high, $r(34) = .81$, $p < .001$. Given the high degree of reliability, the average of the two ratings was used as each child's expressiveness score.

RESULTS

The means and standard deviations for the indexes included in Study 2 are presented in Table 5. Comparisons of these means to those for the CCNES in Study 1 reveal comparable levels and patterns of responses (e.g., that parents endorsed more positive than negative coping responses). Moreover, the alpha coefficients for each of the subscales of the CCNES generally were comparable (although higher) to those in Study 1, ranging from .71 (PR) to .87 (EFR).

There were no significant sex differences found in the subscales of the CCNES and age of the child correlated only with PFR, $r(34) = .46, p < .005$. Thus, parents were more likely to report using problem-focused coping responses when dealing with older rather than younger children's negative emotions.

Children's scores on the decoding and expressiveness tasks were moderately correlated with each other (see Table 6). Tests for sex differences also revealed no significant differences. Not surprisingly,

TABLE 5. Means and Standard Deviations for Measures Used in Study 2

Measure	Mean	SD
CCNES		
Distress Reactions	2.73	.51
Punitive Responses	1.89	.81
Minimization Responses	2.18	.81
Expressive Encouragement	5.44	.96
Emotion-Focused Responses	5.51	.75
Problem-Focused Responses	5.75	.67
Decoding Task	1.18	.14
Expressiveness Task	4.25	1.48

Note: $N = 36$.

TABLE 6. Partial Correlations (controlling for age) of the CCNES with Decoding and Expressiveness Tasks: Study 2

Measure	Decoding	Expressiveness
CCNES		
Distress Reactions	−.57***	−.02
Punitive Responses	−.12	−.40*
Minimization Responses	−.19	−.24+
Expressive Encouragement	−.10	.62***
Emotion-Focused Responses	.42*	−.13
Problem-Focused Responses	.38*	−.01
Decoding		.39*

Note: $dfs = 33$.
+$p < .10$; * $p < .05$; ** $p < .01$; *** $p < .001$

older children tended to score at least marginally higher than younger children on the expressiveness and decoding tasks, $rs(34) = .43$ and $.31$, $ps < .005$ and $.06$, respectively.

To examine the predictions regarding the relations of the CCNES to children's emotional decoding and expressiveness performance, we computed partial correlations (controlling for age). The results of these analyses are presented in Table 6 and reveal differential patterns of interrelations. As predicted, children's decoding performance was positively correlated with PFR and EFR and inversely correlated with DR. Thus, children whose parents were supportive when they expressed negative emotions were relatively able to decode others' emotions, whereas children whose parents tended to become upset and distressed when exposed to their children's negative emotions were relatively unable to decode others' emotions. For the expressiveness task, children whose parents were encouraging of their emotional expressions tended to score relatively high, whereas parents who were punitive or minimized when children expressed negative emotions were at least marginally lower on spontaneous emotional expressiveness.

DISCUSSION

The results of Study 2 add further confirmation to the reliability and validity of the CCNES. In this study, the subscales of the CCNES were differentially related to young children's emotion-related competencies. Specifically, children's ability to accurately decode others' emotions was related to supportive parenting responses (EFR and PFR) and inversely related to parental distress. In contrast, children's observed expressiveness was positively related expressive encouragement and inversely related to punitive coping responses. These findings suggest that parental responses to children's negative emotions appear to have important consequences on children's emotional expressiveness and decoding. The findings also suggest that specific parental responses have individuated effects. Supportive parental responses to children's negative emotions promote children's readiness to learn about others' thoughts, feelings, and behaviors in emotional contexts (Eisenberg et al., 1998), whereas parents who are easily distressed when exposed to children's negative emotions may undermine their children's ability to decode others' emotions by interfering with their ability to deal effectively and supportively with their children's negative emotions. We did not, however, find the expected stronger findings with EFR than PFR, again suggesting that these scales may not be tapping different aspects of parents' reactions to children's negative emotions.

Parental encouragement of emotion was, not surprisingly, related to children's observed expressiveness. This finding is consistent with evidence that parents who are accepting and supportive of the expression of emotions have children who are expressive and emotionally competent (Gottman, Katz, & Hooven, 1996). In contrast, parents who are not supportive have children who are relatively unexpressive. Although these children may not express emotions overtly, they may become internally dysregulated and have difficulty managing emotions–a hypothesis that is consistent with existing data and theorizing (Buck, 1984; Fabes et al., 2001).

GENERAL DISCUSSION

The overall patterns of findings from both of the studies in this paper reveal that the CCNES is psychometrically sound and predicts in accordance with theoretically and empirically derived relations. Measurement of reliability and validity of the CCNES and its subscales were well within the acceptable ranges and test-retest analyses revealed little difference in the mean scores over a 4-month period of time. Even when statistical differences were found in the test-retest analyses, the magnitude of the differences was small and may not reflect meaningful differences. As such, the CCNES appears to tap parents' tendencies to use different coping responses when exposed to children's negative emotions and these generally are stable across time. Concurrent validity analyses revealed that the subscales of the CCNES generally related in logical ways to other measures with similar or same constructs.

Examination of the relation of the CCNES to demographic variables revealed few significant findings. These data suggest that responses on the CCNES did not vary by sex of child, age of child, or by family/parental characteristics. As such, it appears that the CCNES is a scale that can be used to examine emotion-related socialization responses in a wide variety of contexts and with a wide variety of families. Of course, the reliability and validity of use of the CCNES with families from different backgrounds and from different countries or cultures will depend on the assessment of its psychometric properties in these different contexts.

Compared to some of the other scales used in this study, the CCNES had fewer relations with social desirability. Only the distress subscale was related to social desirability (negatively). These findings add further support for validity and reliability of the CCNES. However, an important step in determining the validity of the CCNES is to relate parents' responses to observed parenting behaviors. Until that is done, the degree to which the CCNES reflects true parental behavior is uncertain.

Although the CCNES is comprised of six theoretically distinct subscales, the data in this study suggest that the CCNES may consist of only four empirically distinct subscales. Given the overlap between EFR and PFR, these subscales are not clearly differentiated from one another and it is likely that they may tap a single supportive parental response dimension. Similarly, the subscales of MR and PR appear to tap nonsupportive, harsh parental responses. Further research with children of other ages and with a more diverse sample of parents may reveal more distinct relations for these subscales. Thus, researchers can consider examining the relation among the subscales to see if reducing the number of subscales to four is appropriate and conceptually sound.

LIMITATIONS AND FUTURE DIRECTIONS

There are several important caveats to the present research. First, the reliability and validity of the CCNES were tested almost entirely with mothers. Unfortunately, there were too few fathers in the present studies to separate out for comparisons. Thus, we do not know if the CCNES holds together in the same way for fathers as it does for mothers. Nor do we know how the combined parenting practices of fathers and mothers work to affect children's outcomes. Furthermore, the sample used in these studies were volunteers and we cannot be certain the degree to which these findings generalize to other groups of parents or children.

Although the scenarios used in the CCNES represent realistic and varied contexts for the expression of young children's negative emotions, the scenarios include a variety of children's emotions to which parents may respond (e.g., fear, anger, embarrassment, etc.). The subscales do not reflect how a parent responds to different emotions—they reflect generalized responses to the aggregate of children's negative emotions. Parents likely respond differently to different emotional states and use different strategies depending on whether the child is expressing one negative emotion versus another. For example, parents may be less likely to tolerate the expression of anger in their children than they are of fear or sadness (Casey & Fuller, 1994). As such, parental supportiveness likely varies for different types of negative emotional expressions. How parents respond to different emotions in their children, and how these differential responses play out in emotion socialization, is an important topic for future research.

The fact that we did not find any sex differences in parents' responses to the CCNES may be a function of the aggregated way in which the CCNES groups parents' responses across the different emotions. Other researchers have found that parents hold differential expectations for boys and girls and respond differently to their sons and daughters—encouraging sons to control emotions like fear and sadness, but not necessarily anger (Birnbaum & Croll, 1984; Casey & Fuller, 1994). Researchers who are interested in these kinds of questions may want to group certain items in the CCNES together according to the type of negative emotion expressed.

In summary, the CCNES appears to be a valuable tool for examining the ways parents respond to children's negative emotions and how these responses influence children's social and emotional outcomes. The scale (available on-line at: *http://www.public.asu.edu/~rafabes/GUEST. HTM#ccnes*) is psychometrically sound and provides researchers with an instrument that can readily be used to collect rich and predictive data related to parents' responses to children's negative emotions. Moreover, given the relatively few measures that exist, the CCNES is one of the more reliable and valid instruments. Certainly, more testing of the psychometric properties of the CCNES is needed, but the initial results appear promising and contribute to an increase in our understanding of the complexities that parental responses and parental emotions play in influencing children's emotion socialization.

REFERENCES

Altshuler, J. L., & Ruble, D. N. (1989). Developmental changes in children's awareness of strategies for coping with uncontrollable stress. *Child Development, 60*, 1337-1349.

Anastopoulos, A. D., & Barkley, R. A. (1989). A training program for parents of children with attention deficit-hyperactivity disorder. In C. E. Schaefer & J. M. Briesmeister (Eds.), *Handbook of parent training: Parents as co-therapists for children's behavior problems* (pp. 83-104). New York: Wiley.

Barkley, R. A. (1985). The parent-child interaction patterns of hyperactive children: Precursors to aggressive behavior? *Advances in Developmental & Behavioral Pediatrics, 6*, 117-150.

Baumrind, D. (1989). The permanence of change and the impermanence of stability. *Human Development, 32*, 187-195.

Birnbaum, D., & Croll, W. L. (1984). The etiology of children's stereotypes about sex differences in emotions. *Sex Roles, 10*, 677-691.

Bryant, B. K. (1987). Mental health, temperament, family, and friends: Perspectives on children's empathy and social perspective taking. In N. Eisenberg & J. Strayer (Eds.), *Empathy and its development* (pp. 245-270). New York: Cambridge University Press.

Buck, R. (1984). *The communication of emotion.* New York: Guilford.

Casey, R. J., & Fuller, L. L. (1994). Maternal regulation of children's emotions. *Journal of Nonverbal Behavior, 18*, 57-89.

Crowne, D. P., & Marlowe, D. (1964). *The approval motive.* New York: Wiley.

Davis, M. H. (1983). Measuring individual differences in empathy: Evidence for a multidimensional approach. *Journal of Personality and Social Psychology, 44*, 113-126.

Denham, S. A., & Grout, L. (1993). Socialization of emotion: Pathway to preschoolers' emotional and social competence. Special Issue: Development of nonverbal behavior: I. Emotional experience and expression. *Journal of Nonverbal Behavior, 17*, 205-227.

Denham, S. A., McKinley, M., Couchoud, E. A., & Holt, R. (1990). Emotional and behavioral predictors of preschool peer ratings. *Child Development, 61*, 1145-1152.

Denham, S. A., Mitchell-Copeland, J., Strandberg, K., Auerbach, S., & Blair, K. (1997). Parental contributions to preschoolers' emotional competence: Direct and indirect effects. *Motivation and Emotion, 21*, 65-86.

Denham, S. A., Zoller, D., & Couchoud, E. A. (1994). Socialization of preschoolers' emotion understanding. *Developmental Psychology, 30*, 928-936.

Dix, T. (1991). The affective organization of parenting: Adaptive and maladaptive processes. *Psychological Bulletin, 110*, 3-25.

Dunn, J., Bretherton, I., & Munn, P. (1987). Conversations about feeling states between mothers and their young children. *Developmental Psychology, 23*, 132-139.
Eisenberg, N., Cumberland, A., & Spinrad, T. L. (1998). Parental socialization of emotion. *Psychological Inquiry, 9*, 241-273.
Eisenberg, N., & Fabes, R. A. (1994). Mothers' reactions to children's negative emotions: Relations to children's temperament and anger behavior. *Merrill-Palmer Quarterly, 40*, 138-156.
Eisenberg, N., Fabes, R. A., Carlo, G., & Karbon, M. (1992). Emotional responsivity to others: Behavioral correlates and socialization antecedents. In N. Eisenberg & R. A. Fabes (Eds.), *Emotion and its regulation in early development* (pp. 57-73). San Francisco: Jossey-Bass.
Eisenberg, N., Fabes, R. A., Schaller, M., Carlo, G., & Miller, P. A. (1991). The relations of parental characteristics and practices to children's vicarious emotional responding. *Child Development, 62*, 1393-1408.
Eisenberg, N., Fabes, R. A., Shepard, S. A., Guthrie, I. K., Murphy, B. C., & Reiser, M. (1999). Parental reactions to children's negative emotions: Longitudinal relations to quality of children's social functioning. *Child Development, 70*, 513-534.
Fabes, R. A., Eisenberg, N., & Bernzweig, J. (1990a). *Coping with Children's Negative Emotions Scale (CCNES): Description and Scoring*. Tempe, AZ: Arizona State University.
Fabes, R. A., Eisenberg, N., & Miller, P. A. (1990b). Maternal correlates of children's vicarious emotional responsiveness. *Developmental Psychology, 26*, 639-648.
Fabes, R. A., Leonard, S. A., Kupanoff, K., & Martin, C. L. (2001). Parental Coping with Children's Negative Emotions: Relations with Children's Emotional and Social Responding. *Child Development, 72*, 907-920.
Folkman, S., & Lazarus, R. S. (1990). Coping and emotion. In N. L. Stein, B. Leventhal, & T. Trabasso (Eds.), *Psychological and biological approaches to emotion* (pp. 313-332). Hillsdale, NJ: Lawrence Erlbaum Associates, Inc.
Gottman, J. (1997). *The heart of parenting: How to raise an emotionally intelligent child*. New York: Simon & Schuster.
Gottman, J. M., Katz, L. F., & Hooven, C. (1996). Parental meta-emotion philosophy and the emotional life of families: Theoretical models and preliminary data. *Journal of Family Psychology, 10*, 243-268.
Greenberger, E. (1988). *New measures for research on work, parenting, and the socialization of children*. Irvine, CA: University of California, Irvine.
Greenberger, E., & Goldberg, W. A. (1989). Work, parenting, and the socialization of children. *Developmental Psychology, 25*, 22-35.
Gross, J. J., & Levenson, R. W. (1993). Emotional suppression: Physiology, self-report, and expressive behavior. *Journal of Personality & Social Psychology, 64*, 970-986.
Halberstadt, A. G. (1983). Family expressiveness styles and nonverbal communication skills. *Journal of Nonverbal Behavior, 8*, 14-26.
Halberstadt, A. G. (1986). Family socialization of emotional expression and nonverbal communication styles and skills. *Journal of Personality & Social Psychology, 51*, 827-836.

Halberstadt, A. G., Cassidy, J., Stifter, C. A., Parke, R. D., & Fox, N. A. (1995). Self-expressiveness within the family context: Psychometric support for a new measure. *Psychological Assessment, 7*, 93-103.

Lazarus, R. S., & Folkman, S. (1991). *Stress and coping.* New York: Columbia University Press.

Leavitt, R. L., & Power, M. B. (1989). Emotional socialization in the postmodern era: Children in day care. Special Issue: Sentiments, affect and emotion. *Social Psychology Quarterly, 2*, 35-43.

Linehan, N. M., Paul, E., & Egan, K. J. (1983). The Parent Affect Test: Development, validity, and reliability. *Journal of Clinical Child Psychology, 12*, 161-166.

MacDonald, K., & Parke, R. D. (1984). Bridging the gap: Parent-child play interaction and peer interactive competence. *Child Development, 55*, 1265-1277.

Malatesta, C. Z., & Haviland, J. M. (1982). Learning display rules: The socialization of emotion expression in infancy. *Child Development, 53*, 991-1003.

Patterson, G. R. (1982). *Coercive family process.* Eugene, OR: Castila.

Roberts, W., & Strayer, J. (1987). Parents' responses to the emotional distress of their children: Relations with children's competence. *Developmental Psychology, 23*, 415-422.

Saarni, C. (1985). Indirect processes in affect socialization. In M. Lewis & C. Saarni (Eds.), *The socialization of emotion* (pp. 187-209). New York: Plenum.

Saarni, C. (1989). Children's understanding of strategic control of emotional expression in social transactions. In C. Saarni & P. L. Harris (Eds.), *Children's understanding of emotion* (pp. 181-208). New York: Cambridge University Press.

Smith, M., & Walden, T. (1996). *Coping with emotionally arousing situations among African-American preschool-aged children.* Nashville, TN: Vanderbilt University.

Tomkins, S. (1962). *Affect, imagery, and consciousness* (Vol. 1). New York: Springer.

Tomkins, S. (1963). *Affect, imagery, and consciousness* (Vol. 2). New York: Springer.

Wahler, R., & Dumas, J. (1987). Family factors in childhood psychology: Toward a coercion-neglect model. In T. Jacob (Ed.), *Family interaction and psychopathology: Theories, methods, and findings* (pp. 581-628). New York: Plenum.

Parental Contributions to Preschoolers' Understanding of Emotion

Susanne Denham
Anita T. Kochanoff

SUMMARY. We hypothesized that parents who express positive emotions and are supportive of their preschoolers' emotional expressions and experiences are likely to engage in talking and teaching about emotions, thereby enhancing children's emotion knowledge. Observational and self-report indices of parents' socialization of emotion were obtained for 134 families when children were 3 and 4 years old, along with children's emotion knowledge from ages 3 to 5. Mothers' valuing teaching about emotions mediated the positive effects of their positive expressions and reactions on the emotion knowledge of 3-year-olds. More limited paternal contributions were found for 4-year-olds' emotion knowledge only. Departures from predicted relations suggested that fathers might see their role in emotion socialization as different from that of

---

Susanne Denham and Anita T. Kochanoff are affiliated with George Mason University.

Address correspondence to: Susanne Denham, George Mason University, Department of Psychology, MS 3F5, 4400 University Drive, Fairfax, VA 22030-4444.

This investigation was supported by R01MH54019, granted by the National Institutes of Mental Health. The authors wish to thank the many children and their families, as well as nursery school and daycare teachers, who gave so much time and good will so that the authors could learn about emotional competence, as well as Sharon Auerbach-Major, Krysti Batt, Kimberly Blair, Cameron Caswell, Sarah Caverly, Bettye Changizi, Alvin Malesky, Teresa Mason, Patrick Queenan, Katie Sawyer, Rebecca Sears, and Meredith Vickery, who assisted in gathering the data presented here.

[Haworth co-indexing entry note]: "Parental Contributions to Preschoolers' Understanding of Emotion." Denham, Susanne, and Anita T. Kochanoff. Co-published simultaneously in *Marriage & Family Review* (The Haworth Press, Inc.) Vol. 34, No. 3/4, 2002, pp. 311-343; and: *Emotions and the Family* (ed: Richard A. Fabes) The Haworth Press, Inc., 2002, pp. 311-343. Single or multiple copies of this article are available for a fee from The Haworth Document Delivery Service [1-800-HAWORTH, 9:00 a.m. - 5:00 p.m. (EST). E-mail address: docdelivery@haworthpress.com].

© 2002 by The Haworth Press, Inc. All rights reserved.

mothers. Prediction of 5-year-old emotion knowledge was not as strong as at earlier ages. *[Article copies available for a fee from The Haworth Document Delivery Service: 1-800-HAWORTH. E-mail address: <docdelivery@haworthpress.com> Website: <http://www.HaworthPress.com> © 2002 by The Haworth Press, Inc. All rights reserved.]*

KEYWORDS. Emotion social cognition, preschoolers

Important social cognitive abilities blossom during early childhood. In particular, preschoolers build on earlier foundations of knowledge about emotional expressions and situations. They extend this understanding to comprehending others' emotions differing from their own, discussing causes and consequences of emotions with reasonable accuracy, and beginning to consider more complex aspects of emotional understanding, such as mixed emotions and display rules of emotion (Denham, 1986; Denham & Couchoud, 1990a, 1990b; Denham & Zoller, 1991; Denham, Zoller, & Couchoud, 1994; Dunn, 1995; Gordis, Rosen, & Grand, 1989; Gross & Harris, 1988). By the end of the preschool period they also are starting to use some personalized information about others' emotional reactions (Denham & Couchoud, 1990b; Gnepp, 1989), and to understand emotion regulation. They are most likely to demonstrate some grasp of these concepts if developmentally appropriate methods are utilized (Banerjee, 1997; Covell & Miles, 1992; Gordis et al., 1989; Kestenbaum & Gelman, 1995; Wintre & Vallance, 1994). However, there are certainly limits to preschoolers' understanding of emotions. In particular, despite preschoolers' emerging efforts to weigh expressions and situations in assessing their own and others' emotional experiences, they often remain wedded to either the outward expression or the eliciting situation when interpreting emotions. This bias, of necessity, hampers their accuracy (Hoffner & Badzinski, 1989).

This age period is thus an opportune time to explore how children learn about emotions. Preschoolers are active social cognizers (Miller & Aloise, 1989), observing their social world carefully to understand it. It should come as no surprise that they watch, listen to, and imitate their parents, and with good reason: Parents' socialization of emotions is ubiquitous in everyday contact with their preschoolers. Parenting can elicit a variety of emotions. Children's emotions often require some kind of parental reaction, and negotiating the world of emotions is considered by some parents to be an important area of teaching (Dix, 1991; Eisenberg & Fabes, 1994; Eisenberg, Fabes, & Murphy, 1996; Eisenberg, Fabes et al., 1999; Gottman, Katz, & Hooven, 1997; Hyson & Lee, 1996; Tomkins, 1991).

Thus, children have much to learn from parents about the appropriate expression of emotions, possible reactions to others' positive and negative emotions, the nature of emotional expression, and the types of situations that are likely to elicit emotions (Eisenberg, Fabes, Carlo, & Karbon, 1992; Izard, 1991). Nonetheless, although the last two decades have seen a growing body of knowledge of young children's understanding of emotion and its correlates (Denham, McKinley, Couchoud, & Holt, 1990; Dunn, Brown, & Beardsall, 1991; Dunn, Brown, Slomkowski, Tesla, & Youngblade, 1991), thoroughly elucidating parents' roles in the development of this knowledge has lagged somewhat behind.

Accordingly, it is our first goal to report new findings on how parental socialization of emotions contributes to preschoolers' emotion understanding, both contemporaneously and across the period from 3 to 5 years of age. Our study focuses on three possible mechanisms of socialization of emotion knowledge: parental expression of emotions, parental reactions to their children's emotions, and parental teaching about emotions (Halberstadt, 1991). These elements of socialization of emotion center upon the emotional transactions between parent and child. Current theorizing and empirical findings would predict that parents' positive emotional expression and experience, their accepting and helpful reactions to children's emotions, and their emphasis on teaching about emotions in the family would contribute to their young children's more sophisticated emotion understanding (Gottman et al., 1997; Tomkins, 1991).

POTENTIAL CONTRIBUTIONS OF PARENTAL EXPRESSIVENESS

Parental expressiveness teaches the child which emotions are acceptable in the family and in certain contexts. By modeling various emotions, moderately expressive parents give children information about the nature of happiness, sadness, anger, and fear–their expression, likely eliciting situations, and more personalized causes. Mothers and fathers capable of maintaining relatively positive affect during challenging circumstances also may be able to make the world of emotions accessible to their children (Denham, Mitchell-Copeland, Strandberg,

Auerbach, & Blair, 1997; Denham, Zoller, & Couchoud, 1994; Dunn & Brown, 1994; Parke, Cassidy, Burks, Carson, & Boyum, 1992).

Conversely, parental expressiveness can make it more difficult to address issues of emotion altogether. Although exposure to well-modulated negative emotion can be related to understanding of emotion (Garner, Jones, & Miner, 1994), frequent and intense negative emotions from parents may disturb children, as well as discourage self-reflection, so that little is learned about emotions. It is easy to imagine the confusion and pain of young children relentlessly exposed to their parents' negative emotions. It is no wonder their emotion understanding is compromised. Likewise, parents whose expressiveness is quite limited impart little information about emotions.

Very little work has been done on parental emotions' specific contributions to more advanced levels of preschoolers' emotion understanding, such as display rule knowledge. Preschoolers' and kindergartners' knowledge of display rules–in situations like losing a game, seeing someone in silly pajamas, not liking a present, watching a parent leave on a trip–was associated with mothers' self-reported emotional expressiveness, even after children's age and receptive language ability were statistically controlled (Jones, Bowling, & Cumberland, 1998). First, knowledge of self-protective display rules was related to maternal negative emotions like anger and contempt. When children knew that their mothers might react intensely, even explosively, they also knew ways to "cover up" emotions to avoid trouble. Less happy mothers might also require their children to be more in control of their expressiveness. In contrast, prosocial display rules were negatively predicted by maternal negative emotions like sadness. Morose, emotionally self-focused mothers were less able to convey to children how expressiveness can be managed for kindness' sake.

POTENTIAL CONTRIBUTIONS OF PARENTAL REACTIONS TO CHILDREN'S EMOTIONS

Parents' contingent reactions to their children's emotional displays are also highly salient to their preschoolers' acquisition of emotion knowledge. Following the contingency hypothesis, parents' emotional and behavioral reactions to their child's emotions also help the child in differentiating among emotions. Rewarding socialization of emotion is associated with the most positive child outcomes (Tomkins, 1991). Children of parents who encourage emotional expression have more access to their own emotions than those of parents who value maintenance of a more stoic, unemotional mien, and thus come to understand emotions better (see also Gottman et al., 1997).

Parents' negative responsiveness, such as reacting with anger to the child's sadness or anger, or with happiness to their sadness, constitutes punitive socialization of emotion that hampers the process of learning about emotion. One pattern of responsiveness initiates escalating cycles of negativity; the other constitutes "making fun" of the child. Neither encourages children to learn about the emotional aspects of life (Denham, Zoller, & Couchoud, 1994).

Other types of punitive socialization, such as directly or indirectly telling the child to stop showing an emotion and ignoring the child's emotions, are also negative predictors of emotion understanding (Denham et al., 1997; Garner et al., 1994). In our 1997 study, the contributions of such reactions were significant even after statistically controlling for the contribution of intrapersonal contributors, such as age, gender, children's own reactions to parental emotions, and cognitive/language ability. Hence, parents who show behaviors that fit the punitive socialization paradigm have children who are less adept at emotion knowledge tasks during preschool; little, if anything, however, is known about the contribution of this aspect of socialization to understanding of mixed feelings and display rules.

POTENTIAL CONTRIBUTIONS OF PARENTAL TEACHING/COACHING ABOUT EMOTIONS

In its simplest form, coaching consists of an adult verbally explaining an emotion and its relation to an observed event or expression (Camras, Sachs-Alter, & Ribordy, 1996). It may also include directing the child's attention to salient emotional cues, helping children understand and manage their own responses, and analyzing the entire social interaction into manageable components (Denham, Mason, & Couchoud, 1995). As extensively outlined by Gottman and colleagues (Gottman et al., 1997), parents who are emotion coaches are aware of emotions, particularly negative ones. They talk about them in a differentiated manner, and assist their children in experiencing, identifying, and regulating them when necessary. In contrast, dismissing parents may want to be helpful, but ignore children's emotions in an effort to "make it better" (Denham, Renwick, & Hewes, 1994). Alternatively, dismissing parents may actively punish children for showing or querying about emotions.

Because emotional understanding depends, in part, upon the ability to reflect upon one's self, conversations about feelings are an important context for coaching children about emotions and how to manage them (Bretherton, Fritz, Zahn-Waxler, & Ridgeway, 1986; Brown & Dunn, 1992). Discussing emotions provides children with reflective distance from feeling states themselves, and space in which to interpret and evaluate their feelings and to reflect upon causes and consequences.

Research evidence confirms that feeling state conversations between mother and child contribute to the preschooler's growing causal reasoning about the common situations in which emotions occur. Verbal give-and-take about emotional experience within the scaffolded context of chatting with a parent helps the young child to gradually formulate a coherent body of knowledge about emotional expressions, situations, and causes (Denham, Cook, & Zoller, 1992; Denham, Zoller, & Couchoud, 1994; Dunn, Brown, & Beardsall, 1991; Dunn, Brown, Slomkowski et al., 1991). These associations between emotion language with mother and preschoolers' emotion knowledge are often independent of the child's linguistic ability.

More specifically, mothers who not only talk about emotions, but spend time explaining emotions also have children who are more adept at understanding emotions (Denham, Cook, & Zoller, 1992; Denham, Zoller, & Couchoud, 1994; see also Dunn, Brown, Slomkowski et al., 1991). Their highlighting of personally relevant emotion information by repeating the child's utterances or explaining their own feelings (e.g., "You make me sad when you don't sit still.") arouses the children and captures their attention. Guilt-tinged, quickly processed, salient "hot" cognitions resulting from this inductive style are fertile ground for the social cognitive development of emotion understanding during early childhood (Hoffman, 1984).

THE PRESENT STUDY

In the present study, we examined the contribution of all three aspects of socialization of emotion, an effort rarely performed. We obtained both observational and self-report indices of each, to examine developmentally appropriate aspects of young children's emotion knowledge. Further, most research to date regarding socialization of emotions has only included mothers; we have included fathers, and hypothesize similar effects on children's socialization to that which mothers have shown. That is, we reassert that both mothers' and fathers' positive emotional expressiveness, positive reactions to emotions of children, and teaching about emotions will positively contribute to young children's emotion knowledge. Based on the theoretical propositions and empirical evidence already reviewed, our first goal is to evaluate a preliminary, theoretically and empirically derived multiple regression model. We consider that parents' own emotions and their reactions to their children's emotions are exogenous aspects of the socialization process. For example, parents who experience and express positive emotions, and who are able to be supportive of their children's emotional expressions and experiences, probably are more likely to engage in talking and teaching about emotions. As Brown and Dunn (1991) have asserted, "Discourse about the social world may in part mediate the key conceptual advances reflected in . . . social cognition . . ." (p. 1352). This teaching directly aids preschoolers in enhancing their emotion knowledge. Thus, parental emotions and reactions to children's emotions may have both a direct and indirect (via their contribution to parents' willingness to teach about emotion) contribution to children's emotion knowledge. Furthermore, parental socialization of emotion when children are 3 years old may contribute to their emotion knowledge at age 5 both directly, and indirectly, via their socialization of emotion when children are 4 years old. We place our findings within the broader context of family interaction and especially focus upon trainable aspects of the socialization of emotional competence in preschoolers.

METHOD

Participants

To begin to meet these objectives, we examined the emotional and social competence of 134 predominantly Caucasian, middle-income 3-, 4-, and 5-year-olds, in a multi-setting, multi-method design (69 boys, average age 46 mos at the initial time of observation in the preschool, standard deviation = 5.03 mos, range = 32 to 59 mos). Seventy-nine percent of children were described as Caucasian, and the annual income for a similar proportion of the families was over $50,000. The modal level of education for both mothers and fathers was graduation from college. Eighty-eight percent of the children lived in two-parent homes.

Procedure

To obtain the data discussed here we both interviewed and observed children, and observed and administered questionnaires to their parents at home. We sought to view various aspects of the preschoolers' emotion knowledge and the parents' socialization of emotion.

Various preschool and daycare centers in a large metropolitan area were targeted based on past liaison relationships and director willingness to participate. Probably because of the time commitment required of the family component of the investigation, approximately 25% of all 3-year-olds' families in these centers asked for information about study participation. Over 95% of those evidencing interest continued on to complete participation, including the elements reported on here. Because of this low initial interest rate, we compared these families with families from two earlier studies, one of which also involved heavy family participation (Denham et al., 1997), and one of which did not involve the burden of home visits, with a greater than 75% participation (Denham et al., 1990). T-tests comparing the current sample and these two earlier samples on demographic and study variables showed virtually no significant differences in mean levels across the samples. Thus, we concluded that the low participation rate for this study did not result in biases. Active informed consent was obtained from all parents and children.

Regarding parental socialization of emotions, families were visited at home twice, when target children were 3 and 4 years old. Parental emotions and reactions to children's emotions were observed using a well-validated procedure (Denham, 1986; Roberts, 1993). During the home visits parents and children were also asked to reminisce about experiences of happiness, sadness, anger, and fear; these conversations were transcribed for coding. In addition, parents completed a series of questionnaires. Thus, for each component of socialization of emotion, there were both observational and self-report measures. Regarding children's emotion knowledge, children were interviewed individually in their preschool classrooms, when they were 3 years old, 4 years old, and in kindergarten at 5 years old.

Socialization of Emotion Measures

Parental expressiveness: Observational techniques. The parents' emotions and reactions to the child's emotions were naturalistically observed in their homes. Home visitors were unaware of specific hypotheses of the study. The first family visit was brief, and focused on getting to know the family and leaving self-report packets with each parent. The next two 2-hour visits involved actual observation (one with mother and child, one with father and child), and took place during a 2- to 4-week period for each family. Families generally were visited from about one hour before until one hour after dinner. This time of observation is fertile ground for discipline encounters in the home, but also for "quality time" spent between parent and child, so that these hours are replete with emotional displays and emotion language.

During these visits, parents were encouraged to go about their business. The only restriction on normal interaction was that the "parent of the day" and the child were to be in the same room during the period. The exigencies of parenting preschoolers while maintaining family routines formed a common overarching context for our visits.

The "parent-of-the-day" and the child alternated as focal subjects. During 5-minute periods, occurrence of each emotion of the focal subject was tallied. The process of coding during each five-minute focal period was as follows: Using laptop computers and observational software (Roberts, 1993), observers entered an emotion's code at its onset, observed the target person's reactions, entered them as they occurred, and then looked back to the focal person; if the same emotion continued, reactions were again searched for, and if no emotions were being displayed, the observer entered the "neutral" code.

Happy, sad, angry, and afraid/tense emotional displays of the focal subject were coded, using facial, vocal, postural and behavioral indicators of emotion. For example, for happiness, these included smiles, singing, laughter, voices with "pearly," relaxed pitch. Such operational definitions for sadness included hypotonicity, possible crying, inner corners of eyebrows lifted and corners of lips down, and slow-pitched speech. Anger was evidenced behaviorally by throwing, pushing, hitting, facially by brows shoved down, tense lower lips, staring; speech was clipped, abrupt, and possibly yelling. Fear or tension was shown behaviorially by jumpiness, worried looks, uncertainty and muscular tension (or even tension bursts, as in tapping feet or fingers), with vigilant posture; brows may be tight, raised and drawn together, with high pitched voices and rapid speech (Denham, 1989, 1993; Denham & Grout, 1993).

For each emotion, an index was created equal to the number of displays for the specific emotion divided by total emotional displays. Next, based on findings in Denham et al. (1990) and Denham and Grout (1993), an affective balance aggregate was created: the standard score for percentage of happy displays minus the standard score for percentage of angry displays. As well, an internalizing negative emotion aggregate was created: the sum of standard scores for sadness and tension/fear. Stability coefficients for affective balance across both years of home visits was .30 for mothers and .41 for fathers, $ps < .001$. Similar coefficients for internalizing negative emotion across years was .14 for mothers and .32 for fathers, significant at $p < .001$ level for fathers only.

Parental expressiveness: Self-report measures. Two measures that tap parents' emotional experience, as well as their expressive patterns, were administered as important adjuncts to the purely observational data. On the Self-Expressiveness in the Family Questionnaire (SEFQ; Halberstadt, Cassidy, Stifter, Parke, & Fox, 1995; see also Halberstadt, 1986) each parent was asked to rate 40 items on a 1- to 9-point scale, indicating the frequency of their own positive and negative emotional displays within their current family setting. Example items included "Telling family members how happy you are" and "Blaming one another for family troubles." Internal consistency reliabilities for maternal and paternal positive and negative emotion subscales ranged from .71 to .92 (mean α for mothers = .86, for fathers = .85). Test-retest reliability across the 2 years of home visits ranged from .38 to .68, all $ps < .001$.

The Parent Affect Test (PAT; Linehan, Paul, & Egan, 1983), the second self-report measure, assessed the relative strength of parents' emotion, from negative to positive, when confronted with specific examples of their children's positive and negative behaviors. Twenty of the 40 items total referred to situations likely to please parents; the other 20 focused on situations likely to displease them. On each item (e.g., "My child gets into some things that don't belong to him/her" or " My child shares a favorite possession with a friend") parents rated, on 7-point scales, the likelihood of six reactions–feeling angry/pleased, bad/good, tense/relaxed, want to spank/kiss, want to yell/praise, want to send to their room/want to be with child. Following our findings and others' (e.g., Garner et al., 1994), in this study we used the PAT-N (negative situations) subscale as an indicator of parents' ability to remain "on an even keel" even when parenting is a challenge. We found internal consistency greater than .90 for each of these aggregates. Test-retest reliability was .31 for mothers and .56 for fathers, $ps < .001$.

Contingency/Reactions to the child's emotions: Observational technique. Frequencies of reactions to parents' emotions were coded after children's emotions: matching positive or negative emotions, inappropriate affective reaction, hurt feelings, positive or negative reinforcing, concern, looking, ignoring, or antisocial reactions. These reactions were considered mutually exclusive, but could be coded successively.

Frequency of each reaction was divided by number of emotions emitted by the child. An aggregate of prosocial reactions was created (standard scores for helping and concern), along with one for positive attention (standard scores for positive matching *minus* antisocial reactions, looking, and ignoring; see Denham & Couchoud, 1991, Denham & Grout, 1993). Rates of negative and positive reinforcement were considered separately from the two aggregates. Test-retest reliabilities across the 2 years of home visits were as follows: for positive attention, .39 and .46 for mothers and fathers respectively, $ps < .001$; for prosocial reactions, .01 for mothers, ns, and .21 for fathers, $p < .05$; for positive reinforcement, .37 for mothers, $p < .001$, .13 for fathers, ns; and for negative reinforcement, .35 for mothers and .20 for fathers, $ps < .001$ and .05, respectively.

Contingency/Reactions to the child's emotions: Self-report measure. Fabes, Eisenberg, and Bernzweig's (1990) Coping with Children's Negative Emotions Scale (CCNES) was administered to each parent. In this measure, parents rated how likely they are to choose emotion- or problem-focused coping, punitive, minimizing, encouraging, or distress reactions to specific scenarios of their children's negative emotions. For example, one item stated "If my child becomes angry because he/she is sick or hurt and can't go to his/her friend's birthday party, I would": send my child to her room (punitive), get angry at my child (distress), help my child think about ways to still be friends (problem-focused coping), tell my child not to make a big deal over it (minimizing), encourage my child to express his/her feelings (encouraging feelings), or soothe my child (emotion-focused coping). Scores for each reaction style were averaged across items. Following the theoretical coaching/dismissing distinction and empirical findings of Eisenberg and Fabes (1994), we created aggregates as follows (1) Dismissing: minimizing, punitive, and distress reaction scales (mean $\alpha = .83$; test-retest reliability = .41 for mothers, .60 for fathers, $ps < .001$); and (2) Coaching: encourages emotion, emotion-focused coping, and problem-focused reaction scales (mean $\alpha = .81$; test-retest reliability = .45 for mothers and .50 for fathers, $ps < .001$).

Coaching/Language about emotions: Naturalistic task. In order to sample the emotion language used by the parents with their children, each dyad was given a semi-naturalistic task. Near the beginning of each home visit, the "parent of the day" was asked to sit down with the child, and, in whatever way was natural, to reminisce about four of the following events: (1) four occurrences in which s/he showed four specific emotions in the child's presence and (2) four occurrences in which the child showed emotion in the parent's presence. No other constraints were put on the conversations, which were audiotaped. We gave each parent leeway when performing the emotion reminiscence. We described it and asked them to do it during the visit, gave them cards with each emotion written on them (happy, sad, angry, and afraid), and then really left it up to them how and when to do it, unless they needed reminding to get started or assistance.

All conversations were transcribed and coded for frequency and function of each emotion utterance, as follows (see Zahn-Waxler, Ridgeway, Denham, Usher, & Cole, 1993). Emotion words were tallied. These may refer to positive or negative discrete emotions, as well as to behavioral expressions of emotion (e.g., hitting, crying, hugging). Functions of utterances containing emotion words were noted as follows: (a) commenting–noting someone's feeling without further explanation or clarification; (b) explaining–explaining the causes and/or consequences of feeling states; (c) clarifying–rectifying misunderstandings; (d) questioning–statements in the form of a question; (e) guiding–redirecting emotional behavior or language; (f) socializing–socialization of emotion by confirmation, disconfirmation, or denial. For the purposes of this study, explaining/clarifying and guiding/socializing aggregates were created. Across three coders, interrater reliability yielded kappas for emotional utterance occurrence averaging .94-.95. Function category kappas averaged .78-.85.

Coaching/Language about emotions: Self-report measures. We wished to expand our coverage of emotion coaching to include parents' own views of their coaching within disciplinary contexts, and their global attitudes toward emotion coaching as a task of parenting. Therefore, parents were administered the Parent Disciplinary Styles measure (PDS; Hart, DeWolf, Wozniak, & Burts, 1992), which elaborates the power assertion-induction dichotomy into a continuum that captures varying degrees of these parenting styles (Hart et al., 1992). Parents gave their likely response(s) to six open-ended disciplinary situations, and their responses were hierarchically coded. Scores higher on the induction continuum reflect parents' encouragement of the child's consideration of others' feelings (e.g., "I would ask my child, 'How do you think your friend would feel if you called him a name like that?' or 'If your friend found their special toy missing, how would they feel?' "). Inter-rater reliability was calculated for 18.1% of the total sample; percentage agreement = .88 and κ = .85. An induction score for the Parent PDS was then created by weighting and then summing all response scores (possible range = 6 to 108), and dividing by the number of responses given (range of number of responses = 6 to 18; parents could give up to three responses for each of six situations).

Also, Hyson and Lee's (1996) Teacher Emotion-Related Beliefs (ERB) measure was adapted for parents. The measure consists of 23 items, which are rated from 1 (strongly disagree) to 7 (strongly agree). Sample items included "Children my child's age really are not ready to control the way they express their feelings," "I spend a lot of time talking to my children about why they feel the way they do," and "As a parent, it's important for me to teach my child socially acceptable ways of expressing their feelings."

Because Hyson and Lee (1996) and Karn and Dunsmore (2000) have had difficulties isolating a replicable factor structure for this measure, we reasoned that perhaps all items that could reflect the coach/dismisser dichotomy could be summed for one total score (with dismissing items subtracted). Examination of items showed that only one could not be seen in this light. Cronbach's α for the remaining 22 items were .85 for mothers and .88 for fathers. As a result, we considered this aggregate an index of parents' valuing teaching their children about emotions.

Understanding of Emotion

Three- and 4-year-old assessment: Affect Knowledge Test (AKT). Children's understanding of emotion (nonverbal recognition and verbal labeling of emotional expressions, identification of emotions unequivocally appropriate to certain situations, and inferences of emotions in equivocal situations) was first assessed using puppets with detachable faces that depict happy, sad, angry, and afraid expressions. Because these measures have been described in detail elsewhere (Denham, 1986; Denham & Couchoud, 1990a, 1990b; Denham, Zoller, & Couchoud, 1994), they are summarized as follows: Children were first asked to identify happy, sad, angry, and afraid facial expressions verbally, by naming them, and then non-verbally, by pointing. In the next two emotional situation identification tasks, the puppeteer made standard facial and vocal expressions of emotions while enacting an emotion-laden story. The child was asked to place on the puppet the face that depicted the puppet's feeling in the situation.

The first emotional situation identification task explored how well children know others' feelings in eight common situations that elicit unequivocal emotional reactions, such as happiness at being given an ice cream cone, or fear at having a nightmare (Denham, 1986). The second emotional situation identification task measured how well children identify others' feelings in situations where the other feels differently than the child. All situations could elicit one of two emotions, as in feeling happy or afraid to get into a swimming pool (Denham, 1986; Denham & Couchoud, 1990b). Children's mothers had reported, via forced-choice questionnaire, how their children would feel in 12 such vignettes. For each vignette, their response determined the emotion expressed by the puppet (i.e., opposite from the study child).

Subjects received 2 points for a correct answer, and 1 point for correctly specifying only the emotion's positivity or negativity (e.g., choosing a sad rather than the correct angry face). Standard scores for each item of these tasks were summed for the emotion knowledge aggregate. Cronbach's alpha for the aggregate equaled .89 for 3-year-olds, and .76 for 4-year-olds. Test-retest reliability for total unstandardized scores = .32, $p < .01$.

Kindergarten Assessment Test: Mixed emotions. Because the challenge posed by the AKT wanes toward the end of preschool, and important developments are taking place in children's emotion knowledge, we administered two new measures in kindergarten. The first is the KAT-Mixed Emotions test, adapted from Gordis et al. (1989; see also Dunn, 1995 for evidence that this measure is related to earlier-administered AKT). For this measure, we told each child eight vignettes, accompanied by pictures, in which the protagonist feels two emotions (e.g., happy and sad that school is over for summer). In this prompted version, children were not expected to spontaneously produce the two conflicting emotions, a more developmentally advanced task. They were asked to explain the existence of the two named emotions. Two points were given for each vignette for which the child explains each emotion, with 1 point given for explaining only one correctly, and 0 for mentioning neither; $\alpha = .84$.

Kindergarten Assessment Test: Display rules. We selected six stories from Gross and Harris (1988). In each story, which in accordance with Gross's procedures were not accompanied by pictures, the protagonist felt a feeling that they should either hide or show. As an example of the three discrepant feeling stories, the protagonist should hide his sadness when his big brother teased him, because if he didn't, the teasing would continue. In one of the three nondiscrepant feeling stories, for example, the protagonist should show her sadness because she was lost in a store and needed help.

In order to gain credit for successfully responding to each story, after standard memory probes, the child had to correctly state how the protagonist feels, how the protagonist looks on his/her face, and how the other characters in the story would think the protagonist felt. Each child was also asked to justify his/her reasoning; these data are not pursued further here. In the nondiscrepant stories, these answers had to be factually correct and identical (e.g., "He really feels sad because he is lost, and he looks sad, so that the store man thinks he is lost and sad and helps him."). In the discrepant stories, the first two (correct) answers had to differ, with the third being the same as the second (e.g., "She really feels sad because her stomach hurts, but she looks 'okay' on her face, and her mother thinks she's OK and lets her go out to play."). In this study, we used a total score for understanding display rules, rather than separately tallying the nondiscrepant and discrepant feeling stories; although the discrepant scores were significantly lower than the nondiscrepant (as would be expected), the two were correlated, $r = .45, p < .001$ (internal consistency = .58).

RESULTS

Description of Emotion Understanding and Socialization of Emotion Data

In general, 3-year-olds were fairly adept on the AKT (mean = 48.13, SD = 8.18) although 4-year-old scores were greater (mean = 52.51, SD = 4.67), $t(133) = -3.00, p < .001$. As a group, the 5-year-olds were moderately successful on the relatively scaffolded KAT-Mixed Emotions measure (mean = 12.78, SD = 1.89), and showed more difficulty with KAT-Display Rules, $t(133) = 26.03, p < .001$ (mean = 1.55, SD = .75).

Descriptive data for all parent measures are shown in Table 1. In general, these data suggest that parents, both mothers and fathers, were relatively positively expressive as indicated by both observational and self-report measures. They showed less negative emotion (albeit a moderate amount), again on both observational and self-report measures, ts (133) ranging from 15.27 to 28.85, all ps < .001. In terms of observed reactions to emotions, their profiles indicated mostly the matching of positive emotion and positive reinforcement, ts (133) = 10.49 to 27.64,

TABLE 1. Descriptive Statistics for Parental Socialization of Emotion

	Mothers				Fathers			
	3-Year-Olds		4-Year-Olds		3-Year-Olds		4-Year-Olds	
	Mean	SD	Mean	SD	Mean	SD	Mean	SD
Observed Emotions								
Happiness	.77	.17	.79	.13	.81	.15	.79	.15
Sadness	.01	.03	.02	.02	.05	.03	.01	.02
Anger	.09	.14	.07	.08	.08	.11	.06	.07
Tension/Fear	.02	.04	.03	.05	.01	.03	.02	.03
Parent-Reported Emotions								
FEQ Positive	149.27	15.51	152.42	13.96	138.52	14.86	136.43	12.79
FEQ Negative	88.73	17.46	95.64	14.99	84.93	21.96	86.39	17.44
PAT-Negative	397.56	59.08	401.35	44.42	416.36	42.12	403.59	36.56
Observed Reactions to Child's Emotions								
Match Positive	.44	.19	.41	.15	.40	.17	.38	.16
Positive Reinforcement	.19	.14	.21	.12	.23	.14	.19	.11
Negative Reinforcement	.03	.05	.03	.04	.02	.05	.02	.04
Concern	.06	.08	.05	.06	.06	.08	.05	.05
Helping	.06	.07	.05	.07	.05	.07	.05	.04
Looking	.08	.08	.10	.07	.11	.09	.13	.09
Ignoring	.10	.11	.10	.08	.09	.09	.13	.11
Antisocial	.04	.06	.02	.04	.04	.06	.04	.04
Parent-Reported Reactions to Child Emotions								
Minimizing Responses	2.11	.83	1.99	.54	2.60	.77	3.11	.71
Distress Responses	2.54	.87	1.60	.55	2.52	.62	2.35	.47
Encourages Emotion	5.00	1.02	5.01	.73	4.25	.81	4.12	.63
Emotion-Focused	5.41	.88	5.40	.56	5.28	.61	5.18	.49
Problem-Focused	5.52	.74	5.58	.43	5.29	.70	5.27	.73
Punitive Responses	2.09	.69	2.20	.45	2.30	.60	2.43	.53
Observed Coaching								
Explaining/Clarifying	25.82	8.97			22.81	9.42		
Guiding/Socializing	3.66	4.98			3.90	4.98		
Parent-Reported Coaching								
Emotion-Related Beliefs	35.58	8.81			27.36	6.07		
PDS	3.56	0.53			3.18	.66		

$p < .001$, with moderate amounts of concern, help, ignoring, and looking in response to their children's emotions. On the CCNES, parents tended to rate the likelihood of their own punitive, minimizing, and distress reactions to their children's emotions as lower than the likelihood of the emotion encouragement, emotion-focused, and problem-focused responses, ts $(133) = 2.35$ to 22.43, ps $< .001$.

Parents explained or clarified in their narratives about past emotions about three times per child/parent emotion, and guided or socialized less than one time per child/parent emotion. On the ERB scale, both mothers and fathers demonstrated moderate scores on their valuing the word of emotion and teaching their preschooler about emotions. On the PDS, their most typical level of disciplinary tactics was equivalent to rule justification—but without the input of the child, the discussion of others' feelings, or the eliciting the child's discussion of consequences of behavior and others feelings that are inherent in higher scores on the power assertion/induction continuum. The range of scores obtained on the PDS for both mothers and fathers spanned from relatively power assertive, non-inductive tactics, to inductive tactics.

Data Aggregation

Aggregation was necessary due to multiplicity of measures used, and desirable in order to increase explanatory power. Exploratory principal component analyses for each domain of socialization of emotion were thus performed for mother and father, separately, for each year.

For expression of emotional displays, observations of emotions (parents' affective balance and internalizing negative emotions), and self-reports of emotions (responding positively to difficult parenting situations, via the PAT, and experiencing positive and negative emotions in the family, via the SEFQ) were included in the analyses. For reactions to emotion, both observational indexes (positive attention to child emotions, prosocial responses to child emotions, reinforcing child emotions positively or negatively) and self-reports (positive and negative coping responses on the CCNES) were included. Finally, for parental teaching about emotions, analyses were again performed for both observational and self-reports (parental use of explaining/clarifying language, and guiding/socializing language during reminiscences, as well as self-reports of the use of affect induction via the PDS and valuing teaching about emotion via the ERB). Parental teaching/coaching about emotions was analyzed for Year 1 only because of our need to code conversations and PDS, as well as administration of Hyson's measure in Year 1 only. Each set of components accounted for approximately 59-76 percent of variance in each set of variables.

Year 1 teaching about emotions was, for maternal data, best described as Emotion Language, Inductive Practices, and Valuing Teaching About Emotion. For fathers these components were best described as Explaining Emotion Language, Guiding/Socializing Emotion Language, and Valuing Teaching About Emotion.

For parents' emotional expressiveness and reactions to children's emotions, components generally were most aptly described along lines suggested by the theoretical and empirical bases for our study, positive emotions and reactions, negative emotions and reactions, and prosocial or reinforcing reactions. Some variations were noted in how fathers' variables loaded (e.g., self-reported emotionality in Year 2 expressiveness), and in the loading of positive reinforcement (e.g., for mothers and for fathers in Year 2 only, high component scores for the "prosocial" component included low scores on positive reinforcement; this dichotomy should be kept in mind when interpreting results).

Given the regression model we wished to test, we next submitted each of the parent emotions and reactions factors to a second principal components analysis, to yield final "emotion and reactions" variables for mother and father for each year of study. Thus, the final maternal expression/reaction components for Year 1 were Positive Emotions and Reactions, Negative Emotions and Reactions, and Prosocial Reactions; for Year 2, these were Prosocial Reactions, Observed Positive Emotions and Reactions, and Negative Emotions and Reactions. For fathers, the final expression/reaction components for Year 1 were Positive Emotions and Reactions, Negative Emotions and Reactions, and Positive Reinforcement; for Year 2 they were Positive Emotions and Reactions, Emotional/Coaching, and Negative Emotions and Reactions. Thus, although there were variations across years and between parents in terms of specific socialization variables that loaded together, the final components/aggregates used as predictors conformed generally to our theoretical and empirical notions about the socialization of emotion.

In terms of evaluating these components, maternal Negative Emotions and Reactions showed stability, $r(132) = .33, p < .001$, one tailed; maternal Positive Emotions and Reactions also showed marginal stability, $r(132) = .13, p < .10$. Paternal Negative Emotions and Reactions showed stability, $r(132) = .17, p < .05$, one tailed; paternal Positive Emotions and Reactions also showed stability, $r(132) = .26, p < .001$. Maternal Positive Emotions and Reactions (Year 1) was related to both Maternal Valuing Teaching About Emotion and Maternal Discussion of Emotions During Discipline, $rs(132) = .19$ and $.33, ps < .05$ and $.001$, respectively. Fathers who valued teaching about emotions were more positive in Year 1, $r(132) = .14, p < .10$, as well as less positive, but more likely to be emotional and use coaching, and less negative, in Year 2, $rs(132) = -.22, -.30,$ and $.33, ps < .01, .001,$ and $.001$, respectively.

Thus, there are coherent relations among the components that increase our assurance about their use.

Prediction of Emotion Understanding

Separate regression analyses including these maternal and paternal predictors were performed. We considered that parental emotions and reactions to children's emotions might have both a direct and indirect contribution to children's emotion knowledge. Our regression analyses follow this model via reduced form equations (Cohen & Cohen, 1991). Thus, parental emotions and reactions to children's emotions were entered on the first step of each equation, with parents' values and behaviors related to teaching children about emotions entered on a second step. For measures of emotion understanding beginning in the child's second preschool year, step three includes factors for parental emotions and reactions to children's emotions from the second year of study, and step four includes earlier emotion understanding measures. Because of the nature of our problem questions, we were examining unique contributors to R^2, over and above the omnibus F test for the significance of R^2.

Three- and 4-year-old AKTs. Mothers' Positive Emotions and Reactions ($p < .10$) and Valuing Teaching About Emotions contributed to explained variance (see Table 2). None of the paternal predictors made any significant or borderline significant contribution.

Four-year-old AKT. For 4-year-olds' emotion understanding, mothers high on Positive Emotions and Reactions in Year 1 and lower in

TABLE 2. Prediction of 3-Year-Old AKT from Maternal Socialization of Emotion

Predictor	β	R^2_{CHANGE}
Step 1: *Year 1 Maternal Emotions and Reactions to Children's Emotions*		
Positive Emotions and Reactions	.146+	.03
Negative Emotions and Reactions	−.021	
Prosocial Reactions	−.095	
Step 2: *Year 1 Maternal Teaching About Emotions*		
Emotion Language	.054	.10**
Inductive Practices	.044	
Valuing Teaching about Emotion	.343***	

+$p < .10$, * $p < .05$, ** $p < .01$, *** $p < .001$

Year 2 had children with higher scores (see Table 3). Fathers' Year 2 Positive Emotions and Reactions and Negative Emotions and Reactions ($p < .10$), as well as lack of Year 2 Emotional/Coaching, and an unexpected negative prediction via their explanations about emotions in conversation (Year 1), predicted 4-year-olds' emotion understanding via the ATK (see Table 4). It should be noted that Emotional/Coaching and Negative Emotions and Reactions were borderline or significant predictors only in concert with Positive Emotions and Reactions (i.e., neither zero-order r was significant, and suppression is suggested). Thus, when fathers are generally positive in their emotions and reactions to their children's emotions (and only then), fathers' negative emotions and reactions contribute to 4-year-old emotion knowledge. Their focus on emotionality (Emotional/Coaching component) negatively contributes to this criterion. The meaning of fathers' use of such language may be to "rein in" more difficult children; as Eisenberg et al. (1999) have noted, parents' socialization of emotion and children's behavior influence one another bidirectionally.

At the last, simultaneous step of each equation (i.e., maternal and paternal prediction) for 4-year-old AKT scores, certain predictors became at least marginally significant. Maternal Prosocial Reactions were negatively weighted, $\beta = -.150$, $p < .10$. Thus, mothers who were more

TABLE 3. Prediction of 4-Year-Old AKT from Maternal Socialization of Emotion

Predictor	β	R^2_{CHANGE}
Step 1: *Year 1 Emotions and Reactions to Children's Emotions*		
Positive Emotions and Reactions	.175*	.05+
Negative Emotions and Reactions	.076	
Prosocial Reactions	−.10	
Step 2: *Year 1 Maternal Teaching About Emotions*		
Emotion Language	−.128	.03
Inductive Practices	−.089	
Valuing Teaching about Emotion	.077	
Step 3: *Year 2 Maternal Emotions and Reactions to Children's Emotions*		
Observed Positive Emotions and Reactions	−.167+	.03
Prosocial Reactions	−.042	
Negative Emotions and Reactions	.079	
Step 4: *Earlier Emotion Knowledge*		
3-year-old AKT	−.102	.01

+$p < .10$, *$p < .05$, **$p < .01$, ***$p < .001$

TABLE 4. Prediction of 4-Year-Old AKT from Paternal Socialization of Emotion

Predictor	β	R^2_{CHANGE}
Step 1: *Year 1 Paternal Emotions and Reactions to Children's Emotions*		
Positive Emotions and Reactions	.125	.025
Negative Emotions and Reactions	−.094	
Positive Reinforcement	−.025	
Step 2: *Year 1 Paternal Teaching About Emotions*		
Explaining Emotion Language	−.255**	.061*
Guiding/Socializing Emotion Language	.083	
Valuing Teaching about Emotion	.074	
Step 3: *Year 2 Paternal Emotions and Reactions to Children's Emotions*		
Negative Emotions and Reactions	.165⁺	.082**
Emotional/Coaching	−.189*	
Positive Emotions and Reactions	.220*	
Step 4: *Earlier Emotion Knowledge*		
3-year-old AKT	−.013	.000

⁺$p < .10$, * $p < .05$, ** $p < .01$, *** $p < .001$

positively reinforcing had children with higher 4-year-old AKT scores when all other socialization variables were taken into account. Similarly, Paternal Valuing Teaching About Emotion was a significant predictor at this last step in its equation, as well, β = .244, $p < .05$. Except in the maternal socialization equation for 3-year-old AKT scores, where mediation was present, all other already-significant predictors retained at least marginal significance on the last step of each equation.

KAT: 5-year-old Mixed Emotions. Mothers' lack of Negative Emotions and Reactions in Year 1 ($p < .10$), and positive reinforcement rather than Prosocial Reactions in Year 2, added to explained variance on this measure (see Table 5). Fathers' socialization of emotions predictors made no significant contribution.

KAT: 5-year-old Display Rules. Mothers' Negative Emotions and Reactions in Year 1 ($p < .10$), as well as the 4-year-old AKT ($p < .10$; this was the only contribution of earlier to later emotion knowledge from earlier assessments), predicted knowledge of display rules (see Table 6). For fathers, only Positive Emotions and Reactions in Year 2 made a borderline significant contribution, β = .157, $p = .10$.

Exploratory analyses of relations among maternal and paternal socialization of emotion. In an effort to understand the relative lack of pa-

TABLE 5. Prediction of KAT-Mixed Emotions from Maternal Socialization of Emotion

Predictor	β	R^2_{CHANGE}
Step 1: *Year 1 Maternal Emotions and Reactions to Children's Emotions*		
Positive Emotions and Reactions	.023	.04
Negative Emotions and Reactions	−.141+	
Prosocial Reactions	−.134	
Step 2: *Year 1 Maternal Teaching About Emotions*		
Emotion Language	−.757	.01
Inductive Practices	−.070	
Valuing Teaching about Emotion	.979	
Step 3: *Year 2 Maternal Emotions and Reactions to Children's Emotions*		
Observed Positive Emotions and Reactions	1.526	.06*
Prosocial Reactions	−2.328*	
Negative Emotions and Reactions	1.029	
Step 4: *Earlier Emotions Knowledge*		
3-year-old AKT	.447	.00
4-year-old AKT	−.484	

+$p < .10$, * $p < .05$, ** $p < .01$, *** $p < .001$

ternal prediction of emotion knowledge, correlational analyses were undertaken to show relations between mothers' and fathers' socialization variables. Although paternal socialization of emotion variables did not predict 3-year-old AKT, 5-year-old KAT Mixed Emotions, or 5-year-old KAT Display Rules, they did predict maternal socialization of emotion variables that were related to these aspects of emotion knowledge. For example, Maternal Positive Emotions and Reactions (Year 1) was related to Paternal Positive Emotions and Reactions, as well as to Paternal Negative Emotions and Reactions, $rs (132) = .36$ and .22, $ps < .001$ and .01, respectively. Maternal Negative Emotions and Reactions (Year 1) was related to the corresponding paternal variable, $r (132) = .17, p < .05$. Mothers' negativity in Year 2 or prosociality in Year 1 were related to corresponding aspects of paternal socialization of emotion in the same year, $rs (132) = .20$ and .29, $ps < .05$ and .01, respectively. Finally, maternal and paternal Valuing Teaching About Emotion were also related, $r (132) = .29, p < .05$.

Paternal Negative Emotions and Reactions in Year 1 was inversely related to Maternal Positive Emotions and Reactions in Year 2, $r (132) = −.21$, $p < .01$. Fathers' positive and positively reinforcing socialization of emo-

TABLE 6. Prediction of KAT-Display Rules from Maternal Socialization of Emotion

Predictor	β	R^2_{CHANGE}
Step 1: *Year 1 Maternal Emotions and Reactions to Children's Emotions*		
Positive Emotions and Reactions	−.011	.02
Negative Emotions and Reactions	.151+	
Prosocial Reactions	.034	
Step 2: *Year 1 Maternal Teaching About Emotions*		
Emotion Language	−.053	.01
Inductive Practices	−.040	
Valuing Teaching about Emotion	.059	
Step 3: *Year 2 Emotions and Reactions to Children's Emotions*		
Observed Positive Emotions and Reactions	.098	.01
Prosocial Reactions	.048	
Negative Emotions and Reactions	.036	
Step 4: *Earlier Emotion Knowledge*		
3-year-old AKT	.019	.02
4-year-old AKT	.155+	

+$p < .10$, * $p < .05$, ** $p < .01$, *** $p < .001$

tion in Year 1 was related to mothers' positively reinforcing socialization of emotion in Year 2, rs (132) = .16 and .14, respectively, $p < .05$.

In sum, perhaps fathers' may see socialization of emotion knowledge as "not their job." This being the case, contributions may be more indirect, via their support (or nonsupport) of mothers. The pattern of correlations between maternal and paternal socialization of emotions bolsters this possibility.

Tests of mediation. Only one of the six regression equations, maternal socialization of emotion variables' predicting 3-year-old AKT scores, met the test of mediation in our model (see Baron & Kenny, 1986). Mediation was suggested by the following information: Both Maternal Positive Emotions and Reactions and Valuing Teaching about Emotions were associated with 3-year-old AKT scores (see Table 2). More importantly, when maternal Valuing Teaching about Emotions was entered into the equation with Positive Emotions and Reactions, the contribution of the latter shrank to nonsignificance, β = .030, $p = .73$.

Based on this evidence of mediation in the overall equation, the four-equation method of evaluating the extent of mediation (Baron & Kenny, 1986: MacKinnon & Dwyer, 1993), along with associated statistical tests for the significance of mediation, were performed. In the first equation, we again found that maternal Positive Emotions and Reactions predicted 3-year-old AKT scores ($\beta = .175, p < .05$). In the second, maternal Positive Emotions and Reactions significantly predicted maternal Valuing Teaching about Emotions ($\beta = .310, p < .001$). In the third, maternal Valuing Teaching about Emotions predicted 3-year-old AKT scores ($\beta = .348, p < .001$). In the final equation, both maternal Positive Emotions and Reactions and Valuing Teaching about Emotions were entered to predict 3-year-old AKT scores. Maternal Valuing Teaching about Emotions still significantly predicted 3-year-old AKT scores ($\beta = .325, p < .001$), but maternal Positive Emotions and Reactions no longer did so ($\beta = .074$, ns).

Given this evidence of mediation unaffected by the contributions of other variables, we determined its magnitude and tested its significance following MacKinnon and Dwyer's guidelines, examining the relative contribution of the mediated pathway compared to the unmediated one. The product of the two unstandardized regression coefficients in the second and third equations, 1.52, is compared to the direct effect in the first equation, 2.46; the contribution of maternal Positive Emotions and Reactions is reduced by about one-third when in concert with maternal Valuing Teaching about Emotions. We tested the significance of this change via a z-score evaluating the change in light of the standard errors of the two unstandardized regression coefficients in the second and third equations. This z-score equaled 2.84 ($p < .001$), thus demonstrating the credibility of this mediation pathway.

DISCUSSION

Our goal for this investigation was to discover parental socialization contributors to young children's emotion knowledge, examining the unique and cumulative contributions of three aspects of parental socialization of emotion—modeling, contingency, and teaching. We considered that the most sophisticated knowledge of emotional expression, situations, ambivalence, and display rules, within developmentally appropriate limits, would be attained by children whose parents were relatively expressive (usually of positive emotions), accepting of emotion, and aware of the need to actively teach preschoolers about feelings. Moreover, we proposed a model in which parents' own emotional lives (i.e., their emotional expressiveness, and contingent reactions to the emotions of their children) would contribute to their teaching about emotions, which would, in turn, contribute to children's emotion knowledge. Hence, the contributions of parents' emotions and emotion-related behaviors (both expressiveness and contingency) would be mediated by their teaching about emotions. In a more exploratory vein, we proposed that fathers' socialization of emotion would contribute to emotion knowledge in a manner similar to mothers'.

Overall Findings

Certain of these predictions were upheld, with more predictive relations obtained for mothers' socialization of emotion than for fathers'. Many of the findings replicate and extend Denham, Zoller, and Couchoud's (1994) findings. However, some results involving later-emerging aspects of emotion knowledge and fathers' contribution to these developments suggest a more complex, differentiated picture than previously demonstrated, or even envisioned.

First, specific aspects of parents' emotion-related expressiveness and behavior, similar to what Gottman et al. (1997) call emotion coaching, were important here. Emotion knowledge at both 3 and 4 years of age were predicted by mothers' positive emotions (particularly observed, but also self-reported for Year 1), their attentiveness to their children's emotions, their willingness to help children address emotional upset via letting the feelings out, figuring out how to deal with the feelings, and solving the problems. As well, mothers who were accepting of their children's emotions during Year 2 had children who demonstrated better emotion knowledge with regard to mixed emotions at 5 years of age. Further, mothers' positive attitudes toward actively aiding their children to learn about emotions were the strongest predictor of emotion knowledge at 3 years of age. In combination, these aspects of maternal socialization of emotion were associated in the predicted ways with children's emerging understanding of emotions. Mounting evidence asserts the importance of these experiences to the development of emotional competence.

Moreover, our proposed mediation model was upheld for the prediction of 3-year-old emotion knowledge. That is, we found support for our notion that parents' (albeit only mothers') own experience of emotional expressiveness and behavior would form a foundation for their attitudes about emotion within childrearing, and that these attitudes about direct teaching about emotion would be the proximal predictor of young children's emotion knowledge.

These findings support the meta-emotion theorizing and findings of Gottman and colleagues (e.g., Gottman et al., 1997). Parents who want their children to become emotionally competent could benefit from learning ways to promote emotion knowledge. Taking care of one's own emotional health, being aware of the importance of emotion, and a willingness to support and address issues emanating from the child's emotional experiences, are all topics that could be profitably addressed in parent education.

Unexpected Findings

Earlier evidence from our own work about the deleterious effects of maternal anger on emotion knowledge (e.g., Denham, Zoller, & Couchoud, 1994; Denham et al., 1997) did not emerge from these results—maternal Negative Emotions and Reactions was a negative predictor only of mixed emotion knowledge at 5 years of age. It is easy to imagine that maternal negativity might prompt children not to dwell deeply on the emotional world, especially the more complex nuances of possibly feeling good and bad at the same time. On the other hand, it may be that some anger or negativity needs to be experienced in order to learn about emotions (Garner et al., 1994)—especially about display rules. Our current results on maternal prediction of 5-year-olds' display rule knowledge, and paternal prediction of 4-year-olds' understanding of expressions and situations, suggest that this possibility may hold true, especially when negativity is low in frequency, duration, and intensity and within the context of a positive background affect.

Of more concern are the weak and partially counterintuitive findings for paternal prediction of emotion knowledge. We know that the same behaviors performed by mothers and fathers do not necessarily have the same effects on children. Yet, in comparison to maternal prediction, paternal prediction of young children's emotion knowledge was much less straightforward. Four-year-old expression and situation knowledge was the only aspect of emotion knowledge predicted by paternal socialization of emotion.

How can this pattern of results be explained? First, perhaps fathers talk and explain more about emotions particularly when their children are poorer at understanding emotions. There is some precedence for this seemingly counterintuitive relation in the literature (e.g., Denham, Cook, & Zoller, 1992); the parents' repetition of the child's emotion language, taking their lead, and the accuracy of their emotion language, may be more important, positively weighted, predictors than frequency of a particular function category.

Another answer may lay in the particular functions and quality of paternal emotion language. For example, fathers of young preschoolers, like mothers of toddlers (Dunn et al., 1987), may be talking more about the control of emotion than about its nature, causes, and more subtle points. Their explanations about emotions also may be of poor quality. We have ample anecdotal evidence that this may be likely. Fathers faced with the task of reminiscence about emotions often said, "You want me to what?" Perhaps the role of fathers really is more as arbiter of emotional control than as teacher about the wider world of emotion. The work of Zeman and Shipman (Zeman, Penza, Shipman, & Young, 1997; Zeman & Shipman, 1997) suggests that this may well be true, at least from the children's own viewpoints–preschoolers reported that they would show sadness and anger more around fathers than mothers, but by middle childhood these emotions were shown more passively to fathers.

Bhavnagri and Parke (1991) also assert that fathers' role in the family is more as playmate, with mothers' more of a manager/advisor role. If this is commonly true, it is not surprising that we obtained the findings that we did. Mothers may play a greater role in shaping children's social cognition, with fathers contributing, but through different pathways. Thus, one possible avenue of future research would be to examine more specifically the socialization of emotion that occurs during active father-child play. Our second suggestion is complementary to findings of Gottman and colleagues (Gottman et al., 1997), who found complex relations between marital quality and parents' likelihood of being good emotion coaches. We did not directly measure marital quality in this study, but will be doing so in followup assessments of the children during elementary school.

In sum, our findings suggest that more fully fleshing out fathers' contributions would be a fruitful line of more pinpointed inquiry. Thus, instead of concluding that fathers have relatively little clear contribution to their young children's emotion knowledge, our analyses suggest two things: (1) that the role of fathers in socializing their offspring needs to be acknowledged; and (2) that investigation of fathers' role as support for the emotion coach in the family, who may usually be the mother, is in order.

Larger Issues

These results also must be placed within the larger context of family functioning and of applications for good parenting. For example, it is a truism that an emotionally positive family is a good thing–so much so that the real meaning may be lost. Does such an injunction mean that parents must be upbeat and chirpy at all times, at least in regards to teaching their young children about emotions? Thankfully, our findings suggest that this is not necessarily true. Our findings do reveal that it is helpful for mothers to feel good not only for their own well-being but also because such ongoing emotional experience fosters their ability to teach their youngsters about emotion. We also can say that emotional well-being is not the only important aspect of socialization. The full range of emotional reactions and expressiveness, as well as different types of teaching, contribute in complex ways to children's adaptive understanding of emotions. What parents may most need is to have a sense of our main take home messages and the notion that there is no one perfect way to help children learn about emotions.

Grappling with these findings also points to a larger issue. Coupled with recent evidence that preschoolers talk more about emotions with siblings and friends than with mothers (Brown, Donelan-McCall, & Dunn, 1996), we must view the transition from the foundation of emotion-language-with-parents to the even more mature, social-competence enhancing emotion-language-with-equals. Unfortunately, very little research has been done focusing on the socializing influence of peers and siblings, or of intrapersonal contributions to emotion knowledge.

As potent as socializing agents' influence can be on young children's developing emotion knowledge, there also are child effects on each aspect of such knowledge. Such child effects include age as a marker for other, unspecified, developmental change (e.g., the meaning of socialization techniques is likely to differ across age), cognitive development, linguistic development and the child's own emotionality. Before expecting certain levels of emotion knowledge, it would be wise to consider each individual child's age, as well as his or her levels of cognitive/linguistic ability and development of self. Moreover, children who are more emotionally expressive may have more experiences to fuel their understanding.

LIMITATIONS AND CONCLUSION

The possible limitations of the current study include losing information because of data aggregation, generalization to only a specific population, and the limited context in which emotion socialization was examined. Despite the need to aggregate in order to get a broader view of all aspects of socialization of emotion, it may now be important to use the leads discovered here, by disaggregating some of these estimates. Although our sample was homogeneous, this study provides some indicators of important pathways to children's emotional competence. Similar parental contributions should be explored in future research with more diverse samples given the evidence, for example, that parenting practices differ based on education level, ethnicity and income. Even within an educated, mostly Caucasian sample, the context observed for the purposes of this study (i.e., requiring parent and child to maintain relative proximity for nearly two hours), may not have been representative of typical shared parent-child activities. Such a discrepancy in contextual typicality may be even more severe for father-child interactions, which could partially account for our weaker findings regarding paternal emotion socialization. Even so, it is not surprising that such a macro examination of so few, very focused potential predictors of emotion knowledge yields findings that are small in magnitude but, nonetheless, important in their implications.

In sum, children's growing emotion understanding is grounded in their relationships: pretending, deceiving, teaching, joking, comforting (Dunn, 1995). The particular relationship between persons talking about emotion makes a difference in the content of preschoolers' feeling state conversations. Children learn much about distinctive aspects of emotion from their parents, and following leads from this research promises to yield even greater, practically applicable, insights.

REFERENCES

Banerjee, M. (1997). Hidden emotions: Preschoolers' knowledge of appearance-reality and emotion display rules. *Social Cognition, 15*, 107-132.

Baron, R., & Kenny, D. (1986). The moderator-mediator variable distinction in social psychological research: Conceptual, strategic, and statistical consideration. *Journal of Personality and Social Psychology, 51*, 1173-1182.

Bhavnagri, N. P., & Parke, R. D. (1991). Parents as direct facilitators of children's peer relationships: Effects of age of child and sex of parent. *Journal of Social and Personal Relationships, 8*, 423-440.

Bretherton, I., Fritz, J., Zahn-Waxler, C., & Ridgeway, D. (1986). Learning to talk about emotions: A functionalist perspective. *Child Development, 56*, 529-548.

Brown, J. R., Donelan-McCall, N., & Dunn, J. (1996). Why talk about mental states? The significance of children's conversations with friends, siblings, and mothers. *Child Development, 67*, 836-849.

Brown, J. R., & Dunn, J. (1991). "You can cry, mum": The social and developmental implications of talk about internal states. *British Journal of Developmental Psychology, 9*, 237-256

Brown, J. R., & Dunn, J. (1992). Talk with your mother or your sibling? Developmental changes in early family conversations about feelings. *Child Development, 63*, 336-349.

Camras, L. A., Sachs-Alter, E., & Ribordy, S. C. (1996). Emotion understanding in maltreated children: Recognition of facial expressions and integration with other emotion cues. In M. Lewis and M. W. Sullivan (Eds.), *Emotional development in atypical children* (pp. 203-225). Mahwah, NJ: Lawrence Erlbaum Associates.

Cohen, J., & Cohen, P. (1991). *Applied multiple regression/correlation analysis for the behavioral sciences (2nd edition)*. Hillsdale, NJ: LEA.

Covell, K., & Miles, B. (1992). Children's beliefs about strategies to reduce parental anger. *Child Development, 63*, 381-390.

Denham, S. A. (1986). Social cognition, social behavior, and emotion in preschoolers: Contextual validation. *Child Development, 57*, 194-201.

Denham, S. A. (1989). Maternal affect and toddlers' social-emotional competence. *American Journal of Orthopsychiatry, 59*, 368-376.

Denham, S. A. (1993). Maternal emotional responsiveness and toddlers' social-emotional functioning. *Journal of Child Psychology and Psychiatry, 34*, 715-728.

Denham, S. A., Cook, M. C., & Zoller, D. (1992). Baby looks *very* sad: Discussions about emotions between mother and preschooler. *British Journal of Developmental Psychology, 10*, 301-315.

Denham, S. A., & Couchoud, E. A. (1990a). Young preschoolers' understanding of emotion. *Child Study Journal, 20*, 171-192.

Denham, S. A., & Couchoud, E. A. (1990b). Young preschoolers' understanding of equivocal emotion situations. *Child Study Journal, 20*, 193-202.

Denham, S. A., & Couchoud, E. A. (1991). Social-emotional contributors to preschoolers' responses to an adult's negative emotions. *Journal of Child Psychology and Psychiatry, 32*, 595-608.

Denham, S. A., & Grout, L. (1993). Socialization of emotion: Pathway to preschoolers' affect regulation. *Journal of Nonverbal Behavior, 17*, 215-227.

Denham, S. A., Mason, T., & Couchoud, E. A. (1995). Scaffolding young children's prosocial responsiveness: Preschoolers' responses to adult sadness, anger, and pain. *International Journal of Behavioral Development, 18*, 489-504.

Denham, S. A., McKinley, M., Couchoud, E. A., & Holt, R. (1990). Emotional and behavioral predictors of peer status in young preschoolers. *Child Development, 61*, 1145-1152.

Denham, S. A., Mitchell-Copeland, J., Strandberg. K., Auerbach, S., & Blair, K. (1997). Parental contributions to preschoolers' emotional competence: Direct and indirect effects. *Motivation and Emotion, 21*, 65-86.

Denham, S. A., Renwick, S., & Hewes, S. (1994). Affective communication between mothers and preschoolers: Relations with social-emotional competence. *Merrill Palmer Quarterly, 40*, 488-508.

Denham, S. A., & Zoller, D. (1991). "When my hamster died, I cried": Preschoolers' attributions of the causes of emotions. *Journal of Genetic Psychology, 152,* 371-373.

Denham, S. A., Zoller, D. & Couchoud, E. A. (1994). Socialization of preschoolers' emotion understanding. *Developmental Psychology, 30,* 928-936.

Dix, T. (1991). The affective organization of parenting: Adaptive and maladaptive processes. *Psychological Bulletin, 110,* 3-25.

Dunn, J. (1995). Children as psychologists: The later correlates of individual differences in understanding of emotions and other minds. *Cognition and Emotion, 9,* 187-201.

Dunn, J., & Brown, J. (1994). Affect expression in the family, children's understanding of emotions, and their interactions with others. *Merrill-Palmer Quarterly, 40,* 120-137.

Dunn, J., Brown, J., & Beardsall, L. (1991). Family talk about feeling states and children's later understanding of others' emotions. *Developmental Psychology, 27,* 448-455.

Dunn, J., Brown, J. R., Slomkowski, C., Tesla, C., & Youngblade, L. (1991). Young children's understanding of other people's feelings and beliefs: Individual differences and their antecedents. *Child Development, 62,* 1352-1366.

Eisenberg, N., & Fabes, R. A. (1994). Mothers' reactions to children's negative emotions: Relations to children's temperament and anger behavior. *Merrill-Palmer Quarterly, 40,* 138-156.

Eisenberg, N., Fabes, R. A., Carlo, G., & Karbon, M. (1992). Emotional responsivity to others: Behavioral correlates and socialization antecedents. In N. Eisenberg & R. A. Fabes (Eds.), *Emotion and its regulation in early development. New Directions for Child Development, 55,* 57-73. San Francisco: Jossey-Bass.

Eisenberg, N., Fabes, R. A., & Murphy, B. C. (1996). Parents' reactions to children's negative emotions: Relations to children's social competence and comforting behavior. *Child Development, 67,* 2227-2247.

Eisenberg, N., Fabes, R. A., Shepard, S. A., Guthrie, I. K., Murphy, B. C., & Reiser, M. (1999). Parental reactions to children's negative emotions: Longitudinal relations to quality of children's social functioning. *Child Development, 70,* 513-534.

Fabes, R. A., Eisenberg, N., & Bernzweig, J. (1990). *The coping with children's negative emotions scale: Description and scoring.* Unpublished manuscript, Department of Family Resources and Human Development, Arizona State University.

Garner, P. W., Jones, D. C., & Miner, J. L. (1994). Social competence among low-income preschoolers: Emotion socialization practices and social cognitive correlates. *Child Development, 65,* 622-637.

Gnepp, J. (1989). Personalized inferences of emotions and appraisals: Component processes and correlates. *Developmental Psychology, 25,* 277-288.

Gordis, F., Rosen, A. B., & Grand, S. (1989, April). *Young children's understanding of simultaneous conflicting emotions.* Poster presented at the Biennial Meetings of the Society for Research in Child Development, Kansas City.

Gottman, J., Katz, L., & Hooven, C. (1997). *Meta-emotion: How families communicate emotionally.* Mahwah, NJ: LEA.

Gross, D., & Harris, P. (1988). Understanding false beliefs about emotion. *International Journal of Behavioral Development, 11*, 475-488.

Halberstadt, A. G. (1986). Family socialization of emotional expression and nonverbal communication styles and skills. *Journal of Personality and Social Psychology, 51*, 827-836.

Halberstadt, A. G. (1991). Socialization of expressiveness: Family influences in particular and a model in general. In R. S. Feldman & S. Rime (Eds.), *Fundamentals of emotional expressiveness* (pp. 106-162). Cambridge: Cambridge University Press.

Halberstadt, A. G., Cassidy, J., Stifter, C. A., Parke, R. D., & Fox, N. A. (1995). Self-expressiveness within the family context. *Psychological Assessment, 7*, 93-103.

Hart, C. H., DeWolf, D. M., Wozniak, P., & Burts, D. C. (1992). Maternal and paternal disciplinary styles: Relations with preschoolers' playground behavioral observations and peer status. *Child Development, 63*, 879-892.

Hoffman, M. L. (1984). Interaction of affect and cognition in empathy. In C. E. Izard, J. Kagan, & R. B. Zajonc (Eds.), *Emotions, cognition, & behavior* (pp. 103-131). Cambridge: Cambridge University Press.

Hoffner, C., & Badzinski, D. M. (1989). Children's integration of facial and situational cues to emotion. *Child Development, 60*, 415-422.

Hyson, M. C., & Lee, K-M. (1996). Assessing early childhood teachers' beliefs about emotions: Content, contexts, and implications for practice. *Early Education and Development, 7*, 59-78.

Izard, C. E. (1991). *The psychology of emotions.* New York: Plenum.

Jones, D. C., Bowling, B., & Cumberland, A. (1998). The development of display rule knowledge: Linkages with family expressiveness and social competence. *Child Development, 69*, 1209-1222.

Karn, M. A., & Dunsmore, J.C. (2000, April). What children learn from their friends: Friendships, maternal beliefs about emotions, and emotional competence in kindergarten children. In M. J. Colwell (Chair), *Socialization mechanisms in young children's development of emotion knowledge and emotion understanding: Parenting, peers and sociocultural influences.* Symposium conducted at the Conference on Human Development, Memphis, TN.

Kestenbaum, R., & Gelman, S. (1995). Preschool children's identification and understanding of mixed emotions. *Cognitive Development, 10*, 443-458.

Linehan, M. M., Paul, E., & Egan, K. J. (1983). The Parent Affect Test: Development, validity, and reliability. *Journal of Clinical Child Psychology, 12*, 161-166.

MacKinnon, D. P., & Dwyer, J. H. (1993). Estimating mediated effects in prevention studies. *Evaluation Review, 17*, 144-158.

Miller, P. H., & Aloise, P. A. (1989). Young children's understanding of the psychological causes of behavior: A review. *Child Development, 60*, 257-285.

Parke, R. D., Cassidy, J., Burks, V. M., Carson, J. L., & Boyum, L. (1992). Familial contribution to peer competence among young children: The role of interactive and affective processes. In R. D. Parke & G. W. Ladd (Eds.), *Family-peer relationships: Modes of linkage* (pp. 107-134). Hillsdale, NJ: Lawrence Erlbaum Associates.

Roberts, W. (1993). *Programs for the field collection and analysis of observational data: A manual.* Unpublished, Cariboo College, Canada.

Tomkins, S. (1991). *Affect, imagery, consciousness, Vol. II, The negative affects: Anger and fear.* New York: Springer Publishing Co.

Wintre, M., & Vallance, D. D. (1994). A developmental sequence in the comprehension of emotions: Multiple emotions, intensity and valence. *Developmental Psychology, 30,* 509-514.

Zahn-Waxler, C. Ridgeway, D., Denham, S. A., Usher, B., & Cole, P. (1993). Research strategies for assessing mothers' interpretations of infants' emotions. In R. Emde, J. Osofsky, & P. Butterfield (Eds.), *Parental perceptions of infant emotions* (pp. 217-236). Washington, DC: International Universities Press.

Zeman, J., Penza, S., Shipman, K., & Young, G. (1997). Preschoolers as functionalists: The impact of social context on emotion regulation. *Child Study Journal, 27,* 41-67.

Zeman, J., & Shipman, K. (1997). Social-contextual influences on expectancies for managing anger and sadness: The transition from middle childhood to adolescence. *Developmental Psychology, 33,* 917-924.

Children's Emotional Regulation and Social Competence in Middle Childhood: The Role of Maternal and Paternal Interactive Style

David J. McDowell
Mina Kim
Robin O'Neil
Ross D. Parke

SUMMARY. Associations among parental behaviors, children's emotional reactivity, and dimensions of children's social competence were examined. Fourth grade children (N = 103) and their parents participated in a laboratory discussion task. Parent-child relationship qualities, parental emotion socialization behaviors, measures of children's emotional regulatory abilities, and social competence (assessed by teachers and

---

David J. McDowell, Mina Kim, Robin O'Neil and Ross D. Parke are affiliated with the Department of Psychology, University of California, Riverside.

Address correspondence to: David J. McDowell, Department of Psychology, University of California, Riverside, CA 92521 (E-mail: wolf@citrus.ucr.edu).

This study was supported by National Science Foundation Grant BNS 8919391 to Ross D. Parke and NICHD Grant HT 32391 to Ross D. Parke and Robin O'Neil.

The authors are especially grateful to Sue Isley, Mara Welsh, Mary Flyr and Shirley Wang for the time devoted to interviewing children. Most importantly, they thank the teachers and staff of the elementary schools, and the children and families that participate in our project for their involvement. Finally, thanks to Dr. Karen Harshman, Superintendent of the Fontana Unified School District, and Bonita Roberts, Superintendent of the Jurupa Unified School District, for their ongoing support.

[Haworth co-indexing entry note]: "Children's Emotional Regulation and Social Competence in Middle Childhood: The Role of Maternal and Paternal Interactive Style." McDowell, David J. et al. Co-published simultaneously in *Marriage & Family Review* (The Haworth Press, Inc.) Vol. 34, No. 3/4, 2002, pp. 345-364; and: *Emotions and the Family* (ed: Richard A. Fabes) The Haworth Press, Inc., 2002, pp. 345-364. Single or multiple copies of this article are available for a fee from The Haworth Document Delivery Service [1-800-HAWORTH, 9:00 a.m. - 5:00 p.m. (EST). E-mail address: docdelivery@haworthpress.com].

© 2002 by The Haworth Press, Inc. All rights reserved.

peers) were obtained. Results indicated that parents' behaviors the discussion task were related to both children's emotional and social competence. Both mothers' and fathers' behaviors were linked to children's emotional regulatory abilities and social competence. In addition, children's emotional regulation was related to children's social competence. Only limited evidence of the mediating role of emotion regulation was found. Implications for relative roles of mothers and fathers in the emergence of emotional and social competence were noted. *[Article copies available for a fee from The Haworth Document Delivery Service: 1-800-HAWORTH. E-mail address: <docdelivery@haworthpress.com> Website: <http://www.HaworthPress.com> © 2002 by The Haworth Press, Inc. All rights reserved.]*

KEYWORDS. Parent-child interaction, social competence, emotions

The development of social competence in childhood has emerged as an important area of research due to the often-cited negative consequences of peer rejection and social incompetence in both childhood and adulthood. These deleterious outcomes include feelings of loneliness and depression in childhood (Asher, Parkhurst, Hymel, & Williams, 1990; Boivin, Poulin, & Vitaro, 1994), as well as poor academic performance, disruptive behavior, truancy, and school drop-out (Kupersmidt, Coie, & Dodge, 1990; Parker & Asher, 1987). Poor peer relationships in childhood have also been linked to adult criminality and mental problems (Parker & Asher, 1987; Patterson & Bank, 1989).

Evidence attesting to the serious nature of peer rejection has caused marked increases in the search for the antecedents of socially competent behavior. Much of this research has centered on children's social knowledge and specific social skills (Crick & Dodge, 1994; Dodge, Pettit, McClasky, & Brown, 1986). However, another line of research, which has rapidly come to the fore, has focused on the affective domain. Constructs such as emotional expression, understanding, and regulation in social relationships are purported by researchers in this area to be at the crux of competent social and emotional functioning (Denham, 1998; Saarni, 1999).

EMOTIONAL REGULATION AND CHILDREN'S SOCIAL COMPETENCE

Research indicates that children's abilities to regulate emotions appropriately are associated with the quality of their relationships with peers (Cassidy, Parke, Butkovsky, & Braungart, 1992; Hubbard & Coie, 1994). For example, children's ability to effectively regulate emotions is related to teacher ratings of social status. Eisenberg, Fabes, Bernzweig et al. (1993) found that for 4- to 6-year-old boys, both the type of emotion coping strategies endorsed (as described by adults) as well as lower levels of expressed negative affect were related to children's social competence. This study found that boys who engaged in externalizing behaviors in response to their negative arousal were rated negatively by their peers. In a later study, Eisenberg, Fabes, and Murphy (1995) found that prosocial behavior and competent social functioning were a function of effective attentional and behavioral regulation as indexed by parent and teacher reports. Furthermore, Eisenberg, Guthrie, Fabes, Reiser et al. (1997) found that relations between children's attentional regulation and their social functioning were mediated by resiliency, as defined by flexible use of strategies to cope with stress. More recently, McDowell, O'Neil, and Parke (2000) found that children's endorsement of negative emotional responses and their inappropriate use of display rules during a disappointing gift task were related to lower social competence as rated by peers. Such studies suggest that the ability to regulate the emotional tone of interactions with others may be a critical ingredient of children's social competence and success in peer relationships.

PARENTAL SOCIALIZATION FOR EMOTIONAL AND SOCIAL COMPETENCE

Arguably, the most salient environmental influence on children's emotional development is parental influence. Thus, parents have been the focus of psychological investigations of emotion socialization as they are the first socializing agents who have extended contact with the developing child. Emotion theorists have recently presented heuristic models for the process of emotion socialization and its links to social and emotional competence (Denham, 1998; Eisenberg, Cumberland, & Spinrad, 1998). In these models it is proposed that the mechanisms of parental emotion socialization, which include modeling, coaching, and contingent responsiveness, contribute to the emotion outcomes of children (expression, understanding, and regulation). In turn, these emotional outcomes are assumed to influence children's relationships with peers. The current study is concerned with the role of parental modeling of expression and parental reaction to children's emotional expressions in the socialization of emotion in children.

Modeling of emotional expression. The parent-child relationship is emotion-laden (Dix, 1992) and as a result modeling of parental emotional expression inevitably takes place whenever a child observes a parental emotion, regardless of the intentions of the parent (Denham, 1998). As significant figures in children's lives, parents provide a myriad of opportunities to provide models of emotional expressiveness and regulation. For example, many studies have shown similarities in parents' and children's expression of emotion. It has been shown that in the first year of life, infants exhibit similar expressions to their mothers in laboratory research settings (Field, Healy, Goldstein et al., 1988; Malatesta & Haviland, 1982). Research also indicates that parental expressiveness has implications for other aspects of children's emotional competence aside from emotional expression, which, in turn, may impact their peer competency. For example, a recent study by Dunn and Brown (1994) found that higher levels of negative affect or distress within the family were associated with children's poor performance on emotional understanding and recognition tasks, less reasoning during conflict, and less perspective taking in joint pretend play. Furthermore, Boyum and Parke (1995) found that parents of highly socially competent children rated themselves as higher in positive and total emotional expressiveness. Similar results are reported by Isley, O'Neil and Parke (1996) demonstrating the predictive influence of observed parental affect expression on children's classroom acceptance from kindergarten through first grade. Specifically, parental negative affect was linked with lower acceptance by peers one year later.

Parenting practices. Another set of emotion socialization behavior that has received attention includes parental coaching and parental responses to children's emotions. Gottman, Katz, and Hooven (1996) expanded this line of research by introducing the concept of parental meta-emotion, which is parents' awareness and thoughts about their own emotions and their children's emotions. Two categories fall under parental meta-emotion philosophy: emotion-coaching philosophy and derogatory philosophy. In this longitudinal study, the investigators found that 5-year-olds whose parents endorsed the emotion-coaching philosophy had a number of positive outcomes at age 8, including favorable ratings of peer competence, high academic achievement, and good physical health. The researchers argued that valuing of emotional expression, awareness of one's own emotions, and willingness and competence to help their children with their emotions, all of which constitute the emotion-coaching philosophy, allowed the 8-year-olds to gain knowledge about their emotions and become sophisticated in generating solutions in emotionally charged situations. The manner in which parents respond to their children's discrete emotional expressions has implications for children's emotional well-being as well as their enduring emotional styles.

The antithesis of the emotion-coaching meta-emotion philosophy is the derogatory philosophy, which is characterized by ignoring, denying, or dismissing children's emotions. Parents with a derogatory philosophy find their children's negative emotions noxious as well as potentially harmful to the child and try to extinguish them as quickly as possible (Gottman et al., 1996). Parents with this philosophy may often try to control their children's emotions, which may have harmful consequences. Roberts and Strayer (1987) argue that when parents suppress children's negative emotions, children store these negative experiences in memory and draw on them when similar situations occur. In addition, Eisenberg, Fabes, and Murphy (1996) found that parents' negative responding to third- through sixth-grade children's negative emotions led to more emotional dysregulation. Similarly, Carson and Parke (1996) found that fathers who respond to their children's negative affect with negative affect of their own during emotionally stimulating physical play had children with low peer competency indexed by physically aggressive and avoidant behaviors, and were, in turn, regarded by teachers as less socially competent. More recently, McDowell and Parke (2000) found that parents' controlling of third-grade children's emotion was negatively related to children's appropriate endorsement of display rules. Such findings may indicate that more controlling parents are depriving their children of opportunities to learn and utilize appropriate emotional competence in their social interactions. Conversely, the extent to which parents tolerate the expression of negative emotions and assist their children with the resolution of emotional upset has been found to be associated with children's social competence. Gottman, Katz and Hooven (1997), for example, found that fathers' acceptance and assistance with children's sadness and anger when children were five was related to children's social competence with peers when they were eight years of age.

Emerging from the aforementioned studies is the growing cognizance of the emotional life of families and the powerful influence that parents have on their children's emotional development. Through the avenues of parental modeling, coaching, and contingent response, children construct a repertoire of strategies for dealing with emotional upset that find their use in interpersonal relationships. Recently, Contreras, Kerns, Weimer, and Gentzler (2000) found that even after controlling for emotionality, more positive coping was related to fifth graders being rated by teachers as more positive. More importantly, these investigators found that coping appeared to mediate the link between mother-child attachment and social competence.

In the current study, both parent modeling of affect and parenting behaviors were assessed in relation to children's emotional and social competence. Specifically, it is hypothesized that parents with more positive relationship qualities and more positive affective behaviors will have children who endorse more socially acceptable coping strategies. Moreover, parents with more positive interaction styles and affective behaviors will have children who are rated as more socially competent by both peers and teachers.

MATERNAL VERSUS PATERNAL INFLUENCES ON EMOTIONAL DEVELOPMENT

Most research in the area of emotional development has relied exclusively on maternal assessments. However, several studies that have incorporated fathers into their design suggest that fathers may play an important and unique role in the development of emotion regulation. Parke (1994) has argued that paternal impact on emotion regulation and, in turn, social competence, is likely due to opportunities to learn to regulate emotional arousal in interactions between fathers and children, especially play. The range of emotional arousal, as well as the degree of unpredictability in the intensity of the emotional stimulation, are greater in father-child than mother-child interaction (Parke, 1996). This, in turn, promotes greater opportunities for learning emotion regulatory skills in father-child exchanges. Several studies provide support for fathers' role in the development of emotion regulation. Isley et al. (1996) found that fathers' expressed negative affect and control during an interaction was related to kindergarten and first-grade boys', but not girls', ratings of social acceptance. More recently, McDowell and Parke (2000) found that fathers' control of children's emotion predicted children's lack of display rule knowledge above and beyond mothers' level of control. In view of the role of fathers in the development of emotion regulation, it is hypothesized that fathers' behavior will show a stronger relation to children's emotional regulation and social competence than mothers'.

SEX OF CHILD

Previous research examining parental influences on children's emotional functioning outside of the classroom has found support for the notion that relations are stronger for same-sex dyads than for opposite-sex dyads (Isley, O'Neil, & Parke, 1996). Other research (Denham, Mitchell-Copeland, Strandberg, 1997) has found that daughters are especially affected by mothers' and fathers' expressiveness. Specifically, these investigators found that girls' positivity in the classroom was related to parents' expressions of happiness relative to anger. In light of this earlier work, sex of child will be treated in an exploratory fashion and no explicit hypothesis is offered.

THE PRESENT STUDY

With few exceptions (i.e., Gottman et al., 1996), previous research has seldom utilized observational measures in assessing emotional exchanges in parent-child interaction (Eisenberg et al., 1993, 1995, 1997). In addition to parent self-report of emotional expressiveness as well as the quality of the relationship with their children, it is equally crucial to conduct independent observations of these behaviors. Thus, the first goal of the current study is to extend previous work to include observations of parents' emotion socialization behaviors in interactions with their children. In addition, the present study will incorporate into the observational analysis, fathers' as well as mothers' emotion socialization behaviors.

A second goal of the current study will be to extend prior work in the area of emotional and social competence to the middle-childhood period. Emotion research, specifically emotion regulation, has mainly focused on infants and young children. It is critical that the middle-childhood period be researched given that children in middle childhood are characterized as having a strong need for acceptance and belonging (Parker & Gottman, 1989).

A third and related goal is to use children's self-reports of their emotionality and coping strategies. Prior research, having primarily focused on infants and younger children, has used only parent or teacher reports of children's emotion regulation. Children in middle childhood may be better able to articulate their feelings and the strategies they use in order to cope with them. A noteworthy strength of the current study in relation to children's self-reports is that age-appropriate vignettes that are relevant to the children's lives are used. Thus, whereas parent reports typically involve de-contextualized statements (i.e., "When my child is upset, he/she watches TV."), the measure used in the current study will include hypothetical situations that the participating children may actually encounter in real life.

METHOD

Participants

One hundred-three fourth-grade children (54 males, 49 females) with a range of social acceptance levels participated in the current study. Children had a mean age of 10.03 years ($SD = .35$). Children attended nine elementary schools in two West Coast communities and together with their parents were participants in a longitudinal study of children's social development. The children have been followed yearly since kindergarten. The socioeconomic status of the families ranged from lower- to upper-middle class. Median family income was approximately $40,500 (ranging from under $10,000 to greater than $58,000), and the educational attainment of parents averaged 12.6 years for mothers and 13.0 years for fathers. Approximately 50% of the sample was Euro-American, 40% Latino, and 10% of the sample was African-American, Asian-American or other ethnicity. Teachers of each of the children also participated by completing paper-and-pencil measures (described below).

Procedure and Measures

Children's social competence. When the children were in the fourth grade, the teachers completed a 12-item classroom behavior inventory originally developed by Cassidy and Asher (1992). Teachers used 5-point rating scales ranging from 1 (not at all like this child) to 5 (very much like this child) to assess children's likability (how liked or disliked the child was by their classmates) and behavioral attributes which included prosocial, friendliness, looking sad, disruptiveness, shyness, verbal and physical aggression, exclusion of peers from activities, and avoidance.

Sociometric interviews (Asher, Singleton, Tinsley, & Hymel, 1979) were conducted in fourth-grade classrooms in order to assess each child's likability by asking students to nominate three classmates with whom they liked to play or spend time, and three classmates with whom they disliked playing or spending time. Children also nominated up to three classmates for each of the following: prosocial behaviors (those good at sharing, helping, and taking turns), looking/acting sad, avoidance, having a good sense of humor, verbal and physical aggression, and keeping others from being included in their group. These nominations were tallied and standardized within each classroom. A principal components analysis with varimax rotation was used to reduce the 21 peer- and teacher-based social competence variables to six composite factors. The following peer ratings were combined to form the (1) *peer-rated avoidant*: spends time alone; looks sad; (2) *peer-rated aggressive:* says mean things (verbal aggression); hits; kicks or starts fights (physical aggression); keeps other kids from being in the group; and dislike; (3) *peer-rated positive social orientation:* has a good sense of humor; liked; good at helping, sharing, taking turns (prosocial); (4) *teacher-rated avoidant:* excludes peers; excludes peers when mad; (5) *teacher-rated aggressive:* ratings of aggression (both physical and verbal); disruptive; prosocial (reverse scored); friendly (reverse scored); (6) *teacher-rated positive social orientation:* well-liked; looks sad (reverse scored); not well-liked (reverse scored); avoidant (reverse scored); and shy (reverse scored). Alphas for sociometric variables ranged from .71 to .78.

Parent-child discussion interaction. A triadic discussion task between the mother, father, and child was adapted from a similar task by Conger and his colleagues (Rueter & Conger, 1995). For the present study, parents and children were individually administered a questionnaire of peer and family issues adapted from the Taxonomy of Problematic Situations (Dodge, McClaskey, & Feldman, 1985) which asked each family member to rate how difficult it would be for the child to handle each of the 34 situations. Ratings were based on a 5-point scale for adults and a 3-point scale for children with higher numbers indicating more difficulty for the family. Seven issues were then chosen by the experimenter for the family to discuss. At least one family member had to identify the situation as being difficult for the child to deal with in order to be presented for discussion. Thus, each family was presented with issues that were salient to that family, rather than a standard set which may or may not have been relevant to the triad. Trained coders independently rated each of the family members on several affective and behavioral dimensions.

Using a principal axis factor analysis, the parent discussion behaviors were converted to composite variables. These composites are listed along with the original variables coded in parentheses: *Positive interac-*

tion (inductive reasoning, use of positive responses, encouraging independence, warmth, problem solving, positive affect and negative affect [reverse scored]), *emotionality* (clarity of expression, intensity of expression, and awareness of child's feelings), *control* (regulation of child's emotions, controlling interaction style), and *child focus* (focusing on child as root of the problem). Reliability was established on 20 percent of the videotapes chosen at random. Interrater reliabilities for the original scales were calculated by correlations and ranged from .62 to .70 for the dimensions listed above.

Children's negative emotional reactivity and coping. Children's strategies for coping with emotionally charged events were assessed using children's responses to a series of vignettes. Five vignettes that were designed to generate anger, frustration, or excitement were presented to the children (see Appendix A for complete text of vignettes). Interviewers asked children to respond to a series of closed-ended items that assessed the intensity of emotion ("How upset or excited would this make you feel?"), latency ("How long would it take you to calm down?"), and ease of calming ("How easy or hard would it be for you to calm down?") following an event using a 10-point, barometer-type response scale (lower scores are indicative of a lower level of excitement/agitation and a higher ease of calming down). The scale reliabilities for these scales were: intensity alpha = .59, latency alpha = .70, and ease of calming alpha = .68. The likelihood of utilization of several types of coping strategies (i.e., responding with anger or sadness) were also assessed using a 7-point scale with responses ranging from 1 (I'd never do this) to 7 (I'd definitely do this). The coping strategy subscales included anger (alpha = .67), sad (alpha = .59), nervous (alpha = .75), and reasoning (alpha = .56) Evidence of the validity of a subset of responses to these vignettes (sad and anger responses) has been found earlier by McDowell et al. (2000) who found that these responses were negatively related to children's appropriate use of display rules and social competence.

RESULTS

Descriptive Statistics

Table 1 shows the means and standard deviations for parental style and children's self-reports of emotion regulation and coping. There were no statistically significant differences between boys and girls or

TABLE 1. Means and Standard Deviations for Parental Style and Children's Self-Report of Emotion Regulation

	Boys		Girls	
	M	SD	M	SD
Mother				
Positive Interaction	2.99	.77	3.09	.80
Emotionality	2.89	.71	3.15	.72
Control	2.53	.88	2.82	.91
Child Focus	2.85	1.15	2.84	1.11
Father				
Positive Interaction	2.89	.80	2.81	.66
Emotionality	2.82	.82	2.65	.66
Control	2.44	.98	2.30	.86
Child Focus	2.77	.94	2.64	.98
Emotional Reactivity				
Intensity	5.37	.90	5.44	1.21
Ease of calming	4.41	1.20	4.52	1.24
Latency	3.96	1.18	4.18	1.19
Coping Strategies				
Anger	2.48	1.16	2.75	1.22
Sad	3.32	1.26	3.42	1.13
Nervous	3.12	1.47	3.71	1.35
Reason	4.77	1.32	4.96	1.03

mothers and fathers on the parental behavior variables. With respect to coping strategies, only the nervous coping strategy showed statistically significant differences between boys and girls with nervous more likely to be used by girls than boys, $F(1, 102) = 4.46$, $p < .05$.

Bivariate Analyses of Parental Style and Children's Emotion Regulation

Table 2 shows the correlations between children's emotion regulation and parental style by child sex. There were no significant relations between ease of calming or intensity and parental style. Boys' latency was negatively related to fathers' positive style. Correlations indicate that boys' emotional response of sadness was related to fathers being more child-focused. Boys that endorsed sad and anger responses had mothers who were more child-focused. In addition, boys endorsing

TABLE 2. Bivariate Correlations of Parental Style and Children's Emotion Regulation by Gender

	Positive Interaction	Emotionality	Control	Child Focus
	With Mothers (With Fathers)			
Boys				
Emotion regulation:				
Intensity	.00 (−.12)	−.01 (−.01)	.12 (−.06)	.03 (.18)
Ease of calming	−.04 (−.18)	−.01 (−.02)	.12 (−.05)	.03 (.10)
Latency	−.06 (−.31*)	.06 (−.10)	.20 (−.01)	.08 (.12)
Coping Strategies				
Anger	−.27* (−.23+)	−.23+ (−.17)	.14 (−.02)	.34* (.10)
Sad	−.21 (−.23+)	−.18 (.10)	−.16 (.19)	.30* (.28*)
Nervous	−.05 (−.22)	−.03 (.02)	−.10 (.07)	.20 (.20)
Reason	−.07 (−.13)	−.07 (.07)	−.02 (.15)	.16 (.12)
Girls				
Emotion regulation:				
Intensity	−.24* (−.06)	−.01 (−.01)	.12 (−.06)	.03 (.18)
Ease of calming	−.37** (−.12)	−.09 (.02)	.32* (−.09)	.23 (.34*)
Latency	−.28* (−.22)	−.20 (.01)	.18 (.10)	.24+ (.41**)
Coping Strategies				
Anger	−.47*** (−.07)	−.26+ (.16)	.29* (−.04)	.36** (.27+)
Sad	−.33* (−.12)	−.23 (.08)	.32* (.11)	.26+ (.14)
Nervous	−.44** (−.10)	−.22 (−.04)	.23 (−.11)	.38** (.43**)
Reason	.05 (.40)	−.05 (−.23)	.04 (−.30+)	−.11 (−.11)

***p < .001; **p < .01; *p < .05; +p < .10; r (54) for boys; r (49) for girls.

higher rates of anger as a response had mothers who used less positive affect and style during the discussion. For girls, the ease of calming was related to fathers' focus on the child as the source of the problem. Similarly, girls' who reported less ease of calming had mothers who exhibited less positive and more controlling behaviors. Girls' latency was positively related to fathers' focus on child and negatively related to mothers' positive behaviors. Girls' intensity was negatively related to their mothers' positive interaction. Girls endorsing more nervous responses had fathers that were more focused on the child. Mothers' positive style was negatively related to girls' anger, sad, and nervous responses. In addition, mothers who focused on the child as the source of the problem had girls who endorsed more anger and nervous responses. Finally, mothers' controlling behaviors were related to more anger and sad responses in girls.

Regression Analyses Predicting Children's Emotional Regulation from Parental Style

Regression analyses were used to predict children's coping from parental style as evidenced during the parent-child interaction. For these analyses all parental behavior variables were entered simultaneously into the regression. For boys, mothers' behaviors were marginally significant predictors of anger responses $F(4, 51) = 2.25, p < .07$. For girls, fathers' behaviors predicted nervous responses, $F(4, 45) = 3.47, p < .05$. Mothers' behavior significantly predicted girls' anger, $F(4, 45) = 4.66, p < .01$, sad, $F(4, 45) = 3.31, p < .05$, and nervous responses, $F(4, 45) = 3.62, p < .01$.

Bivariate Analyses of Parental Relationship Qualities and Children's Social Competence

As can be seen in Table 3, when teachers rated boys as aggressive, their mothers were more likely to be controlling. Boys rated more positively by teachers had fathers who used more positive behaviors during the interaction and were more child-focused. When boys were rated by peers as more avoidant, they had fathers who used less positive interaction style and more focused on the child as the source of the problem. Boys rated as more aggressive by peers had mothers who used less positive behaviors, were more child-focused, and controlling. Finally, boys rated positively by peers had mothers who used more positive behaviors during the interaction.

For girls, being rated by teachers as more aggressive was related to fathers' controlling behavior. Teachers' ratings of positivity for girls was related to more positive behaviors of the mother during the interaction. When peers rated girls as more aggressive, fathers exhibited more controlling behaviors.

Additional Analyses

Regression analyses indicated that only peer ratings of boys' aggression and positivity were significantly predicted by mothers' behavior in the interaction, $F(4, 51) = 3.34$ and $2.50, p < .05$, respectively. In the bivariate analyses, girls' emotional intensity was related to being rated

TABLE 3. Bivariate Correlations of Parental Style and Children's Social Competence

	Positive Interaction With Mothers (With Fathers)	Emotionality	Control	Child Focus
Boys				
Teacher ratings				
Avoidant	−.12 (.00)	−.16 (−.06)	−.01 (−.16)	.00 (.15)
Aggressive	−.24 (−.22)	−.15 (.17)	.36* (.24)	.06 (.23)
Positive	−.02 (.34*)	.07 (−.07)	−.04 (.13)	.04 (.28*)
Peer ratings				
Avoidant	−.02 (−.29*)	.00 (−.12)	.02 (.11)	.05 (.28*)
Aggressive	−.28* (−.14)	−.01 (.06)	.31* (.08)	.32* (.08)
Positive	.32* (.11)	.26⁺ (.00)	−.25⁺ (.02)	−.18 (−.20)
Girls				
Teacher ratings				
Avoidant	.02 (−.18)	−.02 (.12)	.27⁺ (.28⁺)	.11 (−.12)
Aggressive	−.06 (−.23)	.05 (.05)	−.06 (.32*)	−.06 (−.14)
Positive	.30* (−.01)	.27 (−.02)	−.07 (.11)	−.22 (.02)
Peer ratings				
Avoidant	−.06 (−.24)	.05 (−.27⁺)	−.15 (−.09)	−.02 (−.13)
Aggressive	−.05 (−.15)	.05 (.08)	−.03 (.32*)	.04 (.08)
Positive	.07 (.25)	.00 (.26⁺)	.00 (.05)	−.01 (.09)

**p < .01; *p < .05; ⁺p < .10; r(54) for boys; r (49) for girls.

as less avoidant and less negative by peers [$r(49) = -.27$ and $-.30, p < .05$, respectively]. Girls' rated by teachers as more avoidant endorsed more sad and less reasoning responses [$r(49) = .30$ and $-.39, p < .05$ and .01, respectively]. Finally, girls' rated by teachers as more positive used fewer nervous responses [$r(49) = -.34, p < .05$].

DISCUSSION

A major goal of this study was to examine the relations among parents' relationship qualities, emotion socialization behaviors and children's emotion regulation and social competence. Our results found that both parental relationship qualities such as warmth, positive responsiveness, and inductive reasoning and more direct forms of emotion socialization (e.g., parental control) are related to children's emotion regulation. This extends research in this area by providing an observational account of these parenting practices as a correlate of children's emotional and social competence. Specifically, correlational analyses revealed that parents with more negative relationship qualities had children who offered more negative responses to the hypothetical vignettes. This link was found for both mothers' and fathers' relationship qualities. Although only fathers' focus on the child as the source of problems in the discussion was related to children's emotion regulation, for mothers a variety of relationship qualities were related to their children's emotional functioning (child-focused, clarity, warmth, etc.). This suggests that only when fathers seem blaming, do children react with less positive emotional functioning. This is consistent with previous research that has found that fathers' controlling behaviors predict children's social outcomes over and above mothers' (Gottman et al. 1996, 1997; McDowell & Parke, 2000; Roberts & Strayer, 1987). Further, when analyses were conducted by sex of child, the relationship remained for both mothers' and fathers' qualities.

The majority of the findings with regard to parental relationship quality and children's emotional functioning suggest that mothers seem to be playing a more central role than fathers. Our results show that there are more relations between same-sex dyads (e.g., father-son, mother-daughter) than for opposite sex dyads, with the vast majority of the significant relations evident for mother-daughter dyads. This is consistent with previous work which has shown stronger relations between same-sex dyads (Isley et al., 1996). The finding that mothers' positive interaction is related to children's emotional functioning is not surprising because mothers are still commonly the primary caretakers (Parke, 1996). Through daily interactions with their children, mothers may be more in tune to the emotional style of their children. It is interesting to note that this effect of mothers being more in tune is not present for children of both genders. It may be that by middle childhood boys are not encouraged to reveal their emotions and that when they do show emotions, they are related to paternal patterns of emotional functioning which may be seen as gender appropriate behavior. This would account for the relations that did emerge for the father-son dyads.

Although there are few relationships between fathers' behaviors during the interaction and their children's emotional functioning, there are significant relations between fathers' interactional style and children's social competence. It is often assumed that the link between interaction style and social competence is mediated by emotional regulatory abilities (Contreras et al., 2000; Parke, 1994). However, in the case of father-son dyads, this was not evident and suggests that boys may directly model fathers' interactive style and, in turn, influence their social competence with peers. Second, fathers may play a more central role in the acquisition of emotional regulatory strategies in younger children. As children become older, they distance themselves emotionally from their fathers more than their mothers and rely more on mothers as emotional confidants and sources of support for daily conflicts or problems (Larsen, 1995). Third, children may use mothers and fathers for classes of problems of differing magnitude and/or mothers and fathers may intervene for different problems. Although mothers are sought out for everyday regulatory issues, fathers may be sought out under circumstances that are well in excess of their children's coping resources. Alternatively, fathers may intervene, especially in a case where children are expressing high levels of negative emotion, such as anger. Given that the hypothetical vignettes were designed to tap into everyday regulatory requirements of the child, these issues may have been more appropriate for detecting mother effects than father effects.

In general, our results confirm the link between parental interactional style and children's social competence (MacDonald & Parke, 1984; Putallaz, 1987). In addition, correlational analyses from the current study support previous research on the link between children's emotion regulation and social competence, and extends these studies to the middle childhood period. As mentioned previously, few studies have examined links among parental emotion socialization, children's emotion regulatory abilities, and children's social competence in middle childhood. Again, this omission is critical, given the unique developmental needs of this period.

This study also extends previous research by including children's self-report of emotion regulation. Most studies use parent or teacher reports of children's emotional functioning. Our results indicate that children's own reports of their coping strategies are related to indices of peer- and teacher-rated social competence. Research on peer reputation in middle childhood further emphasizes the importance of explicating the correlates of social competence. Investigation in this area has revealed robust relations between positive peer reputation in middle childhood and broad adaptation in adolescence (Morison & Masten, 1991). Conversely, negative peer regard, associated with a disruptive and aggressive reputation, was related to externalizing and antisocial behavior in adolescence.

Limitations and Future Directions

The current study builds upon prior research by utilizing an observational measure of parents' affect and behavior. Future research in this area should incorporate observations of children's emotion regulation and/or coping strategies. While children's reports of emotion regulation are consistent with some observational indices, observational measures predict child outcomes better than self-reports (McDowell et al., 2000). These studies could examine the use of children's coping strategies in natural settings (i.e., school, home) or in laboratory settings (i.e., using a disappointing gift paradigm, etc.) as a function of parental behavior and affect. In addition, longitudinal and experimental designs could be useful to establish the direction of effects. It is possible that the parental strategies assessed in this study were a result of previous interactions with the children. The current study's use of a single time point does not allow for assessment of how children with poorer coping skills may elicit particular parental behaviors. Finally, our measures were not able to determine how relevant the particular vignettes may have been for the children. Associations between parent variables and child outcomes (both emotional and social) would benefit from examining situations in which children have had to regulate their emotions in the past, rather than speculating what they might do.

Implications for Families and Emotion Socialization

The findings of this study suggest several implications for understanding the role of family in the development of emotional competence. First, it is clear that both mothers and fathers play significant, but separate, roles in emotional socialization. However, as argued above, fathers may play a major role in learning self-regulatory abilities in younger children because their physical play style is a more central aspect of father-child interaction. Second, the pathways through which parental impact on emotional competence is achieved is underspecified and perhaps, mothers and fathers impact their children's emotional regulatory abilities through different pathways. In addition, to direct interaction as a context for socialization of regulatory abilities, the quality of the marital relationship, especially parental conflict resolution strategies, may play a role in teaching children about emotional regulatory strategies. The marital context may be a particularly important avenue through which fathers impact their children, given that the level of expressed emotion may be higher than in the context of parent-child interaction during the middle childhood period. This argument suggests that more attention needs to be paid to different contexts (i.e., parent-child, marital, etc.) in the socialization of emotions and specifically how the importance of these contexts shifts across development.

REFERENCES

Asher, S. R., Parkhurst, J. T., Hymel, S., & Williams, G. A. (1990). Peer rejection and loneliness in childhood. In S. R. Asher & J. D. Coie (Eds.), *Peer rejection in childhood* (pp. 253-273). New York: Cambridge University Press.

Asher, S. R., Singleton, L. C., Tinsley, B. R., & Hymel, S. (1979). A reliable sociometric measure for preschool children. *Developmental Psychology, 79,* 443-444.

Boivin, M., Poulin, F., & Vitaro, F. (1994). Depressed mood and peer relationships in childhood. *Development and Psychopathology, 6,* 483-498.

Boyum, L. A. & Parke, R. D. (1995). The role of family emotional expressiveness in the development of children's social competence. *Journal of Marriage and the Family, 57,* 593-608.

Carson, J. L. & Parke, R. D. (1996). Reciprocal negative affect in parent-child interactions and children's peer competency. *Child Development, 67,* 2217-2226.

Cassidy, J. & Asher, S. R. (1992). Loneliness and peer relations in young children. *Child Development, 63,* 350-365.

Cassidy, J., Parke, R. D., Butkovsky, L., & Braungart, J. M. (1992). Family-peer connections: The roles of emotional expressiveness within the family and children's understanding of emotions. *Child Development, 63,* 603-618.

Contreras, J. M., Kerns, K. A., Weimer, B. L., & Gentzler, A. L. (2000). Emotion regulation as a mediator of associations between mother-child attachment and peer relationships in middle childhood. *Journal of Family Psychology, 14,* 111-124.

Crick, N. R. & Dodge, K. A. (1994). A review and reformulation of social information-processing mechanisms in children's social adjustment. *Psychological Bulletin, 115,* 74-101.

Denham, S. A. (1998). *Emotional development in young children.* New York: Guilford Press.

Denham, S. A., Mitchell-Copeland, J., Strandberg, K., Auerbach, S., & Blair, K. (1997). Parental contributions to preschoolers' emotional competence: Direct and indirect effects. *Motivation and Emotion, 21,* 65-86.

Dix, T. (1992). Parenting on behalf of the child: Empathic goals in the regulation of responsive parenting. In I. E. Sigel & A. V. McGillicuddy-DeLisi (Eds.), *Parental belief systems: The psychological consequences for children* (pp. 319-346). Hillsdale, NJ: Lawrence Erlbaum Assoc.

Dodge, K. A., McClaskey, C. L., & Feldman, E. (1985). A situational approach to the assessment of social competence in children. *Journal of Consulting and Clinical Psychology, 53,* 344-353.

Dodge, K. A., Pettit, G. S., McClaksy, C. L., & Brown, M. M. (1986). Social competence in children. *Monographs of the Society for Research in Child Development, 51,* 1-85.

Dunn, J. & Brown, J. (1994). Affect expression in the family, children's understanding of emotions, and their interactions with others. *Merrill-Palmer Quarterly, 40,* 120-137.

Eisenberg, N., Cumberland, A., & Spinrad, T. L. (1998). Parental socialization of emotion. *Psychological Inquiry, 9*, 241-273.

Eisenberg, N., Fabes, R., Bernzweig, J, Karbon, M., Poulin, R., & Hanish, L. (1993). The relations of emotionality and regulation to preschoolers' social skills and sociometric status. *Child Development, 64*, 1418-1438.

Eisenberg, N., Fabes, R. A., & Murphy, B. C. (1996). Parents' reactions to children's negative emotions: Relations to children's social competence and comforting behavior. *Child Development, 67*, 2227-2247.

Eisenberg, N., Fabes, R., Murphy, B., Maszk, P., Smith, M., & Karbon, M. (1995). The role of emotionality and regulation in children's social functioning: A longitudinal study. *Child Development, 66*, 1360-1384.

Eisenberg, N., Guthrie, I. K., Fabes, R. A., & Reiser, M. (1997). The relations of regulation and emotionality to resiliency and competence social functioning in elementary school children. *Child Development, 68*, 295-311.

Field, T., Healy, B., Goldstein, S., Perry, S., Bendell, D., Schanberg, S., Zimmerman, E. A., & Kuhn, C. (1988). Infants of depressed mothers show "depressed" behavior even with nondepressed adults. *Child Development, 59*, 1569-1579.

Gottman, J. M., Katz, L. F., & Hooven, C. (1996). Parental meta-emotion philosophy and the emotional life of families: Theoretical models and preliminary data. *Journal of Family Psychology, 10*, 243-268.

Gottman, J. M., Katz, L. F., & Hooven, C. (1997). *Meta-emotion: How families communicate emotionally.* Mahwah, NJ: Lawrence Erlbaum Associates, Inc.

Hubbard, J. A., & Coie, J. D. (1994). Emotional correlates of social competence in children's peer relationships. *Merrill-Palmer Quarterly, 40*, 1-20.

Isley, S., O'Neil, R., & Parke, R. D. (1996). The relation of parental affect and control behaviors to children's classroom acceptance: A concurrent and predictive analysis. *Early Education and Development, 7*, 7-23.

Kupersmidt, J. B., Coie, J. D., & Dodge, K. A. (1990). The role of poor peer relationships in the development of disorder. In S. R. Asher & J. D. Coie (Eds.), *Peer rejection in childhood* (pp. 274-305). New York: Cambridge University Press.

MacDonald, K. & Parke, R. D. (1984). Bridging the gap: Parent-child play interaction and peer interactive competence. *Child Development, 55*, 1265-1277.

Malatesta, C. Z. & Haviland, J. M. (1982). Learning display rules: The socialization of emotion expression in infancy. *Child Development, 53*, 991-1003.

McDowell, D. J., O'Neil, R., & Parke, R. D. (2000). Display rule application in a disappointing situation and children's emotional reactivity: Relations with social competence. *Merrill-Palmer Quarterly, 46*, 306-324.

McDowell, D. J., & Parke, R. D. (2000). Differential knowledge of display rules for positive and negative emotions: Influence from parents, influences on peers. *Social Development, 9*, 415-432.

Morison, P. & Masten, A. S. (1991). Peer reputation in middle childhood as a predictor of adaptation in adolescence: A seven-year follow-up. *Child Development, 62*, 991-1007.

Parke, R. D. (1994). Progress, paradigms, and unresolved problems: A commentary of recent advances in our understanding of children's emotions. *Merrill-Palmer Quarterly, 40*, 157-169.

Parke, R. D. (1996). *Fatherhood*. Cambridge, MA: Harvard University Press
Parker, J. G., & Asher, S. R. (1987). Peer relations and later personality adjustment: Are lower-accepted children at risk? *Psychological Bulletin, 102*, 357-389.
Parker, J. G. & Gottman, J. M. (1989). Social and emotional development in a relational context: Friendship interaction from early childhood to adolescence. In T. J. Berndt & G.W. Ladd (Eds.), *Peer relationships in child development* (pp. 95-131). NY: Wiley.
Patterson, G. R. & Bank, C. L. (1989). Some amplifying mechanisms for pathologic processes in families. In M. R. Gunnar & E. Thelen (Eds.), *Systems and development* (pp. 167-209). Hillsdale, NJ: Lawrence Erlbaum Associates.
Putallaz, M. (1987). Maternal behavior and sociometric status. *Child Development, 58*, 324-340.
Roberts, W. L. & Strayer, J. (1987). Parents' responses to the emotional distress of their children: Relations with children's competence. *Developmental Psychology, 23*, 415-422.
Rueter, M. A. & Conger, R. D. (1995). Interaction style, problem-solving behavior, and family problem-solving effectiveness. *Child Development, 66*, 98-115.
Roberts, W. L. & Strayer, J. (1987). Parents' responses to the emotional distress of their children: Relations with children's competence. *Developmental Psychology, 23*, 415-422.
Saarni, C. (1999). *The development of emotional competence*. New York: Guilford Press.

APPENDIX A
Emotional Reactivity Vignettes

1. You have been waiting a very long time to play a video game at a friend's house and just when it is your turn your friend says, "I'm tired of playing this game. Let's play something else," and you never get a turn to play the game.

2. Your class has been planning a really great field trip and the big day has finally arrived. It is going to be a very long ride on a bus that is filled with all your classmates. You can hardly wait to arrive because there is going to be so much to see and do!

3. You get to bring a pet hamster home for the weekend from school. On Monday morning, when it is time to return the hamster, you discover that the hamster has died.

4. Your family has company one evening. There are two other children your age visiting and you've been having a lot of fun playing all evening. Now your parents tell you that you must go to bed because it is a school night.

5. You're riding your bike home from school one day when another kid whizzes by you and knocks you off your bike into the gutter. Your knees are scraped and your favorite jacket is ripped.

Monographs "Separates" list continued

Intermarriage in the United States, edited by Gary A. Crester, PhD, and Joseph J. Leon, PhD (Vol. 5, No. 1, 1982). *"A very good compendium of knowledge and of theoretical and technical issues in the study of intermarriage." (Journal of Comparative Family Studies)*

Cults and the Family, edited by Florence Kaslow, PhD, and Marvin B. Sussman, PhD (Vol. 4, No. 3/4, 1982). *"Enlightens not only the professional but the lay reader as well. It provides support and understanding for families . . . gives insight and . . . enables parents, friends, and loved ones to better understand what happens when one joins a cult." (The Family Psychologist)*

Family Medicine: A New Approach to Health Care, edited by Betty Cogswell and Marvin B. Sussman, PhD (Vol. 4, No. 1/2, 1982). *The history, rationale, and the continuing developments in this medical specialty all in one readable volume.*

Marriage and the Family: Current Critical Issues, edited by Marvin B. Sussman, PhD (Vol. 1, No. 1, 1979). *Covers pluralistic family forms, family violence, never married persons, dual career families, the "roleless" role (widowhood), and non-marital, heterosexual cohabitation.*

Index

Acceptance, emotional, 171
Accommodation, 120
  in marital relationship, 170-171
Adolescents
  aggression in, parental
    conflict-related, 17
  depression in, parental
    conflict-related, 17
  emotion communication among, 221
  Multidimensional Family Therapy
    for, 172
  peer allegiance of, 37
  relationship with parents, 172
    emotional negativity in, 216-217
    with mother, 222
  self-disclosure by, 222
Adolescent twins, fathers' negative
    expressiveness toward, 216
Affection
  children's expression of, 226
  as interpersonal emotion, 117
  in sibling interactions, 185
Affective involvement, family systems
    paradigm of, 232-233
Affective responsiveness
  family systems paradigm of,
    230-232
  as inappropriate male behavior,
    233-234
Aggression
  in adolescents, parental
    conflict-related, 17
  in children
    domestic violence
      exposure-related, 219
    parental emotional unavailability
      and, 231

    parental marital conflict-related,
      17,28
  parental rejection-related, 269
  confrontation-related, 121
  parental, domestic violence-related,
    218-219
  in relationship conflict, 120
  in sibling interactions, 185
Alcohol abuse
  parental, 90,234-325
  parental rejection-related, 269
Alcoholics, children of, 231,234-235
American Psychological Association,
    PsychInfo database of, 39
Anger
  behavioral and relational activities
    associated with, 5
  children's understanding of, 65
    effect of parental negative
      emotions on, 68
    of maternal anger, 75,76,77-78,
      79,80-81
  infants' expression of, 244-245,247,
    248,249-250,251,252-253,
    254-255,256
  interpersonal tension-related, 117
  marital conflict-related, children's
    responses to, 17-18,26,
    27,29-30
  maternal
    children's solutions to, 78-79
    children's understanding of,
      67-68,75,76,77-78,79
  parental
    children's understanding of, 64-65
    domestic violence-related,
      218-219

between siblings, 187
Anxiety
  behavioral and relational activities associated with, 5
  domestic violence-related, 219
  interpersonal tension-related, 117
Attachment relations
  with caregivers, 223
  effect of parental emotional sensitivity on, 232
  effect of parental empathy on, 224
Attachment theory
  of emotion-focused couple therapy, 169-170
  mother-child, 208
  of siblings, 208
Aversive stimuli response, in infants, 245
Avoidance, as relationship conflict response, 120,121-122

Bailey examination, 268
Biases
  emotional, 235
  hostile attributional, 236
Boys, gender socialization of, 233-234
Brief Ways of Coping (BWOC), 120, 124-125
Buddha, 3
Bühler, C., 217, 218

Caretaking, by older siblings, 186
Child Behavior Checklist, 268
Child maltreatment
  children's affective responses to, 231
  effect on children's emotional understanding, 68
Children
  aggression in
    domestic violence-related, 219
    parental emotional unavailability-related, 231
    parental marital conflict-related, 17,28,219
    parental rejection-related, 269
  of alcoholics, 231,234-235
  emotional regulation in, 266
    basal vagal tone as predictor of, 273-280
  emotional understanding in, 65-67
    older siblings' influence on, 188-189
    role in emotional regulation, 65-66
    role in social competence regulation, 65-66
  negative emotions in
    Coping with Children's Negative Emotions Scale measurement of, 285-300
    Family Expressive Questionnaire measurement of, 287,288
    as parental distress cause, 290, 295,297-298,299,300
    Parent Attitude toward Children's Expressiveness Scale measurement of, 287-288,291-292,293
    parents' emotion-focused responses to, 288-289,292-293
    parents' problem-focused responses to, 288-289,292-293
    parents' punitive responses to, 287,289,290
  effect of parental conflict on, 16-18,28,219
  effect of parental emotional expressiveness on, 35-62,215
    age factors in, 38,39,46,47, 48-49,51,52,53-54,57
    developmental issues in, 57
    on emotional understanding, 49-52,54
    family size effects, 56

gender factors in, 55
global expressiveness effects, 44,45,47,52,54
negative-dominant emotional expressiveness effects, 45, 48,52,54-55
negative expressiveness effects, 46,47,48-49,50-51,52-54
negative-submissive emotional expressiveness effects, 45,47,48,52,54-55
parental marital relationship effects, 55-56
positive expressiveness effects, 44,46,47,49,50-51
role of interpretive structures in, 57
physiological reactions to stressful parental interactions, 265-283
basal vagal tone, 267,273-280
as emotional regulation predictor, 273-280
"recovery from arousal" hypothesis of, 268-269, 277-279
"stress inoculation" theory of, 268,274-277
vagal tone suppression, 267-269,274-277
responses to parents' marital conflict
behavioral responses, 27-30,31
diary study of, 21-31
emotional responses, 26-27,30
emotional security hypothesis of, 19-21
multilevel modeling of, 31
response to parental emotionally-expressive behavior, 215
China, emotional expressiveness restraint in, 222
Classroom behavior, disruptive, parental rejection-related, 269

Closeness
effect on emotion communication, 221-222
as interpersonal emotion, 117
within stepfamilies, 117-118,125, 126,127-129,130,131
Close Relationship Framework, 90-91,97,108-109
Coaching role, of older siblings, 190-191,208
Coercion, by siblings, 187
Common-law relationships, 116
Communication
about emotions, 190-191
of emotion. *See* Emotion communication
Competence, emotional/social, older siblings' influence on, 183-212
caretaking and, 186
coaching function, 190-191,208
contingency function, 189-190,202
dealing with parents function, 188
differentiation function, 188
direct services function, 188
identification function, 188,203
modeling function, 188-189, 203,208
mutual regulation, 188
Competition, among siblings, 186
Compromise
among friends, 220
as relationship conflict response, 120-121
within stepfamilies, 127,128, 131,134
Conflict. *See also* Anger; Aggression; Marital conflict
emotional regulation during, 266
emotion communication related to, 226
metaperception errors-related, 218
parent-child, verbal behavior during, 216
with peers, 228

scripts and narratives in, 228
in sibling relationships, 186,187
Conflict resolution. *See also*
  Negotiation
 among friends, 220
 as peer social competency, 266
Confrontation, in relationship conflict, 120,121
 within stepfamilies, 127,128,129, 131,133,134
Contempt, in marital relationship, 169
Cooperation
 reciprocity in, 120-121
 as relationship conflict response, 120-121
 risk associated with, 134
Coping
 confrontational, 120,121
 definition of, 119
 emotion-focused, 119
 with negative emotional communication, 236
 problem-focused, 119
 relationship-focused, 119
 scripts for, 227
 by stepparents, 115-138
  compromise strategy, 127,128, 131,134
  confrontation strategy, 127,128, 129,131,133,134
  diary study of, 122-135
  husbands' coping strategies, 125,126-130,131,132,133, 134-135
  interpersonal withdrawal strategy, 127,128-129,131, 132,133-134,135
  as parent-child closeness cause, 125,126,127-129,130,131
  effect on parent-child relationship, 122-135
  as parent-child tension cause, 125,126,128,129-130,131, 132

effect on stepgap, 118,125, 127-132,133-135
  wives' coping strategies, 125, 126-127,128,129,130,131, 132,133,134-135
Coping with Children's Negative Emotions Scale (CCNES), 9,285-300
 correlation with
  Interpersonal Reactivity Index, 294,298-299
  Parent Affect Scale, Parental Anger subscale, 293-294, 299,300
  Parental Control Scale, 293,299
  parent and child demographics, 296-297
  Parent Attitude Toward Children's Expressiveness Scale, 293,299,300
  Social Desirability Index, 294, 296
 Distress Reaction subscale, 295, 297,298,299,300
 Emotion-Focused Reactions subscale, 288-289,292-293, 295,297-298,300
 Expressive Encouragement subscale, 289,297-299,300
 internal consistency of, 294-295, 299
 interrelation of parent measures of, 297-299
 Minimization Reactions subscale, 289,295,297-298,299,300
 Problem-Focused Reactions subscale, 288,289,292-293, 295,297-298,300
 Punitive Reactions subscale, 289, 295,297-298,300
 reliability of, 291,294-296
 validity of, 291,297-300
Criticism
 among friends, 220,221
 in marital relationship, 169

parental, effect on children's vagal tone, 269,273,274,275, 276,277,278-279
by siblings, 190
Cultural factors, in family emotional expressiveness, 58n
Cybernetics, 166

Defensiveness, in marital relationship, 169
Delinquency, parental rejection-related, 269
Dependency, as marital stress modulator, 93,97-98,101,102, 103,104
Depression
  in adolescents, parental conflict-related, 17
  domestic violence-related, 219
  marital conflict-related, 90
  maternal, 231
    effect on infants' emotional reactivity, 246
  parental, effect on empathy, 224-225
  parental rejection-related, 269
Desire, 5
Diagnostic and Statistical Manual of Mental Disorders-DSM-IV, 160
Diary studies
  Brief Ways of Coping (BWOC) use in, 120,124-125
  of coping within stepfamilies, 122-135
    methodology, 122-125
  of marital conflict, 17-18,21-31
    children's behavioral responses, 27-30,31
    children's emotional responses, 26-27,30
    children's response component, 23,24,26-30

husband's reports, 25,26-28, 29-30
of psychosocial modulators, 89-113
wives' reports, 25,26-29
Disciplinary style. *See also* Punishment
  effect on emotion communication, 224
Discourse analysis, of emotion communication, 230
Disgust, behavioral and relational activities associated with, 5
Divorce rate, 116
Domestic violence
  effect on children, 18
  emotion communication related to, 218-219
Dominance, nonverbal expression of, 219-220

Eating disorders, 229,233
  marital conflict-related, 90
Educational level, as marital conflict modulator, 98,101,102-103
Emotional expressiveness, family context of. *See* Family emotional expressiveness
Emotionally-expressive behavior, consequences of, 214-217
Emotional reactivity
  in infants, 243-263
    anger expression frequency, 251, 252-253,254,256-257
    anger expression intensity, 251,252-253,254,256
    bi-directionality in, 246,255-256
    caregiving behavior effects on, 244
    cluster analysis of, 252-253
    environmental factors in, 244
    maternal intrusiveness effects on, 250,251-252,254-256, 257-258

maternal sensitivity effects on, 245-260
  as negative affect, 249-250,251, 252-253,256
  physiological processes in, 244
  as positive affect, 249-250,251, 252-253,245,258
  as temperament component, 244-245
marital conflict-related, psychosocial modulators of, 89-113
  acute life events, 94-95,98,101, 102,103-104,106,107
  children, 95,98,101,102,103, 106,107
  chronic stress, 94-95,101,102
  Close Relationship Framework of, 90-91,97,108-109
  dependency, 93,97-98,101,102, 103,104
  diary study of, 89-113
  educational level, 98,101, 102-103
  extraversion, 97,101,102-103, 104
  first marriage *versus* remarriage, 98,101,102-103,104
  frequency of arguments, 94,97,98,102,103-104
  gender factors, 91,100,104-105
  individual factors, 91,92,97, 101,104-105
  intimacy, 94,98,100,101, 102-103,105
  introversion, 93
  length of marriage, 98
  marital argument/daily mood relationship, 101-104
  marital history, 93,101
  mastery, 100,101,102,104
  neuroticism, 97,100,101,102, 103,104
  perceived social support, 94, 98,100-101,102,103-104,106
  personality factors, 91,92,93
  relationship factors, 92,97-98, 105-106
  self-esteem, 97,100,101, 102-103,104,105
  sex-role orientation, 98,101, 102,103
  social environment, 91,94-95, 97,98,101,102,106-107
  socioeconomic status, 95,101
  stress, 94-95
  total household income, 103-104,106,107
  trust, 94,98,101,102-103, 104,105
  wives' contribution to income, 94,98,101,102-103,104, 105-106
  parental perception of, 215
Emotional regulation
  in infants, 244, 246
  physiological factors in, 266-267
  social referencing in, 218
  vagal tone as predictor of, 273-280
Emotional security, definition of, 19
Emotional security hypothesis, of marital conflict, 18-21
Emotion communication
  appeal function of, 217
  children's understanding of, 213-242
    family context of, 235-236
    family systems paradigm of, 228-235
    of functions of emotion communication, 217-219
    interpersonal negotiation in, 214, 225-226
    intersubjectivity in, 214,222-225
    McMaster model of family functioning of, 214
    as metacommunication, 214-215,216-217,219-221
    as metaperception, 214-215
    nonverbal behavior and, 214-215

older siblings' influence on,
188-189,198,199,200,
202-203,210
as reflected appraisals, 236
relationship dimensions and,
219-222
of relationship quality, 222-228,
229-230
report and command aspects of,
214,220
role in emotional regulation,
65-66
role in emotional social
competence regulation, 65-66
scripts and narratives in, 223,
226-228,235
verbal behavior and, 215
among friends, 220-221
symbolic function of, 217
symptomatic function of, 217
Emotion Facial Action Coding System
(EMFACS), 248-250
Emotion-focused couples therapy, 168,
169-170,171,172,175,176
Emotions. *See also* specific emotions
as cognitive function correlates,
18-19
definition of, 19
effect on family interaction
patterns, 4-5
functionalist perspective on, 18-19,
20,31
as interpsychic processes, 4
as intrapsychic processes, 4,166,
167
measurement of, 6,10-11
as regulator of interpersonal
relationships, 214-219
relational perspective on, 4-5,166
role in family development, 3-4
transactional nature of, 8,10
Empathy
parental, 224-225,232
as affective involvement, 233
as peer social competency, 266

Expressiveness, familial. *See* Family
emotional expressiveness
Extraversion (extroversion), as marital
conflict modulator, 97,101,
102-103,104

Facial expressions
children's biased labeling of,
217-218
children's understanding of, 217
as expression of dominance,
219-220
in infants, in response to maternal
sensitivity, 245-260
anger expression frequency, 251,
252-253,254,256-257
anger expression intensity, 251,
252-253,254,256
bi-directionality in, 246,255-256
cluster analysis of, 252-253
maternal intrusiveness effects,
250,251-252,254-256,
257-258
negative affect frequency,
249-250,251,252-253,256
positive affect frequency,
249-250,251,252-253,254,
258
parental, negative, 216
Family emotional expressiveness
effect on children's emotionality,
35-62
age factors in, 38,39,46,47,
48-49,51,52,53-54,57
children's emotional
understanding, 49-52,54
children's interpretive structures,
57
developmental issues in, 57
gender factors in, 55
global family/children's
expressiveness correlation,
44,45,47,52,54
methodology, 39-43

negative-dominant emotions,
  38-39,45,48,52,54-55
negative expressiveness
  correlation, 46,47,48-49,
  50-51,52-54
negative-submissive emotions,
  38,39,45,47,48,52,54,55
positive expressiveness
  correlation, 38-39,44,46,47,
  49,50-51,53
studies used in, 39,42-43
cultural factors in, 58n
effect of family size on, 56
effect of marital distress on, 55-56
effect of parental homogeneity on, 56
suppression of, 36
systems perspective on, 14-15
Family Expressive Questionnaire
  measurement, 287,288
Family Inventory of Life Events
  (FILE), 72
Family of origin system, of emotion
  communication, 230
Family size, effect on children's
  emotional understanding, 56
Family structure, heterogeneity of,
  173-174
Family systems
  of anorexic individuals, 233
  role of emotions in, 166
Family systems-based therapies. *See
  also* Family therapy; Marital
  therapy
  role of emotions in, 165-179
  structural and development
    complexities of, 173-174
  theoretical assessment of,
    174-175
Family systems model
  of children's emotional
    understanding, 228-235
  of emotions, 172-173
  of marital conflict, 13-34
    application to diary study, 21-31

children's behavioral responses,
  27-30
children's emotional responses,
  26-27
emotional security hypothesis
  about, 18-21
Family therapy
  narrative model use in, 235
  role of emotions in, 171-176
  historical overview of, 166-168
  interactional perspective on,
    166-167
  in Multidimensional Family
    Therapy, 172,175,176
Fathers, negative emotional
  expressiveness by, 216
Father-son relationship, effect of
  father's marital conflict on, 17
Fear
  behavioral and relational activities
    associated with, 5
  children's understanding of, 65
  marital conflict-related, children's
    responses to, 26,27,29
Friends. *See also* Peer relationships
  disclosure of secrets to, 221
  emotion communication among,
    220-221
Frustration, in infants, 245
  effect of maternal sensitivity on,
    246-247
  facial affect during
    anger expression frequency,
      249-250,252
    cluster analysis of, 252-253
    coding of, 248-250,258-259
    happy (positive) affect
      expression, 249-250,251,
      252-253,254,258
    negative (distress) affect
      expression, 249-250
    relationship with maternal
      intrusiveness, 250,251-252,
      254-255,257-258

relationship with maternal sensitivity, 250

Gender factors, in marital conflict modulation, 91,104-105
Gender roles, socialization into, 233-234
General systems theory, 166
Greene, Bob, 7-8

Happiness
  behavioral and relational activities associated with, 5
  children's understanding of, 65
  infant's expression of, 249-250,251, 252-253,254,258
  maternal, children's understanding of, 75
Heart rate. *See also* Vagal tone
  correlation with response to novelty, 267
  as indicator of emotion, 10
Hidden Markov Model-based classification, of marital relationship quality, 139-163
  components of, 145-148
  rationale for, 141-143
  socio-affective process recognition in, 141-144,145, 148-161
Hostility
  confrontation-related, 121
  in sibling interactions, 185
Hyper-vigilance, domestic violence-related, 219

Income, as marital conflict modulator, 103-104,106,107
Indian girls, emotionally-expressive behavior management in, 222

Individual factors, as marital stress modulators, 91,92,97, 101,104-105
Infants
  aversive stimuli response in, 245
  basal vagal tone in, 268
  emotional reactivity in, 243-263
    anger expression frequency, 251,252-253,254,256-257
    anger expression intensity, 251,252-253,254,256
    caregiving behavior effects on, 244
    environmental factors in, 244
    maternal intrusiveness effects on, 250,251-252,254-256, 257-258
    maternal sensitivity effects on, 245-260
    negative affect, 248,249-250, 251,252-253,256
    positive affect, 249-250,251, 252-253,254,258
    as temperament component, 244-245
  emotional regulation in, 244,245
  reactions to parents' marital conflict, 18
  smiling in, 245-246
  social referencing in, 218
Inhibition, novelty-related, 267
Insecure behavior, in response to parental conflict, 27-28,29-30
Integrative behavioral couples therapy, 170-171,172,175,176
Interest
  behavioral and relational activities associated with, 5
Interest, infants' expression of, 244-245
Interpersonal Reactivity Index (IRI), 291-292,294,298-299
Interpersonal relationships
  emotion as regulator of, 214-219
  within stepfamilies, 117-118

Intersubjectivity, in emotion
    communication, 214,222-225
Intimacy, as marital conflict
    modulator,
    94,98,100,101,102-103,105
Introversion, as marital conflict
    modulator, 93
Intrusiveness, parental, effect on
    children's vagal tone, 269,
    273,274,275,276-277,278

Joy, infants' expression of, 244-245

Kahen Affect Coding Systems
    (KACS), 271
Kahen Engagement Coding System
    (KECS), 271

Language, emotional expression in,
    215-216
Language acquisition, 215
    of emotion-descriptive language,
    226
Laughter, 189
Locke-Wallace Marital Adjustment
    Test, 151,154-155
Love, as interpersonal emotion, 117

Male role, socialization into, 233-234
Marital conflict, 16-18
    aggression in, 120
    as alcohol abuse cause, 90
    as anger cause, children's reactions
        to, 17-18
    avoidance and withdrawal response
        to, 120,121-122
    children's emotional responses to,
        16-18,19
        aggression, 17,28
        diary study of, 21-31

emotional development, 259
emotional security hypothesis
    of, 19-21
emotional understanding, 55-56
emotion-laden behavior,
    235-236
confrontation response to, 120,121
    within stepfamilies, 127,128,
    129,131,133,134
cooperation and compromise
    response to, 120-121
    within stepfamilies, 127,128,
    129,131,133,134
as depression cause, 90
diary studies of, 17-18,21-31
    children's behavioral responses,
        27-30,31
    children's emotional responses,
        26-27,30
    children's response component,
        23,24,26-30
    husbands' reports,
        25,26-28,29-30
    of psychosocial modulators,
        89-113
    wives' reports, 25,26-29
dyadic family context of, 17
as eating disorder cause, 90
effect on empathy, 224-225
family systems model of, 13-34
    application to diary study, 21-31
    children's behavioral responses,
        27-30
    children's emotional responses,
        26-27
    emotional security hypothesis
        about, 18-21
mediation of, 28-29
parent-child subsystem effects, 16
psychosocial modulators of, 89-113
    acute life events, 94-95,98,101,
        102,103-104,106,107
    children, 95,98,101,102,103,
        106,107
    chronic stress, 94-95,101,102

Index

Close relationship Framework
  of, 90-91,97,108-109
  dependency, 93,97-98,101,
    102,103,104
  educational level, 98,101,
    102-103
  extraversion, 97,101,102-103,
    104
  frequency of arguments, 94,
    97,98,102,103-104
  gender factors in, 91,104-105
  individual factors, 91,92,97,
    101,104-105
  intimacy, 94,98,100,101,
    102-103,105
  introversion, 93
  length of marriage, 98
  marital argument/daily mood
    relationship, 101-104
  marital history, 93,101
  mastery, 100,101,102,104
  neuroticism, 97,100,101,102,
    103,104
  perceived social support, 94,98,
    100-101,102,103-104,106
  personality factors, 91,92,93
  relationship factors,
    92,97-98,105-106
  self-esteem, 97,100,101,
    102-103,104,105
  sex-role orientation, 98,101,
    102,103
  social environment,
    91,94-95,97,98,101,102,
    106-107
  socioeconomic status, 95,101
  stress, 94-95
  total household income,
    103-104,106,107
  trust, 94,98,101,103-104,105
  wives' contribution to income,
    94,98,101,102-103,104,
    105-106
relationship with marital
  satisfaction, 169

triadic family context of, 16-17
verbal competition in, 120
Marital relationship, role of emotions
  in, 168-169
Marital relationship quality, Hidden
    Markov Model-based
    classification of, 139-163
  components of, 145-148
  rationale for, 141-143
  socio-affective process recognition
    in, 141-144,145,148-161
Marriage therapy, role of emotions in,
    165-179
  in emotion-focused couples
    therapy, 168,169-170,171,
    172,175,176
  historical overview of, 166-168
  in integrative behavioral couples
    therapy, 170-171,172,
    175,176
  interactional perspective on,
    166-167
Mastery, as marital conflict modulator,
    100,101,102,104
Maternal emotional expressiveness,
    children's perception of,
    63-88
  effect of poverty on, 69-84
  extrafamilial influences on, 68-69
  familial influences on, 67-68
  story-stem narrative assessment of,
    66-67,72-75,80-81
    accuracy in, 67,76-77,80-81
    emotional intensity assessment,
    67,77-78
    responses to negative emotions,
    78-80
Maternal sensitivity, effect on infants'
    emotional reactivity, 245-260
  bi-directionality in, 246,255-256
  cluster analysis of, 252-253
  facial affect assessment of, 248-250
    anger expression frequency, 251,
    252-253,254,256-257

anger expression intensity, 251, 252-253,245,256
maternal intrusiveness effects, 250,251-252,254-256, 257-258
negative affect frequency, 249-250,251,252-253,256
positive affect frequency, 249-250,251,252-253,254, 258
maternal responsivity assessment of, 250
prediction of, 254-255
McMaster model, of family functioning, 228-235
affective involvement dimension, 232-233
affective responsiveness dimension, 230-232
application to emotion communication, 214
communication dimension, 229-230
problem-solving dimension, 234-235
roles dimension, 233-234
Meaning, interpersonal exchange of, 215
Metacommunication
definition of, 214
effect of power on, 219-221
in emotion communication, 219-221
interpersonal consequences of, 215
in interpersonal negotiation, 225
messages conveyed in, 216
negative effects of, 216-217
report and command features of, 214,220
Metaperception, 236
definition of, 214-215
errors in, as conflict cause, 218
interpersonal consequences of, 215
Mockery, parental, effect on children's vagal tone, 269,273,274,275,276,277, 278
Modeling, in sibling relationship, 188-189,190
Mother-child relationship
with adolescent children, 222
emotion communication in, 224
Mothers
children's disclosure of secrets to, 221
stability of emotionality in, 225
Multidimensional Family Therapy, 172,175,176

Narratives
effect on children's emotion understanding, 215
in emotion communication, 227-228,235
Narrative story-stem technique, 66-67, 72-75,80-81
Negative emotional behavior, as parental disengagement cause, 224
Negative emotions. *See also* specific emotions
of children
Coping with Children's Negative Emotions Scale measurement of, 9,285-300
Family Expressive Questionnaire measurement of, 287,288
as parental distress cause, 290, 295,297-298,299,300
Parent Attitude toward Children's Expressiveness Scale measurement of, 287-288,291-292,293
parents' emotion-focused responses to, 288-289, 292-293
parents' problem-focused responses to, 288-289, 292-293

parents' punitive responses to, 287,289,290
in infants
  correlation with maternal intrusiveness, 250,251-252, 254-256,257-258
  correlation with maternal sensitivity, 245-260
  effect on family relationships, 259
maternal, children's understanding of, 63-88
  accuracy of, 67,76-77,80-81
  emotional intensity assessment in, 67,77-78
  extrafamilial influences on, 68-69
  familial influences on, 67-68
  perception of response to negative emotions, 78-80
in parent-adolescent communication, 216-217
among siblings, 187
Negotiation, interpersonal, 225-226
  scripts and narratives in, 226-228
Neuroticism, as marital conflict modulator, 97,101,102, 103,104
Nonverbal behavior, as expression of power, 219-220
Novelty, as inhibition cause, 267

Parent Affect Scale-Parental Anger subscale, 291-292,293,299
Parental Control Scale, 291-292,293,299
Parent Attitude toward Children's Expressiveness Scale, 287-288, 291-292,293,299,300
Parent-child relationship
  of adolescents, 172
  emotional expression regulation in, 266
  role of emotions in, 7-8,10

in stepfamilies
  closeness in, 117-118,125,126, 127-129,130,131
  stepgap in, 118,125,127-132, 133-135
  tension in, 117-118,125,126,128, 129-130,131,132
Parenting, emotional stability in, 225
Parents
  emotional expressiveness of. *See* Family emotional expressiveness
  response to children's negative emotions
    Coping with Children's Negative Emotions Scale measurement of, 9,285-300
    distress responses, 290,295, 297-298,299,300
    emotion-focused responses, 288-289,292-293,295,297-298,300
    expressive encouragement responses, 289,297-299,300
    Family Expressive Questionnaire measurement of, 287-288
    minimization responses, 289, 295,297-298,299,300
    Parent Attitude toward Children's Expressiveness Scale measurement of, 287-288,291-292,293
    problem-focused responses, 288,289,292-293,295, 297-299,300
    punitive responses, 287,289,290, 295,297-298,300
  role in child's emotional socialization, 266
Peer relationships
  adolescents' allegiance to, 37
  comparison with sibling relationships, 186-187
  hostile attribution bias in, 217-218

Peer social competence, 266
Personality factors, as marital stress
    modulator, 91,92,93
Physical abuse, domestic
    violence-associated, 219
Physiological processes, in infants'
    emotional reactivity, 244
Physiological reactions, to stressful
    parent-child interactions,
    265-283
  basal vagal tone, 267
    as emotional regulation
      predictor, 273-280
    measurement of, 271-272
  follow-up assessment of, 272-273
  individual variations in, 267
  vagal tone suppression, 267-269
    "recovery from arousal"
      hypothesis of, 268-269,
      277-279
    "stress inoculation" theory of,
      268,274-277
Play
  cooperative/complementary, 184,
    187
  peer social competency in, 266
  with siblings, 187
Positive affect, interpersonal
    emotions-related, 117
Poverty, effect on children's
    understanding of maternal
    emotions, 69-84
  children's accuracy of
    understanding, 76-77
  children's story-stem narratives of,
    66-67,72-75,80-81
  children's understanding of
    emotional intensity, 77-78
  maternal self-report measures of,
    71-72
Power, nonverbal behavior associated
    with, 219-220
Preschoolers, emotional and social
    competence development in,
    183-212
  as developmental task, 184
  parental influence on, 187,202
  peers' influence on, 186-187
  siblings' influence on, 185-208
    affective balance variable,
      198,199,207
    age factors in, 197-198,200,201,
      203,204-205
    caretaking role and, 186
    coaching function in, 190-191,
      208
    contingency function in,
      189-190,202
    dealing with parents function in,
      188
    differentiation function in, 188
    direct services function in, 188
    emotion understanding, 198,199,
      200,201,202-203
    future research in, 207-208
    gender factors in, 197,199,200,
      201,202,203,206
    identification function in, 188,
      203
    modeling function in, 188-189,
      203,208
    mutual regulation function in,
      188
    peer-rated sociometric
      likeability variable, 198,200,
      204,205,206
    positive responsiveness,
      197-198,199,200,201,
      202-205,206-208
    prosocial responsiveness, 197,
      198,199,200,201,205
    provocative responsiveness, 197,
      198,199,200,201,204,205,
      206-207
    teacher-rated social competence
      variable, 198,199,200,201
  socialization in, 184-185
Problem-solving, family systems
    paradigm of, 234-325

Prosocial behavior, in sibling
    interactions, 185
Psychiatric disorders, effect on
    parental empathy, 224-225
PsychInfo database, 39
Punishment, as response to children's
    negative emotions, 287,
    289,290

Reciprocity, 120-121
    of expressive behavior, 215
Reflected appraisals, 236
Rejection, parental
    children's physiological response
        to, 269-280
    basal vagal tone, 271-272
    as emotional regulation
        predictor, 273-280
    follow-up assessment in, 272
    observational coding of,
        271-272
    parental gender factors in, 274,
        275-277,278-280
    verbal and nonverbal
        behaviors-related, 216
Relational perspective, on emotions,
    4-5,166
Relationship factors, as marital conflict
    modulators, 91,92,93-94,
    97-98,105-106
Relationship quality, effect of emotion
    communication on, 222-228
    interpersonal negotiation in,
        225-226
    intersubjectivity in, 222-225
Remarriage, 116
    as marital conflict modulator,
        98,101,102-103,104
    marital relationship after, 117
Remarried families. *See also*
    Stepfamilies
    coping strategies of, 119
Resilience, in children, 82,219
Roles, familial, 233-234

Runaway behavior, parental
    rejection-related, 269

Sadness
    behavioral and relational activities
        associated with, 5
    children's understanding of, 65
    infants' expression of, 244-245
    marital conflict-related, children's
        responses to, 26,27,29-30
    maternal, children's understanding
        of, 75-76,77-80
    parental, children's understanding
        of, 64-65
Satir, Virginia, 167,215-216,217
Scripts, in emotion communication,
    223,226-228
Secrets, disclosure of, 221
Self-disclosure, 221-222
Self-esteem
    low, domestic violence-related, 219
    as marital conflict modulator, 97,
        100,101,102-103,104,105
Self-Expressiveness in the Family
    Questionnaire (SEFQ), 71-72
Self-reports, of emotion, 6. *See also*
    Diary studies
    of marital conflict, 17-18
Self-soothing, role of vagal tone in,
    267,279
Sex-role orientation, as marital conflict
    modulator, 98,101,102,103
Sibling relationships, comparison with
    peer relationships, 186-187
Siblings
    influence on younger siblings'
        emotional/social
        competencies, 183-212
    affective balance variable, 198,
        199,207
    age factors in, 197-198,200,201,
        203,204-205
    caretaking role and, 186

coaching function in,
190-191,208
contingency function in,
188-189,202
dealing with parents function in,
188
differentiation function in, 188
direct services function in, 188
emotion understanding, 198,
199,201,202-203
future research in, 207-208
gender factors in, 197,199,
200,201,202,203,206
identification function in, 188,
203
modeling function in, 188-189,
203,208
mutual regulation function in,
188
peer-rated sociometric
likeability variable, 198,200,
204,205,206
positive responsiveness,
197-198,199,200,201,
202-205,206,208
provocative responsiveness, 197,
198,199,200,201,204,205,
206-207
teacher-rated social competence
variable, 198,199,200,201
twins as, 216
Smiling
among friends, 220
as emotionally-expressive behavior,
214
in infants, 245-246
Social Desirability Index, 294,296
Social dilemmas, compromise in,
120-121
Social environment, as marital conflict
modulator, 91,94-95,97,98,
101,102,106-107
Socialization
emotional, 9,215
maternal influence on, 259,260

older siblings' influence on,
189-190,191
paternal influence on, 81-82,
223-224,266,259
in preschoolers, 184-185
theory of mind of, 223
parental, effect on children's
emotional development,
68-69
social, 233-234
Social referencing, in emotional
regulation, 218
Social skills, peer-related, 266
Social support, as marital conflict
modulator, 94,98,100-101,
102,103-104,106
Stepchildren
differential treatment of. See
Stepgap
as divorce risk factor, 116
Stepfamilies
parent-child relationships in
closeness in, 117-118,125,
126,127-129,130,131
stepgap in, 118,125,127-132,
133-135
tension in, 117-118,125,126,
128,129-130,131,132
prevalence of, 116
stepparents' coping strategies in,
115-138
compromise, 127,128,131,134
confrontation, 127,128,129,131,
133,134
diary study of, 122-135
husbands' coping strategies,
125,126-130,131,132,
133-134
interpersonal withdrawal, 127,
128-129,131,132,133-134,
135
as parent-child closeness cause,
125,126,127-129,130,131
parent-child relationship effects,
122-135

as parent-child tension cause, 125,126,128,129-130,131, 132
stepgap effects, 125,127-132, 133-135
wives' coping strategies, 125, 126-127,128,129,130,131, 132,133,134-135
stress experienced by, 116-117,119
Stepgap, 118
effect of stepparents' coping strategies on, 125, 127-132,133-135
Stress
acute, as marital conflict modulator, 94-95,98,101,102,103-104, 106,107
children's physiological reactions to, 265-283
basal vagal tone, 267,271-280
as emotional regulation predictor, 273-280
"recovery from arousal" hypothesis of, 268-269, 277-279
"stress inoculation" theory of, 268,274-277
vagal tone suppression, 267-269, 274-277
chronic, as marital conflict modulator, 94-95,101,102
effect on maternal emotional expressiveness, 76k
in stepfamilies, 116-117,119
Substance abuse, affective repression response to, 231
Suicidal behavior, domestic violence-related, 219
Symbolic systems, for expression of meaning, 215

Teasing, 186
Temperament
of children, effect on maternal expressiveness, 83-84
of infants, 244-245
Tension, interpersonal, within stepfamilies, 117-118, 125,126,128,129-130,131, 132
Toddlers, social referencing in, 218
Truancy, parental rejection-related, 269
Trust, as marital conflict modulator, 98,101,102-103,104,105

Vagal tone
role in infants' emotional reactivity, 244
in stressful parent-child interactions, 273-280
"recovery from arousal" hypothesis of, 268-269, 277-279
"stress inoculation" theory of, 268,274-277
Verbal competition, in relationship conflict, 120

Withdrawal
as conflict management technique, 121-122
interpersonal, 121-122
in marital relationship, 169
as relationship conflict response, 120,121-122
Wizard of Oz, The (movie), 270, 271-272